Also by PHILIP ZIEGLER

Omdurman

King William the Fourth

The Black Death

Addington

The Duchess of Dino

MELBOURNE

MELBOURNE

A Biography of William Lamb
2nd Viscount Melbourne

PHILIP ZIEGLER, *1929 –*

ALFRED A. KNOPF   NEW YORK   1976

FOR CLARE
Who took Caroline's side

CONTENTS

ILLUSTRATIONS

following page 156

The 1st Viscount Melbourne
From a painting by Stubbs *(National Gallery)*.

Lady Melbourne with her father,
Sir Ralph Milbanke, by Stubbs *(National Gallery)*.

William Lamb with a dog, and George Lamb with lion cubs,
both by Maria Cosway *(Lady Ravensdale)*.

William Lamb at Eton in Montem dress, by Hoppner
(By Gracious Permission of Her Majesty the Queen).

Emily Lamb, by Hoppner *(Lord Gage)*.

Lady Caroline Lamb. From a mezzotint at Melbourne Hall *(Mrs Kerr)*.

Brocket Hall, Hertfordshire *(Victoria and Albert Museum)*.

Melbourne Hall, Derbyshire *(English Life Publications)*.

William, Augustus and Caroline Lamb,
a sketch by Caroline Lamb *(Henry Blyth)*.

Mrs Norton, by Stone *(National Portrait Gallery)*.

William Lamb aged about 35, by Lawrence *(Lord Sudley)*.

Receiving the Fatal News! and *The Galley Slaves.*
Cartoons by John Doyle.

Lord Grey, after Lawrence, circa 1828 *(National Portrait Gallery)*.

Lord Brougham, by Lonsdale *(National Portrait Gallery)*.

Lord Palmerston, by Partridge, circa 1844 *(National Portrait Gallery)*.

Lord John Russell, by Grant, circa 1853 *(National Portrait Gallery)*.

The First Council, by Wilkie
(By Gracious Permission of Her Majesty the Queen).

Melbourne riding with the Queen at Windsor, by Grant
(By Gracious Permission of Her Majesty the Queen).

Frederick Lamb in 1846, by Partridge *(National Portrait Gallery)*.

The Diner-Out. From *Punch,* September 1841.

Lord Melbourne in old age, by Landseer *(Earl Mountbatten of Burma)*.

ACKNOWLEDGMENTS

By gracious permission of Her Majesty the Queen I have been allowed to study all Lord Melbourne's papers in the Royal Archives at Windsor as well as the papers of King George IV, King William IV and Queen Victoria. I have also been permitted to reproduce certain pictures from the Royal Collection.

I am indebted to the following for allowing me to use manuscript material in their possession or to which they hold the copyright: The Duke of Devonshire and the Trustees of the Chatsworth Settlement, the Duke of Wellington, the Marquess of Anglesey, the Marquess of Lansdowne, the Marquess of Lothian, Earl Fitzwilliam and his Trustees, the late Earl Spencer, the Earl of Shelburne, Lord Lambton, General Sir Michael Carver, the Hon. Mrs Samuel Allsopp, Mrs Andrew Kerr, and the Trustees of the National Library of Scotland.

Many of the above have also been of the greatest help in my work. In addition I would like to thank Lord David Cecil for his characteristic generosity and wisdom, Lord Egremont, Lord Ravensdale, Mrs Georgina Battiscombe, Mr John Bebbington of the Sheffield City Library, Dr Ann Burton, Mrs Iris Butler, Miss M. E. Cash of the Hampshire County Record Office, Dr Donald Cameron, Dr D. M. Close, Mr Hugh Cobbe and Mr John Hudson of the Department of Manuscripts at the British Museum, Professor Richard Davis, Mrs Joan Exton, Mr J. E. Fagg of Durham University, Dr I. D. Newbould, Colonel Olivier, Miss Felicity Ranger of the Royal Commission on Historical Manuscripts, Miss Joan Sinar of the Derbyshire County Record Office, Mr S. B. Still of the Staffordshire County Record Office, Miss Margot Strickland, Mr Brian Trainor of the Public Records Office of Northern Ireland, Mrs Elizabeth Trotter, Mrs Juliana Wadham, Mr P. Walne of the Hertfordshire County Record Office, and Mr T. S. Wragg, Librarian and Keeper of the Devonshire Collections.

I am most grateful to Lord Arran and the late Lady Helen Nutting for their efforts to persuade the Trustees of the British Museum to relax the embargo on certain of the Lamb family papers.

Sir Robert Mackworth-Young, Librarian at Windsor Castle, gave enormous assistance and I am particularly grateful to Miss Jane Langton and Mrs Sheila de Bellaigue, who is currently at work on the cataloguing of the Melbourne MSS at Windsor.

Sir Oliver Millar, Surveyor of The Queen's pictures, and Drs John

Hayes and Richard Ormond of the National Portrait Gallery have been most helpful over the tracing and selection of illustrations. In addition to those to whom I have already acknowledged my gratitude I must thank for permission to reproduce pictures the National Gallery and the National Portrait Gallery, Viscount Gage, Lady Ravensdale, Lord Sudley and Mr Henry Blyth.

Finally I owe much gratitude to my editor, Mr Richard Ollard; to my father and my brother who read the proofs; to Mrs Wilber, who helped at every stage; and above all to my wife without whom this book might have been finished more quickly but would have lacked much of whatever quality it possesses.

FOREWORD

Melbourne is already the subject of one of the most delightful biographies of our age. Why then write another? For one thing, it is nearly thirty years since Lord David Cecil completed his biography, nearly forty since he published the first volume. I have been able to consult many papers which, for one reason or another, were not then available. On the political side the most relevant are probably those of Lord Brougham and Edward Ellice, of Earl Grey and his son, Lord Howick. On the personal side I have had the great good fortune to stumble on 25,000 words or so of Melbourne's autobiography as well as a massive series of letters to and from Lady Branden and from Mrs Norton.

But more important even than this is the fact that my understanding of Melbourne differs sharply from that of Lord David. When I first read *Lord M* many years ago I could not understand how a man so insouciant, detached and free from ambition, could have held together a cabinet of warring prima-donnas over seven such difficult years. I still do not think he could have. I agree with Lord David that Melbourne as a friend or relative must have been one of the most delightful, wise and entertaining of men, but in public life I believe him also to have been ambitious, cynical and almost wholly without political principle. He was, in short, much less of a carefree amateur, much more of a politician. Every biographer perhaps to some extent is a victim of his generation and of his prejudices. If so, Lord David has enjoyed incomparably the happier lot. But, almost regretfully, I fear that I am right.

MELBOURNE

———— ◆•◆ ————

CHAPTER I

The Child

WILLIAM LAMB, 2nd Viscount Melbourne, was not born into the Whig oligarchy; that 'Sacred Circle of the Great-Grandmotherhood'[1] which considered itself entrusted with the guardianship of the British constitution as laid down at the time of the Glorious Revolution. He was not even tenuously related to the Dukes of Bedford or of Devonshire, of Portland or, indeed, of Omnium. By title he was an aristocrat, but by ancestry his claims must have seemed frail to his better-bred contemporaries. Some purists might even have denied him the title of gentleman. Such comments may seem unnecessarily negative as an opening to a biography. The concept of Lamb, however, as a member of a privileged élite who was propelled almost against his will into positions of great responsibility is so misleading that it cannot too rapidly be dispelled.

It would, of course, be absurd to deny that he enjoyed a privileged position. The Lambs were an exceedingly wealthy family. Much of their money was accumulated by the uncle of William's grandfather, Peniston. In 1842 a Mr Richard Sprye conducted an exhaustive enquiry into the family's origins and could come up with nothing more romantic than a 'citizen and saddler' on one side and a coachmaker on the other, who lived in Southwell at the end of the seventeenth century.[2] Peniston emerged from this shadowy background to study law, become a conveyancer and amass a large fortune, mainly, it would appear, at the expense of his most loyal patrons, the Cecils of Hatfield.[3] Peniston's nephews, Matthew and Robert – 'who their father was I haven't the least idea,' admitted William cheerfully[4] – inherited their uncle's money and continued the good work. Matthew, William's grandfather, greatly increased the family fortune and carried on the tradition of despoiling the Cecils. A visitor to Brocket Hall, the Lambs' home in Hertfordshire, was surprised to find that some fishing close to the house belonged to this family. 'Well,' William is supposed to have said, 'I believe my grandfather did the Salisburys out of some land in that direction, and was generous enough to leave them the fishing.'[5] He did no less well out of Lord Egmont, though no doubt also well *by* him since Matthew Lamb was a business-man of singular dexterity. As perpetual solicitor to the Post Office he feathered his nest still further and by 1741 was able to afford the luxury of a seat in parliament.

But Matthew's main achievement was not pecuniary. In 1740 he won the hand of Charlotte Coke, heiress of Melbourne Hall in Derbyshire and the rich lands that surround it. In an age when *mésalliances* were rare and attorneys held by the gentry to be little better than tradesmen, the feat was astonishing. The Cokes were an eminent family who had played a part in national affairs for two centuries or more. Nor were they now impoverished: the farms around Melbourne alone brought in some £6000 a year. Melbourne Hall was and mercifully is one of the most exquisite of the smaller stately homes of England, while the formal gardens, laid out by Henry Wise, pupil and rival of Lenôtre, are as close to perfection as any in the country. When Matthew Lamb, by then a baronet, died at the age of sixty-four, he left to his son Peniston, money, land and investments worth something close to a million pounds in the currency of the time.

Peniston Lamb was hardly worthy of such affluence. He was affable, generous and not ill-looking – though the Duke of Sutherland described him as short and fat.[6] With that humble tally concludes the catalogue of his virtues. He was lazy, self-indulgent and lecherous; a weak and stupid man who allowed himself to be led by those around him except when injured vanity provoked him into usually ill-judged activity. He did little harm but less good. Thrust into parliament when only twenty-two he achieved nothing and, left to himself, would have squandered his fortune inconspicuously: gambling here, fornicating there, and leaving no mark behind him.

He was not left to himself. In 1769 he married one of the most formidable women of the age. Elizabeth Milbanke came from an old Yorkshire family. One of her ancestors had been cup-bearer to Mary Queen of Scots and his descendants had languished in the distinguished obscurity which such an office might be expected to foreshadow. Distinguished obscurity was not at all to Miss Milbanke's taste. At the age of nineteen she bore her wit, her beauty and her breeding to the London marriage market and traded them in for the vast wealth and high degree of independence which she knew a wedding with Peniston Lamb would offer her.

He could have done a lot worse. Lady Melbourne, as she was to become when her husband was given an Irish barony the year after their marriage, had many admirers, most of them men, and a few harsh critics, almost all of them women. Friend and foe, however, united in admitting her cool cleverness, her discretion and her inflexible determination. She was a beautiful and sensual woman, who got much satisfaction from both these attributes; she was well read and intelligent, a good talker and a sympathetic listener; but all her talents for pleasing, intellectually as well as physically, were harnessed to a driving ambition. She wanted to be at the centre of London society, she wanted influence, she wanted power. Lady Holland spoke for the opposition when she wrote that Lady Melbourne put her in mind of Madame de Merteuil in *Les Liaisons Dangereuses*,[7] but the jibe, though not wholly unjustified, was far from the whole story. She was to be a loving mother, a loyal friend, within her own terms of reference a conscientious wife, and one of the most delightful of companions. Byron wrote of 'the magical influence . . . that you possess not only over me but anyone on whom you please to exert it,'[8] and her power to fascinate left its mark upon her generation. Nor was it only men whom she could beguile: the Duchess of Devonshire, undisputed queen of London society, adopted her as her most cherished confidante and bore her into the innermost sanctum of the Whig *beau monde*.

It was not probable that such a woman should long be contented with her serviceable but unsatisfying husband. It was, however, Lord Melbourne who began the rot. Within a year of his marriage he was busily wooing Mrs Baddeley, a fashionable courtesan who was equally sought after by the Dukes of Northumberland and Queensberry. He lavished jewellery upon her, was constantly making her presents of £200 or £300, writing her love letters in which the grammar and spelling were as original as the sentiments were trite: 'I should be happey in seeing my love evry minnit, with sending you a thousand kisses'.[9] Lady Melbourne was said to have been aware of the liaison and to have ignored it. Any other behaviour would have been out of character, and her husband's infidelity gave her licence – if licence she needed – to conduct as many affairs of her own as she felt inclined.

A few days before he died William was found by his nephew Spencer Cowper seated in front of his mother's portrait and muttering to himself: 'A very clever woman, kindhearted, not chaste, no not chaste, but sagacious and of excellent judgment'.[10] One of the problems of the biographer is assessing the value of scandal which was taken for granted by contemporaries but for which no documentary evidence exists. If everyone, meaning everyone in London society, assumed that Lady Melbourne was the mistress of Lord Coleraine or the Prince of Wales, then everyone may well have been right – yet it is only necessary to consider some of the palpable nonsense which 'everyone' has believed in our own time to realize how unreliable popular report can be. The late eighteenth century was, however, not a period in which marital fidelity was a virtue highly esteemed among the upper classes, nor was Lady Melbourne the woman to let convention stand in the way of the discreet enjoyment of her pleasures. There is no reason to doubt that, from the birth of their eldest son Peniston in May 1770, the Melbournes' marriage became increasingly an affair of social convenience. Lord Melbourne may not have relished the arrangement but at least he was thrown various sops along the way: an Irish viscountcy in 1781, a post as gentleman of the bedchamber to the Prince of Wales in 1784 and the long awaited English peerage with its seat in the House of Lords in 1815. On 15 March 1779 he was also presented with a second son.

Lady Melbourne's marital aberrations are of little interest except in so far as they bear on the paternity of William Lamb. At the time of his birth and for some time previously William's mother had been conspicuously allied with Lord Egremont, a man magnificent in his riches and in his generosity, connoisseur and collector of all things beautiful among which women were not the least. There is, there could be, nothing on paper to prove that William was Lord Egremont's son – even the claim that he inherited a large sum from his putative father does not survive a reading of Egremont's will.[11] Yet at the time, those who had some reason to think themselves well-informed had no doubts on the subject: Greville and Creevey took it for granted in their journals; Lord Holland, when Hobhouse remarked that he had never seen Egremont, replied, ' "You have often seen someone very like him", meaning our master Melbourne'.[12] Portraits are uncertain evidence, yet it does not require too active an exercise of imagination to see some likeness between Egremont and the adult Melbourne. Probably one can get no nearer the truth than in Hayward's anecdote, apocryphal or not. Landseer, when inspecting the portraits at Brocket, came to one of Lord Egremont, started and looked round at his host. 'Aye, you have heard that story, have you?' commented William. 'It's all a damned lie, for all that!' Then, half aloud, 'But who the devil can tell who's anybody's father?'[13]

In 1813, when temporarily out of the House of Commons, William Lamb decided to divert himself by writing the story of his life. Though disarmingly frank about many features of his life he says little about his family and is reticent on many details about which the biographer longs to know. A letter written to his brother Fred shortly before he died makes it clear that he envisaged its eventual publication. It is nevertheless a fascinating document and by far the best source available on the first thirty years of his life.* The opening sentence is admittedly discouraging – 'Of my childhood I recollect nothing which even to myself appears worthy of being recorded' – but fortunately it is possible to find other material to fill this unsatisfactory blank.[14]

Until the age of seven, when he was put in the charge of a private tutor, most of William's childhood was passed on the banks of the River Lee at Brocket Hall, with occasional ventures into the more rarified atmosphere of Melbourne House in Piccadilly. After the nine years' gap between Peniston and her second son, Lady Melbourne lost no time in enlarging her family. Frederick followed early in 1782, George in 1784, Emily in 1787 and finally the short-lived Harriet in 1789. Frederick was also generally attributed to Lord Egremont, George to the Prince of Wales – though the dates make this seem somewhat fanciful – while the two girls were held to be the acts of God, the Duke of Bedford, Lord Fitzwilliam, or indeed almost anyone except Lord Melbourne.

This ebullient gang – for the Lambs swiftly established a well-earned reputation for noisiness and high spirits – was entrusted for its early upbringing to a cantankerous old woman from Jersey whom Lady Melbourne, for some reason that the children were never able to fathom, adored and admired. William detested her and showed it. He was 'dreadfully passionate' when young, he told Victoria, and he battered his childish heart out against the inflexible armour of a professional nanny. Most frequent battlefield was the dining table. William was convinced that his enemy first found out what he most hated and then served it up on every occasion. The dish was boiled mutton and rice pudding, and meal after meal would end in defiance and hysterical tears. As a result he lost his appetite almost entirely, a curious affliction for a man whose gluttony was to be one of his most noted features. In the end the dragon from Jersey married Mr Bignor, a Swiss clergyman

---

* From here until p. 68 all quotations from William Lamb, unless otherwise attributed, are from this source.

who had travelled with Peniston as tutor. An eighteenth-century household was not disposed to accommodate itself to so disreputable a romance; the husband continued to dine with the family, the wife in the servants' hall. 'One couldn't do that in these days,' said William wistfully many years later.[15]

No doubt because he had no intention of being indebted to a woman whom he so heartily disliked, William was slow in learning to read; 'a work of heavy labour and most grievous suffering', he described it. Writing went better, since he enjoyed the services of a Mr Cuppage whom he quite liked. Almost before he had mastered the elements of English, however, he had been promoted to Latin – a course of study which tormented him. In anguish he would gaze out of the schoolroom windows into the farmland which ran close up to the house: 'I used to think how I wish I was one of those happy fellows in the field instead of learning this consumed Latin!' It was a thought that, in one form or another, he was to voice throughout his life – with as much sincerity as is usually to be found in those who have never tried nor are likely to try the way of life they envy.

In the autumn of 1785 William was removed six miles from his family to board with the Rev. Thomas Marsham, curate of Hatfield. Marsham was a classicist of distinction, a scholar of Eton and a fellow of King's. He was a dour, unimaginative man; not unkind by intention but making no concessions to human frailty and inclined to assume that any failure was the result of idleness or malevolence. His method of teaching was to place his pupil in front of a Latin text which, if not actually beyond his powers, would at least strain them to the uttermost, and leave him to get on with it. No relief was permitted until the task was done. 'I have often thus remained with very short intervals during the whole day, and a great part of the night, and have resumed the same task the next morning without either hope or chance of accomplishing it. In this manner my mind lost all power of applying itself, or even of comprehending what it had to do . . .'

William did not take kindly to this regime. He evolved a form of passive resistance in which his chief weapon was to pretend to be ill: 'I soon learned all the symptoms which were considered as the most alarming, pain in the head, weight at the stomach, and had no objection to swallow any potion provided by these means I could save myself from the punishment of returning to Mr Marsham.' His mother, who was unusually attentive by the standards of the age, used anyway to enjoy rescuing her son from his durance whenever she was at Brocket. Furnished with so convincing an excuse she was quick to have him at home and if possible keep him there, whether or not she was taken in by his performance.

These interludes at Brocket or in London – when he was held to be too ill to play with his brothers and sisters and yet was in fact ready for anything – in one way changed his life. He discovered the delights of reading. His idea of heaven, he later said, was a bedroom with three libraries leading out of it. His taste was precocious and eclectic; he would read anything that he could lay his hands on and hungrily come back for more. From this period he particularly remembered Cook's *Voyages*, Plutarch's *Lives*, Goldsmith's *History of Rome*, Voltaire's *History of Charles the Twelfth* in translation, Robertson's *History of America*, Pope's translations of Homer. He spent days on end stretched on the couch in his mother's room in Piccadilly gulping down Johnson's *Lives of the Poets*. He even borrowed a translation of Ariosto from one of the footmen, a circumstance possibly connected in some way with his remark to Queen Victoria that everything useful he had learnt had come from a nurserymaid.[16] One would like to know more about the footman.

But his leading passion, at the age of eight and for the rest of his life, was Shakespeare. He read the plays again and again until he could recite long passages by heart, often only understanding a little of what he read but intoxicated by the words and the sense of vast events shaping themselves on the periphery of his consciousness. He would act whole scenes by himself and composed an epic drama in Shakespearian style based on the life of Charlemagne. Though he was never taken to the theatre, the excitement he gained from reading plays was enough to kindle an obsessive ambition to be a dramatist, or better still an actor.

Mr Marsham thought all this deplorable: promiscuous reading weakened the intellect, sapped the concentration and could only lead to immorality. Lady Melbourne, on the other hand, was wholeheartedly in favour. It was by now becoming evident that Peniston, her eldest son, though handsome, friendly and by no means a fool, was without a particle of ambition. Lady Melbourne has usually been portrayed as insatiably anxious for her children's advancement. There seems in fact no reason to think that she pushed them extravagantly far or fast; temperate in that as in all things she was as much concerned about their happiness as their advancement. But she did esteem success and with Peniston likely to win little glory except perhaps on the race-course, she transferred her hopes to her second son. William's precocity delighted her, the pleasure which he gained from books and plays seemed to her natural and proper, his talents were obvious.

William responded eagerly to her encouragement and was proud of her good opinion. 'Almost everybody's character was formed by their mother,' he told Victoria, and, 'if the children did not turn out well, the mothers should be punished for it.'[17] He would have applied this rule most emphatically to himself. Lady Melbourne was too wise and too cool to choke her children with an excess of maternal love, but her interest was keen and her influence great. On the whole it was beneficial. By the time he was ten William had learned to think for himself, to question dogmas and to delight in new knowledge and new experience. He also enjoyed the stability which comes from being part of a happy and united group of children. It was not a bad basis on which to build a life.

In September 1788 Peniston Lamb returned from a visit to the continent. Sophisticated, elegant, moderately debauched, he seemed to his younger brother a prodigy of adult splendour. When he descended on Mr Marsham and swept William away to stay with their parents at Melbourne, it was as if Prince Charming had broken the magician's spell and set the prisoner free. There followed a baby grand tour of the stateliest Whig houses. Chatsworth, Newborough and Castle Howard in turn amazed and delighted the impressionable child. After such glimpses of paradise it would have been hard indeed if he had been recalled to the dingy discipline of the curate's house at Hatfield. Luckily he was not to be tested so unkindly. In the middle of November the family returned to London; at the end of the month Lord Melbourne, for once playing the father's role, bore his apprehensive but optimistic son away with him to Eton.

———◆◆◆———

CHAPTER 2

The Student

ETON, like other leading schools, was, in academic terms, a factory for the production of classicists. Other subjects might figure in the curriculum but they were of little significance: the making of Latin verses, as William regretfully noted, was 'almost the exclusive road to reputation at Eton'.

To be fair to the school, however, academic performance was by no means the only, or even the main purpose of its education. Eton was a forcing ground for the boys who would be entering parliament over the next ten years and governing Britain for the following thirty. It was taken for granted that the way of the Etonian would lie in public places and that he must be equipped for all the exigencies of such a role. Much emphasis was put on declamation and the boys were encouraged to debate and to orate formally at each other. But it was not so much what was taught that was important as the fact that the air itself seemed suffused with politics. The boys' fathers ruled Britain and the boys not only assumed that they would take on the mantle but also that they were already associated in the work. In William's first year the regency crisis was in issue. The school was split into two warring camps and each side urged its cause by methods perhaps more brutal but certainly little less sophisticated than those used by their fathers in the Houses of Lords and Commons.

In later life William was fond of quoting Talleyrand's aphorism: '*La meilleure éducation, c'est l'éducation Publique Anglaise; et c'est détestable.*' At first, at least, he found plenty to detest. Life was a series of disagreeable shocks for a gentle, slightly bookish child used to a home where he was treated as a civilized and almost adult being. On his arrival he was taken directly into chapel. A boy dropped his marble and William saw a master scowl at him 'in menace of future punishment'. He thought no more about it, but as soon as the school reassembled the luckless child was called out of class and flogged. If this was the sort of punishment meted out for trifles, what could be reserved for more serious offences? Nor were the boys any less violent to one another. The proper way of settling any difference was by one's fists. William became involved in some quarrel with a bigger boy 'who had much longer arms and pounded amazingly. I stood and reflected a little, and *thought* to myself, and then gave it up. I thought that one of the most prudent acts, but I was reckoned very dastardly for it.'[1] Undiscomfited, he made it a rule always to give up after the first round if he found that he was going to lose. Such behaviour could hardly have been more rational but a little boy who stood around and *thought* rather than knocked down his enemies was hardly likely to be a hero among his contemporaries.

It was not so much the violence as the neglect which disconcerted William. At midday on the first schoolday he found himself despatched to a field on the banks of the Thames where he was told to amuse himself for the next two hours. In alarm and perplexity he wandered around, wishing that someone would tell him what to do. 'I thought it then very odd, for I had been accustomed to have two or three nursery maids after me, not allowing me to wet my heels . . .'[2] He solaced himself by gorging at the tuckshop. His father had given him an extravagant amount of pocket money, more than ten guineas a term, and though he later discovered the delights of the dog-fighters, the rabbit-catchers and the boatmen, at the start every penny was spent at the pastry cooks. He stuffed himself with tarts, made himself sick, and, by the time he went home for the Christmas holidays, had spots all over his face.

At least the work did not pose any serious problems. In spite of his criticism of Mr Marsham, William found that he was well ahead of his contemporaries. His house-master was Dr William Langford, one of the most ferocious of Eton's floggers at a time when corporal punishment was considered to be the panacea for almost every ill. He was a chaplain to George III and the harshness of his regime was mitigated by his frequent absences when he trailed off behind the court to Weymouth. He equally moved up to Windsor when the court was in residence but here there was no relief since he was close enough to Eton to know what was going on and his victims merely added the tedium of a walk to the Castle to the pain of their beating. He could have been worse. 'A schoolmaster of more than thirty years standing who either preserves a tolerable degree of temper or is not worn down into complete carelessness and apathy is a man of considerable merit,' wrote William. 'Such a man was Dr Langford.' But he was also vain, unimaginative and rather silly. He was so anxious that his boys should do him credit that he would sometimes write their verses for them and then bask in vicarious glory when the headmaster was told of their accomplishment. Even though William's Greek was lamentable and he was never one of the outstanding Latinists, he was one of Dr Langford's favourites. Indeed, he escaped with only three floggings in as many years. 'I don't think he flogged me enough,' William told Victoria, 'it would have been better if he had flogged me more.'[3]

A spotty and studious boy who refuses to fight and is a favourite of the teachers would seem destined to unpopularity, if not persecution. William escaped it. He was tolerably good at games, which may have helped; his lavish pocket money perhaps bought him a few friends and, more important than either of these, he was cheerful, friendly and relaxed. It was possible to ignore William Lamb but very hard to quarrel with him. He had too a kind of insouciance, an indifference to the woes which usually trouble schoolboys, which won the admiration of his contemporaries. He was not unconventional; he did not clash with the authorities; yet he went his own way and somehow contrived to give the impression that, when he conformed, he did so because he wanted to and not through lack of independence. For the first year or two of his Eton life he was tolerated, then he became popular, finally he found himself the height of fashion.

His last two years at Eton were happy ones. His Greek got no better but his masters comforted themselves with the fact that he was reasonably proficient in other subjects. For William himself the theatre became increasingly important. With a group of fellow enthusiasts he set up a stage in a room thirty feet long and ten wide and acted every kind of play. He was assistant stage manager and played Faulkland in a particularly ambitious performance of *The Rivals*. Mrs Malaprop was acted by Montgomery minor and Lamb minor, William's brother Frederick, was cast as Sir Lucius.[4] Some of the parents protested that their sons were spending too long on such diversions. The headmaster blandly agreed that the whole thing was unfortunate and should be stopped; then urged the boys in future to hold their rehearsals secretly. All did not run smoothly. 'Our society,' recorded William, 'was disturbed by envy, jealousy and all the various passions, which produce intrigue and dissension in other theatres . . .' The group broke up in disarray, to set up rival theatres and to write angry prologues and epilogues denouncing the amateurish bungling of the opposition.

On reflection William was more inclined to support the parents than the headmaster. For one thing he thought it possible that the boys who took the female roles might assume a 'character of effeminacy' which they would find hard to shake off in after life. Montgomery minor no doubt survived his stint as Mrs Malaprop, but what about the innocent ephebe who starred as Lydia Languish? More seriously, he thought that boys might become enraptured with all things theatrical and never escape the thrall. This was not as foolish as it might sound; it was a stage-struck age. Of William's contemporaries at Eton one became a professional actor, several more wrote for the stage, while William himself thought nothing of devoting two months at a time to elaborate amateur theatricals in some country house. But nonetheless he felt that acting was a healthier pursuit than the likely alternatives: 'drinking, racing, badger-baiting and the low company into which such amusements lead.'

His time on the stage was bought at the price of his concern for matters political. Unlike the preceding generation, of which Canning had been the golden boy, William's immediate contemporaries took relatively little interest in what went on at Westminster. His division included Beau Brummel; a future Archbishop in Charles Sumner; Charles Stuart, who was to become Lord Stuart de Rothesay and a distinguished diplomatist; the next Duke of Atholl but one: but no one else who was to play any great part in government.[5] Politics were part of their life but rarely a subject for passion.

By the time he was seventeen, William had had enough of school. Afterwards he regretted he had not stayed on for another year but at the time he was hungry for the world outside. He looked back benignly on his time at Eton – 'seven years of as much enjoyment and satisfaction and as little vexation and discontent, as can fall to the lot of the years of childhood'. But he never felt that the public schools did a proper job of education; arithmetic and geometry were neglected to meet the demands of the teachers of the classics; modern languages or scientific subjects were unheard of. He told Victoria that the only things he learnt at Eton were punctuality and the value of time – he had never carried a watch in his life or had a clock in his room yet he always knew the hour with fair precision.[6] Nor did he think well of the boarding school as a system of education. Too often a handful of 'disagreeable, bad, blackguard boys' would establish a reign of terror and intimidate or corrupt a whole generation. Boys learned to lie and cheat so as to escape from trouble, habits which they found hard to get rid of in later life.

Yet, in the long run, it probably mattered little. 'The fact is, everybody is self taught,' he wrote to Lord Holland in 1835. 'Everybody learns a great deal more by himself and his own efforts, than he is taught by others . . .'[7] He would have said much the same thing forty years before. At the time, however, he can have had little energy to spare for musing over the irrelevance or inadequacy of his education. His mind was filled with bright visions of what lay ahead in London and the world beyond, with 'hope and anticipated pleasure and exultation at obtaining the liberty which I had so long desired'.

In October 1796 William Lamb went up to Trinity, Cambridge. For a young man in quest of a brave new world Trinity was a barren hunting ground. For fifty years it had mouldered intellectually, indeed physically. In 1786 four of the senior fellows were either mad or notoriously immoral and the other four had never had an original idea between them.[8] William Wordsworth eyed these deplorable dotards from his window across the road in St John's:

> . . . grave elders, men unscoured, grotesque
> In character, tricked out like aged trees,
> Which through the lapse of their infirmity
> Give ready place to any random seed
> That chooses to be reared upon their trunks.[9]

Under their baleful sway entries dwindled to a mere forty a year. Since then things had improved a little. Thomas Postlethwaite, the new Master, though no reformer, was at least sane and sober; Thomas Jones, the senior tutor, did much to raise academic standards until his energies petered out in the quicksands of professorial opposition; but though Trinity had become more respectable it was still without that intellectual ferment which distinguishes any seat of learning worth the name. In this it was sadly representative of the whole university: William was later to tell Victoria that Oxford was for people of no talents, while Cambridge was best for clever people, but this was an uncharacteristic burst of chauvinism which in no way reflected his opinions at the time.[10]

William Lamb was entered as a Fellow Commoner, a device by which, on payment of an extra fee, an undergraduate could procure the privileges of a nobleman. William thus wore a hat instead of an academic cap, had elaborate gold embroidery on his gown and dined at the fellows' table in knee breeches and stockings. More important, he was exempt from certain rules, lectures and examinations; the presence of a nobleman at Cambridge was felt to confer an honour on the institution which should not be tarnished by undue emphasis on discipline or hard labour. It was enough that he should divert himself in the time-honoured ways of 'boating; fighting the bargees and the town; riding and walking; shooting and fishing', and, of course, drinking and gambling.[11]

'It would be difficult at any time,' wrote William of himself at this period, 'to find a person more completely conceited, presumptuous and self-confident, who had a greater contempt for most of the rest of mankind.' He was an advanced example of that unattractive type, the boy who has been a success at school and considers that the same role is his of right in later life. His Etonian friends had assured him that he was possessed of transcendent talents and that any setbacks in the academic field were due to his natural reluctance to let himself be shackled by the bonds of scholasticism. His mother, who should have known better, told him that he was possessed of poetic genius. With his elder brother Peniston away from home and covering himself in no kind of glory he was free to lord it at Brocket, warmed by the reverence of his siblings. It was small wonder that he arrived at Cambridge convinced that the university had nothing to teach him but that he might, if he felt so inclined, teach the university a thing or two.

An inspired teacher could have engaged his interest and made him work, but inspiration was not a quality esteemed among the fellows of Trinity. The chief lecturer, with the unmerited name of Mr Lax, was a distinguished mathematician whose approach to Euripides was to analyse every sentence on principles derived from his favourite study. Grammatical construction was the main consideration, meaning or grace of expression of trivial importance. To a boy who had a real if still immature feeling for beauty in literature, such pedantry seemed intolerable. But at least Mr Lax tried. Mr Jones, when lecturing on metaphysics, 'told us that Mr Locke's ideas upon this subject were the most sound, that it was impossible that he should state them more clearly than they were stated in Mr Locke's own work, to which he referred us, strongly recommending its perusal, and so dismissed us'. Though he still read largely, for life without books was never tolerable to William, he found *The Sentimental Journey* or Rousseau's *Confessions* more stimulating than Mr Locke or Mr Lax, cut most of his lectures and almost entirely neglected his studies.

Instead he took up with the bloods, the gang of rich young men who made Trinity a by-word in the university for intemperance and indiscipline. Their wickedness was not particularly ambitious, but even in the foothills of debauchery they contrived to spend a lot of money, make more noise and do themselves a fair amount of harm. This might have been all right for William if he had got fun out of it; if he had indeed been, as biographers have painted him, in carefree quest of new sensations and much too happy in his independence to buckle down to a dour curriculum. But he was not. He aspired to the character of a libertine without having the temperament: 'I got drunk without at that time loving drinking, affected amours which in fact would have turned me sick with disgust, and bought caps and whips without the least intention of going out a-hunting.' When he was not tagging along behind the fast set he relapsed into idleness, lounging around with no idea how to divert himself. He suffered from a teen-age *accidie*, no less painful for being exaggerated. In later life he quoted approvingly Dr Langford's indignant exclamation: 'I had rather see you engaged in vice than doing nothing.' But in his first year at Cambridge William had no stomach for vice and no energy for anything more rewarding.

After that things began to go better. His first long vacation he spent up at Cambridge and at last did some serious historical reading. He was seduced from these studies only by the discovery of Rousseau's *Nouvelle Héloïse* which produced in him 'sensations of delight and enthusiasm which I hardly ever felt before or since'. Enraptured, he settled down to write a novel in the same style but the enterprise foundered. So did his entry for the Latin Ode competition; perhaps fortunately since the subject was Napoleon in Italy and William's panegyric of the young republican general would hardly have endeared him to the Tory dons.

In the middle of the summer vacation he fell seriously ill. No clue remains as to the nature of his illness, but the doctors mismanaged it and it was eight months before he could return to Cambridge. By this time most of the raffish crew who had dominated Trinity the previous year had moved on and William felt free to follow his own inclinations. He by no means became a recluse but henceforth he shunned the more raucous forms of revelry. His progress as a classicist showed little improvement and he earned a rebuke from the senior fellow for his deplorable showing in the mathematics examination, but he began to win a reputation for declamation. In his final year he won a college prize and was called on to declaim, on any subject he chose, in the chapel at Trinity. He selected 'The Progressive Improvements of Mankind', a good Whig theme which would have caused a wry smile among those Radicals who were to complain in later years about Melbourne's stubborn resistance to progress of any kind. The speech,

anodyne enough and calculated to offend no one, was well received
and was even honoured by Charles James Fox who borrowed a few
sentences from it to decorate one of his speeches in the House of
Commons.

William Lamb, therefore, left Cambridge with kinder feelings than
when he had arrived. On the whole, however, he looked back on his time
there with distaste. 'It was spent neither in improvement nor in pleasure,
but in listlessness and inactivity which leave behind them a sensation
more uneasy than even a certain degree of contrition and repentance.'
It was said of the Duke of Newcastle that he lost two hours in the
morning and spent the rest of the day running after them. Lamb took
these words as the epitaph for his Cambridge career, only in his case it
was three wasted years which he was never to recapture. In part he
blamed the college authorities but far more he held himself responsible.
Something, however, he had learnt, and he was never to forget it.
When he left Cambridge he did so bearing with him 'a consciousness of my own ignorance, a desire to learn, and a willingness to be
taught'.

At the end of the eighteenth century, with the opportunities for a
Grand Tour limited by the war with France, the fashion had grown up
for a young gentleman of family to round off his education with a year
or so in Scotland. Palmerston, Lansdowne, Dudley and John Russell,
to mention only a few of Lamb's future colleagues, all did their stint in
the north. But this was in Edinburgh, a capital city admitted by the
most bigoted of southerners to have a history and traditions, even a
certain grandeur of its own. When Lord Lauderdale and the Duke of
Bedford urged the merits of Glasgow on Lady Melbourne as a place
for William's further education, she may well have wondered where it
was. So uncouth a provincial city could hold little to attract this most
soignée of hostesses. Tobacco had made it rich but had hardly em-
bellished it and its reputation was that of the dirtiest and most violent
of Britain's cities. Even the university was violent: student riots were
frequent and the dons quick to retaliate. An undergraduate named
James Mathie, suspected by Professor Moor of ridiculing him, was
beaten to the floor by blows from a heavy wooden candlestick, accompanied by cries of 'Wretch! Scoundrel! Puppy!' 'You old blinker, you
shall pay for this!' cried Mathie, gallantly tottering to his feet; but the
Professor survived without serious criticism.[12]

In spite of such excesses the university had a deserved reputation for learning. Dr Johnson visited it with Boswell in 1773 and pronounced it worthy academically; he found 'the habit of application much more general than in the neighbouring university of Edinburgh'.[13] He did not take kindly to any of the professors but this is hardly surprising since the chief ornament of Glasgow, Professor John Millar, was a doctrinaire Whig of the most perfervid nature. He had rejoiced at the fall of the Bastille, remained undiscomfited by the Terror and earned discredit in 1798 by opposing a contribution of £300 from university funds for the defence of the realm. His book on the British government and constitution was dedicated to Charles James Fox. He was a brilliant lecturer on Scots Law and Jurisprudence and the father of the Scottish school of Roman Law. Originally destined for the church, he never lost his evangelical zeal but preached the gospel according to Adam Smith until his dying day.

James Mylne, Lamb's other professor, was Millar's son-in-law and henchman. Though he could not match his father-in-law's scholarship he vied with him in ultra-Whiggery. In 1815, on the day that Napoleon's return from Elba was announced, he selected for the morning service the psalm beginning:

> Behold he comes! Your leader comes,
> With might and honour crowned.

This somewhat partial comment on events was taken in bad part by certain of his colleagues. Charges of sedition were lodged against him but the matter was smoothed over and Mylne survived.[14]

As eager to heed his preceptors at Glasgow as he had been loath to do so at Cambridge, Lamb showed himself as good a Whig as any of his seniors. His views were orthodox Foxite with a flavour of Scottish sanctimoniousness. He wrote to his mother in indignation at the 'low scurrility and weak reasoning' which marked Grenville's rejection of Bonaparte's peace overtures early in 1800:

> We have certainly been for a long time for freedom of thought and opinion, for public spirit and for toleration, the first nation in Europe. We have now certainly lost our superiority, and there is every reason to fear that we shall never regain it. We shall shortly be the last. We are fixed in bigotry and prejudices. We think there is no liberty but our liberty, no government but our government and no religion but our religion. Some time ago perhaps we were right in thinking so, but we have occasions enough before our eyes at present to induce us to alter our opinions.[15]

But though he delighted in laying down the law about matters political he devoted more of his energies to systematic study. He was hindered by the presence of his seventeen-year-old brother, Frederick. Though by no means a fool, Frederick had none of William's intellectual curiosity. William was apparently self-confident and carefree but in fact racked by inner doubts; Frederick was sure about everything, above all his own capabilities. His leading fault was flippancy which matured into corroding cynicism. 'He sees life in the most degrading light,' complained Lady Granville, 'and he simplifies the thing by thinking all men rogues and all women ***.'[16] It was thought that a period in Glasgow before he went to Cambridge would steady him and perhaps help him to avoid some of the pitfalls into which his elder brother had stumbled. The experiment was moderately successful but William must often have been irritated by the presence of his ebullient junior.

'There is nothing heard of in this house but study,' grumbled Frederick.[17] William was alternately appalled and exhilarated by the way of life to which he was now committed. It was, he recorded, 'a course of study and exercise, of debate, doubt, contradiction and examination such as I had never witnessed nor been engaged in before'. Every morning there was a lecture on the Institutes of Justinian, with an examination the following day on the ground which had been covered. An hour a day was devoted to French. Three evenings a week there were lectures on government, every Saturday evening a formal debate; and at breakfast, dinner, supper and on every walk, endless conversation and argument about religion, metaphysics, law or politics. William enjoyed the talk but deplored the debating, mainly because he found it impossible to get to his feet and speak without 'much awkwardness and hesitation'. He could not bear to make a fool of himself, particularly among people to whom secretly he felt himself superior, and so took the easy way of poking fun at the practice until his fellow students were contaminated by his disdain and abandoned the debates altogether.

There was not much in the social life of Glasgow to lure him from this austere regimen. He told his mother that he had dined out once with a wealthy merchant and that there had been several parties at Professor Millar's. He seems to have been genuinely disconcerted to discover that the Glaswegians were not only human but even recognizably similar to their politer brethren from the south. 'We drink healths at dinner, hand around the cake at tea and put our spoons into our cups when we desire to have no more; exactly in the same manner we used to behave at Eton and Cambridge.' The only marked difference was 'a devilish good one which ought to be adopted everywhere. After the cheese they send round the table a bottle of whisky and another of brandy, and the whole company male and female in general indulge in a dram. This is very comfortable and very exhilarating, and affords an opportunity for many jokes.'[18] The trouble about the girls was that, though some of them were pretty enough, they were all of them blue-stockings at heart. William quoted poetry at them but Frederick noted that he seemed to be making no impression. It would be interesting to know the views of the Glasgow girls on these two brash and supercilious young men from London.

William was pleased enough with Glasgow to go back there for a second season but after that he had had enough. The climate depressed him, his companions seemed increasingly dour and earnest, he began to question a school of learning which could condemn poetry and painting as irrelevant trivialities and preach that utility was the sole test of value. Worst of all, he began to lose faith in Professor Millar. He found him impracticable, limited in his views, absurd in his claims for the Scottish schools of law and metaphysics. Even politically William began to waver and he finally parted company from his teacher when Millar convinced himself that it would be in the best interests of Britain to be conquered by France so as to rid her of her monstrous government. It was one thing, William felt, to stick up for the rights of the French; quite another to talk about the British being conquered by a bunch of foreigners.

William Lamb never denied the debt he owed to Millar. He came to Glasgow idle, shiftless and distracted; he left it having recaptured the will and the capacity to work. His casual scepticism had been transformed into a true spirit of enquiry, an unwillingness to accept dogma merely because it was preached by all around him. Above all he had learnt to listen to the arguments of others and, even though not converted, to respect the views of those who differed from him. He had acquired tolerance at an age when most young men shed one prejudice only to acquire another. He wrote to his mother that he disliked the dissenters, not because they dissented, but because they were:

more zealous and consequently more intolerant than the established church. Their only object is power. If we are to have a prevailing religion let us have one that is cool and indifferent and such a one we have got. Not that I am so foolish as to dread any fire and faggot and wheels and axes but there are other modes of persecution.

Toleration is the only good and first principle, and toleration for
every opinion that can possibly be formed.[19]

Such a sentiment might have been unremarkable if offered by Lord
Melbourne to Queen Victoria in 1837. From William Lamb, aged just
twenty, it was an observation of some significance.

CHAPTER 3

———— ◆◆◆ ————

A Way to Make

EUROPE in 1800 offered the English patriot little cheer. The war with France had been dragging on for seven years. At the end of 1799 Pitt's second continental coalition was well established, the French were making overtures for peace and the end seemed in sight. Then Marengo and Hohenlinden shattered that rosy dream, the coalition crumbled, Austria retreated into neutrality, Russia into alliance with the French. There was no immediate reason to fear military defeat but as little to hope for victory; meanwhile the cost of the war became ever more intolerable. To add to the woes of the country, the harvest of 1800 was as bad as any for decades and the price of wheat rose alarmingly.

To generations whose idea of war is conditioned by black-out, rationing and air-raids the aspect of London would have appeared perplexing. A few more younger sons than usual were with their ships or regiments but society made no other concession to the perils of the hour. There were still balls and dinners; people grumbled about Mr Pitt's iniquitous income tax but rarely indeed did they find it necessary to put down their carriages or discharge their servants. The face of politics, however, had been transformed. In 1794 the Duke of Portland had brought over the bulk of the Whigs to support Pitt's Tory government. Only a handful of irreconcilables under the leadership of Charles James Fox remained to keep the banners flying. The Whig party, of course, in any contemporary sense of the word 'party', had never existed, but it had still achieved a certain cohesion of outlook and purpose.[1] This cohesion was now shattered.

But though the Whig party might have disintegrated, the spirit of Whiggery was hardly affected. The Duke of Portland and his group did not consider themselves to be Tory converts but patriotic Whigs. Though they might differ with Fox and Grey on the proper attitude towards France and the French revolutionaries, on all the essential tenets of the Whig faith they were still as one.

So much is easily said, but to define those tenets is less easy. The perennial problem of the Whig party was indeed its search for an identity, a quest which only ended when it defined itself out of existence far on into the nineteenth century. The touchstone of the Whig faith could hardly be a belief in the need for parliamentary reform, for there were almost as many attitudes towards this problem as there were members of the party. Nor could it be retrenchment. Every Whig, it is true, preached tax reductions and strict economy, but then every opposition in every country habitually condemns the wanton extravagance of the sitting government. Grey perhaps summed it up as well as anyone when he wrote in 1817 that 'the party principle which distinguishes us as Whigs is a principle of moderation and liberality, both in religion and government . . . complete toleration, or to speak more properly the rejection of all intolerance whether in the severer form of penal, or the milder form of disqualifying statutes; in short no imparity that cannot be proved to be necessary for the security of the state'.[2] The Whigs stood, therefore, for Catholic Emancipation and the removal of restrictions on dissenters; within limits, for free speech and a free Press.

That all sounded properly liberal and right-minded but it must also be remembered that the Whigs were, for the most part, conservative by nature, drawing almost all their strength from a thousand or so rich, land-owning families, more than three hundred of which were titled.[3] They were strong on principles but weak in practice, theoretical progressives who accepted the need for reform only as a lesser evil than revolution and to every liberal proposal appended a string of reactionary postscripts. Their limitations as reformers were to become apparent in the 1830s. In 1800, however, especially with many of its more traditionalist members in defection, the party showed only its more progressive side. To William Lamb – young, iconoclastic and more nearly an idealist than at any other moment of his life – it seemed the only force in politics which stood even approximately for what he believed in.

It would, indeed, have been surprising if Lamb had supported any other party. His father, it is true, had started as one of the dullest and dumbest members of North's sheep-like army of supporters but since he had joined the Prince of Wales's household in 1784 he had thrown his inconsiderable weight behind the Whigs. Lady Melbourne valued the Prince's friendship and the entrée to Devonshire House far above any political principles. Peniston was said to be a Tory but his appearances in the House of Commons were so rare that he hardly affected the image of a family generally considered to be ranked with the opposition.

Even if the Lambs had been Tories however, William would still probably have retained enough Whiggish leanings from his time in Glasgow to steer him in that direction. Though in some ways he had outgrown Millar he never doubted the lucidity of his mind and the force of his reasoning. He reappeared on the London scene convinced of the superiority of his own information and logical powers, stoutly defending those extremist views which had offended him in Glasgow a few months before and viewing with somewhat priggish disdain those of his friends who failed to live up to his own self-righteous standards. Lady Holland observed him quizzically and found him 'pleasant but supercilious, as he shut himself up in his own thoughts as soon as he saw Lord G[ranville?], Morpeth and Boringdon. He affects to hold them cheap for being anti-Jacobins'.[4]

It was left to Charles James Fox both to confirm William Lamb in his Whiggish sentiments and to cure his self-righteousness. Rare indeed was the young man who could resist that most beguiling of statesmen and Lamb responded gratefully to the warmth, the generosity and the charm which render Fox as vivid a myth today as he was in his own lifetime. Lamb idolized him. Trying to catch the evanescent image many years later he wrote of Fox's 'perfect truth and simplicity . . . in the total absence of anything like pompous reserve, in the candour and openness of his conversation, in the just weight which he allowed to whatever dropped from any other person, in the youthful energy of his mind, in the free communication of his knowledge and the open avowal of his ignorance'. He consciously tried to model his own behaviour on that of his hero and it is notable how many of the characteristics he thus noted were in turn remarked in him by the young men who approached him when he had won high office. Under Fox's guidance Lamb learned that Morpeth and Boringdon were not necessarily imbecile in failing to perceive the splendour of the Jacobin revolution, but also that his principles were to be cherished and protected against all who might assail them.

Politics, however, did not bulk particularly large in Lamb's mind

after his return to London. There were so many other things to distract
him. Sociable, amusing, exceptionally good-looking, well-connected
and with plenty of money behind him, it was inevitable that he would
succeed in the London drawing-rooms. He arrived, too, with an inflated reputation for intelligence. His prize-winning declamation had
been printed and circulated as a pamphlet. Lady Bessborough read it
and sent a copy to her son – 'the style a little too flowery in some places,'
she commented, 'but it certainly proves great genius'. Lady Holland
was equally impressed by his contribution to 'Monk' Lewis's translation
of the Thirteenth Satire of Juvenal: 'twenty-eight of the best lines are
by William Lamb, a rising genius, who is to dine here for the first time
today'. His absence of fortune saved him from the fate of those eligible
bachelors who were yearly thrown to the wolves of the London season,
but in every other way he was a most desirable adjunct to any party.[5]

Flattered and cosseted in this way a young man will usually become
spoiled. William Lamb was no exception. He and his brother Frederick,
Tom Sheridan, Lord Kinnaird, became the *enfants terribles* of London
society: arriving ostentatiously late and often drunk; talking too loud,
too coarsely and too much; swaggering around with arrogant indifference to the impression they made on those around them. Harriet
Cavendish reported meeting him very drunk at a reception at Melbourne
House; he talked to her 'in a loud voice the whole time of the danger
of a young woman believing in weligion and pwactising mowality'.
Lamb could never dance in time and so affected to despise it, indeed to
despise all music. When others danced he lounged on a sofa and looked
supercilious. The impression he created can hardly have been attractive
but the phase did not last long. Lamb was far too fond of rational
conversation to waste many evenings in drunkenness; too kind-hearted
to get satisfaction out of hurting people's feelings; too attached to
reading to wish to fritter away a lifetime in society.[6]

Though his family contrived to remain on good terms with the
King and Queen they were part of the Carlton House set and the
Prince of Wales was a frequent visitor at Melbourne House, by this
date to be found in Whitehall in a building which is today the Scottish
Office. Lamb was dining there with his parents and the Prince the night
in May 1800 when the lunatic Hatfield fired at King George III as he
entered his box at Drury Lane. The Prince was disposed to finish his
dinner in peace but Lady Melbourne, who always knew what was
proper and usually persuaded somebody else to do it, packed him off
to the theatre to congratulate his father on his escape.[7] William Lamb
was taken along as an extra equerry and the Prince, who liked to have

personable men about him, henceforth often invited him, with or without his parents, to Carlton House. It was hardly the ideal surroundings for an impressionable young man but Lamb quickly acquired a capacity for taking what he wanted from a situation and ignoring the rest. It is doubtful whether the garish opulence of Carlton House impressed him much, certainly it did not corrupt him.

He found time to dabble in literary pursuits, though with mixed success. He had first found his way into print in a London newspaper when the *Morning Chronicle* published an anonymous poem attacking Canning and the other editors of that satirical Tory journal, the *Anti-Jacobin*.[8] The climax of this pasquinade read:

> Proceed – be more opprobrious if you can;
> Proceed – be more abusive every hour;
> To be more stupid is beyond your power.

The somewhat limp conclusion perhaps justified Canning's reply in the next issue of the *Anti-Jacobin*, claiming that the editors rejoiced in 'Censure, cloth'd in vapid verse like thine'. The effort was, however, approved of in Whig circles, which is more than can be said for a comedy *The Fashionable Friends* which was put on at Strawberry Hill in 1801. Lamb was said by some to have written the whole play. Certainly he wrote the epilogue which described what preceded it as being intended not merely to entertain but also:

> To form the infant mind, and to explode
> The old morality's mistaken code.

Alas for such hopes, the play closed quietly after only three days; leaving the old morality unshaken.

But Lamb's principal pastime at this period was both more demanding and less innocent. Some time towards the end of 1801 he became deeply involved with one of those fashionable *poules de luxe* who preyed on young men of good family and long purses.

> I had fallen into the power of a lady of no very strict virtue and was entirely devoted to her. Morning, noon and night I was at her house or pining after the moment when I should be there. All my hours were passed in attending upon her, in flattering her vanity by exposing myself in public with her, in gratifying her fancies and obeying her caprices.

She seems to have been cold-blooded and unscrupulous even by the standards of her class. She decided quickly that Lamb did not have enough money to make him a really interesting victim but held on to him for want of someone better. Lamb's infatuation continued until the summer of 1802 when he had promised to go to Scotland with his friend Kinnaird. Half anxious to escape, half loath to go, he told his mistress of his plans. She opposed them but with an unflattering lack of energy, 'not, I believe, thinking me worth any very violent efforts and speculating upon more leisure, and vacancy for more advantageous connections'. Lamb broke away, and every mile he travelled the pains of parting seemed to grow less sharp and the pleasures of liberty more delectable. Ten days' shooting completed the cure: he concluded that he had wasted his time and money and degraded himself into the bargain. He vowed to break off the connection and never to get himself into the same sort of mess again.

Diverting himself in Mayfair drawing-rooms and producing *jeux d'esprit* for the fashionable stage were not of great service to a young man with a way to make in the world. Though Lord Melbourne was still a rich man he had been outspending his income for twenty years and the bulk of what was left of his fortune was destined for Peniston, the eldest son. William would never starve, but he would not have enough money to keep him in the style to which he was accustomed, still less to maintain a wife in the same state. Somehow he must earn his living.

There were not many paths open to a young man of family. Politics was the only career which immediately attracted Lamb and he had a private arrangement with Kinnaird that he would take over the latter's seat at Leominster when his friend's elderly father died and he was thus propelled into the House of Lords. Where the money was to come from, however, was less easy to settle. Getting and keeping a seat in the Commons was usually an expensive, often a cripplingly expensive business, and there were few pickings to be expected by a young man notoriously opposed to the policy of the government. It is said that Lady Melbourne once played with the idea of the church for her second son but that Lord Egremont dissuaded her.[9] If true he acted wisely. Lamb might have made an excellent Renaissance or perhaps eighteenth-century prelate but he would have fitted unhappily on the bench of bishops in the early days of Queen Victoria. He had no taste for the army or navy; commerce was, of course, unthinkable; literature too uncertain. Diplomacy was a possibility but he loved London and did not think that he much cared for foreigners.

There remained the bar. This was a highly respectable profession: Campbell when he entered his chambers in 1801 noted gleefully that, 'Almost all my neighbours are people of large income – Honourables, Rt Honourables, etc. A card with Lincoln's Inn upon it is as genteel for a young man as Grosvenor Square'.[10] It could also – given a judicious combination of brains, industry and good connections – prove uncommonly lucrative. Finally Lamb felt himself well suited for it, priding himself on his logical mind and powers of persuasion. He moved into his chambers in Lincoln's Inn just before Christmas, 1801, but devoted his first year almost exclusively to the pursuit of his courtesan and shooting in Scotland. It was not till November 1802 that he settled down to serious study.

It was Cambridge all over again. Lamb wrote that he took to the Law 'with contemptuous notions both of the system and its professors'. He knew it all already or would find it out within a few weeks, and what is more 'would be able to elucidate it with a clearness and reduce it to an order hitherto unknown either in Lincoln's Inn or Westminster Hall'. It took him only a few weeks to realize how irrelevant were his principles and reflections amid the maze of precedents which composed the law of England; two years to discard all he had learned in Glasgow and memorize the tedious rituals which were the life-blood of the barrister. Lamb loathed the drudgery, but concluded that the price must be paid. In Michaelmas 1804, on the same date as Charles Pepys, the future Lord Chancellor, he was called to the bar.

His career must have been one of the briefest in legal history. He elected to work in the north, partly because the area was one of the less fashionable and therefore less competitive but mainly because he was invited to accompany on the circuit a family friend who was just breaking through into the first rank of contemporary barristers, Charles Scarlett, later to become Lord Abinger. Lamb's intention had been to tag along, watching what went on and perhaps devilling for his friend to justify his presence. Scarlett, however, did better than that and actually obtained a guinea brief for his protégé at the Lancashire sessions. It was to be the last money Lamb earned for nearly a quarter of a century. Before the sessions at Manchester were half concluded he was posting back to London on urgent family business.

Over the last few years the Lamb children had become ever more united. William and Frederick had been much together; two handsome, noisy and, at least superficially, self-confident young men. Frederick was now just down from Cambridge and preparing for the diplomatic service. His closest confidante, equally beloved but not as well known by William, was their younger sister, Emily. 'She was always like a pale rose,' William said, and with her grey eyes, hair clustered in dark curls around her face, slender waist and elegant, precise movements, the description did somehow catch her grace and cool beauty. She also had the thorns. Frederick called her a 'rattle-pate' and said that he would not love her so much if she had been otherwise. Not everyone would have agreed, for she had a sharp tongue and delighted in gossip, preferably malicious. To Lady Bessborough she seemed neither good-natured nor sincere and such was her general reputation. Though she might criticize one brother to another, however, she was fiercely loyal to them against the outside world and was to prove their most valued friend throughout their lives.[11]

Between Frederick and Emily had come George. Beside his tall, glamorous brothers George appeared short and thick, red-haired and red-faced, a clumsy, uncouth creature. But he was blessed with an excellent brain, quick wit and immense good nature. 'A more amiable jovial man I never knew,' wrote Haydon,[12] and though he was some-times dismissed as a buffoon it was usually with affection. Harriet, by far the youngest child, had died two years before of consumption. Pretty and bright, she had been something of a pet to William but though her death moved him greatly at the time, he had never known her well and was soon to forget her.

Peniston was always the odd man out. Considerably older and richer than his brothers, slightly frightened by his mother, he rarely appeared at home and devoted himself to hunting, his clubs, the race-course and his mistress, Mrs Musters. In 1803, when his sister was dying of con-sumption, he was afflicted by the same disease. He recovered, but never completely, and by the autumn of 1804 was once more seriously ill. William grew closer to him during his final illness and claimed that he was at last beginning to tire of his dissipated life and to be planning to devote more time to parliament. His regeneration was never put to the test. While William was in the north, Peniston's condition grew dramatically worse and on 24 January 1805 he died.

William was undoubtedly distressed, not only by Peniston's death but also by the misery of his parents and whispers that Emily had the same complaint.[13] Try as he might, however, he 'could not be entirely insensible to the change which the event produced in my own situation'. He was now the eldest son, heir to the peerage, the estates at Brocket and at Melbourne, the coalfields in Derbyshire and Nottinghamshire, a rich fortune besides. Now he could expect to inherit his brother's place in the Commons, and abandon the drudgery of the bar. Contentedly he settled down to wait until a seat became vacant. Meanwhile he indulged himself by reading all those books which he had wanted to read over the previous years but had put to one side because of his legal studies.

He did not enjoy this tranquil existence for long, nor did the prospect of a seat in the House of Commons play the most important part in his mind. 'A passion which I had long cherished, but had repressed while prudence forbade the indulgence of it, now that it felt all obstacles removed out of its way, broke forth and became my master.' In May 1805, William became engaged to Lady Caroline Ponsonby.

CHAPTER 4

'An exaggerated woman'

THE MARRIAGE between William Lamb and Caroline Ponsonby, or to be more precise the affair between Caroline Lamb and Lord Byron, has found an honoured place in the pages of English romantic folk-lore – tame stuff perhaps compared with the loves of Tristram and Iseult or Abélard and Héloïse, but evidently as sublime as this lack-lustre realm can offer. It is indeed a tale so much too often told that it is tempting to pass it by with no more than a cursory mention. To do so would, of course, be wrong. Lamb's marriage affected every aspect of his life. To ignore it would be to ignore an element crucial in the development of his personality and of his career. It would also be to pass by an episode as dramatic as it was bizarre, featuring protagonists who all, in their own way, were of exceptional quality.

Caroline Lamb would have proved professionally absorbing to any contemporary psychiatrist. It is only too easy to imagine her, flitting from couch to couch and revelling in the attention which her host of the moment was obliged to bestow on her. To be eschewed, however, is the temptation to apply modern psycho-analytical techniques to the scraps of information which survive about her and thus to arrive at some glib formula which would 'explain' her as a textbook example of the latest fashionable neurosis.

If one had to sum up Caroline's personality in a single word, it would be excess. 'She is such a mixture of good and bad, of talent and absurdity,' wrote Byron, 'in short an exaggerated woman.'[1] In all she did and said she trembled on the fringes of hysteria. Her irritation became rage; her disappointment, despair; her pleasure, unbridled joy. She lacked the internal thermostat which normally controls the emotional temperature of the adult human being. To apportion the blame for this between heredity and environment would be a futile exercise. It is hardly venturesome, however, to hazard that symptoms so extreme as Caroline's suggest that there was something wrong with her from birth. Equally there is every reason to think that her upbringing contributed substantially to her final predicament.[2]

Caroline Ponsonby was the daughter of the 3rd Earl of Bessborough, a dim Whig grandee who has left only the most vestigial traces of his existence. His wife Henrietta was altogether more formidable. Daughter of Earl Spencer, sister of the Duchess of Devonshire, her intelligence was as acute as her connections were resplendent. She produced three sons who ensured the succession; then indulged herself with a daughter. Unfortunately she indulged the daughter too. The facts about Caroline's upbringing are obscured by her inability to tell the truth about anything in which she herself was concerned, but there is no doubt that it was erratic and unsettling. Her childhood was divided between protracted tours of the Continent with – or at least generally in the same city as – her parents; sojourns with her austere, devoted yet somehow ineffective grandmother, Lady Spencer; and the nurseries of that gilded birdcage, Devonshire House. Her uncontrollable rages, followed usually by equally intemperate remorse, alarmed her parents, who referred her to the fashionable specialist in nervous diseases, Dr Warren. The doctor recommended that she be treated delicately, allowed to do more or less what she liked without being coerced into the harness of formal education. As a result she became still more self-willed and unstable; reading rapaciously in fields which appealed to her, such as poetry, but ignoring the more mundane elements in the curriculum.

William Lamb knew her as a child in Devonshire House. Afterwards he was accustomed to say that he had picked her out from the start as the girl for him. He met her again staying at Brocket in August 1802, significantly the moment at which he had just made his break for freedom from the *belle dame sans merci* who had held him in thrall for the previous year. The contrast between the professional courtesan and this fey child could not have been more complete. Caroline was not beautiful, often she was plain, sometimes even ugly. Her hair was cropped, her figure angular and boyish, her chin too pointed, her mouth too small, her eyes perpetually smudged as if she had just been crying or intended soon to do so. 'Her countenance had no other beauty than that of expression,' wrote Lamb, '*that* charm it possessed to a singular degree.' 'I won't talk to you about beauty,' echoed Byron, 'I am no judge, but our *beauties* cease to be so when near you . . .'[3]

Passive she was nothing, in animation she was transformed. On form she was one of the most enchanting companions men could imagine. She lacked the wit of her mother-in-law but was capable of blotting out almost any woman in an explosive fount of gaiety. Her rococo imagination was tempered by sensibility and enlivened by a delighted appreciation of the absurd. She had skill at drawing and singing but was too undisciplined ever to be more than a gifted amateur; only in the less rigorous arts of companionship was she truly mistress of her *métier*. To be with her was to be amused, stimulated, sometimes enraged, always interested; for Caroline could never be dull. Once again Byron's comment says it all: 'I have always thought you the cleverest, most agreeable, absurd, amiable, perplexing, dangerous, fascinating little being that lives now or ought to have lived 2000 years ago.' Above all, perhaps, she was capable of real and warm devotion. It was not the least of her charms to William Lamb that she made her affection for him evident from the start; in her cousin Lady Lyttelton's words she 'acted the gentleman's part and told him of her passion'.[4]

For three blissful days during a Brocket house party they whispered together in corners, William read her poetry and explained the meaning, partnered her at hunt-the-squirrel and hunt-the-slipper, told her tales of wonder as they sat together on the tither-tother. When she left they were mutually captivated and Caroline 'roared all the way from Brocket to Roehampton'.[5] But it seemed that it could never be more than a country house flirtation. The only daughter of the Earl of Bessborough must aim at higher game than the second son of a *nouveau riche* Irish viscount. It was generally assumed that she would marry her gentle, sensitive cousin Lord Hartington, heir to the Duke of Devonshire and already crippled by the deafness which was to dictate the pattern of his life. The Spencer heir, Lord Althorp, was another eminently proper possibility. Caroline, anyway, was only seventeen and a decision could safely wait for a year or two.

Peniston's death changed everything. Though still not as good a match as the other two William Lamb was now heir to an Irish peerage and a considerable fortune. After the smallest delay that propriety demanded he moved into the attack. The Bessboroughs were dubious. Caroline's mother thought he had many good qualities and great intelligence but deplored his manners, his principles and, above all, his mother. On the whole she would have preferred a safer suitor. But she had the sense and the charity to realize that her views were of secondary importance. As her sister wrote, 'this has brought about such happiness in her [Caroline], such evidence of the most boundless attachment, that

I really believe . . . that any check would be productive of madness or death'. In the face of such a conviction any serious resistance seemed impossible.[6]

I have loved you for four years, loved you deeply, dearly, faithfully – so faithfully that my love has withstood my firm determination to conquer it when honour forbade my declaring myself – has withstood all that absence, variety of objects, my own endeavours to seek and like others, or to occupy my mind with fix'd attention to my profession, could do to shake it.[7]

William Lamb can have had little doubt that his appeal would be favourably answered. Lady Bessborough gave him the good news in a corridor at Drury Lane; William embraced her with enthusiasm, then looked up to see the surprised and interested face of Mr Canning observing them from the staircase. He fled, leaving his future mother-in-law to explain the matter as best she could. She told Canning the truth and the news was soon all over London. At Lady Stafford's a few nights later Lamb was overwhelmed with congratulations. Lord Carlisle, it is true, appeared to believe Caroline to be eight years old and would only say 'come, come, this is a very good joke!' but the Prince of Wales was enraptured, clasped William by the hands and, beaming all over his face, repeated, 'I *am* so happy, oh! but so very happy!' Only the Melbournes, who had wanted William to marry money, were not wholly satisfied, and they, too, never contemplated trying to stop the match.[8]

By the wedding day – 3 June 1805 – Lady Bessborough was wholly won over. Caroline seemed almost miraculously to have calmed down and found a new sense of security. 'I believe all her ill-health, all the little oddities of manner and sauvagerie that us'd to vex me, arose from the unhappiness that was preying upon her . . .' But miracles do not happen, or not as easily as that. She survived the wedding with equanimity, spoke the responses with aplomb, then crumbled when the time came to leave her family. Her aunt found consolation in William's behaviour: 'she was very bad indeed, but he was so gentle and seems to know how to manage her so well that I have not any fear about her.'[9]

The couple honeymooned at Brocket: a transitory interval of peace broken by incursions from Caroline's relations. Their chances of establishing a mutually satisfactory way of life might have been greater if they had been left in peace. As it was benevolent observers seemed constantly to be arriving, taking the emotional temperature and reporting to all and sundry on what they had found. Lady Spencer was kept waiting an hour to allow her grandchild's nerves to settle; 'when she did at last come in she desired to see me alone and began panting and throwing herself in a chair'. All agreed that William's patience and devotion were exemplary and that few couples could ever have been more in love. Cautious optimism was the prevailing mood.[10]

Probably it was William's mood as well, yet even in these first few weeks he must have begun to wonder what he had taken on. Many years later he told Victoria that he had married too early, at thirty a man was more competent than at twenty-six to meet whatever demands were put upon him. He would have needed the wisdom of a philosopher, the patience of a saint, to support him through the trials ahead. To Victoria again he gave a simple explanation of why marriages broke up: 'Why, you see, a gentleman hardly knows a girl till he has proposed, and then when he has an unrestrained intercourse with her he sees something and says, "This I don't quite like".' Even before familiarity took the edge off the initial rapture there must have been a lot that Lamb did not quite like.[11]

Why did he do it? Caroline's instability, her sulky melancholy, her rages, her self-absorption, were notorious among all who knew her. Neither her beauty nor her riches were remarkable enough to redress the balance. The answer perhaps lay in her very frailties. She had the defencelessness which so many men long to protect, the fears which they long to appease, the vices which they long to cure. Intellectually she stimulated William, but she also stirred in him latent impulses of virility. He would have been vulnerable to any woman who demonstrated clearly that she loved and needed him. '. . . I do believe if I had been refused,' he once said, 'I should have died of it; it would have killed me; I was so very vain.' Caroline left him in no doubt that he would *not* be refused, that he would be eagerly welcomed, that life without him, indeed, would be intolerable.[12]

In one of the many perceptive passages in her novel *Glenarvon*[13] Caroline described what must have been her life among the Lambs:

What talents she had were of a sort they could not appreciate; and all the defects were those which they most despised. The refinement, the romance, the sentiment she had imbibed, appeared in their eyes assumed and unnatural; her strict opinions perfectly ridiculous; her enthusiasm absolute insanity; and the violence of her temper, if contradicted or opposed, the pettishness of a spoiled and wayward

child . . . There was a liberality of opinion which she could not at
once comprehend; and she said to herself daily, 'They are different
from me . . .'

Anyone might have found the Lambs a difficult family into which to
marry. Singularly united, censorious, contemptuous, they lived in an
atmosphere of fierce but amiable argument, of raucous jokes, of a
conversational free-for-all in which no holds were barred and no
subjects eschewed. Some found it bracing but those of lesser stamina
were deafened by the 'scarcely human though cheerful' laughter, aghast
at the freedom of their language, the hugeness of their appetites, the
informality of their manners. A typical Lamb joke was to send Lord
John Townshend into the bedroom of a young female visitor on the
pretence that he was sleeping there. Harriet Cavendish viewed a
forthcoming visit to Brocket with alarm. 'How they will crow and
shout over us when we are so entirely at their mercy. I am sure they
trod on Lord Morpeth's foot and I dare say they will knock out my
tooth. It is like getting among savages, there is no knowing how far
their vivacity may carry them.'[14]
For Caroline there was no escaping them, for she and William installed themselves on the second floor of the Melbournes' town house
in Whitehall. Though they had their own entrance and their own
establishment it was inevitable that the two households should often
mingle. Apart from William the Lambs treated Caroline with an irritated tolerance. Lord Melbourne had no idea what she was going on
about; Lady Melbourne knew but thought it silly. Emily, who in July
married the stolid, silent and enormously rich Lord Cowper, thought
her wholly unworthy of her beloved brother and a sly, mischief-
making *intrigante* into the bargain while George and Frederick dismissed her as absurd and felt the worse of William for not controlling
her excesses. In such an atmosphere it was hardly surprising that
Caroline should flee the family circle whenever possible. Elsewhere,
however, the whims and fancies which seemed so fatuous to her
husband's family, won her a certain reputation. The William Lambs
were sought-after guests and the occasions were rare indeed that they
had to spend an evening in each other's company.
A glimpse of their early married life comes from the various reports
of a lengthy house party at the Abercorns' house, The Priory, in the
winter of 1805. Amateur theatricals were Lord Abercorn's delight and
the centre piece was to be a performance of Lamb's old favourite from
Eton, *The Rivals*. This time he played Captain Absolute and yielded

Falkland to his close friend, the future Tory prime minister, Lord Aberdeen. George Lamb, whose own play *Whistle for it* was also given a performance prior to a Covent Garden production the following year, was generally agreed to be by far the most polished actor. William was also excellent but, observed Harriet Cavendish maliciously, 'too much occupied with his beauty and expression of countenance and makes crooked smiles to the audience when he ought to be attending to his companions. He is also rather tame as a lover and looks much alarmed as Caroline sits and watches him and would probably go into fits if an expression or look of well-acted tenderness was to escape him.'[15]

Caroline was pregnant, which on this occasion at least may have excused her possessiveness. Even so, William must have found it trying: she could not bear to have him out of her sight and, when restrained from following him into the lavatory, parked her maid outside to report as soon as he was on the move again. Lady Bessborough made various descents on The Priory – 'which is more like Bedlam than a house in the country' – to minister to her daughter, but found Lord Abercorn unsympathetic. 'No pain to be felt at *my* house,' was his edict and Caroline's disabilities were classed as treason. Luckily William's parts in both the plays were important enough to protect them from expulsion.

Apart from the play it was a leisurely life. William and Caroline would get up at ten or ten-thirty, breakfast, talk a little and read Thomas Newton's new book on the prophecies in the Bible. Caroline would then hear his lines after which William would go for a walk, leaving her to finish dressing. After a drive or some other excursion they would meet again to read Shakespeare together for an hour or two before the dressing bell. Dinner was at six, after which people read, talked, sang or played chess and backgammon. Supper came in at half past ten and by eleven there was a movement towards bed. Few sat up after midnight. Caroline and William were very conjugal, noted Harriet Cavendish, reading out of the same book and sharing the same chair, while the Aberdeens 'played at spillikins with their arms round one another's necks', and the Hinchinbrookes sat on a couch 'very civil and simpering'.

Such glimpses of the Lambs are often to be had at this period: 'living almost a London life' at Cowes; shooting at Brocket or with Lord Palmerston in Hampshire; at balls and dinners; at the play in Lady Holland's box, 'talking considerably louder than the actors'; at the famous masquerade party at Wattier's. William wore a magnificent Italian dress. 'He looked so stupid,' commented Harriette Wilson, 'I

could not help fancying that Lady Caroline had insisted on him showing himself thus beautiful, to gratify her vanity; for to do William
Lamb justice, his character is in truth a manly one . . .' The emphasis
is always on the almost ostentatious devotion which the couple showed
each other, but already there were stories of rows, disagreements over
trivial matters which flared up into violence, only to cool quickly in an
orgy of pleasurable reconciliation. Caroline relished such outbursts,
William was less enthusiastic. 'Remember,' he warned his nephew
many years later, 'that happiness is neither in marriage nor in celibacy
. . . but in a calm, settled and satisfied mind . . .'[16]

'The measure of married happiness,' William once told Victoria, 'is to
have a great number of children.'[17] She heeded the advice better than
her mentor. Caroline miscarried in February 1806. Lamb rushed back
from electioneering at Leominster to meet the little coffin going out
of the house. In August of the following year she produced a boy.
George Lamb took an early look at his nephew and pronounced him
'the most frightful creature he had ever beheld', but everyone else
agreed that Augustus was a most handsome baby. Caroline broke into
verse to express her rapture:

> His little eyes like William's shine –
> How great is then my joy,
> For while I call this darling mine,
> I see 'tis William's boy.

Then in January 1809 she had a daughter who died after only a few
hours. 'Caro really bears it with the greatest resignation,' wrote Lady
Bessborough, 'but it is a cruel disappointment.'[18]

It was not to be the only one. Augustus was christened with great
éclat, with the Prince of Wales as godfather, but he was only three or
four when doubts began to form about his progress. Physically he was
fair and fat enough but his ferocious temper and convulsions while
teething suggested that he was only too much his mother's son. Two
years later, when he could still barely speak and his fits grew no less
violent, his parents became seriously alarmed. Experts were called in
and pronounced that everything would probably right itself in due
course but his father at least was not satisfied. By 1812 or so William
Lamb must have been convinced that his only son would never lead
a normal life.

Some compensation was provided by a mysterious child, known as

Susan St John, who appeared in the household some time before 1820 with no explanation as to her origins. It has been suggested that she was Lamb's illegitimate daughter* and the contrary can not be proved but it seems more likely that she was an orphan adopted on some whim of Caroline's. Lamb treated her with avuncular affection but showed no special interest in her. After Caroline's death his various women friends were recruited to give advice on the girl's future and even to take her on holiday; in the end she married a Swiss and slipped back into the obscurity from whence she had come.

Perhaps if Caroline had borne children in whom she could have taken a pride it would have settled her in the coming years. Certainly it would have been some consolation to her husband. As it was their marriage was soon drifting towards disaster. Those who had hoped that matrimony would somehow provide a solution to Caroline's problems were quickly proved vain optimists. Merely, she widened the focus of her egocentricity to include her husband. She demanded from him constant and concentrated attention: love was desirable, flattery acceptable, abuse or even violence tolerable, so long as always she was the centre of his life.

William would not, could not oblige. Caroline wrote to Lady Holland from the bedside of a husband recovering from influenza:

> I am at home with William Lamb
> And he, I think, is rather better.
> He says he does not care a d—n
> Whether I prate or write a letter.[19]

The words were written in jest, but there was still a note of real bitterness. William's indifference was, to Caroline, more chilling than any rebuke. He cared certainly, cared about her excesses and her follies, her unhappiness and her tormented furies, but he did not care enough to make a determined stand. Caroline accused him of allowing her too much liberty, of laughing her out of prudishness yet offering no new set of standards to replace it.[20] Whether a more authoritarian approach would have made much difference in the long run can never be decided but certainly William's refusal to act as more than a by-stander, sometimes amused, sometimes appalled, can have done nothing to check her decay. Always he shied away from the confrontation which might have achieved some improvement in Caroline's conduct but would certainly have cost much in domestic uproar. She responded with ever more erratic flights of volatility. One moment she would abuse him or hurl

* Notably by Miss Margot Strickland, author of *Those Byron Women* (London, 1975).

crockery, the next be all charm and sweetness:

> I think lately my dearest William we have been very troublesome to each other which I take by wholesale to my own account and mean to correct . . . I will . . . be silent of a morning, entertaining after dinner, docile, fearless as a heroine in the last vol. of her troubles, strong as a mountain tiger.[21]

William would always succumb to such blandishments; her charm, when she chose to use it, he found invincible. But just as the outrage which preceded such a display failed to provoke the explosion of rage for which she hankered, so the reconciliation was calm and affectionate rather than passionate. Always William was temperate and reasonable; qualities which to Caroline smacked of apathy, even of rejection.

It was this urge for madder music and for stronger wine which drove her into the arms of Sir Godfrey Webster, son by the first marriage of the great Whig hostess, Lady Holland. Webster was a debauched rake, a former soldier of courage but no other noticeable quality who had established himself as a leading figure in London society. Caroline flung herself at his head with abandon: not so much for his attractions as because no one could have provided a greater contrast to her husband. Sir Godfrey accepted the gift horse quizzically: she was not at all his sort of woman but she was fashionable and celebrated and as such added a creditable notch to his tally of conquests. For a few months their liaison was notorious, then Sir Godfrey lost his appetite for emotional explosions, Caroline sickened of his earthy sensuality, the affair withered and died.

It had achieved some of its objects. Lady Melbourne had been enraged by behaviour 'so disgraceful in its appearance and so disgusting from its motives that it is quite impossible it should ever be effaced from my mind'. Lady Holland was offended by the scandal which her son and Caroline had fomented and still more by the impertinent letters which the latter had sent her. Now Caroline, uneasily aware that she had gone too far, indulged herself in a welter of repentance. 'I know I have sinned beyond all hope of pardon,' she told Lord Holland. 'From this hour I promise to give up all further acquaintance with Sir Godfrey . . .' Lady Holland was one of the few people whom Caroline feared. 'How wrong I have been William will never know,' she now wrote to that redoubtable matron. 'I do not think that were I to tell him he would believe it.'[22]

Worse still, he would not have listened. The affair with Godfrey Webster had failed in its prime object, the provocation of William into some violent reaction. 'My husband is angry with me,' she wrote hopefully, but if he was his anger was moderate and well-concealed. He cannot have been unaware of what was going on but must have decided that the matter was of little moment and that, publicly at least, he would ignore it. Such dignified restraint was to be harder to maintain with Caroline's next escapade.

George Gordon, 6th Lord Byron, graduated almost overnight from the obscure station of an impoverished backwoods peer to that of London's foremost literary lion. The world-weary romanticism of *Childe Harold* prepared the way for the coming of the Lord, but it was the fine head, the haunted beauty of his features, the low musical voice, the well-cultivated taste for melancholy which completed the conquest of London society. Byron was one of the funniest and gayest of companions yet, for those who craved it, could instantly register the appropriate degree of gloom with artistry and apparent satisfaction. Any serious attempt at analysing this most elusive of human beings is perhaps fortunately beyond the scope of this book. What is relevant is that to Caroline reality and legend proved equally bewitching.

The tragi-comedy of Byron and Caroline is too well known to call for lengthy recapitulation. The first abortive meeting followed by Caroline's celebrated comment in her journal, 'Mad, bad and dangerous to know'; the second meeting at Holland House, 'that beautiful pale face is my fate'; Byron's first present of a single rose, 'Your Ladyship, I am told, likes all that is new and rare – for a moment': though the libretto is clearly written by accomplished artists, the plot is that of a third-rate operetta.

Through the summer of 1812 the affair raged vehemently. Despite the flamboyance it bears a curious air of innocence. 'I really believe that the public see the worst of it and that there is no real harm,' wrote John Ward. 'But then the world in general does not make so charitable a conclusion, and the scandal is infinite.' There may be no smoke without fire but here most monumental billows of smut seem to have issued from the meagrest flames. Little by little Caroline's demands for emotional satisfaction became more strident and Byron's disinclination to gratify her more implacable. At root he found it impossible to believe that any real feelings could lie behind the histrionics: 'I need not repeat that I lay stress upon no attachment, *two* balls and one admirer will settle the last to her heart's content.' He was not alone in his judgement, but was no less wrong for that.[23]

The climax came on 12 August, when Caroline was lectured by her mother and hectored by Lord Melbourne in his most tactless vein. Beside herself, she threatened to leave the house and fly to Byron. 'Go and be damned!' said her father-in-law robustly. She went, but took refuge not with her lover but in the house of a surgeon in Kensington. There she was discovered by a thoroughly alarmed Lord Byron and persuaded to return home. 'O Lady Caroline,' wailed the faithful housekeeper, Mrs Petersen, '. . . you have exposed yourself to all London, you are the talk and [sic] of every groom and footman about the town.' Lady Bessborough was so overcome that she collapsed unconscious in her carriage but recovered in time to accompany her daughter to Melbourne House. 'I went in before her, and William most kindly promised to receive and forgive her . . . But how long will it last?'[24]

The most interesting feature of the whole affair was the dog that did not bark in the night, the failure of William Lamb to take any steps to protect his household or his honour. He knew that many of his friends and all his acquaintances were waiting for some violent reaction, knew that he was being sneered at as a cuckold. He must have had his own case in mind when many years later he reminded Grey about Dean Burrows, whose 'wife was caught with another man and he took no steps upon it, nor said anything about it. This was at that time considered a conclusive reason against a man being made a bishop . . . it being held decisive evidence that a man's own conduct in those matters would not stand investigation.' Certainly he was not influenced by any fondness for Byron. On the contrary, he disliked him, describing him to Victoria as 'treacherous beyond conception . . . he dazzled everybody and deceived them'.[25]

And yet he did nothing. To his contemporaries this seemed amazing: 'I wonder he don't throw her out of the window,' wrote Ward '. . . and then send *Childe Harold* after her.'[26] Yet his conduct was in character. Throughout his life it was his preoccupation to avoid taking any active measure until it was forced upon him, above all to avoid any action of which the results could not readily be predicted. For this he has been accused of laziness, cowardice, an over-delicate shrinking from unpleasant confrontations. None of these harsh epithets is wholly unjustified. Yet Lamb's attitude was founded on the rational if pessimistic belief that human beings are not merely fallible but usually inefficient and often malevolent. Consequently any attempt they might make to extricate themselves from messes of their own contriving would be likely merely to embroil things further. Leave well alone and *a fortiori* do the same for bad. No one can state with confidence that a more energetic policy would have worked better. With two characters as volatile as Caroline and Byron there is indeed reason to doubt whether it would have helped if Lamb had played the virile and indignant husband. It might have been just what Caroline desired and needed; equally it might have provoked even worse excesses or breathed life into an affair that would otherwise soon have died naturally.

In so far as anyone intervened it was Lady Melbourne. 'Lord Byron had bewitched the whole family, mother and daughter and all . . .' Lord Melbourne indignantly told the Prince of Wales.[27] His wife was not bewitched, though she certainly found Byron both attractive and entertaining. Having packed William and Caroline off to Ireland with the Bessboroughs she settled down to win the poet away from her daughter-in-law and eventually to redirect him towards her equally unsuitable but less committed niece, Annabella Milbanke. In the process she won Byron's trust and part at least of his heart.

The death throes of Byron's affair with Caroline were protracted and undignified. The more she clamoured for attention, the more violently he recoiled, lashing out with a fury that may have been defensive in origin but soon acquired elements of the sadistic. Her crowning exploit, in which as so often with her, tragedy teetered on the edge of farce, came at Lady Heathcote's ball in July 1813. Distraught with jealousy at Byron's attentions to Lady Oxford, Caroline made an hysterical scene which concluded with her breaking a glass and attacking her wrists with the fragments, then continuing the work upstairs with a pair of scissors. 'I could not have believed it possible for anyone to carry absurdity to such a length,' commented Lady Melbourne acidly. 'I call it so, for I am convinced she knows perfectly what she is about all the time.'[28] There was some justice in the jibe, but Lady Melbourne could never understand the real pain that lay below the extravagance. The incident too was typical in another way. Byron was there, Lady Melbourne was there, Lady Bessborough was there, but William Lamb had stayed quietly at home.

The affair was over. Byron's farewell is part of romantic tradition, but bears repeating once more. Caroline had invaded his rooms and, seeing a copy of Beckford's *Vathek* lying open, had scrawled 'Remember me' across the title page. Byron took up the injunction with bitter relish:

> Remember thee! Remember thee!
> Till Lethe quench life's burning streams

Remorse and shame shall cling to thee
  And haunt thee like a feverish dream
Remember thee! Ay, doubt it not,
  Thy husband too shall think of thee,
By neither shalt thou be forgot,
  Thou false to him, thou fiend to me!

Gradually the dust settled, but William Lamb's marriage was never to return even to its former unsatisfactory state. For one thing, Caroline could not bring herself entirely to accept defeat. In the face of the most brutal rebuffs she continued to bombard Byron with letters, three in a week at the beginning of 1814. Throughout the spring and summer she would invade his rooms whenever she found an open door: 'I can't throw her out of the window,' complained Byron to Lady Melbourne, 'but I will not receive her . . . she has no shame – no feeling – no one estimable or redeemable quality.' Not until Byron's engagement was announced did Caroline seem to recognize that all was over; even then she was suspected by Byron of inserting in the *Morning Chronicle* a paragraph denying that the wedding was to take place.[29]

She had been gravely tried by her experience. Harriet Cavendish described her on her return from Ireland. 'She is worn to the bone, as pale as death and her eyes starting out of her head. She seems indeed in a sad way, alternately in tearing spirits and in tears . . . She appears to me in a state very little short of insanity.'[30] Hary-O, as Harriet was nicknamed, was not the most charitable of observers but many other reports paint the same picture. She was not mad, in the sense that she would be certifiable by contemporary standards, but her carapace of self-control, always thin, had been eroded to a point where hysteria was just below the surface. Only the slightest stimulus was needed to provoke outbursts of rage or grief.

Yet Lamb stuck to her. It was not for want of advice to the contrary from relations and friends. Constantly the gossips reported that a separation was imminent. Lord Auckland in October 1814 told his sister that the terms had actually been worked out and that Lady Melbourne had driven triumphantly down to Brocket to arrange the final details, only to find 'the happy couple at breakfast, and Lady Caroline drawling out – "William, some more muffin?" – and everything made up'. Three months later it was Lord Byron anxiously asking Lady Melbourne, now his aunt, whether it was true that the Lambs were about to separate – 'If it is so I hope that this time it is only on account of incompatibility of temper – and that no more serious scenes have occurred.'[31]

Lamb must seriously have contemplated the idea, yet when it came to the point he shrank from it. Partly this must have been out of loyalty, partly inertia, partly compassion, partly a fear of unpleasant scenes. Yet as important as anything was the fact that he still loved Caroline; not with the zest of ten years before but with a weary tenderness, so that she could still melt him by any sign of grief or affection. Still more, he knew that she loved and needed him. 'She has no real affection,' judged Byron, 'or if any it is to the very man she has most injured.'[32] She had been true to William in her fashion, though the fashion was not one which could have commended itself to her husband. However excessive her passions, she never forgot that he was the one constant force for good that remained to her. That she deserved ill of him she recognized, she was ashamed of the mischief she had done him, she was grateful for the kindness that he had always shown. 'She is most *dangerous* when *humblest*,' Byron warned a friend. 'Like a Centipede – she crawls and stings.'[33] Yet the humility was real and William reacted to it with chivalry. Byron one day told Lady Melbourne what seemed to him an absurd story. Lamb had come home to find Caroline in tears. He asked the reason and was told that Byron had insulted her. On hearing this he showed greater indignation towards his wife's former lover than he had ever done when the affair was prospering. Such conduct might indeed have seemed absurd to Byron, but it was also generous in the grand style. It was the sort of grandeur which Caroline appreciated.

In 1815 Frederick Ponsonby, Caroline's brother, was seriously wounded at Waterloo. The Lambs had been contemplating a continental tour for some months, this news stimulated them into action. By the end of June they were in Brussels. Ponsonby, wrote Lord Fitzroy Somerset unkindly, was 'in dread of Caro's sisterly persecutions, but she was soon prevailed upon to prefer parading about the town at all hours'. While she thus diverted herself William visited the battlefield – the stock entertainment for English tourists who would make up large parties and return laden with skulls, old shoes or other evocative souvenirs.[34]

By August Caroline's brother was on the mend and the Lambs moved on to Paris, taking a house in the Place Royale near where the Bessboroughs were similarly installed. Indeed, a large section of London society seemed to be there and the English colony managed to recreate a fair simulacrum of the life it had left behind. Wellington was, of course, the prize catch for every hostess and Caroline only one of many who made a set at him. 'I have no doubt that she will to a certain extent succeed,' noted Harriet Cavendish, 'as no dose of flattery is too strong for him to swallow or her to administer.'[35] She throve in Paris, surrounding herself with a raffish group of admirers – 'Lovers and tradespeople' as her cousin haughtily assessed them – while William lurked disconsolately in an adjoining room.

For him the trip to the Continent must have been something of a last throw. If his marriage was ever to return to normality then it must be now, in new surroundings and away from the baleful presence of Byron. He can have been left in little doubt that the experiment had failed. Caroline's extravagance was unchecked, she flaunted herself publicly half naked or in purple riding habit, held the floor noisily at dinner parties and tormented her husband with violent scenes. One night she was described as smashing glasses and ornaments, upsetting furniture, hurling vases and candlesticks to the ground. William Lamb looked 'worn to a bone' noted Harriet Cavendish. It was perhaps no coincidence that at this time his hair began to go grey. At first he was seriously concerned. 'I had all the grey hairs pulled out,' he told Queen Victoria. 'I had three women at it, and in a week's time there were just as many; and you have no idea how painful it is, when you go on doing it for an hour together.'[36]

By the time the Lambs returned to London he had abandoned the battle and accepted the grizzled dignity that lasted the rest of his life. He had abandoned another battle too and resigned himself to a marriage which, if it survived at all, could bring him no satisfaction and allow him little peace. He was thirty-six years old.

———◆◆◆———

CHAPTER 5

The Doldrums

TO DESCRIBE a man's private and public life in neatly insulated chap-
ters is to present a false dichotomy. Inevitably the two interact, often
events in the one may wholly alter the development of the other.
William Lamb must have been less effective as a parliamentary performer
because of the strains of his home. With a wife whom he could have
respected and consulted, he would probably have reacted with less
asperity to the disappointments of his career. If he had done so, it is
conceivable that he would have had less reason to feel disappointed
in the future. 'I know enough of domestic disquietude,' he told Lansdowne, 'not to be surprised at any step, which a man may take under
the pressure of it.'[1] Nevertheless, such variations would have been of
minor importance. There was little room for manoeuvre on the part
of any of the main protagonists. Let Caroline have been the most wise
and considerate of wives, William the most contented of husbands, and
it still seems unlikely that by 1815 his place in the political sphere
would have changed to any marked degree.

Even before his marriage Lamb was launched into the political career
on which his heart was set. He was pressed to stand for Hertford in the
place of his brother Peniston but refused because of his earlier arrangement to take over Leominster from his friend Kinnaird. He went to
Hertford, however, to take the chair at the county meeting and was
deemed a success. Tom Lloyd, the vicar, roared across the church to
Lord John Townshend, 'What a damned shame it was that you did not
come to hear William Lamb t'other day. His speech has done him more
than a three years canvas, by God!' Kinnaird's father died in the

summer of 1805 and Lamb was elected to Leominster with a minimum of trouble. The arrangement, however, was never meant to be more than temporary and at the general election of 1806, as a result of a complicated deal between the Duke of Bedford and Lord Lauderdale, Lamb was brought in for the Haddington Boroughs. The seat was in Lord Lauderdale's gift and only the most token obeisance to the wishes of his constituents was imposed upon the would-be member.[2]

Lamb would, of course, never have been sponsored in this way if it had not been known that he would support the Whigs. As a parliamentary force this group was still numerically weak, though the quality of its membership sometimes disguised its powerlessness. The phrase 'His Majesty's Opposition' was not coined for another twenty years and George III certainly considered the Whigs a most dissident rabble but they did in fact operate more nearly as a regular opposition party than had been the case before, setting themselves against Pitt's belligerent policy and hence, by extension, criticizing almost every piece of legislation which the Pittite administration introduced.[3]

Of this band Fox was still undisputed chief; without him, indeed, it is hard to see how the party would have survived. He was dropsical now, almost visibly in decay, but his brilliant mind and the delights of his personality were as potent as ever. Of his followers, Lord Lansdowne was generally agreed to be the most eminent. 'The damnedest idiot that ever lived,' Creevey described him irascibly many years later, but in 1806 he was generally held to be sensible and serious. His great possessions and powers as an orator assured him an important role but in the last resort he lacked the will to govern others, still more the common touch. '. . . there was some resemblance between him and his London residence,' observed Guizot, 'capacious, imposing, well-furnished, but somewhat cold in the nature of its ornaments.'[4]

Lord Howick, later to be Lord Grey,[5] was the most impressive of the younger Whigs. He had 'the patrician thoroughbred look . . . which I dote upon,' said Byron,[6] and the fact that the Duchess of Devonshire doted upon it too did nothing to diminish his standing in the party. Lamb admired him and believed that his 'commanding figure, his lofty yet gracious deportment' stamped him as a future leader, but he never felt towards him the love he bore for Fox. Nor did other members of the party: Howick was a distant figure; to be respected certainly, followed perhaps, but not a man to die for.

Brougham, a mountebank of genius, commanded more affection. His learning was immense, his eloquence sublime; yet already he showed signs of the vanity and instability which were to cripple his career. Lord Holland commemorated him in doggerel:

> There's a wild man at large doth roam,
> A giant wit! – they call him Brougham
> And well me thinks they may;
> He deals, whene'er he speaks or acts,
> With friends and foes and laws and facts
> In such a *sweeping* way![7]

Holland himself, nephew of Fox and with much of his uncle's charm, was another member of the Whig inner circle. His great wealth, his conviviality and the zest of his wife turned his mansion in Kensington into the virtual headquarters of the Whig party. Lady Holland had been divorced and was thus *persona non grata* to the stricter ladies but she revenged herself by drawing away their husbands night after night. Lamb never admitted to liking or admiring her – her manners were appalling, her house too cold or too hot, her table too crowded – yet like everybody else he went on coming. He would explain that he was drawn there by her husband but in fact he was in search of the unique stimulation provided by that 'great lady – fanciful, hysterical and hypochondrical, ill natured and good natured, afraid of ghosts and not of God', who would not for the world have begun a journey on a Friday evening but was quite ready to run away from her husband on any other day of the week.[8] She would dearly have loved to see her second husband as Prime Minister but he was a light-weight and knew it, all the more esteemed by his colleagues because of his limited ambitions.

The most attractive of the Whig leaders was Lord Althorp, eldest son of Earl Spencer and thus, like Howick and Lamb, destined eventually to join Holland and the other grandees in the House of Lords. He was a monument of integrity, one of the few politicians who really meant it when he said that he preferred country life to even the most triumphant role in Westminster. Though slow, he had a good brain; though no orator, he talked sense; but it was his decency and his generosity which endeared him to his colleagues and, for that matter, to his opponents.

Althorp was Caroline's cousin and William Lamb liked and trusted him. But the two men were not close friends. Throughout his life Lamb was to be surrounded by men who enjoyed his company, but he had few male intimates; his brothers, Frederick and George, had more of his confidence than anyone else and were the only men with whom he could completely relax. Outside the family circle it was always in the company of women that he felt most at ease. Though he was a member of Brooks's, the leading Whig club, his use of it was sparing. This backwardness, rooted in social rather than political inclination, nevertheless affected his public life since it effectively excluded him from the small, informal conclaves in which party policy was evolved. A readiness to discuss, argue, plot until far into the night is a desirable attribute for any politician; Lamb always preferred to read a book or talk to a pretty woman. Though his attitude may seem eminently sensible it was not to help him in his career.

Lamb's first election coincided with a violent transformation of the political pattern. William Pitt died in January 1806. Lamb had neither known him personally nor admired him politically but he felt as much as anyone that a giant had passed. As a graduate of Cambridge, he had a vote in the election for Pitt's seat as member for the university. Within forty-eight hours of the seat being vacated he received a note from Pitt's would-be replacement, soliciting his support. 'Damn him!' he exclaimed, crumpling the letter. 'Can no feeling but party enter his cold heart?'[9]

Pitt's death opened the way for the 'Ministry of All the Talents' – an uneasy coalition of Foxite Whigs, followers of Lord Grenville and dissident Tories under Lord Sidmouth. Homogeneous only in the fact that, for one reason or another, most of its members had been opposed to Pitt, it nevertheless seemed almost impregnable in its massive majority. Lamb, knowing that Fox liked him, had confidently expected to be offered some kind of post. He was disappointed. The difficulty of satisfying the two main groups, he wrote, 'one very needy and the other very grasping', meant that there was little room for bright young men of unproven ability. Philosophically he reflected that a chance was bound to offer itself soon and that it would do him no harm to establish himself as a debater in the meantime.

Within a few months of taking office, Fox was dead. Lamb lost not merely a family friend and the man who had inspired him politically and philosophically, but also a powerful protector. Now the effective leadership of the Foxite Whigs fell to Lord Howick, a man to whom Lamb felt far less close. Howick, however, showed goodwill. In December 1806 he asked Lamb to move the address – a task normally offered to young men on the verge of office. After nearly a year in the House of Commons, Lamb had still to make his maiden speech. 'I think he has lately fallen into a want of confidence in himself,' commented his brother Frederick.[10] Lamb affected to treat the matter lightly;

maintaining that he had nothing particular which he wished to say. In fact, as he admitted in his autobiographical notes, he was in terror at the prospect. His dramatic training, he said, had made him dependent on learning speeches by heart. Those who had seen him confidently stride the stage as Captain Absolute took it for granted that he was a natural orator. In fact, 'I was always very nervous, I was too vain to expose myself to what I considered the disgrace of speaking in a hesitating manner, and I had not taken the measures necessary for a more fluent and striking performance.' Time after time he braced himself to speak; then, when the day ended, found himself mute, secretly humiliated, never having even tried to catch the Speaker's eye.

Moving the address was a relatively painless way of starting. He was able to prepare his speech carefully and memorize it in the confidence that it would not have to be adapted to meet the demands of the debate. The result was adequate if not memorable. Lamb emphasized the need for a strong army, deplored the equivocation and insincerity shown by the French in the recent negotiations for peace and extolled the blessings enjoyed by the British at home, 'not only by the superior classes of society but by a great majority of the meanest and most illiterate of the people'. The House applauded this comforting reflection and Sheridan told his wife that Lamb had acquitted himself admirably.[11] Lamb, however, was little encouraged, since he knew his success was irrelevant to his performance as a debater. It was to be seven years before he overcame his nervousness and even then he was never rated a considerable orator. For the next few years his speeches were almost always contrived and artificial; he would launch himself into laboured periods which he had worked out conscientiously in advance, then flounder like a tyro if he was interrupted or lost his train of thought.

In March 1807 the ministry sank, torpedoed by the King and Lord Sidmouth on the issue of Catholic Emancipation. In its place came in the solid, humdrum team of the Duke of Portland, Perceval and Hawkesbury which, though modified from time to time by deaths or resignations, was to remain in power for some twenty years. At the election which followed Lamb transferred to Portarlington, an Irish borough, a move necessary because the Duke of Bedford could not provide him with a seat in England.

In the autumn of 1807 the British launched a pre-emptive strike against Copenhagen, an unpalatable step justified by ministers on the grounds that otherwise Napoleon would have laid his hands on the Danish navy. Lamb wrote to rebuke his wife for referring to the 'naughty Danes'; as far as he could see, he said, 'they are much more sinned against than sinning'.[12] But though he thus supported the official Whig line, he did so only with many reservations. He argued that the government had on the whole acted 'wisely and resolutely', though he allowed himself to be talked into sticking with his party in the House of Commons. The issue was of significance for it was on questions of this kind, in which patriotism pulled one way, party loyalties the other, that Lamb's relationship with the Whig leaders was to be put under heavy strain in the next few years. Eighteen months later he was deploring the 'impolitic and unfortunate course' taken by his colleagues in opposing English intervention in the war in Spain.

Yet on other matters, in so far as the terms 'left' and 'right' make any sense when applied to the political spectrum of the early nineteenth century, Lamb was at this time usually to be found on the activist left of the Whig party. 'I had always been eager and almost extreme in popular opinions,' he wrote, joining with his party in their dislike of the King and delight in thwarting him. In 1809 a golden opportunity arose. The Duke of York, George III's second son and Commander-in-Chief of the British army, was accused of conspiring with his mistress to sell military commissions and promotions. He had in fact been no more than foolishly indiscreet but there was much material for making scandal. A split opened in the party between the sober leaders – Grey, Ponsonby and Tierney – who found the affair distasteful, and the fanatics who would happily have hounded the Duke into his grave. Though Lamb as usual shrank from speaking he did not miss a day of the proceedings and was with the final minority of thirty who pressed for a general inquiry into corruption in the administration.

This vision of Lamb as angry young radical may appear curious to those acquainted with his subsequent career. The limits to his radicalism were indeed always apparent. In April 1810 Brougham wrote to him about parliamentary reform. In this 'greatest and most momentous subject', Brougham said, it was essential that the party should proceed with moderation, the existing system should be tinkered with not swept away, healing was preferable to amputation.[13]

Lamb's reply unhappily does not survive but it is not difficult to imagine its content if he volunteered the 'candid sentiments' for which Brougham asked. No parliamentary reform could be too moderate for Lamb. Healing was certainly better than amputation but inactivity would be best of all. He believed this not because he felt the parliamentary system to be perfect but because, with all its faults, it worked reasonably well, there was no certainty that reforms would improve it and there was a risk that any movement towards change would unleash forces beyond the control of those who had called them into being. Look before you leap and then don't do it, was Lamb's political philosophy; a passivism tempered only by the reflection that it might be better to leap if otherwise you would certainly be pushed.

Though parliamentary reform was the issue which brought into the open Lamb's distrust of what he called 'the high popular party', a more general dislike of their policies and principles was forming in his mind:

> I began to perceive the folly of some and the ill designs of others, that they were for the most part entirely ignorant of the constitution and the laws, which they pretended to restore and amend; that their arrogance and presumption were equal to their ignorance and incapacity; that either from passion or prejudice they were guilty of every species of misrepresentation . . . Their sweeping condemnation of all who differed from them, their exclusive claims of credit for integrity and abilities, the haughtiness with which they demanded from all, who had not satisfied them, explanations of their conduct . . . proved amply to me that from them, if ever they should obtain power in the country, might be expected measures more illegal and oppressive in themselves, than any, which had ever been attempted by kings and nobles, and aggravated by the low insolence of vulgar and illiberal minds.

This diatribe was, of course, directed against 'the Mountain', the activist wing of the party where Whiggery shaded into radicalism. But this wing was in many ways the driving force of the Whig party, some of the best and most constructive minds were concentrated there, its influence was out of all proportion to its numbers. When Lamb deplored its growing power he cast doubts on the future of the party.

On Catholic Emancipation, that central pillar of the Whig temple, he felt no doubts. The dividing line between tolerance and indifference is notoriously hard to draw. Lamb can often fairly be accused of straying across it. On the question of a man's religious beliefs, however, his views were based on principle and firmly maintained in the face of any opposition. He was mildly anti-Semitic; not that he knew any Jews but he suspected that he would not like them if he did. Though disapproving of dissenters he still boasted to Queen Victoria about his gardener: 'Great thing to have a dissenter; they don't go to races, they don't hunt, and don't engage in any expensive amusements.'[14] But neither in the one case nor the other did he feel that he had any right to interfere in the way that they chose to worship, nor that religious beliefs as such should be a criterion for deciding whether a man should vote or hold some post in the public service.

In May 1810 he chose this subject for what was till then by far his most considerable speech in the House of Commons.[15] He did not deny that the influence of the Roman Catholic Church could sometimes be dangerous to British interests: 'Good God! Sir, danger from the spiritual influence of a foreign power! . . . Whoever doubted, whoever disputed it? . . . There is danger, Sir, a danger which makes me shudder day and night – a danger which makes the empire totter to its very foundations!' But as he lay awake shuddering he asked himself how the danger was to be countered. Not by persecution, of that he was sure: all sects throve on persecution and 'became supine and negligent as soon as they were established in security'. To treat Roman Catholics with trust and respect, to treat them as British citizens, was the only sure way to disarm them.

His peroration caused some comment. He said that he had 'for the most part, acted in opposition to His Majesty's ministers'. He had, he felt, been right to do so. Their foreign policy had been mistaken, their expeditions ill-conceived, their commercial measures unwise. But in all these cases some defence was possible. Only when their attitude towards the Catholics in Ireland was considered did he see no possibility of justification. 'Ireland is the great cause, the root and foundation of my opposition. My hostility to them is persevering as it is because they hold their offices pledged . . . not to adopt those measures which are necessary for the conciliation of Ireland, and the consolidation of the empire.' To some it appeared that he was signalling to those on the Tory benches who felt like him on the Catholic question, above all to Canning and his followers. Let this one issue be resolved, he seemed to suggest, and I am yours.

In October 1810 the old King made the final descent into the black night of his insanity. Politics, for so long imprisoned within the framework of his prejudices, now seemed to offer a new flexibility. The predilection of the Prince of Wales for the opposition had for so long been accepted that it was generally assumed a Whig government would follow his taking power. Perceval managed temporarily to thwart this intention by allowing the Prince only limited powers during his first year as Regent. The Whigs indignantly opposed this ploy, Lamb moving the amendment in the House of Commons, but consoled themselves with the thought that the Regent would be even more certain to make them his ministers when the restrictions lapsed.

So certain were they that the prize would be theirs, that in February 1811 Grenville and Grey formed a shadow administration. Lamb was approached and offered a post either as a Lord of the Treasury or as one of the Under Secretaries. It was not sensational; equally, for a man of thirty-one with no experience in office, some doubts about his loyalty and a pretty undistinguished record in the House of Commons, it was as much as could have been expected. To Lamb, however, it seemed wholly inadequate. He reacted with a querulous indignation which in later years he was to recall with mingled shame and amusement. 'This proposal,' he wrote, 'mortified me extremely. It placed clearly before my eyes the consequences of my own hesitation and irresolution, it showed me of how little value I was considered, and what was to me the most galling of all, it told me plainly that many were to be preferred before me, whom I knew to be in every respect my inferiors.' He declined the offer on the curious ground that he had been dismayed by the abuse always heaped on those in receipt of public money.

Unfortunately for the Whigs the Regent had been quietly growing disenchanted by them over the last few years. After a somewhat brusque suggestion that Grey and Grenville should form a coalition with the Tory ministers, the Whig Lords were suffered to return to outer darkness. Lamb made appropriate noises of disapproval and did indeed deplore what he called the 'cold and hollow offer' of the Regent, but he must have viewed with some relish the chagrin of those whom he felt had recently misused him.

The liberal, Canningite wing of the Tory party had particular appeal for Lamb. Canning himself was one of the most brilliant and in some ways attractive of contemporary politicians, yet to many his intelligence seemed meretricious, his oratory flamboyant, his high principles hypocritical. Lamb himself was always ambivalent, In 1800 he was dismissing him as either a 'degraded fool' or an 'infamous calumniator'; forty years later he impressed Howick with his low opinion of Canning, describing him as a schemer and fundamentally dishonest; yet frequently in the interval he was classed as, indeed behaved like a dedicated Canningite. 'William was completely devoted to him . . .' wrote his sister Emily in 1827, and Emily knew as much of her brother's mind as anyone.[16]

The man whom Lamb liked best among the Canningites was the rich, talented and eccentric John Ward, future Earl of Dudley, but his closest association was with the more prosaic Huskisson. Physically uncouth, intellectually pawky, inadequate in society and incompetent in the House of Commons, Huskisson was yet curiously formidable. He was a connection of the Lambs by marriage and was generally derided by them – 'as yet I never saw a man not bred a gentleman who became one,' observed Frederick loftily. As William Lamb got to know him better he felt more and more admiration for his clear mind, integrity and capacity for hard work. Huskisson, he told Greville, was 'the greatest practical statesman he had known', and, though he never warmed to him, he was always a man under whom Lamb would have been happy to serve.[17]

Lamb markedly drew apart from the main stream of the party during the debates of 1812. The most clear breach came when questions of civil order were discussed. He urged ferocious penalties against the operatives who smashed frames in the cotton factories in the belief that otherwise their jobs would be lost and, in July, directly challenged Whitbread and Burdett in a debate on the preservation of public peace.[18] There was, he maintained, sufficient evidence of a 'system of outrage' which threatened every person and all property in the land. He could not go along with all the measures that the Tories proposed but some extension of the powers of the authorities was essential. By the standards of the day such an attitude was neither extreme nor particularly reactionary, being shared by men of good will such as Wilberforce as well as by Whigs in the mould of Lansdowne and Grenville. He was, however, directly opposing his own party leadership in the Commons. 'I offended, and in some measure alienated many of my friends by so doing but I approve my conduct upon reflection.'

Several times during 1811 Perceval had conveyed hints to Lamb that a job in the administration was his for the asking. In February 1812, he tried again. The Regent in person was enlisted to offer Lamb one of the Lordships of the Treasury. Once more he was offended. 'In the cabinet there were at that time many persons of whose abilities it was impossible to entertain any but a low opinion and by such a ministry I was told not only that a seat at the board of Treasury was sufficient for my present parliamentary character, but that it was a bribe ample enough to persuade me to abandon my friends, my party, my principles and my reputation.' To the Regent he wrote in appropriately obsequious terms, regretting that he disagreed with so much of the government's policy that to join them would destroy his reputation as a man of honour. To the rest of the world he concealed his chagrin as best he could. This did not conclude his dealing with the Tories. In October of the same year, after Spencer Perceval had been assassinated and

Hawkesbury, now Lord Liverpool, installed in his stead, the Regent again approached him. The details are unknown, but according to Lady Bessborough the offer was of a seat in the cabinet. Lamb had no doubt that, like the earlier invitation, it must be refused. At least – if it were really made – it may have done something to solace his wounded vanity.[19]

In September 1812, Liverpool decided to take advantage of the good harvest and a run of military successes by holding an election. It is commonly said that Lamb lost his seat because of the 'No Popery' cry which wreaked havoc among the Whigs and Canningites. There seems no evidence to support this. He abandoned Portarlington because his support of the Prince Regent had unfairly stamped him as an enemy of emancipation in the minds of the Irish voters[20] and the seat had any-way been sold to another opposition member.

Lord Melbourne refused to put up the money to secure the election of an enemy of government, even though that enemy was his own son, and Lamb himself had barely enough to make both ends meet. The only hope seemed to be that some benevolent grandee would place a borough at his disposal. The Duke of Bedford did, indeed, make a tentative offer but since the Duke at that time stood for everything that Lamb most deplored in Whig policy, the possibility was not pur-sued with any vigour. With Romilly, Horner, Brougham and Tierney all in search of a seat it was not surprising that nothing could be quickly found for this unreliable and unproven junior.[21]

Lady Melbourne thought that her son was making a fuss about nothing. If he had wanted to he could perfectly well have displaced the sitting member at St Albans and kept the seat at relatively small expense. It is indeed hard to reconcile Lamb's inertia with his extrava-gant cries of dismay: 'It is impossible that anybody can feel the being out of parliament more keenly for me than I feel it for myself. It is actually cutting my throat. It is depriving me of the great object of my life . . .' A clue, of course, lies in his private life. He was writing on 30 September 1812 from Lismore, the Duke of Devonshire's seat in Ireland, where he and Caroline had taken refuge. The emotional wear and tear of Caroline's Byronic escapades had been more damaging than Lamb was ever to admit. He was depressed and on edge, physically and mentally exhausted by the strain of coping with the demands of his tormented wife.[22]

Certainly in his usual equable form he would never have been guilty of the outburst which he directed at Grey in November of the same year. After stressing the loyalty which he had shown the party and the sacrifices which he had endured as a result, he wailed that he was:

> . . . deserted and abandoned. The expressions may be too strong but it must be admitted to me, that I am not maintained and supported. When I reflect on my own situation, when I remember that all the avenues to public distinction are for the present closed against me, that I have not, as others have, a profession to the prosecution of which I may turn my exertions, I cannot but feel that my friends have failed me at the most critical moment of my political life . . . I have never before stood in need of aid. Perhaps I may never stand in need of it again; but it will be difficult for me to forget that when I did stand in need of it, it was not afforded me.[23]

Grey's answer was predictable: distress at this sad misunderstanding; protests of his total inability to find seats for even the most senior of Whig politicians; assurances that, if a vacancy could be found, 'there are very few persons indeed whose claims upon me I should think preferable to yours'. He had, indeed, already approached Fitzwilliam and been turned down. Lamb was soothed but not satisfied. What he objected to, he said, was not Grey's inability to help him, 'but to the arrangements, or rather to the no-arrangements, to the want of concert, plea, co-operation, mutual sacrifice and accommodation'. The soul had gone out of the party: a deficiency which he felt was demonstrated by the failure of the Whig proprietors of parliamentary seats to place them at the disposal of would-be members as deserving as himself. He was misused and despised, the leaders of his party neither trusted nor esteemed him.[24]

In this he was not wholly wrong. Brougham considered him a secret Canningite, whom he would much rather see frankly ranged against him than 'grumbling and doing us no earthly good'. He classed Lamb with Ward and Granville, bright young men of some talent who were masters of 'little prize essays of speeches, got up and polished, and useless, quite useless, for affairs'. Grey felt better disposed towards him but not so strongly that he would bring much pressure on Whig supporters to free one of their few seats for his benefit. As so often, the man unjustly accused of some offence feels disposed to go out and commit it. Before the election Lamb had admired Canning but had always considered him an inveterate opponent; in October 1812 he rejoiced at Canning's victory in the Liverpool election and openly hoped that he would soon gain high, perhaps the highest, office. When a seat came free he rejected it because he could not bring himself to accept the terms on which it was offered him.[25] 'My principles are, as I believe, the Whig principles of the revolution,' he told Holland. 'The main foundation of them is the irresponsibility of the crown, the consequent responsibility of ministers, and the preservation of the power and dignity of parliament as constituted by law and custom. With a heap of modern additions, interpolations, facts and fictions, I have nothing to do . . .'[26] Since these 'modern additions' included virtually every point of importance likely to be debated in the next twelve months, it must have seemed to Holland that the gap between Lamb and the Whig party was now unbridgeable.

For the twelve years after 1815 William Lamb, both personally and politically, was adrift. He seemed to have lost not only the means to progress but also any clear idea as to where he wanted to go. His marriage was a mockery, and yet he could not bring himself finally to break off the relationship. His loyalty to the Whigs had worn thin almost to the point of extinction, yet he was still reluctant to commit himself to any other party. He was stuck in the melancholy doldrums and it seemed that only a political earthquake could extricate him.

The end of the Napoleonic wars and the restoration of the Bourbons eased the way for a reconciliation with the Whigs. 'This subject at rest,' Lamb told Fitzwilliam, 'we shall again unite, hand and heart, in the common cause of a well-constituted administration . . .' Lamb, however, did not quickly forget his indignation at what he felt to be the spite shown by the Whig leaders and in March 1816 was still refusing an invitation to Holland House in protest at the 'sly suspicious' attitude of Lord Grey. Holland's good-natured reply did something to appease him but the Holland House dinner book, no bad barometer of a man's standing in the Whig establishment, shows that it was not until June 1818 that he appeared once more within the sacred walls.[27]

In the House of Commons he made an earlier come-back. In April 1816 Peterborough fell free for Lord Fitzwilliam to bestow on his old protégé. Fitzwilliam was a strong enemy to parliamentary reform and he imposed on anyone who sat for one of his boroughs the obligation of taking the same line. To Lamb this did no more than reinforce his own prejudices, and since reform was anyway not a cause close to the hearts of the more conservative Whigs he did not find himself in immediate conflict with his colleagues.[28]

A fundamental divergence was, however, about to open. The previous fifty years had witnessed the disintegration of a pattern of life that had lasted substantially unchanged since the Middle Ages. The industrial revolution, vastly accelerated by the demands of the Napoleonic wars, had created a new proletariat whose problems were either ignored or misunderstood by those who drew wealth from their labours. The face of Britain was defiled by squalid shanty towns, clustered around the mines and factories which they served; ill-built, evil-smelling, disease-ridden, where comfort and hygiene were unknown and beauty a concept so remote as to belong to another world. Badly fed, badly housed, badly clothed; without education, without religion, often without work; the industrial classes rotted in sullen acquiescence; too weak and ill-organized to resist, yet dreaming that one day vengeance would be theirs. In the countryside the situation was a little happier, some of the traditional values lingered on. But even where a landlord wished to look after his tenants there was not much he could do when the crops failed or the price of wheat slumped. The margin between prosperity and pauperdom was always paper thin and a single bad year could plunge a rich farming area into abject misery.

With the end of the war such economists as existed assumed that things would now go famously. All the money that had been blazed away as gunpowder or poured into the pockets of continental allies would now remain in the national coffers, enriching industry and agriculture alike and in its turn breeding still greater prosperity. Disillusionment followed swiftly. The demobilized soldiers and sailors returned to a country in which government spending dropped by more than £40m in a single year, exports were dwindling as industry revived on the Continent and almost every factory was laying off its workers. Nor could agriculture absorb the surplus; wheat prices had tumbled, the fields lay fallow and even those lucky enough to be employed often found their wages harshly cut. Looting and rioting were widespread and when a summer of ceaseless rain led to the almost total failure of the potato crop and a dramatic rise in the cost of the now largely imported corn, the only question seemed to be whether famine or revolution was the more pressing danger.

It never occurred to Lamb, any more than to other leading statesmen, that the government either could or should concern itself with the underlying ills which brought about this situation. The function of ministers was to hold the ring while the inexorable and inexplicable economic forces worked out their purpose. Law and order were fit subjects for debate, together with such meagre distribution of national charity as might be authorized to mitigate the disaster. Even though the isolated sabotage and acts of violence of the previous years were being subsumed into a mighty popular demand for reform, the issues concerning ministers remained the same. If a few hundred or thousand radicals met to discuss the future of the nation it was proper to enquire whether the meeting was legal and if any threat to security were involved, but no minister would have contemplated asking what was said, still less reconsidering his party's policies in the light of it.

The more important debates in the House of Commons, therefore, concerned not economic or social policies but the degree of repression that was necessary to keep the discontented workers – or more often the unemployed – securely in their place. Even within these narrow bounds, however, there was room for differences. The Whig opposition, in general, considered that there should be as little interference as possible with the liberties of the individual; the Tory ministers that the welfare and security of the state were more important than the rights of any particular subject. It was a debate which had pre-occupied governments since organized society began, but in 1816 it seemed peculiarly urgent.

William Lamb found himself temperamentally on the side of the more liberal Tories. He laid down his guide lines at the beginning of 1817 when he urged the 'vigorous and immediate repression' of any assembly which seemed likely to resort to violence. 'This conduct he would recommend,' he said, 'not only from motives of public security, but from motives of tenderness and mercy to the deluded persons themselves . . . Tumult for liberty and right was not only dangerous and destructive, but was a liar and never kept its promises. It led in the end, through scenes of anarchy and blood, to a political tyranny, or military despotism.'[29] One must be cruel to be kind; must protect the benighted from the consequences of their folly. Such paternalism is not necessarily unjustifiable; but when the power and the prosperity are all on the side of authority, the misery and weakness on the side of those who stand to be repressed, then those who draw the line must be doubly sure that they do not do so exclusively to their own advantage.

In 1817 all Lamb's major speeches were made against his fellow Whigs and in defence of the repressive policies of the government. In February a secret committee was set up to investigate the conspiracy which was believed to underlie the widespread disorder. Milton, Elliot and Lamb, 'three Whigs likely to be alarmist', were recruited to join in its deliberations. When the Committee recommended the suspension of Habeas Corpus, Grey and the more libertarian Whigs fiercely opposed the measure, Lamb supported it. The radical Lord Folkestone denounced him as pressing for 'the intimidation of the people'. Lamb's answer was that he agreed with those Whigs who would rather see the country 'revolutionized than enslaved', but that his was the only way by which such enslavement could be prevented.[30]

Two years later the Whigs were temporarily reunited. The incompetence of the local yeomanry and the injudicious use of the 15th Hussars turned a peaceful meeting at St Peter's Fields on the edge of Manchester into a scene of carnage. In the event only eleven people were killed but the Peterloo Massacre has always enjoyed a position of peculiar distinction in radical hagiography. The Whigs seized on an issue which they felt must embarrass the government and demanded a thorough investigation: 'everyone wants enquiry, even the most moderate,' noted William's sister Emily, and Lamb himself rallied to the party. But his support was never whole-hearted. In October he was urging Lord Fitzwilliam not to put in jeopardy his post of Lord Lieutenant by sponsoring a public meeting on the issue. He even defended the use of government spies, a particularly sore point with the Whigs. To Brougham this was the last straw. In the House of Commons he bemoaned the fact that a person of Lamb's respectability, 'of so much weight in that house and in the country, from his accomplishments, his talents, his character, should have lent himself to the support of such a measure'. Lamb may have felt sorrow at this assault from an old ally, but certainly no remorse for the conduct which had provoked it.[31]

Lamb's differences with the Whigs did not prevent him energetically supporting his brother George in the Westminster election of February 1819. George Lamb was the candidate of the Whig establishment against the radical Hobhouse. 'He is not of sufficient consequence in the party to make his failure a party disgrace,' wrote Lambton loftily, 'and he has declared his attachment to principles which his brother disavows and attacks. If he had not done so, I would not have supported him . . .'[32] George was grilled at a party meeting and made to promise that he would never imitate his brother's apostasy.

William Lamb can hardly have been pleased to find his wife beside him on the hustings. Caroline had evidently decided to take a leaf out of the book of the Duchess of Devonshire who had fought so celebrated a campaign for Fox in 1784. It was inevitable that she would do so with excessive zeal. 'She made no bones about going into taverns and dancing and drinking with the electors: what else she did is shrouded in mystery,' commented Princess Lieven drily. The value of her contribution must be uncertain but she was still capable of short bursts in which her vitality seemed as astonishing and her charm as irresistible as ever. Undoubtedly George Lamb had cause to regret her absence when his majority of several hundred was turned into heavy defeat at the general election the following year.[33]

Later the same year it was suggested that William Lamb should stand for Hertfordshire, his own county. He coveted the seat, yet could not quite screw up his courage to face what might prove a difficult conflict. He would not stand, he said, unless it seemed that the current of opinion was running strongly his way. This sort of feebleness enraged his sister Emily. Always the channel for family gossip, she wrote to Frederick to tell him that George Lamb had been staying at Brocket 'patting William on the back and trying to give him a little courage, but he is quite disgusted with his irresolution and want of decision . . . He is in all the nervousness possible, not daring to look the case in the face, not able to summon the courage to say he will stand a contest, and has worked and agitated himself quite thin.' In fact Lamb had nothing to fear. When it came to the point there was no contest and the prize was his for only trifling labour.[34]

George III died in January 1820. One of the new King's first acts was to inform Lord Liverpool that he proposed to divorce his wife. Queen Caroline had indeed been leading a life of flamboyant indiscretion but no blacker pot had ever abused a kettle and ministers looked forward to endless muck-raking and mutual acrimony. On the whole the Whigs supported the Queen, with enthusiasm on the part of some, distaste of others. Lamb was anxious to offend no one. He stayed away from the Queen, so as not to upset her husband, but openly spoke of the divorce as 'the most unfortunate and the most useless question, that had ever been proposed'. In the House of Commons he said that the Queen's name ought by rights to be included in the liturgy – the particular point then at issue – but that she should be prepared to accept her omission in the interests of peace. 'I don't like Wm's speech,' remarked Emily, 'it is twaddling and foolish, speaking on one side and voting on the other, splitting hairs . . . When you differ with *your party* about trifles, it is better to hold your tongue.' His efforts to please everyone ended by giving offence all round. The Whigs thought that Lamb was up to his tricks again, ostentatiously taking a different line to the rest of the party; while the King refused to speak to him at a dinner at Devonshire House and behaved even more offensively to

Caroline, who had been seen riding around in the company of the Queen.[35]

The embarrassment which Caroline Lamb caused her husband at the time of the Queen's trial was in no way unusual. Though the Byronic episode was now far behind she was still obsessed by it, following his activities with hungry interest, demanding the return of her letters, threatening to publish her memoirs which would expose Byron to the world. The memoirs never came but in May 1816 her autobiographical novel *Glenarvon* burst upon a delighted London.

Glenarvon is a lurid shopgirl shocker, the plot of which would fit happily into the lowest category of romantic Gothicks. Set amidst this farrago of absurdity, however, are thinly disguised portraits of Caroline's intimates which are witty and perceptive and an account of herself as clear-headed as anyone could wish for: 'Calantha was esteemed generous; yet indifference for what others valued and thoughtless profusion were the only qualities she possessed . . . Never did she resist the smallest impulse or temptation . . .' The picture of Byron was the centrepiece of the book and also its weakest part, for on this subject there could be no objectivity, no trace of humour. '*Elle aurait été plus ressemblante si j'avais voulu donner plus de séances*,' as Byron acidly remarked when asked by Mme de Staël how he liked his portrait. Her husband was better treated. Lord Avondale 'displayed even in his countenance the sensibility of a warm, ardent and generous character. He had a distinguished and prepossessing manner, entirely free from all affectation . . . Of his mind it might be truly said that it did not cherish one base, one doubtful or worldly feeling . . . If Lord Avondale had a defect it was too great good nature, so that he suffered his vain and frivolous partner, to command and guide . . . With all his knowledge, he knew not how to restrain; and he had not the experience necessary to guide one of her character.' The sting, though sugar-coated, was in the tail, which exhibited Caroline's often articulated belief that her husband had been offered the chance to mould an unformed and impressionable girl but had callously elected to leave her to her own devices. 'It is,' wrote Creevey, 'a *plaidoyer* against her husband addressed to the religious and methodistical part of the community, accusing him of having overset her religious and moral principles by teaching her doctrines of impiety.'[36]

Glenarvon was not surprisingly an instant best seller but it earned Caroline many enemies. The Cavendishes were upset because the central incident, involving an exchange of children, seemed to be based on one of their old family scandals. Lady Holland was outraged at the spiteful attack on her in the guise of the Princess of Madagascar. The Lambs were angriest of all. Emily called it 'that infernal book' and wished Caroline to damnation, George wrote to beg his brother to part with her, while Lord Melbourne declared he would never live in the same house as her again.

William Lamb defended her, but his heart was not in it. For him it was the most crippling blow that she had yet struck him; crippling because he could pretend to ignore her liaisons with other men but nothing of the sort was possible when the book in all its horror was thrust under his nose. To Lord Holland he wrote to excuse his failure to call on the grounds of:

> shyness and embarrassment which the late cursed events have not unnaturally occasioned. They have given me great trouble and vexation, and produced an unwillingness to see anyone and more particularly those who have been the objects of so wanton and unjustifiable an attack. I did not write, because what could I say? I could only exculpate myself from any previous knowledge, the effect of which must be to throw a heavier load upon the offending party . . .[37]

The fact that he had not known his wife was even writing a novel until she brought it to him on the day of publication was the most humiliating part of the whole affair. He did not hesitate to tell his friends the truth but he must have realized in how poor a light it showed him – a man who had failed to protect his wife from her lovers and now could not even keep her works out of the bookshops. 'No woman should touch pen and ink,' he said many years later; they had too much passion and too little sense.*

To Emily Cowper and Lord Melbourne – Caroline's only use, according to Emily, was that she gave Lord Melbourne employment in abusing her – *Glenarvon* had a silver lining. Surely now William would separate from his termagant wife? But still he was not ready: the usual combination of weakness, loyalty and residual tenderness prevented him taking any decisive action. 'The only chance we have of getting rid of her is by committing murder . . .' wrote Emily glumly. Lord Melbourne was so outraged by Caroline's continued presence that he threatened to close up his house in Whitehall and send off the Lambs

---

* Queen Victoria, recipient of these words of wisdom, conspicuously failed to profit from them.

to keep house for themselves.[38]

Caroline was only inspired into fresh excesses. She now made a fool of herself by making up to the Scottish doctor hired as a tutor for Augustus. Dr Roe was a gauche, harmless youth who had no understanding of the wasps' nest in which he found himself. For some reason displeased at his behaviour, or more probably his lack of response, Caroline 'kicked his door open, threw a looking-glass at him and a bottle, and poured a jug of water over him'. The unfortunate doctor fled the house and the servants reported that Caroline had been drunk for a week. The story came from Emily Cowper who could be relied on to present it in the blackest light, but there are too many similar reports for it to be improbable. Princess Lieven described Caroline at Brighton, breaking two hundred pounds worth of glass and crockery in a fit of rage, while in July 1824, once more drunk, she tried to force her way through the Horse Guards at night, challenged the sergeant on duty to a fight and was only rescued by William Lamb and some servants who sallied out to her rescue from near-by Melbourne House. After this latest escapade she was banished to Brocket and limited to a single bottle of sherry a day.[39]

The worst of it was that Caroline had contrived to make William Lamb's beloved Brocket almost impossible to live in. She veered between the wildest extravagance and bouts of equally intemperate economy. 'Avarice is at present her darling vice, and starving her servants her occupation,' wrote Ellis to the Duke of Devonshire. The result, of course, was that the servants left in droves, 'like the figures in a magic lanthorn – they come on and go off'. One new cook was offered fifty guineas a year – a huge salary by contemporary standards – but found the atmosphere so intolerable that she left within a week. Only the old butler, Hazard, stood constant, morosely telling Emily that at least Lady Caroline could get no worse. Early in 1819 she decided to give a ball to rival a recent triumph of the Cowpers at near-by Panshanger. She chose the worst possible weather and left insufficient time. The county largely boycotted the occasion. When one family refused on the grounds that their horses were out she was so desperate that she sent her carriage for them. It returned empty and the masquerade was played out to a handful of family, four guests and twenty-four musicians. 'And Wm all the time miserable,' recorded Emily, 'fretted to death, flying into passions continually and letting her have quite her own way.'[40]

Things would never have come to such a pass during Lady Melbourne's life but in the spring of 1818 she had died. It had not been a

peaceful end. For two or three years she had been in excruciating pain
and had resorted to increasingly large doses of opium which had
dimmed her mind and broken down what was left of her health. Her
last three days were passed in almost uninterrupted convulsive fits.
William was constantly with her: he was, wrote Emily with the
tartness of a younger sister, 'all that is attentive and kind . . . but he has
no observation and no judgment and not likely to suggest anything
that might be of use'. The death agonies were torture for son as well as
mother but William had learnt to do without her during the last few
years and the sense of loss was not overwhelming. Though objectively
he could understand the role she had played in the Byron affair and her
continued friendship with the poet, it must still have hurt him deeply;
injuring both his sense of propriety and his pride and cutting into a
bond which till then had been the most stable and in many ways the
most intimate of his life. They had never been estranged yet equally he
had lost the habit of confiding in her, wrote to her with less freedom.
The death of Lady Melbourne merely set the final seal on a relationship
which had withered long before.[41]

There was no hope that his son would offer him the companionship
which mother and wife could not provide. Augustus showed many of
the symptoms of arrested development. The doctor hired to attend
him, Robert Lee, referred to 'the lamentable appearance of vacancy in
his look'. To love, to anger, to derision, he offered the same blank
apathy; he would sit for hours staring dully into space, showing no
resentment if disturbed yet unable or unwilling to emerge from his
trance and establish any sort of relationship with his interlocutor. To
Lamb, most responsive of men, this was both inexplicable and alarming. He was convinced that, by some effort of will, his son might
suddenly emerge as a mature and normal human being:

> If you wish to be written to [he told Augustus] you must write
> yourself; if you wish to be spoken to you must speak; and if you
> wish others to have confidence in you, you must have confidence in
> them. This I say, because when you was with me, I observed you
> had a foolish disagreeable way of not answering anything you was
> asked, nor talking of anybody else's concerns or of your own, under
> a silly mistaken idea of prudence.[42]

When Augustus did show animation it was almost worse because
his intellectual development, always slow, had become finally blocked
at the age of eight or nine. His old nanny had to lock the drawing-room
door when she was doing out the room since otherwise, a bulky boy

of eighteen, he would run half naked down the stairs, bowl her over and sit on her. Such bouts of activity were often followed by violent fits, any one of which seemed, to the terrified onlookers, as likely as not to kill him. The only way in which such outbursts could be prevented was by keeping him perpetually underfed and applying leeches if, in spite of this, he showed signs of excitement. At least this treatment must have been less painful than the remedies which Caroline procured for him from the currently fashionable quacks. For a time Augustus was magnetized every morning, 'metallic tractors' being applied to draw off 'the obnoxious fluids'. Another time his skull was scorched with caustic acid. Such drastic therapy did not seem to do him any harm – but nor, it soon became clear, did it do good.

While Augustus vegetated, Lord Melbourne rapidly decayed. The death of his wife had removed the last restraint on the drunkenness which had grown to dominate his life. From the moment he woke until two or three the following morning his intake of sherry seemed continuous till he reached such a state of alcoholism as to be almost permanently intoxicated. Even when he cut down to one glass of negus a day he contrived 'somehow or other to be drunkish . . . it must be the fog that makes him so', commented his daughter sadly. Her father rode her like the Old Man of the Sea 'and gets drunk without falling off, which is worse'. But his children stuck by him. Lady Holland recorded a dinner at Melbourne House when old age and alcohol between them had reduced him to squalid senility. 'This hopeless state is made less cruel from the attention of his family. He is never without one or more in his house, and they are careful and contribute all they can to his comfort.'[43]

Against this sombre family background it was difficult for William Lamb to employ himself in ways both profitable and pleasurable. He read enormously but with little system. At one time he plunged deeply into English comedy as a preliminary to writing a book on Sheridan and, having an excellent memory, was able ever after to shine by quoting lengthy passages from Wycherley or Congreve. When it came to the point, however, he got no further than a preliminary sketch of the early part of Sheridan's political life; then resigned the enterprise with some relief to the readier hands of Thomas Moore.[44]

Some residual loyalty to Caroline seems at this time to have inhibited any close relationship with another woman. He was as likely as not to spend his leisure hours at Brooks's, the great Whig club, where every night during the session parliamentarians would drop in to discuss the day's events, to drink, to gamble and to gossip. Lamb, Brougham,

Scarlett, Ward, Mackintosh were usually among the most conspicuous; sometimes Grey would look in but he was stiff and reserved and would quickly blight the easy atmosphere.[45] It was pleasant enough, but not what Lamb wanted. Still less did the balls and routs, the endless dinners, grand or casual, the country house visits, the evenings at the theatre, convince him that he was contented. Such pleasures were no substitute for what he craved; a happy family and a woman in whom he could confide.

Towards the end of 1822 Lamb visited Panshanger to talk things over with his sister Emily. '. . . He says he is quite miserable,' she wrote to Frederick, 'and does not know what to do about her, that he never has a day's peace, and that her violence increases so much that he is always afraid of her doing some serious mischief to some of her servants . . . He says she is the greatest bore in the world, and that there never was such a temper, because her fits of passion, instead of being succeeded by a calm, are only changed for the most eternal crossness and ill-humour. He is a *great* ass for having borne her as he has done . . .'[46]

He was becoming less and less ready to bear her in the future. In 1824 she conducted a brief and flamboyant flirtation with the young Edward Bulwer Lytton, nearly twenty years her junior but dazzled by the brilliant high spirits which she could still at her best display. Caroline flaunted her latest captive, then dropped him abruptly in favour of a bastard son of the Duke of Bedford. Meanwhile her conduct towards her husband became ever more intolerable and his armour of good humour began to crack more frequently. Caroline's French maid Thérèse told of her mistress, hysterical and bemused by brandy, beating at her husband's door. 'I must and will come into your room. I am your lawful wife. Why am I to sleep alone?' 'I'll be hang'd if you come into my room, Caroline, so you may as well go quietly into your room.' Then, as she persevered, 'Get along, you little drunken . . .!'[47]

It could not go on. The picturesque story of Caroline encountering Byron's funeral cortège and stumbling off into total insanity is almost certainly apocryphal but the poet's death dealt another injury to her wavering self-control. 'He has long long been absent from me,' she wrote, 'yet I hope I shall be forgiven if I say how deeply I feel his death. To me it is an awful blow . . .' Her behaviour degenerated to a point where life in London became insupportable. Still hoping to avoid a formal separation William banished her to Melbourne Hall. His brother George had married Caroline St Jules, illegitimate daughter of the 5th Duke of Devonshire, and the pair had made their home at Melbourne. Caro George, as she was called to distinguish her from her sister-in-law, Caro William, was a woman of generosity and endless patience. She accepted the charge without enthusiasm but also without protest. At first all went reasonably well. Caroline was irritating but not outrageous, her misdeeds no worse than walking through the muddy lanes in feathers and thin shoes and losing her temper with the local children. 'Come and see how gentle, amiable, healthy, wealthy and wise I will be in future . . .' she told the Duke of Devonshire, 'no more mad than a March Hare only now and then rumbustious when misunderstood.'[48]

Soon however she was back in London and on the rampage again. By the spring of 1825 William Lamb had finally screwed himself, or been screwed by his family, to the point of demanding a legal separation. He then fled the scene, leaving it to his brother Frederick to face the fury and work out the details. Caroline was agonized. '. . . tell me, must this take place?' she wrote to her regular confidant, the Duke of Devonshire. 'It is destruction to me . . . 20 years I have not only been tolerated but loved – with such devotion that when I have offered and begged to go away I have been detained. I see too by William's letter to Frederick Lamb that he is wretched at the step he is taking, but he has been urged to do it . . .' William was indeed wretched but he had finally concluded that the pain of his marriage was still greater than that of separation. If he had seen her misery he would probably have relented, but by the time that he returned to confront her she had become more or less reconciled to the idea. 'She was not violent,' he told his sister in some surprise. 'She was cross and abusive at first, but at length grew quite good-humoured and rattled away saying everything about everyone in such a manner that I could not help laughing immoderately . . .' There might be storms ahead, he concluded, but at least things had got off to a tolerably tranquil start.[49]

Emily Cowper and William's brothers were terrified lest Caroline might win him back again by a show of humility and distress. Instead she exploded into characteristic violence. She told her brother, William Ponsonby, that her husband had beaten and misused her. Ponsonby, 'reckoned an ass and a jackanapes by everybody', wrote Lamb an offensive letter implying that Caroline had married beneath her and that the honour thus conferred on her husband outweighed any peccadilloes on her own part. Lamb took offence and was stiffened in his resolve. Still, however, he shrank from any confrontation. 'Wm can only do a thing of this kind by a great effort,' wrote Emily perceptively.

'He has not courage to stand against scenes and entreaties.'[50]

Once again he took to flight, this time to Paris. Little is known about the visit except that many years later he boasted to Queen Victoria about the opera-singer, Madame Grassini, 'the prettiest woman I had ever seen', with whom at least once he dined. The interlude did not last long, he was back in London long before the financial details of the separation had been thrashed out. What was agreed was generous enough. Caroline was to have £2500 a year, to be raised to £3000 at the death of Lord Melbourne, against the £2000 guaranteed her under the marriage settlement. Even so, he was still nervous that Caroline would avenge herself by running up enormous debts for which he would be responsible. Lord Althorp, Caroline's cousin, who was asked to act as trustee of the deed of separation, had similar fears. Eventually Scarlett was called in to consider the case and pronounced that Lamb, and still more the trustees, would be protected by the terms of the settlement from any such liability.[51]

Generous or not, Caroline seemed in no hurry to sign. One moment she threatened suicide, the next dire vengeance. 'She is in a strange state,' wrote Emily on 15 June, 'good-humoured, but always muddled either with brandy or laudanum.' Emily believed that Caroline was trying to wear down William's patience and win him back again, but her brother, she reported with relief, was 'completely stout and completely disgusted, and aware of her tricks'. If only he would cut himself off entirely from his wife all would go well; so long as Caroline was given a chance to exercise her wiles the issue remained uncertain. William 'wants energy so much and somebody at his back to push him on'.[52]

And then, suddenly, it was over. Caroline 'marched out without beat of drum last Friday morning at 8 o'clock by the steam boat to Calais'. From France she wrote angry letters denouncing all those who had misused her. William himself, she said, she could never curse 'but if it be permitted me to return I will come and look at you even as Lord Byron did at me'. Permitted or not, she was back within two months, only to find herself confined in a house on the outskirts of London in the charge of Dr Goddard and two women provided by the prominent mad-doctor, Sir George Tuthill. Lady Caroline had 'a predisposition to the high form of insanity', reported the doctor, but if she could be treated kindly yet firmly and kept away from alcohol, there was no reason why she should not live out the rest of her years in comparative tranquillity. William is 'in great glee' reported Emily Cowper, a distasteful phrase which probably reflects more her own feelings than her brother's but still suggests the immense relief he must have felt.[53]

Caroline's confinement could not last for ever unless she were formally consigned to Bedlam – a fate so horrible that even her sister-in-law would hardly have wished it on her. A compromise was worked out by which she rarely came to London but lived either at Brocket or Brighton, with Dr Goddard usually in attendance. She was the more ready to submit to this because her health had been broken. She was soon to show the first symptoms of the dropsy that eventually killed her. In the eyes of London society she was dead already. From time to time her husband would visit her but usually the effort only provoked an outburst of fury which left William aghast and Caroline weak and failing. Alone and forlorn, rambling in mind and crippled in body, she lived out her final years. Her husband could never forget her, nor was there any question of the marriage being ended by divorce, but to all intents and purposes the relationship was over.

CHAPTER 6

Ireland

POLITICALLY TOO new possibilities seemed to be opening. In 1822 Canning joined the cabinet as Foreign Secretary. No job was offered Lamb and it is unlikely that he would have accepted if it had been, but he wished the new government well. When J. W. Ward was asked by Canning to serve under him at the Foreign Office, Lamb urged him to accept – adding the characteristic rider: 'Do not take it unless you can make up your mind, in the first place, to bear every species of abuse and misrepresentation and the imputation of the most sordid motives; in the second place, to go through with it if you undertake it and not to be dispirited by any difficulties or annoyances which you may find in the office, and which, you may depend upon it, no office is free from.'[1]

Whether William Lamb was or was not a 'Canningite' is one of those irritating semantic problems which would be better ignored if it were not for the fact that it pre-occupied not only Lamb himself but also many of his fellow politicians. Lamb's relationship with this brilliant and enigmatic statesman was to shape his own career for the next five years, indeed until long after Canning's death, and an assessment of their respective attitudes lay at the bottom of every overture which was made to him at this period. It was almost two years since Emily Cowper had thought that she detected signs of an incipient union: 'I rather think *notre frère* has a mind to attach himself to Canning . . .' Since then they had if anything grown closer together politically, while Ward and Huskisson seemed to be more Lamb's close associates than Brougham, Grey or any of the Whigs. It was indeed Brougham in one of his historical studies who, twenty years later, stung Lamb into a categoric denial that he had ever been a Canningite. 'Not that I consider it a reproval or wish to disclaim it as such; but it is not the fact. I was acquainted with Canning, liked him, admired him, agreed with him upon some great questions, in his opposition to Parliamentary reform and in his support of the Roman Catholic claims, but never acted with him, was not in his confidence, nor had any political connection with him until I accepted office in the year eighteen hundred and twenty-seven.'[2]

A man is not necessarily the best authority on his own political allegiance but in this case there is no reason to doubt his words. Indeed one can sometimes detect in Lamb's attitude towards Canning the faint contempt of the amateur for the professional; or still more, perhaps, the hauteur of one who had passed his youth in the halls of the Grand Whiggery, played in the nurseries of Devonshire House and sat at the feet of Fox. 'Without the experience of a clerk,' he wrote of Ward to his brother Frederick in 1827, 'he has the tone of one, a tone by the way which Canning never got rid of and which characterizes all his followers.'[3]

Canningite or not, he drew steadily closer to the government. Every step he took was hailed as fresh apostasy by his former colleagues. Once he was rash enough to accuse a Whig member of inconsistency. 'If there is one member of this House to whom the charge of an abandonment of former principles could attach more deservedly than another,' retorted Dr Lushington, 'it is the hon. member for Hertfordshire.'[4] Lamb offered the traditional defence, that it was not he who had changed but the Whig party. The facts were against him. Whether he had changed or merely revealed his true disposition, he was now a very different political creature from the Lamb of twenty years before. As much responsible as anyone was that clerk to end all clerks, William Huskisson. In 1823 Canning procured Huskisson's entry into the cabinet, where it quickly became evident that he knew more about financial and commercial matters than any of his colleagues. Lamb still found him faintly comical, the clod-hopping cousin from the country, but the fact of that cousinship made possible a closer rapport than he could have established with any other minister. Huskisson he could at least trust implicitly, a fact more important than the admiration which also grew as the two exchanged views on economics or ideology. If Huskisson was a Canningite, Lamb perhaps was a Huskissonian.

It was through Huskisson that, in 1824, Liverpool seems to have made cautious overtures to Lamb. He still shrank from taking such a plunge but his indecision was now notorious and the source of exasperation to his family. 'Wm's speech the other night was bad,' wrote Emily Cowper, 'such milk and water. I wish he would join one side or the other . . .' Emily herself probably had more influence on her brother even than Huskisson and she was now imbibing her politics from her lover Palmerston, himself a member of the government. She was a Whig only by marriage, commented Emily Eden, and 'a regular courtier at heart'. Huskisson and Lady Cowper, though personally they were never close, proved a formidable team in overcoming Lamb's lingering doubts. Palmerston, too, Whig by birth and Tory by profession, Lamb's contemporary, old friend and future brother-in-law, provided a strong push in the same direction. His energy and self-assurance was viewed by Lamb with mingled admiration and alarm; the two men complemented each other admirably and were to work together in something as near to harmony as the turbulent Palmerston could hope to establish with any colleague.[5]

If there was one thing which Canning held more passionately at heart than any other it was his opposition to parliamentary reform. Ever since 1821, when Grey officially espoused the doctrine as a plank in the party platform, the Whigs had grown more united on this issue. In April 1826 they made an effort of particular vigour and Lord John Russell spoke long and eloquently in the House of Commons. Among those whom he failed to impress was William Lamb. He could not see, Lamb said, 'what real benefit could be derived from it'. Though he did not wish to diminish democratic influence, still less did he want to increase it. Democracy was perhaps better than despotism but 'the Sultan of Constantinople, the Shah of Persia, or the Bey of Algiers, were subject to a more efficient responsibility than the leaders of a democratic assembly'. To enfranchise the masses was a road not to liberty but to a new form of slavery. Canning remarked that he could not follow the speech, 'for I could not have gone so far'. The Whigs, of course, were far from gratified.[6]

They had their revenge almost immediately. Even before this debate Lamb had so far fallen out with the Whigs as to forfeit any hope of electoral support. On the other hand ministers showed no particular wish to help him. The result was that his seat in Hertfordshire seemed in danger in the forthcoming election of 1826. He dithered, now determined to fight it out, now minded to run away. 'I believe he could certainly carry it if he would exert himself,' wrote Emily, 'but I never saw such a want of energy, or they say a worse canvasser. He never talks the people over, but takes an answer at once, always seeing things in the view of his opponents, as he did in politicks, and too candid, and doing the thing by halves, and always despairing . . .' The radicals put up a lively candidate in Tommy Duncombe, who fought the contest in a knockabout style most distasteful to his more squeamish opponent. By mid-April Lamb had more or less made up his mind to abandon the fight and was planning a visit to his brother Frederick.[7]

Apart from anything else, it seemed foolish to spend several thousand pounds and much energy when the fruits of battle, even if gained, might be lost again at any moment by the death of his ailing father. 'It did not suit with my views,' he told his putative electors in his farewell address, 'to run the slightest risk of failure.' Their votes would have been gratefully received but 'they were not to me so precious an object as to be sought and struggled for against difficulty, ill-will and opposition'. His sister Emily, for her surprisingly uncritical, described this as 'a very good address' and said that it had 'quite cleared him from blame'. Presumably she knew the electors of Hertfordshire as well as most people but it seems unlikely that anyone confronted by this curious mixture of arrogance and oversensibility would be particularly well-disposed to the author in the future.[8]

Lamb was said to bear his eviction from parliament with equanimity, indeed to be noticeably cheerful.[9] No doubt he put as good a face on it as he could but he quickly had reason to regret his electoral fiasco. Early in 1827 Lord Liverpool was found unconscious in his library, victim of an apoplectic fit. He lingered on, but it was clear that he could not carry on the government. No ministry could be formed without Canning and Canning would serve under nobody. George IV tried every device to avoid the inevitable but in the end had to give way. In April Canning was called on to form a government. At last the way seemed clear for the sort of liberal/conservative coalition in which Lamb might hope to make his way. And at this moment of all others a mixture of pride, folly and feebleness had banished him from the House of Commons.

The categoric refusal of the Duke of Wellington and the high Tories to serve under what Londonderry described as a 'charlatan *parvenu*'[10] meant that Canning had to look outside Liverpool's old ministry for his support. There were not enough independents like Lamb to give him a majority. Nothing was left but to turn to the Whigs.[11] The Whig response, habitual in moments of crisis, was to split into warring fragments. Grey, Althorp and the other purists felt that they should join no government not specifically pledged to Catholic Emancipation and parliamentary reform. Brougham was prepared to take Canning's good will on trust and accept office on almost any terms. In the middle a group of moderates under Lansdowne wavered fretfully, standing out now for one thing, now the other. Palmerston wrote to Lamb that the most likely solution seemed to be a union of liberal Tories with Lansdowne, Holland, Brougham and a few other Whigs – a combination which carried with it the risk that Canning 'in calling in the Saxons to beat the Danes might change and not get rid of masters'.[12]

Lamb's trouble was that he was neither Saxon nor Dane and risked missing the battle altogether. The key to the situation was Lansdowne, who took the line that, even though Catholic Emancipation could not be guaranteed, at least the main offices in Ireland should be held by pro-Catholics and that these should also be in a majority in the cabinet. Lamb saw him on 20 April, then moved on to Brooks's where a group of thirty or forty Whigs was debating the issue. Brougham carried the day and a deputation set off to try to persuade Lansdowne to moderate his terms. Lamb was gloomy about their chances. 'This crotchet about the Irish government,' he wrote to Canning the following day, 'is felt by almost everybody to be just such another obstacle as the Whigs have always contrived to raise up against their own entrance into power.'[13]

In the end it was Lamb who helped break the deadlock. Lansdowne was prepared to accept that Wellesley should remain as Lord Lieutenant in Ireland but insisted that he should be supported by a Catholic Chief Secretary.* The King maintained that this place should be filled by a Protestant. Canning was reluctantly prepared to accept this ruling but could find no suitable candidate to take the place of the strongly Protestant Goulburn. Without much hope he suggested Lamb. 'William Lamb, William Lamb – put him anywhere you like,' George IV is supposed to have replied. Whether or not he was quite so obliging he certainly seemed to have got over the irritation which he had felt at the time of the Queen's trial and rightly considered Lamb as a moderate who would do nothing to exacerbate existing differences. Lamb was to be offered the job, though only until such time as a true Protestant was found. Somewhat disingenuously Canning then sold the appointment to Lansdowne on the promise that, if Lamb were moved elsewhere, he would be replaced by an equally emancipationist Secretary.[14]

'What Wm will be I don't exactly know,' wrote Emily Cowper on 27 April. '. . . perhaps he may go to Ireland now, but I hope he will eventually be Home Sec'y of State. He and Canning are very thick, and all seems to be going on prosperously.' 'Eventually,' almost turned

* 'Catholic' in this context, of course, means favourable to Catholic Emancipation, not Roman Catholic by religion.

out to be within a few days. Lansdowne talked himself into a position where he was ready to advise anyone but himself to join Canning's government. If he refused to come in, said Canning, then he would ask Lamb to fill the gap.[15] Indeed he seems even to have reached the point of discussing it with Lamb, since on 24 April he reported that, if Lansdowne finally let him down, Lamb would 'not refuse to undertake the office of Home Secretary of State'.[16]

Lamb must have been disappointed when Lansdowne finally took the job. He had no particular interest in or knowledge of Ireland; suspecting, like most Englishmen, that its people were incomprehensible and its problems insoluble. Nor had he any wish to travel at the moment: with his wife secluded at Brocket he was finding London society agreeable enough and, anyway, was uneasy at the thought either of taking his son with him or of leaving him behind. Finally, the office of Home Secretary was one of the two or three most important in any ministry; to be Chief Secretary in Ireland, though the effective power was perhaps almost as great, did not even carry with it at that time a seat in the cabinet.[17]

Nevertheless, he was well pleased. After floating irresolutely for more than fifteen years, now, aged 47, he had at last found a home and a job, serving moreover with a man whom he admired and who seemed to admire him – 'not one of, but *the* cleverest person going', Canning told Princess Lieven. He was confident that, if the government survived, he would win promotion in a few months. 'Brother Wm looks more happy and comfortable than I have ever seen him . . .' wrote Lady Cowper. What was more, he was back in the House of Commons again; Canning had put him in for his own borough of Newport, a seat which was almost immediately exchanged for another ministerial borough at Bletchingley.[18]

The only matter for regret was the fragility of the government. Most of those Whigs who had refused to serve under Canning still felt that they were bound to support him, 'as the least of two evils' in Althorp's unenthusiastic phrase. But Lord Grey was not disposed to go even so far. A great man capable of astonishing pettiness, he was offended that Lansdowne and the other Whigs should thus have ignored his advice, outraged that he had not been consulted at every stage. He told Lansdowne that, while he would stop short of outright opposition, his status now was that of 'an individual almost totally without political connections of any sort'.[19] With such shaky support from the uncommitted Whigs and the inveterate opposition of both radicals and ultra-Tories it was obvious that the ministry would be hard put to it to survive. But its real feebleness was summed up by E. J. Littleton. 'Were Canning to die,' he wrote, 'there is not a soul on the Treasury bench who could succeed him. No party would follow Brougham as a leader; Mr Lamb, who is competent, is the elder son of a peer who is 82, and Mr Stanley, a young man competent to any post, is not brought into office.' 'If Canning lasts, the ministry will last,' as John Russell put it more tersely. But Canning was a sick man who had acceded to the office he had so long coveted at a moment when his tenure of it seemed likely to be quickly and cruelly terminated. If Canning did not last, then could the ministry?[20]

The roots of the Irish problem, like those of some monstrous weed, can be traced ever downwards through the centuries. For the purposes of this book, however, the critical date is probably 1796, when a French fleet off Bantry Bay kindled hopes of liberation which, two years later, exploded into revolution. It was this revolution, harshly repressed, which in its turn led to the Act of Union of 1801. By this the Irish parliament was extinguished and Ireland became part of the United Kingdom. If Union had been followed by immediate emancipation for the Roman Catholics, as Pitt had hoped, it is conceivable that it would have prospered. The feebleness of successive Tory ministries and the intransigence of Kings George III and IV ensured, however, that the experiment was given no chance. In 1827 no Catholic could vote or sit in parliament, serve as a magistrate or occupy any of the more profitable offices under the crown.

This injustice was aggravated by economic troubles. Almost entirely dependent on agriculture, Ireland had been far worse hit than England by the depression which followed the Napoleonic Wars. In a country of well over six million Catholics, five-sixths of the land was owned by the same eight hundred thousand Protestants as monopolized all the political power. The Catholic peasantry largely subsisted on uneconomically small agricultural plots for which they nevertheless often had to pay extravagant rents to their English landlords. Nor were the English landlords often there to receive their rents; for the most part they existed in absentee splendour on the other side of the Irish Channel while their agents enforced their bidding. The final twist – adding insult to insult, injury to injury – was that the peasant was required to surrender a tenth of his exiguous produce as tithe to support an inflated Anglican church establishment which would never serve him and which he usually detested. Meanwhile the Roman Catholic church was starved for funds. As Sydney Smith put it, 'the bell of a neat parish church often summons to worship only the parson, and an occasional conforming clerk, while two hundred yards off, a thousand Catholics are huddled together in a miserable hovel and pelted by all the storms of heaven'.[21]

As a prescription for disorder, the situation could hardly have been improved. That there had been no major explosion for nearly thirty years can be attributed to the capacity of the Irish for falling out with each other in circumstances which, in any other nation, would induce at least a measure of unity. Nevertheless, from the early 1820s, Richard Sheil and Daniel O'Connell, the twin heroes of Irish liberation, finally decided that the English imperialists were even more pressing a target than each other. From their co-operation sprang the Catholic Association, a body of equivocal status and uncertain objects but dedicated without question to the removal of all the disabilities under which the Catholics laboured. Lamb had been one of the foremost in defending measures to restrict the powers of this body. He was, he asserted, as much a friend as ever of emancipation but, 'if any assembly of persons met, and, under the pretence of seeking redress for particular grievances, proceeded to discuss the whole political affairs of the empire, then he maintained that such a society was a fit subject for legislative interference'.[22] Since the Catholic Association was indeed guilty of the dangerous crime of discussing the affairs of the empire to which it was alleged to belong, then it was evident that it must be curbed.

With such a background it was not surprising that the Irish Catholics should look with some caution on their new Chief Secretary. Their suspicion was reciprocated. 'The people of Ireland are not such damned fools as the people of England,' Lamb once remarked, but the compliment could not be called extravagant and he never really felt any affection for or understanding of the people he had to govern. The Irish could not be separated from the Catholics and in spite of his support for Catholic rights, he objected strongly to any attempt on their part to win those rights by tumult. The first duty of every citizen was to acquiesce in the law as it stood at the time. 'As to the Roman Catholics,' he wrote to Brougham, 'it is of course better that they should be tranquil and prudent than the contrary, but it is of importance that they should not think that they confer great obligation upon the government by their tranquillity and forbearance.'[23]

The role of Chief Secretary is a difficult one to define, if only because it varied so much according to the personality of the Lord Lieutenant.

He was, in a sense, a middleman between the Lord Lieutenant and the British government; spending the parliamentary session in London, the rest of the year in Dublin. But he was also chief executive of the administration in Dublin, a kind of Managing Director to the Lord Lieutenant's Chairman, responsible for the smooth running of affairs from day to day. He had to be efficient and business-like; a requirement which Lamb initially found troublesome. Canning, indeed, was forced to write to urge him in future to number his letters – so as 'to give them an appearance, if not a reality, of method'.[24]

Lamb's terms of reference were vague, almost non-existent. Catholic Emancipation was bound in the end to come but probably not for some years yet. The Irish Catholics were to be kept happy in the interim. Anything that could be done to mitigate their miseries would be desirable, provided, and the provision was a crippling one, it did not upset the Protestants too severely. Lamb knew only too well that the Protestant minority viewed him with greater suspicion even than the Catholic majority. It was indeed the rabidly Protestant clique in the Castle at Dublin who were the main obstacle to any satisfaction being given the Catholics. These people had been running Ireland to their own advantage for many years and were not now disposed to change their ways to suit the vaguely liberal views of a newcomer from London. The most nefarious influence was that of William Gregory, who had been Under Secretary for fifteen years and knew every trick in the book with which to confound his masters. An 'arch jobber', Anglesey called him. 'A man who has the press at his command – a determined intriguer. False as hell. A violent anti-Catholic – a furious Tory . . .'[25]

Previous biographers have tended to assume that Lamb did good work in Dublin; manfully tackling the Augean stables left by his predecessors, laying about him with a will in the jungle of prejudice and jobbery. It would certainly be wrong to ignore his achievement, yet to praise it too highly is to confuse the deed with the intention. Lamb was in fact largely inactive, but he was inactive with style and affability and his patent good will, after the ultra-Protestant Goulburn, was enough to endear him to the Catholics. He understood the value of public relations and was shrewd enough to identify, in Daniel O'Connell, the man whose good will was essential if Ireland were to be pacified. Lamb had little liking for O'Connell, considering him a braggart and bully whose word was worth nothing and whose objective was to make good government impossible. Nevertheless he was astute and persuasive, and commanded the loyalties of his fellow Catholics. Somehow he must be conciliated.

One of the first things Lamb did when confirmed in office was to send a message to O'Connell through Richard Bennett, the latter's trusted friend. 'Tell Mr O'Connell I must for a time be worse than Peel but when we can we will do all the good we can. Beg of him to have confidence, though we cannot do much, or worse men will come.' Judge me, appealed Lamb, not by what I am doing but by what I tell you secretly I would like to do. Not surprisingly this did not seem irresistibly attractive to O'Connell. Lamb, he replied angrily, 'has taken up the notion that in order to show his *candour* and *liberality* he will patronize men of the Orange faction . . . It is idle to expect anything of Mr Lamb . . .' But in spite of this unpromising beginning Lamb did in fact persuade O'Connell of his sincerity and win a measure of support for his Fabian policy. Within three months O'Connell was classing him among those people in the administration who were 'perfectly free from guile and too honourable themselves to believe in the existence of duplicity'. Nor did he ever change this opinion. He liked Lamb personally and believed that, given a free hand, the Chief Secretary would put things right in Ireland. But he was not going to be given a free hand, nor had he got the temperament to seize the initiative himself. 'You know well,' wrote O'Connell to Spring Rice at the end of 1827, '. . . that Mr Lamb has done nothing, that although Lord Wellesley spoke the Catholics fair, all his countenance was given to the enemies of Irish tranquillity.'[26]

Wellesley, elder brother of the Duke of Wellington and Lord Lieutenant since 1822, was not likely to breathe much fire into his Chief Secretary. He was a man of great talent corroded by vanity and self-indulgence who had come to Dublin with the best intentions but quickly allowed himself to be defeated by the forces of inertia and reaction. Lamb arrived in July to find him 'exceedingly hurt and irritated' with Canning for giving him no news about the intentions of the government. Worse still, Canning made it plain that he thought Wellesley had been in Ireland long enough and tried to fob him off with the Embassy in Vienna. Wellesley was tired and ready to go, but not on terms like that. 'He is become irresolute and indecisive,' Lamb told Lansdowne, 'and is particularly very nervous with respect to the situation of the government upon the R.C. question.' But Lamb still thought that, on the whole, Wellesley had done well by Ireland and that it would be a pity to replace him. 'I never saw two men better suited to each other than Mr Lamb and Lord Wellesley,' wrote

Wellesley's friend and former private secretary, a comment perhaps not quite so flattering to Lamb as was intended.[27]

The most urgent task was to open public offices to Catholics, in particular within the legal system. In 1828 only one county-court judge in all Ireland was a Roman Catholic. Yet when it came to the point there was little that could be done to remedy the situation, at any rate by a Chief Secretary who was only to remain in Dublin for a few months. Nor was he likely to make much headway on education, a problem rendered particularly intractable by the fact that what few facilities Ireland possessed were for the most part firmly in the grasp of the Anglican church. He wrote to ask Brougham's advice. Had he ever contemplated 'the establishment of a general system of education in this country', perhaps on the Scottish pattern? 'Nothing can equal the general anxiety for something of the kind,' – and then came the characteristically gloomy afterthought – 'except the difficulties which stand in the way of its adoption.' Somehow in Lamb's mind it was always the difficulties that bulked largest. He wrote to Lansdowne stressing the importance of the subject; but it was one of 'great delicacy and difficulty'; when so many different interests were involved and passions ran so high 'it is impossible to proceed otherwise than with the greatest caution and deliberation'. To charge baldheaded at an obstacle is not necessarily the best way of overcoming it, but no one yet has crossed a fence by standing still and deploring its height.[28]

Yet Lamb did try in his own way, and did not wholly fail. 'You can do almost anything by feeding, from a man down to a goat or a deer,' he once remarked, and he fed the Irish with a will. To say that he kept open house would be to overstate his liberality but he certainly entertained many enemies of the *status quo* who would have been anathema to his predecessors. As far as possible, too, he kept open office. 'When Mr Lamb was here the only orders were, Show him in,' was supposed to be the comment of the porters at the Castle many years after his departure.[29] He set his face against jobbery and did his best to appoint to vacant positions men who had some qualifications for the work. In doing so he caused much offence among the Irish nobility, who were accustomed to treat the public service as a pasture in which their needy relatives might safely graze. Lord Clare was a particular irritant in this respect. In October Lamb wrote in indignation:

That damned little man-milliner Clare. He knows that I promised him nothing but like all Irishmen, if you drop one single civil word in your communication with them, they immediately convert it into a promise, and charge you with a breach of faith if they do not get what they have asked. I always now end every letter and every interview with these words – 'Now, Sir, remember that I have made you no promise whatsoever . . .' You cannot think how bleak it makes them look, finding their future ground of application cut from under their feet.[30]

Above all Lamb listened, and listened sympathetically. Sometimes what he heard must have seemed close to treason but he bore it with equanimity. When Sheil dined with him – in itself a daring departure – he heard without interruption a lengthy dissertation on the forces which drove the peasants to attack and sometimes murder the agents and tithe-collectors who persecuted them. His only comment was: 'And why don't they go at the big ones,' meaning the great landlords whose selfish irresponsibility was at the root of the trouble. He told Lansdowne bluntly that they should look with more forbearance on the excesses of Roman Catholics than of Protestants, 'because we feel that the former are labouring under a galling exclusion, whilst the latter are striving to maintain an unjust superiority'. 'We hear on all sides of Wm's popularity at Dublin . . .' wrote Lady Cowper proudly; Lamb was 'popular beyond all precedent', reported Villiers. Kind words may not seem much for a nation hungering for radical reform, but they were more than the Irish had learned to expect. They were not unappreciative.[31]

On 8 August 1827 Lansdowne wrote to Lamb to tell him that Canning was dead. Goderich had been sent for by the King. 'You shall hear from me when things assume a more decisive turn.' Where Goderich was concerned a decisive turn was the last thing to be expected. A kindly, gentle man, he was totally inadequate to the demands of his position. It was uncertain whether Lansdowne would agree to serve under him – especially when the King refused to accept Lord Holland as Foreign Secretary. In the end he grumblingly agreed. Isolated in Dublin, Lamb was in no position to influence events. He knew little of Goderich but thought that, under the guidance of Lansdowne and Huskisson, he could probably run quite a decent government. With the King still opposed to a predominantly Whig ministry it seemed that the only alternative would be a return to the ultra-Tories. This would not have suited Lamb at all: he was enjoying office and would have resented a change in ministry which cost him it. To Brougham he wrote with relief of 'what I hope I may now call the *late* difficulty'. It was a pity that the Whigs at Brooks's were angry but there was plenty of time for them to simmer down before the meeting of parliament.[32]

The Whigs did not simmer down and their initial restiveness was doubled when Goderich, once again under pressure from the King, foisted on them as Chancellor of the Exchequer John Herries, a man popularly believed to be in the pay of Nathan Rothschild. 'The disposition to act for himself in the King is the devil,' wrote Lamb apprehensively. Harassed by the King, the ultra-Tories and half his own cabinet, the always frail nerve of Lord Goderich failed him. The 'damned, snivelling, blubbering blockhead', as George IV described him, failed to resolve a row between Herries and Huskisson about the leadership of the Finance Committee and resigned in a flood of tears. Satisfied that there was no hope of resuscitating the uneasy coalition under new management the King sent for the Duke of Wellington. Token overtures were made to Lansdowne's wing of the Whig party but the Duke can have had little expectation that they would be accepted. The Whigs duly resigned; it remained to decide the fate of Huskisson and his little band of former Canningites.[33]

On 12 January 1828 the Duke of Wellington wrote to William Lamb in Dublin urging him to continue in his present post and assuring him that there would be no sudden switches of policy. Lamb replied cautiously: 'there is no man, either with whom, or under whom personally, I should be more happy to serve'; but first he must find out what his friends were doing and more about Wellington's plans. In private he doubted whether the new government would provide a framework in which he could work. No doubt the Duke's intentions were excellent but, as he wrote to his brother Frederick, 'In politics, tone and impression are everything, and whatever may be the real feelings and merits of the Duke of Wellington, Peel, Goulburn, etc. they have got such a damned character for intolerance in this country that their accession to office would encourage the violent Protestants and depress the Roman Catholics to such a degree as would make it impossible for me to pursue my course . . . with credit and the appearance of consistency.' He told Wellington that he would defer his decision until he reached London, a visit which anyway he was bound to pay within a week or so because of the illness of his wife.[34]

His absence prevented Lamb playing any part in the deliberations of Huskisson and his supporters. It is unlikely that he would have adopted a different approach. Both Huskisson and Palmerston, the two chief negotiators, were anxious to stay in the government if they could reconcile it with their consciences. The Duke insisted that he did not want to revive the traditional Tory governments of the last decade. Ultras like Eldon and Westmorland would not be included, half the cabinet at least would favour Catholic Emancipation, the Lord Lieutenant and Chief Secretary in Ireland would be picked 'from among persons not known as decidedly hostile to the Catholic claim'. Palmerston wrote to give the news to Emily Cowper. He hoped Anglesey, who had already been asked by Goderich to replace Wellesley as Lord Lieutenant, would still go to Ireland. If he did not the post would be offered to Aberdeen 'who would do very well and is a Catholic though not an *enthusiastic* one. In that case he ought to make Wm Lamb Chancellor of Lancaster and bring him into the cabinet at once, provided he consents to remain, which I hope and trust he will.'[35]

Lamb therefore arrived in London to be faced by what was virtually a *fait accompli*. Georgiana Ellis reported that he was 'very wavering' but such wavers as there were must, one suspects, have been assumed largely for the benefit of his Whig friends; intended to demonstrate that he was not acting without first scrupulously scanning his conscience. He called on Wellington and emerged aglow with satisfaction: 'nothing,' he told Frederick, 'could be more satisfactory or in fact more agreeable to my own opinions than the language and views of Peel and the Duke.'[36] But, like the other members of the group, he was sensitive about charges of treachery from the Whigs. 'Canning's friends are very busy negotiating with his enemies,' wrote Lansdowne; 'One thing it is impossible for me to do, to unite with Mr Canning's murderers,' was the Duke of Devonshire's lofty comment. Even Wellington seems to have felt that their behaviour was shabby; at least if one is to accept his reported answer when asked why Huskisson had been retained – 'as a bridge for rats to run over'.[37]

According to Durham, Lamb made Anglesey's appointment to Ireland a condition of his remaining.[38] It is doubtful whether he would have gone so far. Lamb was glad to see the last of Wellesley and quite content with his replacement, but he never found Anglesey easy to work with. All Pagets, he told Victoria, are 'very proud, very passionate, and see no need to correct their pride and their tempers'. He must have had 'One Leg', the swashbuckling, aggressive yet generous-minded First Marquess much in mind. In the event they were only in office together for some four months and for almost all that time Lamb was in London.

The relationship between Wellington and Huskisson, never cordial, degenerated rapidly. East Retford, a particularly corrupt and rotten borough, was to be abolished. The official government line was that the seat should be transferred to the adjoining country districts; Huskisson and Palmerston held that it should rather go to the grossly under-represented city of Birmingham. When the matter came to a vote the two dissenting ministers sided with the opposition. Huskisson the same evening wrote to the Duke in somewhat brusque terms, saying that his place in cabinet was at the Prime Minister's disposal. Wellington believed, or affected to believe, that this constituted a formal letter of resignation and promptly informed the King. Dismayed, Huskisson claimed that his letter had been misunderstood; he had intended to do no more than offer to resign if this were thought essential. Dudley bustled to and fro trying to cure 'this silly, provoking quarrel, if quarrel it can be called' but Huskisson was too proud to ask for his place again, and Wellington, who was heartily glad to be rid of him, had no intention of taking him back on any other terms.[39]

For Lamb this was peculiarly annoying. He had no wish to resign, considered that Huskisson had behaved like a fool and, worst of all, had voted with the majority on the issue of East Retford. However, as he was prone to remark, anyone can support their friends when they are in the right, the important thing is to support them when they are wrong. If Huskisson and Palmerston were going, then he must go too. As he regretfully told Peel, the resignation 'so entirely alters the character and aspect of affairs and so completely subverts the principles upon which I understood the government to have been formed in January last, that I feel it impossible that I should continue in office'.[40]

Palmerston in his journal (written long after the event and often unreliable but in this case sounding true to life) described how he, Lamb and Dudley discussed what they should do. Lamb said there was no choice, it was clear the Duke was determined to get rid of Huskisson and therefore they must follow. Dudley 'stroked his chin, counted the squares of the carpet three times up and then three times down, and then went off in an agony of doubt and hesitation'. Later the same day they met again. Dudley announced that he was in some embarrassment: 'The King has been pleased to take a great fancy to me . . .' Lamb, who had already been told privately through Bulwer Lytton and the Duke of Cumberland that George IV was particularly anxious that he above all others should stay on, was not impressed by the news of his friend's sudden favour. Dudley then said that he was happy to be able to assure them that the Colonial Office was to be filled by 'a moderate Tory, a man of promise, a member of a noble family'. Lamb commented that he did not know any such man existed – anyway, the appointment must still indicate a decided swing towards the right. With the air of a man playing his last card Dudley said that there was, after all, something to be said for attaching oneself to so great a man as the Duke. 'For my part,' said Lamb, 'I do not happen to think that he is so very great a man; but that's a matter of opinion.' Next morning the three men resigned.[41]

'William's resignation has produced great consternation in the government, the King and all rational people of all sides,' wrote Emily Cowper, 'and they all express it openly.' She was being somewhat partial but Lamb, who by his absence in Ireland had escaped much of the discredit earned by his colleagues for agreeing to serve under Wellington in the first place, now won more than his due proportion of the credit by resigning on an issue in which he had not been personally involved. Some thought he had been imprudent, even irresponsible, but none denied that he had acted with honour and courage. 'Wm is very well satisfied to resign,' continued his sister, 'is as usual in very good spirits and stands higher in character with all parties than anybody else in England, so that I think we shall still see him some day Prime Minister . . .'[42]

CHAPTER 7

Lady Branden

It is a bold biographer who ventures any categoric statement about the sexual predilections of his subject. The relationship between William and Caroline was understood, if by anyone, then only by the two protagonists; even to them it must have seemed inconstant and obscure, varying from hour to hour and rarely appearing to one of them in the same guise as it wore for the other. There is at all events no evidence to suggest that Lamb was unfaithful to his wife between their marriage and his departure for Ireland in 1827. During the last two years they had lived apart, for a dozen years before that their life together had been stormy, offering little real companionship to either party. Yet Lamb's name was never linked seriously with that of another woman; in an age and social group in which fidelity was ranked low among the virtues, he stayed constant to his volatile and tiresome wife.

In so doing he deprived himself of the greatest pleasure of his life. From his letters and what is known of his behaviour he does not seem to have been a man of strong sexual urges; on the whole only those who knew him slightly or not at all referred to him as a promiscuous womanizer. Yet women were, or perhaps more *a* woman *was* indispensable to his happiness. He relished the society of attractive women, rejoiced in the range of quasi-erotic experiences which lie between introduction and consummation, what Landor described as 'the middle state between love and friendship more delightful than either'. He did not pour out his heart to them, since no Lamb poured out his heart, but he confided in them in a way which was otherwise denied him. His mother and his wife had, in their own ways, supplied the needs of the first thirty years of his life. Then had come the arid interregnum. From 1827 until he left the service of Queen Victoria in 1841, three women in turn filled his life and occupied a high proportion of his thoughts and energies: Lady Branden, Mrs Norton, and the Queen herself.

In London the interregnum might have been tolerable. Lamb was protected by a carapace of clubs and conviviality; more important, in his sister Emily he had someone whose judgement he valued and in whose loyalty he could have confidence. In Dublin he realized that he was lonely. No Chief Secretary need ever spend an evening by himself, but the concept of the lonely crowd was not invented by contemporary sociologists. In the middle of his hectic office, besieged by the best that Dublin had to offer in the way of society, Lamb was profoundly alone.

He first met Lady Branden a few weeks after his arrival in Dublin, probably at the house of Peter La Touche – '94 years old past. They keep him upon a strict regimen of sherry and water, but if he can get at a bottle of wine now, he drinks it off in a crick. There is a fine old cod for you . . .'[1] The La Touches were one of the most respectable, indeed distinguished of Dublin families. Huguenots who had fled from France in the early eighteenth century, they had founded one of the largest of Irish banks and bought several fine estates within striking distance of the capital. Elizabeth Branden's father, Colonel David La Touche, married the daughter of the Earl of Miltown, from the great house of Russborough. In 1815 their daughter married the Rev. William Crosbie, a clergyman considerably her senior and shortly to succeed his cousin as Lord Branden. Branden seems never to have taken his pastoral duties with noticeable seriousness and, after succeeding to the title, abandoned them altogether. Within ten years of his marriage he was crippled by debts and gout, to the first of which disabilities his wife had undoubtedly contributed and which together rendered him unfit to meet her financial and sexual expectations. Though they were never formally separated he passed most of the year taking the waters in Buxton or sunning himself in the south of France, while she led the life of a merry widow in the house in Fitz-William Square which her family had bought her.

Traditionally Lady Branden has always been assigned a minor role in Lamb's life – a mistress who would barely have deserved a biographer's attention if it had not been that her indiscretion dragged her lover into the law courts. The sequence of some two hundred letters which survive among the Panshanger papers and which Lamb wrote to her between 1828 and 1832 prove however that she meant a great deal more to him than that, indeed that she pre-occupied him almost to the

exclusion of any other close relationship. It is all the more unsatisfactory, therefore, that she remains a shadow figure who must be built
up from casual references in contemporary journals and the letters of
William Lamb. She was without doubt beautiful and educated above
the usual level of women of that age. She was intelligent, perceptive
and shrewd, and her vivacity served as an acceptable substitute for wit.
She had spontaneous gaiety and the gift of communicating it to others;
many people in Dublin had better cooks, more numerous servants,
grander houses, but no one had created a salon in which it was more
agreeable to pass an hour or two.

So much for her virtues. She was also kind and generous on issues
which mattered little to her and thereby enjoyed a reputation for
amiability which her husband at least would have argued was scarcely
deserved. She was, in truth, selfish and egocentric, exigent in matters
material and still more emotional, but she was skilled at concealing
these weaknesses. Her minimum demand was that she should be the
centre of attention, to those who claimed to love her she must be the
unique source of light and life. To find pleasure outside her society
was treason.

'The six months we have just passed,' Lamb wrote to her in January
1828, shortly after he left Dublin, 'seem to me as if they were the last
sunshine that would gleam upon my life.'[2] Within a few weeks of their
first meeting he was visiting her house every evening, often arriving
as late as 11 p.m. He went with her regularly to balls and theatres and
those who wished to ingratiate themselves with the Chief Secretary
knew that it was wise to invite him to the same parties as Lady Branden.
The couple behaved with striking indiscretion, and in her case at least
probably got as much pleasure from the excitement which the liaison
caused as from the relationship itself. Whether they actually made love
is a problem to which there can be no final answer. It was taken for
granted by all their friends and acquaintances that they did, yet Lamb,
in a letter most emphatically not intended for the public eye, urged her
to 'assist and maintain that innocence of which you are conscious'[3]
and on other occassions referred to his regret at missed opportunities
during their time together.

Sunshine, as Lamb soon discovered, could burn as well as warm.
The dulcet hostess of FitzWilliam Square turned nasty if in any way
thwarted. 'Pray come this evening,' she wrote on one occasion. 'I will
not do anything to annoy you such as biting *hitting* and so forth – but
you must do something more to quiet me than looking *stern* and
cunning. This is all a most unsatisfactory way of spending an evening,

designed for better purposes . . . One might as well be in company with an old woman as with you . . .' She congratulated herself on her restraint – 'I had no idea that I could have felt so strong an aversion and almost thirst for revenge as I did after you left me the night that you nearly broke my arm'. Now she had got over her anger and 'this morning I love you as much as ever'. Lamb's crimes, it seems, were in part at least those of non-commission – though he was sometimes denounced as brutal it was his failure to respond to her sexual or other demands which caused Elizabeth Branden the deepest upset.[4]

Whether his offence lay in his inability to give her what she wanted once he had reached her house or his failure to get there at all, he found her exigence equally displeasing. 'I have just got your note,' read one anguished letter, 'you are really very unreasonable. I tell you that I am ill, that my cough is worse, that I am subject to very bad coughs, and yet you wish me to go to the play on one of the coldest nights that we have yet had. I think this very selfish, and does it not show a readiness to sacrifice to your own inclinations the welfare of one for whom you profess a friendship?' Her determination to make scenes on the slightest provocation and her gluttonous appetite for admiration must have seemed painfully familiar to her lover. He told his sister-in-law, Caro George, that Elizabeth Branden 'was very like in her ways' to Caroline; on which Emily Cowper commented, 'he does not appear to like her at all'.[5] The remark was curiously imperceptive. It is impossible to study his liaisons with Caroline, Lady Branden and Mrs Norton, even with Queen Victoria, without concluding that violent reactions, extravagant jealousy, insatiable demands for attention, were in some way an essential part of his relationship with any woman whom he truly loved. They seemed a stimulus without which the affair lacked flavour. He told Mrs Norton that he disliked rows, to the extent of taking sides against those who made them, however good their cause.[6] In political terms that might have been true, but no man who involves himself with *four* assertive and strident women can legitimately claim that he values a quiet life above all things.

In January 1828 the change in government made it essential for Lamb to go to London. A fortnight before he had received an appeal from Caroline to return at once because of her failing health. 'My heart is almost broken that I cannot come over directly . . .' he replied. 'How unfortunate and melancholy that you should be ill now and that it should be at a time when I, who have had so many years of idleness, am so fixed and chained down by circumstances.'[7] The strongest chain that held him was that provided by Lady Branden. But Caroline had often cried wolf about her health before and Dr Goddard had recently reported that she was on the mend. When Lamb set sail for Holyhead he had no reason to think that she was in immediate danger.

It was a dreadful passage. 'Heavy gale of wind right against us,' Lamb told Lady Branden. 'More than fifteen hours – suffered horribly . . . Never was a worse scene on this side the infernal regions. I believe these pains were inflicted upon me for any harshness which I may have been guilty of. Will you accept them as an expiation?' A worse scene was awaiting him. Caroline had in fact been dying for the last three months; bloated and dropsical, tormented by the foul potions of the doctors – 'blue pills, squills, and sweet spirit of nitre, with an infusion of cascarella bark'; what little strength she had drained by incessant tapping – 'it turns you deadly cold and sick', she told her husband. She accepted her fate with tranquillity. 'I consider my painful illness a great blessing', she had told her sister-in-law a few weeks before. 'I feel returned to my God and my duty and my dearest husband . . .'[8]

To write to your mistress from the deathbed of your wife is an exercise difficult to carry off with grace or even decorum. Lamb made as good a shot at it as could be expected. 'I am afraid you will think me negligent,' he wrote, 'but you do not know the melancholy here, which I have come to witness. She is dying, dying rapidly, and that with a perfect knowledge of it and the greatest composure. The only bitter feelings which affect her, are those under which I knew she would suffer, if ever she came to think calmly and to have the unclouded use of her own powerful understanding, namely deep regret and repentance of the course which she has run, and the conduct, which she has pursued.' Within a few days she was dead, 'without any pain and from complete exhaustion . . . She only fetched one sigh and she was gone.' Her husband had been with her only a few hours before; according to her brother William Ponsonby the visit gave her much comfort. 'Lamb acted as I always knew he would do,' he wrote later the same night.[9]

It could hardly be expected that William Lamb would mourn for long. Lady Carlisle, a childhood friend from the days of Devonshire House, found him at first in great distress: 'However he got over it, after crying a good deal, and talked with very great interest on political subjects; he cannot be expected to feel it really as a loss, tho' very much affected whenever he mentioned her.' Emily Cowper rated his grief still lower: 'He was hurt at the time and rather low next day, but he is now just as usual, and his mind filled with politicks.' The twin pulls of

Lady Branden in Dublin and the political crisis at home prevented him brooding over a loss which can have meant little to him in terms of the present but re-opened many vivid recollections of the past. He had loved Caroline deeply in his time, would probably never have brought himself to part from her but for the pressure of his family, was never to forget her. She was buried on 7 February and ten days later Lamb wrote of it to Elizabeth Branden. 'I felt upon that occasion in a manner which I have often heard others describe, but in which I never felt before myself, and did not think that I could feel, a sort of impossibility of believing that I should never see her countenance or hear her voice again, and a sort of sense of desolation, solitude and carelessness about everything, when I forced myself to remember that she was really gone . . .'[10]

Five months later Lord Melbourne followed his daughter-in-law to the grave. Here there was indeed no room for grief. For several years he had been no more than a drink-sodden hulk; an embarrassment to his family when at his best, a vegetable when not. William Lamb's regrets were largely selfish. 'I am very sorry to part with my name,' he told Lady Branden, 'which had become as it were part of myself, and by which I was so well known. Everybody now will be asking who this new gentleman is.'[11] The new gentleman would, of course, thenceforward sit in the House of Lords. The most important consequence of this was that he no longer had to worry about the arduous and expensive hunt for a seat in the Commons; the only serious drawback that certain posts, in particular that of Chancellor of the Exchequer, were traditionally barred to peers. Since Lamb had no aspiration to dabble in economic affairs, the deprivation cost him little.

Lamb, to call him by his old name for a few months longer, did not intend that his departure from Dublin should sever him from Lady Branden. On the contrary, their love seemed to thrive on separation; the longer the distance between their meetings, the stronger grew the note of hungry desire in his letters. Lamb's personality comes across admirably in the casual, affectionate, hurried notes which he dashed off at meetings or in stolen moments between ball and dinner-party. He loved to teach, and one of the charms of Elizabeth Branden was that she was always ready to learn and quite intelligent enough to keep her master up to the mark. He lectured her lovingly: 'Put the day of the month as I do, learn a little punctuality and accuracy, which women hardly ever have, principally because they are not in their youth subjected to that discipline which alone can teach it'. He mocked at her temperamental rages: 'There is nothing like a little irritation sometimes, it stirs the blood, moves the energies and does more good than all the tonics and stimulants in the world.' He chided her impetuosity: 'What a foolish thing to quarrel with Ld Abergavenny. It seems to me like quarrelling with one's bread and butter, which even in the nursery one knows to be very absurd.'[12]

Another, less attractive note was struck throughout the correspondence. Lamb began to reveal a curious obsession with beating and 'discipline', particularly involving girls or women. The subject arose innocently enough when he urged Lady Branden, half-jokingly, to have greater resort to flogging in dealing with her children. Then he suggested the same treatment for an idle maid, wishing he could order the application of the birch 'upon that large and extensive field of *derrière,* which is so well calculated to receive it'. From that they were soon exchanging anecdotes in which beating was in one way or another involved, and Lamb cut from a book to send his mistress a print showing a woman beating a naked child, accompanying the gift with a long dissertation on the subject and praising the 'great heartiness and grace' with which the rod was being applied. The flavour of erotic zest became more and more obtrusive – there was no use beating a dog protected by its hair, 'but a few twigs of a birch applied to the naked skin of a young lady produces with very little effort a very considerable sensation'.

That he practised as well as preached is shown by a letter from his ward, Susan, written many years later, in which she reminisced about the whippings which Lamb had administered, boasted that she was following the same practice with her three-year-old daughter and excused herself for sparing her son on the grounds that he was only ten months old. 'I remember,' wrote Susan, 'as though it was yesterday, the *execution,* then being thrown in a corner of a large couch there was at Brockett – you used then to leave the room and I remember your coming back one day and saying "Well cocky does it smart still?" at which of course I could not help laughing instead of crying.'[13]

'A letter from you excites me more than the full possession of others,' Melbourne was to write nearly three years after his first meeting with Elizabeth Branden. It was the emphasis on flagellation that seemed to give the excitement its especial potency. Inevitably Lady Branden herself became the putative target: 'So you are duller and fractious, are you? I wish I were with you. I would administer promptly what is necessary upon such occasions'; 'If I did not think that you were too

angry to be jested with, I should say that I would certainly get a rod
for you and apply it smartly the first time that I see you'. In a sequence
of forty letters only four do not allude in some way to his obsession.
Nor was it confined to his relationship with a single woman. Ten years
later, in a letter written to him from Italy, Mrs Norton told him of an
inlaid box which she had seen in an antique shop and had nearly bought
him because the design was of 'your favourite subject of a woman
whipping a child'.[14]

Whether Lamb did or did not indulge in erotic fantasies of this kind
is not a matter of the first importance. Nor, however, can it be ignored.
His hall-mark, almost his stock in trade, was his complete normality.
Decent, honourable, straightforward, you knew where you were with
Lamb. He enjoyed his paradoxes and read rather more than might be
felt quite normal, but at bottom he was safe. His nonchalance, his calm
good-sense, his flippancy, his ostentatious freedom from ambition,
were surely the signs of a mind at peace, without complexes or in-
hibitions. With Lady Branden to some extent he gave himself away.
If these quirky appetites could flourish in what to the outside world
seemed so conventional a relationship, could everything else be as
uncomplicated as it seemed? To say that no one is exactly as they
appear on the surface can hardly be called an original or even helpful
observation; yet when the surface is as urbane and impenetrable as
that of William Lamb, the point is one that should be borne in
mind.

Lamb's love for Elizabeth Branden involved him in the first of the two
scandals which were to threaten his career. Rumours had filtered
through to Dublin that the Rev. Lord Branden was put out by his
wife's behaviour. Discreet adultery was one thing, a flamboyant affair
with the Chief Secretary quite another. When Lamb had been back in
London for a few weeks he called on Branden; uncertain about his
reception but feeling that failure to do so might be still more dangerous.
To his relief: 'He received me quite with rapture and expressed himself
greatly obliged at my calling'. But Lamb, when away from Lady
Branden, soon reverted to his habitual caution. 'Men with quick
feelings are always the worst men,' he once pronounced, referring to
Brougham and matters political but with just as much application to
affairs of the heart. In spite of Branden's friendliness he wrote to warn
Elizabeth: 'do not let your desire to see me make you do any thing imprudent or unwise for yourself. Do not come over to him too hastily,

when you have once rejoined him you will have put yourself in his power . . .'[15]

Two months later the storm broke. In May 1828 Lord Branden brought an action against Lamb, alleging the seduction of his wife. He seems to have laid his hands on some correspondence between the two which he felt conclusively proved their guilt. Creevey alleges that he tried to blackmail Lamb into procuring him a bishopric and that it was only when this came to nothing that he resorted to the courts.[16] Given Branden's subsequent conduct this might not seem improbable if it were not for a letter from Lamb to Lady Branden in which he gloomily commented that her husband's passions were so violent 'and as I understand so much excited that they will make him blind to all reason and common sense, and even to his own interests and the disgrace and danger of his situation'. He seemed, complained Lamb, to have got the most extraordinary notions into his head – that his wife had several times dined alone with the Chief Secretary at Phoenix Park and that she had had a key cut so that her lover could have easy access to her through a side door of her house.[17]

Whether or not he could have proved such allegations it seems Lord Branden had assembled a regiment of witnesses who would show the couple to have been, if not adulterous, at least guilty of the grossest indiscretion. The time came and nothing of the sort occurred; the plaintiff's case was so ludicrously weak that Lord Tenterden dismissed it without even hearing counsel for the defence. Officially, at least, Lamb's honour had been vindicated. It was not astonishing that so tame a conclusion should have been greeted with derision by those who fancied themselves in the know. 'The verdict of *Not Guilty* pronounced in consequence of the witnesses not appearing,' observed Campbell weightily, 'raised a not improbable suspicion of compromise.'[18]

The suspicions were justified. That Lamb bought off Lord Branden can be proved by a letter from Michael Bruce which now lies among a handful of other personal papers in the Melbourne archive at Windsor.[19] In this letter Bruce, who seems to have been acting as go-between, reported that 'the noble and reverend cuckold' had been making difficulties. 'Our friend Lord B has had a fit of delicacy which in him was truly ridiculous. He did not wish the money to be paid to him, or to affix his signature to any receipt. This is straining at gnats after swallowing a camel. To obviate all difficulties I went myself to Snow's Bank and presented your draft and got from them two one thousand pounds notes, which I have this instant paid into Farquhar's Bank.' Two years later the reverend cuckold was writing to Bruce to promise

not to renew the suit and at the same time complaining that some condition in the agreement had not been observed, 'thereby constantly
adding to the heavy wrongs he has already heaped on one who never
did him any injury'.[20] Branden was an ignoble creature and deserves
little sympathy. He carried his grudge to the grave and beyond; his
will reading: *'Quant à ma très infame et vicieuse épouse dont l'infidelité à
mon égard est le moindre de ses crimes, je donne et je legue la somme d'un
schilling'*. In the same document he urged his daughter not to marry
unless she was determined to stick faithfully to her husband and to
abandon all other men for him.

Lamb had told his sister when the threat of an action was first broached
that 'he would rather die than leave any woman in that situation'. On
the whole he lived up to these words, yet he was always cautious and
temperate – qualities alien to his extravagantly demanding mistress.
Constantly she abused him for not proclaiming his love for her from
the rooftops; ideally calling out her husband and running him through
for good measure. 'Reason and common sense you call coldness and
calculation,' complained Lamb.[21] It was a complaint he had often
levelled at his wife and in time was to level at Mrs Norton. The next
few months were to prove full of such tribulations. Nothing Lamb did
would have seemed adequate to Lady Branden, equally he must have
irritated her beyond measure by his acceptance of what she felt to be
intolerable impositions. Always he was urging her to give way; to
compromise; to avoid direct conflicts with her husband. She was not
to show resentment when she got an offensive letter from her sister:
'It serves no end and generally by creating irritation hardens people
in their hostility. Pray preach patience and tolerance, a lesson which to
the female sex is generally preached in vain.' She was to propitiate the
lawyers who seemed set upon ruining her. 'Attornies and solicitors
are of all human beings the most irritable, the most consequential and
can the least bear anything that seems disrespectful and wounds their
sense of their own importance . . . It is madness to offend them and
like Evil Beings they ought to be propitiated by any sacrifice.'[22]

Lady Branden was not the woman to accept unpalatable advice
meekly. She turned elsewhere for counsel, began to talk wildly and
almost to include Lamb in the roll-call of her enemies. 'You seem to
have no confidence in me and to be inclined ever to act hostilely and
against me . . . You also appear to me to take other advice than mine
and to have the fault, common to all women I have known, of listening
and trusting to any trumpery fellow, rather than to the person in whom
they profess the utmost confidence.'[23] Lady Branden, who was some-

thing of a feminist, can not have found his strictures the more palatable for being presented as general assaults on the female sex.

It seemed as if the affair must disintegrate under this endless bickering. And then, without any meeting between them, all was light and love again. From early in 1830 Melbourne was once more writing to her with the enthusiasm of a lover wooing his mistress. It is impossible not, in some degree, to relate this new enthusiasm to the obsession with flagellation which Melbourne now revealed, but it would anyway not be surprising if Lady Branden's qualities proved more apparent and her vices less vexatious when she was far away. At all events, for the rest of 1830 and throughout 1831 he lived in eager expectation of her letters and reacted with alarm and distress if they did not arrive. 'Why do you not write?' he would ask again and again, and then, 'Surely I can not have offended you? Why do you not write?'

Finally, early in 1832, came a fresh dwindling of correspondence. For the rest of his life Melbourne was to feel some responsibility for Lady Branden's well-being; even after his death his brother continued to pay the £1000 a year which he had been giving her for the last twenty years. Letters continued to arrive addressed to 'dearest Lord M', reproaching him with being late in his payments. 'Oh dearest Ld M just consider the painful position I am placed in and pray, pray I beseech you do not add to it. I have suffered enough in various ways God knows! I have nothing to look back to with *pleasure* or to look forward to with *hope*.'[24] Always he responded to such appeals, but he did so from duty and not from love. He had found comfort elsewhere, the memory of Lady Branden grew dim, the affair was over.

———◆◆———

CHAPTER 8

The End of the Huskissonians

W HETHER OR NOT Melbourne should properly be called a Canningite there is no doubt that in 1828 he was a committed Huskissonian. The pre-eminence which this impressive yet curiously unalluring figure enjoyed among his motley band of followers was unquestioned. Yet Huskisson was not only the greatest asset of the little party, he was also in a way its greatest liability. Melbourne, Palmerston, the Grants, Wortley, Sturges-Bourne had each their critics and even enemies but on the whole were liked and trusted. Without too much difficulty they could have fitted into almost any ministry short of the radical on one wing or the ultra-Tory on the other. Huskisson was a different matter. The Whigs had long considered him devious and self-seeking; since his retreat from Wellington's administration the Tories would have described him by harsher words. Though both parties accepted that, in certain circumstances, he might be necessary, there was no doubt in their minds that he would be a necessary evil. With him at the helm it seemed that the Huskissonians, like some politically-powered *Flying Dutchman*, might tack for ever across the seas in search of a welcoming port.

In such straits they clung together, not so much from loyalty, as from a conviction that their bargaining power was greater as a group than as individuals. Mrs Arbuthnot was too close a friend of the Duke of Wellington to be deemed impartial but she was not being wholly unfair when she commented in June, 1828: 'There is not one of them that is not dying to be in again, and what specially provokes me with the whole party is that not one of them affects to think or say he thought Mr Huskisson in the right. They all went because they considered themselves a separate party and bound to act together, right or wrong; it was intended to be what Mr Wilmot calls a *general strike*, and they fancied they sh'd be too strong for the Duke.'[1]

'United we stand, divided we fall' is not a bad slogan for a group of political exiles. The trouble was that they did not know *where* they stood. Ideally, of course, they would be the nucleus of a coalition which would draw away the moderates from both sides: that will-o'-the-wisp of a centre party which haunts political life whenever times are bad for the big battalions. Twice in the first months of 1829 a group of Huskissonians was invited to Windsor and the King was particularly gracious to Melbourne. It was an open secret that he was in a mood to welcome an escape from the Duke, and the Huskissonians would have been restrained indeed if they had not seen themselves as heading the rescue party. 'They passed the whole time plotting against the Govt,' wrote Mrs Arbuthnot, 'and plotting how their *expected cabinet* sh'd be formed. Lord Melbourne was to be prime minister.'[2] But such illusions did not survive long. Whatever the King's wishes, he could not conjure parliamentary majorities out of nothing. The future of the Huskissonians must in the end lie in union with one of the major parties. The problem was to decide which. Huskisson himself and Palmerston – though the latter always claimed to have been a Whig at heart[3] – would probably have preferred the Tories, especially if Wellington had given some hint that he would one day espouse a modest measure of parliamentary reform. Melbourne for his part inclined towards the Whigs. He cared nothing for parliamentary reform but felt that the Whigs were sounder on the other great issue of the day, Catholic Emancipation. Besides, he had a residual loyalty towards the party of his youth; other things being equal, he would feel more at home with the heirs of Charles James Fox. Essentially, however, the group was uncommitted: 'no reasonable offer refused' would perhaps be over-simplifying their philosophy but certainly no reasonable offer would automatically have been rejected, on grounds either doctrinaire or personal.[4]

Austin Mitchell has referred to the Huskissonians as 'a group of generals without soldiers, weak in numbers, strong in ability'.[5] The comment is an apt one. Huskisson had the preponderant voice but he was *primus inter pares*, he must have looked nervously each morning at his flock in case one of them had deserted during the night. Their collective weakness and individual quality made them a tempting target for party leaders anxious to enlist notable outsiders under their standards. Melbourne himself seems to have been one of the first to be thus solicited. In August 1828 the Duke of Clarence ended his capricious career as Lord High Admiral. It was at once rumoured that Melbourne was to take on the Admiralty. From Panshanger came embarrassed denials; no such offer had been made and if it were to be it would be refused. But Lord Grey knew better, or thought he did. 'I see now, to use the sporting term, that Lord Melbourne is the favourite for the Admiralty. I thought this at first the most likely arrangement. But I was assured so positively that it was not to be, that I gave up my opinion. I return to it in consequence of the renewed report . . .' He was wrong again, but it is probable that there was some basis for the gossip in the shape at least of a tentative suggestion from the Duke.[6]

One of the main obstacles between Melbourne and the Tories was about to be removed. In July 1828 O'Connell was returned by a massive majority in a by-election for Clare. As a Catholic he could not take his seat but the event was enough to convince Wellington that the Catholic Association could not be crushed and that it would be impossible to govern Ireland if no relief were given. That most pragmatic of all statesmen cajoled and bullied the King into accepting the same point of view and early in 1829 emancipation was passed with only the most trivial qualifications.

The right wing of the Tory party, already offended at being largely excluded from office, now moved into inveterate opposition. If the Duke were to survive he would have to find help elsewhere. In the autumn Mrs Arbuthnot was deploring the possibility of a union with the Huskissonians. 'There is not one among that party who have one grain of honour or principle. Ld Melbourne talked the other day to a person, who repeated it to me, of having given the best living vacant while he was Secy for Ireland to Mr La Touche that he might help to support his mistress, Ly Branden. I think a man who could do that wholly unfit to be trusted with anything.'[7] Her facts were wrong – the only clerical La Touche, the Rev. John, did not change his parish while Lamb was in Ireland – but she was still voicing the opinion of a sizeable wing of the Tories that the Huskissonians were tricky time-servers, to be avoided if at all possible.

Wellington, however, had in mind a more ambitious coalition. His plan was to send Lord Grey as Lord Lieutenant to Ireland and to absorb the leading Whigs into his government. It seems clear that Grey and Russell at least would have been ready to co-operate – 'I confess I should have been glad to have been able to support the men who carried the Catholic Question . . .' Russell wrote wistfully – but the attempt foundered on the King's intransigent hostility. The good will caused by emancipation soon died away and relations between Wellington and the Whigs became as frigid as ever. For Melbourne and his friends the turn of events must have been something of a relief. If Grey and Wellington united there would have been few pickings indeed for the rump of the Canningites, they might even have found themselves excluded altogether. Grey asked Princess Lieven what she thought Melbourne and Palmerston would do next. 'Judging from their antecedents,' she replied, 'it seems natural enough that they should take part with the opponents of Govt. But . . . are they sufficiently united – sufficiently determined? It appears to me more than doubtful. I would wager that no one of the party yet knows on which side he will ultimately find himself . . .'[8]

Though neither she nor even the members of that party realized it, the decision had in effect been taken. If Wellington had made overtures to the Huskissonians directly after the grant of emancipation they could hardly have refused but by now it was too late. They were edging inexorably towards the Whigs, though still professing publicly that what they wanted was the widest possible coalition. For the Whigs Grey confessed that he distrusted Huskisson but that, 'I do not see how it would be possible to form an administration that could conduct things satisfactorily . . . without his assistance and that of those who are supposed to be connected with him'.[9]

In the middle of June came the death of King George IV and the political situation took on a new flexibility. His brother and successor, William IV, had a not unmerited reputation as a buffoon but was believed also to be honest, decent and conscientious. As a political figure, however, he was an unknown quantity. In his youth he had associated mainly with the Whigs and he had fallen out with Wellington when he lost his job as Lord High Admiral. So far, so good for the opposition, but the new King showed no inclination to turn out his ministers. On the contrary, he made it almost embarrassingly clear that he was prepared to support them so long as they continued to command a majority in the House of Commons. It was generally assumed that he had suffered a change of heart and was now as Tory as his government; the fact that he was perfectly ready to accept the Whigs if they, in their turn, could win the support of the country, was far from being apparent. For Grey and his followers William's accession, therefore, proved something of a disappointment. It still, however, removed Grey's greatest enemy. From the new monarch he could expect no particular favour, yet equally need fear no hostility.

Melbourne did not feel that the change touched him closely. For most of the time George IV had treated him with singular kindness, even if the royal favour had been worth little in the way of patronage.

There seemed no reason to expect less or more from William. Melbourne observed with tolerance the King's well-intentioned and on the whole successful efforts to win popular approval. William ambled up St James's and had to be rescued by the members of Whites' from the embraces of an exuberant Irish tart, chatted affably with old ladies on the pier at Brighton, made innumerable speeches professing his love for the Duke of Wellington, the British people, the constitution. What the King does is generally sensible, thought Melbourne, 'but perhaps there is something a little burlesque in his manner of doing things, and in the language with which he accompanies them'.[10]

Melbourne himself spent much of the summer at Panshanger, the vast castellated Gothick mansion a few miles from Brocket where the Cowpers entertained lavishly and often. 'Full to the brim of vice and agreeableness, foreigners and roués,' Emily Eden described it.[11] Palmerston, now established for several years as Emily Cowper's lover, was there almost as often as either her husband or her brother, and the house became something of a centre for the Huskissonians. Traditionally Lord Cowper was a Whig and his house a party stronghold, but in fact any kind of doctrinaire commitment would have been deplored in this blandly free-thinking establishment. In so far as there was any prevailing tone it was that of a mild and sceptical Toryism. In such an atmosphere fanaticism faded, dogmas were questioned, simple faith dismissed as gullibility. Melbourne relished the ease, the sophistication, the cultivated debauchery. But though neither he nor Palmerston felt any loyalty to the Whig leaders, they recognized that their best interests would probably be served by entry into the fold. It was a question of choosing the time. Since the death of George IV made the formation of a Whig government marginally more probable, the advantages of reunion became more evident and the urgency more pressing.

Wellington was uneasily conscious of what was going on and anxious to arrest the process. At the end of June, when it was clear that the new King intended to keep his present ministers, he decided to make a further attempt on Melbourne's loyalties. By way of Lady Burghersh and Frederick Lamb he sent a message saying that he 'would be glad if they could come together again, and did not see why they should not do so'. Melbourne, he suggested, had only left office in 1828 because of 'the scrape he got into with Lady Branden, which made it unpleasant to him to return to Dublin'. Wellington himself would have been perfectly happy to offer him a cabinet post in London but had been deterred by George IV's notorious dislike of giving jobs to people who had once resigned. Now, with a new king on the throne, the rift need not remain unhealed for another day.[12]

Melbourne was not flattered by the suggestion that his resignation – an act which not without reason he felt had been disinterested and even noble – had been inspired by such base motives. He replied that he had left the government not for any personal reason but because the Duke had treated Huskisson so shabbily. He could not now return to office alone. 'Why, who does he want with him?' asked Wellington. 'Does he want Palmerston? I have no objection to him. As to Huskisson, I do not know what to say . . .' The Duke announced that he would think it over, and then call on Frederick Lamb with his final offer. Alarmed by the imminent approach of the mountain, Mahomet conferred with his friends. They could not put back the clock two years, they decided; even if the Duke were prepared to welcome Huskisson they would still refuse unless Grey and one or two other Whigs were included in the deal. Such a reply was tantamount to flat rejection and the Duke so interpreted it. The promised call on Fred Lamb never took place.

In September the opening of the new Manchester railway offered Wellington a chance to renew his overture. This time he decided to start at the top. Two days before the ceremony Huskisson wrote to commiserate with Melbourne on the illness which would prevent him attending the ceremony. 'The great Captain comes here tomorrow and great are the preparations for his reception. The feeling is not confidence or admiration of his political character, but rather that of awe at the man that subdued Bonaparte and forced the Catholic question. It is the Indian worshipping the devil, because he is not conscious where he shall find a protecting deity.'[13] That Wellington intended to make use of the meeting is certain; quite what he would have said we will never know. Huskisson succumbed to a mixture of clumsiness and panic, was run over by an approaching train, and ensured a modest niche in the book of records as the first statesman to die in a railway accident.

Canningites without Canning and now Huskissonians bereft of Huskisson; Palmerston and Melbourne anxiously conferred about their future. In Torrens's excellent phrase, they were not so much sheep without a shepherd as sheep-dogs without a master. They found the prospects of a union with the Tories still less alluring: as Palmerston told Littleton, if they were to enter Wellington's cabinet without Huskisson they would be 'more completely destitute of means or influence to carry their opinions into action, and would be more decidedly considered by the public, as submitting to be instruments, instead of being admitted to be colleagues'. But it did not follow from this that they should immediately coalesce with the Whigs – 'co-operation whenever possible, but no incorporation', should be their rule.[14]

The Whigs would have liked to take things a little further, at least as far as a firm engagement if not actually consummation. In Brougham's view the death of Huskisson had cost the group more than half its value, 'but there are men among them of most valuable talents, as Pam and Grant, and of excellent sense and disposition as Ld Granville, and of excellent talents and dispositions and temper too, as W. Lamb'. An argument against open union in the past had been that it would rule out any chance of a working arrangement with the ultra-Tories, to whom Huskisson was anathema. With this danger vanished, an unholy alliance of extremist Tories, Canningites and Whigs seemed a real possibility. On 25 September Grey sent Holland to discuss possibilities with Melbourne. Though there was still to be no fusion of the two groups, Melbourne made it plain that he and his colleagues would be happy to serve under Grey in any future government. As for joining Wellington, Palmerston roundly assured Littleton, they would as soon jump off Westminster Bridge. Brougham still busily retailed rumours that 'our excellent Countess Emily' was trying to 'organize a rapproche-ment between Canningites and Duke of Wellington' but he hardly be-lieved them himself, let alone convinced anyone else.[15]

Wellington, with the hostility of his own right wing becoming ever more menacing, decided to have one last try. The deaf but affable Lord Clive was sent off to Palmerston with a fresh offer. There was still no suggestion that any leading Whigs should be admitted to the cabinet but Grey, at least, could perhaps be satisfied with the job of Lord Lieutenant in Ireland. The position of the Canningite group in the cabinet was to be safe-guarded by the simultaneous inclusion of Lord Goderich. Not surprisingly Melbourne and Palmerston did not feel that this would afford them the protection that they required. A hint to Melbourne that he might like to come in by himself if a reshuffle left vacant the post of Lord Privy Seal was given equally short shrift. The die was cast. As Melbourne wrote to Palmerston, they were now in a position where they 'could not fairly and honourably accept office' unless Grey and Lansdowne at least accompanied them. 'We might do ourselves credit and the country service, but a cabinet formed upon a principle of balance and difference and commenced in distrust and hostility can never be of much use to the public nor, to the members of it, any other than a source of annoyance and disquiet.'[16]

A few days after his final approach to Palmerston, Wellington signed his own political death-warrant. The pressure for some measure of parliamentary reform had now become so great that it was generally expected the Duke would at least hint at his willingness to introduce changes in the speech from the throne at the beginning of November. No such hint was given, and to compound his error Wellington, in the course of the debate, declared that not only was he satisfied with the present basis of representation but that, if called upon to start from scratch and devise the perfect system, he would arrive at something indistinguishable from the contemporary House of Commons. He maintained subsequently that any attempt to introduce concessions would have undermined his own support: 'I saw that it was a question of noses – that as many as I gained on one side I should lose on the other.' To everyone else, however, it seemed that he had staked the future of his government on a wild gamble.[17]

From Melbourne's point of view it was not the ideal issue on which to see the Tories defeated. Though he was now privately prepared to concede that the force of public opinion made some concession on parliamentary reform essential he hardly relished the idea of appearing as its champion. His associates, however, who had for some time been converted to the principle, convinced him that he was being over-squeamish. At a meeting on 6 November, they agreed to support a Whig motion in favour of parliamentary reform provided it was worded vaguely and they were not committed to any precise proposals. Palmerston passed on the news to the Whigs, who were well satisfied. 'Though he and his friends do not yet seem disposed to go as far in reform as we think necessary,' recorded Howick, 'they are quite prepared to vote for a general resolution and I hope if it came to be necessary to form a govt they would consent to do a great deal more than they would now pledge themselves to.'[18]

All was now set for a change of ministry. The general election which followed William IV's accession had shown a marked swing away from the Tories and towards a majority who supported reform. The well-ordered and virtually bloodless July Revolution in France, though it came too late to have much influence on the British elections,[19] strengthened the cause of those who argued that radical change was possible without civil war. Whigs, Canningites, Radicals, ultra Tories – united in nothing except a conviction that Wellington and his ministers must depart – defeated the government by nearly thirty votes in the House of Commons. On 16 November 1830 Wellington resigned. After so many years in the wilderness, the Whigs had at last returned to power.

That the Canningites would be included in the new government was taken as certain by everyone; the only question was what they would pick up in the distribution of the spoils. In view of later developments it is interesting to see how clearly Palmerston was considered to be chief of the little band. In earlier negotiations, whether with Whigs or Tories, it was he who had taken the lead. Now Grey reported 'a very satisfactory conversation with Lord Palmerston' as a result of which 'I have every reason to believe that he and his friends will form a part of the new government'.[20] 'He and his friends' had every reason to feel satisfied as well. Two of the plum jobs fell to them: Palmerston was to be Foreign Secretary while Lord Melbourne took the Home Office.

Except for a few months as Irish Secretary, Melbourne had passed the first fifty years of his life in something close to idleness. He had, it is true, read a lot; had no doubt got thoroughly bored out of a sense of duty in the House of Commons; had studied now and then in a desultory way. In essence, however, his life had been one of self-indulgence. Now all was transformed. His next eleven years were to be ones of intense activity, making heavy demands on his stamina and his fortitude. He was to fill, almost without interruption, the highest offices of state; a burden which had broken several of his immediate predecessors. At this point it seems, therefore, appropriate to consider what sort of a man he had become, and how far his life to date qualified or disqualified him for what was to lie ahead.

Winthrop Mackworth Praed made such an examination in the poetical sketch which he did of parliament at about this period.[21] He had been describing Wellesley and now turned to a more congenial theme:

> In stalwart contrast, large of heart and frame,
> Destin'd for power, in youth more bent on fame,
> Sincere, yet deeming half the world a sham,
> Mark the rude handsome manliness of Lamb! . . .
> Gossip accords him attributes like these –
> A sage good-humour, based on love of ease,
> A mind that most things undisturb'dly weighed,
> Nor deemed their metal worth the clink it made.

But under this urbane exterior lurked another Lamb:

> His was a restless anxious intellect,
> Eager for truth and pining to detect;

Each ray of light that man can cast on soul,
Chequering its course, or shining from its goal,
Each metaphysic doubt – each doctrine dim –
Plato or Pusey, had delight for him.
His mirth, though genial, came by fits and starts –
The man was mournful in his heart of hearts . . .
I mark not one concealing from mankind
A larger nature or a lovelier mind,
Or leaving safer from his own gay laugh
That faith in good which is the soul's best half.

The verse, hardly memorable in itself, is worth attention since it encapsulates not only several shrewd judgements but also those illusions about himself which Melbourne industriously fostered all his life. To pick a few phrases from Praed's doggerel – was Melbourne in youth or in maturity really 'bent on fame'? Certainly he was not bent on the baubles which customarily attend it. No man who refused the Garter four times, who was said to have vetoed the Order of the Thistle for a Scottish nobleman on the grounds that he would eat it, who asked indignantly when a much-decorated marquis pleaded for yet more honours: 'God, does he want a Garter for the other leg?' can be accused of undue reverence for the symbols of power and rank. Lady Lyttelton remembered him commenting on a mutual friend who had just received some accolade or other: '. . . I don't know how it is – one ought not, perhaps, to say it – but *don't* you think those *ribbons* are rather over-valued?'[22]

But a disdain for empty honours did not imply indifference to power or the office which produced it. 'No fellow who likes office,' he once told Ellice, 'should ever talk as if he disliked it or was indifferent to it. It always results like pretence and affectation.'[23] It was advice which he rarely followed himself; an appearance of disinterest, of finding the whole thing a damned bore, was a prominent element in his style as a public man. Yet few of those who knew him well doubted his eagerness to hold office or his tenacity in retaining it. His pages of autobiography betray both his conviction that he was suited to the highest positions and his pique when he was denied them. For the politician fame is the inevitable concomitant of power, the overt proof that he has in fact achieved his ends. Melbourne had as little vanity as anyone in a similar position, he disliked self-advertisement and in an age of television would certainly have distrusted and despised the medium. But he would also have mastered it and exploited equally any other device by which his reputation could be enhanced and his position strengthened. Fame was not so much the spur as a useful tool which served his ends. In so far as he could not exercise power without enjoying it, then he was indeed 'bent on fame'.

'Deeming half the world a sham,' is a less questionable judgement. Melbourne had a cool, rational eighteenth-century mind, he deplored all fanaticism, *'surtout, pas trop de zèle'*, could have been his slogan as well as Talleyrand's. Few things gave him more pleasure than to mock the earnest efforts of the well-intentioned. 'In the past history of the world,' he told the Archbishop of Dublin, 'no feelings have been more extravagant or expensive, nor have imposed heavier burdens upon mankind, than those of piety and charity'. To the youthful Queen Victoria he couched his advice more simply: 'You had better try to do no good, and then you'll get into no scrapes'.[24] Such sayings were deliberately extravagant, but they reflected a conviction that those who sought to change the lot of their fellow-men were generally either fools or hypocrites. Displays of excessive sensibility seemed equally distasteful to him, if less dangerous to the life of the nation. The artistic temperament bred disorder and tended to produce flamboyant or *outré* results rather than products of solid worth: Sir Joshua Reynolds was his favourite painter; Mme de Sévigné the leading female writer, though even she 'was a great humbug'. Men of letters, he felt strongly, should be kept in their place. When Waddington was put forward for a bishopric, Melbourne commented that he was 'a mere literary man, and literary men are rarely good for anything practical', while Serjeant Talfourd was suspect as a future Solicitor General: 'He writes plays, and I don't think a man who writes plays is ever good for much else . . .' Worst of all, Talfourd was 'a great friend of Wordsworth'.[25]

A benevolent scepticism is probably a desirable attribute in a minister; there will always be a sufficiency of idealists around him. But scepticism can easily degenerate into corroding cynicism, and the man of power who is also a cynic may prove dangerous. It is hard not to detect the note of cynicism in Melbourne's outburst to Archbishop Whately: 'I say, Archbishop, what do you think I'd have done about this slavery business, if I'd had my own way? I'd have done nothing at all! I'd have left it all alone. It's all a pack of nonsense! Always have been slaves in all the most civilized countries; the Greeks and Romans had slaves; however, they *would* have their fancy, and so we've abolished slavery; but it's great folly.'[26] Melbourne may have been half-joking, seeking to tease a worthy prelate. If so, it was a bad joke. It was not – priggish though the judgement may appear – the sort of joke which should be made by a man charged with the welfare of a nation at a time of deep social and economic disturbance.

If the unacceptable face of scepticism is a crippling cynicism, then that of tolerance is indifference. Melbourne had, said Praed, 'a mind that most things undisturb'dly weighed'. Objectivity, indeed, was among the most valuable of his qualities. He was genuinely ready to judge arguments on their merits and to hold it against no man that he differed from the majority. But always this tolerance verged on apathy. Guizot, the French Ambassador and a shrewd observer, considered that Melbourne was 'impartial from clear sense and indifference; a judicious epicurean; an agreeable egotist, gay without warmth, and mingling a natural air of authority with a carelessness which he took delight in proclaiming. "It is all the same to me", was his habitual expression'.[27] Guizot had put his finger on one of Melbourne's weaknesses. He did not care enough about any issue, or indeed any person outside the tiny circle of those he loved, to fight hard in their defence. Conversely, nothing seemed to him so evil that it was worth going to great pains to oppose it.

The strength, yet also the weakness, of Melbourne's tolerance is clearly shown in his attack on Pusey's bigotry: 'The danger of religious zeal is the spirit of ill-will, hatred and malice, of intolerance and persecution, which in its own warmth and sincerity it is too apt to engender.'[28] It is easy to condemn religious bigotry if you do not think it matters greatly whether a man is a papist, an anglican, or for that matter a Mahometan. Similarly, tolerance in matters political comes more easily to those who cannot see any significant difference between the parties. Yet Melbourne's indignation when it was suggested to him that the best man should not be appointed to some non-political post because of the prior claim of a party hack was genuine and admirable. His dislike of cant and bigotry, of slipshod reasoning based on prejudice and nurtured in ignorance, stamped his whole career. He rarely deceived himself and found it hard to forgive those who did otherwise.

And yet the 'restless anxious intellect' with which Praed credited him had limitations. He was certainly interested in the recondite points raised by the sixteenth- and seventeenth-century theologians and his knowledge of their works, if not that of a scholar, was more than dilettante. Of economics, however, he knew and cared nothing. Scientific problems alarmed or bored him. He had the perception to realize that the accumulation of facts was no substitute for thought – 'People who have industry enough to collect information rarely have the ability to use it' – but at times his learning seemed little more than a magpie collection of undigested texts. His knowledge of English history was profound yet it is hard to think of an instance where his political conduct seems to have been shaped by lessons he had learnt from the past. He had an endearing faith in the osmotic power of literature, defending himself for not having read *The Excursion* on the plea: 'I've bought the book; its amazing when you leave a book on the table how much you know what is in it, without reading it.'[29]

'I generally find that nothing that is asserted is ever true, especially if it is on the very best authority.' Here again the note of cynicism is perhaps more conspicuous than the eagerness for truth which Praed extolled. Yet Melbourne was indeed one of the most truthful of politicians – 'truthful' meaning not merely that he eschewed lies but that he consistently presented the full truth as he saw it, avoiding the mystification and evasion so beloved by most of his peers. His honesty was rarely questioned, indeed there were times when his colleagues must have wished him more devious than in fact he was. It was characteristic that he ranked Schiller far above Goethe: 'the one all truth, clearness and beauty; the other, principally mysticism, obscurity and unintelligibility'. If he could not be simple and straightforward he preferred not to speak at all, loathing the meaningless clichés which are so often substituted for opinions in both public and private life. When asked by his coachmaker for a letter of recommendation to the Bishop of Ely he obliged with a brisk note: 'My dear Lord, Mr Robson has been my coachmaker for many years, and I believe him to be a very good one, but so he ought, for I must say he is a very dear one'.[30]

From the above Melbourne emerges as a detached, quizzical figure, keeping the world at bay with the weapons of flippancy and profound scepticism. Yet, says Praed, 'the man was mournful in his heart of hearts . . .' It would be rash to deduce a deep-seated melancholia from occasional moments of moroseness, but too many people detected an underlying sadness in Melbourne's nature to dismiss their vision as a romantic fantasy. Howick described him at dinner with Lord Auckland, when he 'fell into such a state of thought and abstraction that it was quite painful to witness . . .' His habit of suddenly lapsing into gloomy silence in the middle of an animated conversation made many people think his cheerfulness no more than a veneer which it cost him a considerable effort to maintain and which cracked when he was tired or under pressure. 'There is a bitterness in Lord Melbourne's humour that betrays something melancholy . . .' was Haydon's comment. It would be extravagant to present him as a tragic figure, a Hamlet who had strayed into drawing-room comedy and was doggedly playing it out

until the final curtain, but he was certainly more introspective, more
subject to doubt and depression, than he cared to let it appear.[31]

Indeed it sometimes seemed that a principal object in his life was to
pass off a spurious version of himself on a gullible public. He occupied
himself in 'concealing from mankind' not merely 'a large nature and a
lovely mind' but a whole complex of fears and hopes which for some
reason he was determined to hug to himself. Sydney Smith put it well
when he accused him of being an impostor, masquerading as a light-
weight who would 'giggle away the Great Charter, and decide by the
method of tee-totum whether my Lords the Bishops should or should
not retain their seats in the House of Lords', and yet was in fact a
conscientious and hard-working minister. 'I am sorry to hurt any man's
feelings, and to brush away the magnificent fabric of levity and gaiety
he has reared; but I accuse our minister of honesty and diligence.'[32]
He carried to the point almost of obsession the trick of every clever
schoolboy who will study late at night under the blankets by the light
of a torch so as to give the impression of effortless success the following
morning. And like every clever schoolboy, he overdid it. At the end of a
three-hour cabinet meeting to discuss a change in the duty on corn he
came out on to the landing to call after his departing colleagues: 'I say,
did we decide to raise it or to lower it? It doesn't really matter, but we
all ought to say the same thing.' It is hard to know whom he thought he
was fooling by this display of insouciance. To an outsider it might have
been entertaining enough but to hard-pressed and weary ministers
who knew perfectly well that he was aware of the issues involved, the
act must have been distinctly irritating.

'My knowledge of Lord Melbourne,' wrote Hobhouse, 'has made me
think better of politicians. I think him one of the most straightforward,
sagacious, disinterested men I ever knew.'[33] Praed's final tribute to
Melbourne referred to his 'faith in good'. Simple faith is perhaps not
the attribute which one would ascribe most readily to this subtle and
sophisticated man, and yet he was at times capable of a disconcerting
innocence; a clarity of vision which is found in children or saints, but
rarely politicians. In cabinet one day he 'assumed a tone not usual with
him, and said he considered England to have been under the special
protection of providence at certain periods of her history, several of
which he then mentioned, from the dispersion of the Spanish Armada
to the retirement of the French squadron in Bantry Bay'.[34] But even
when the mystic fires thus burnt within him, he retained a grasp on the
intractable facts of the situation. In spite of the prior claim which
England enjoyed to the benevolence of providence, he concluded that

'no men ought to count upon such interposition of divine favour, and use no human effort'. In the context of the immediate discussion, the country should put its faith in God and its money into new warships.

Praed's portrait was an attractive one and by no means unfaithful. But it did not tell the whole story. It omitted characteristics which grew in the fertile soil of his scepticism and indifference and came to dominate his political philosophy. Lytton wrote of him that his political life contained no imprudence. 'Not to commit himself was at one time supposed to be his particular distinction. His philosophy was less that which deals with abstract doctrines than that which teaches how to command shifting and various circumstances.'[35] He was a superb tactician, a negligible strategist. When confronted by any situation he would see clearly the arguments against each possible course of action and usually conclude that all were undesirable. Allied to a moderate but fundamental pessimism – a belief that it was not within man's power to better his lot on earth – and an innate conservatism which inclined him to regret any deviation from the traditions of the past, the whole added up to a prescription for almost total inactivity. He was that most dangerous of all reactionaries: the intelligent sceptic who is perceptive enough to see the force of his opponents' case and meets it not with blind hostility but with adroit, humorous and totally unconstructive argument.

A curious illustration of this urbane negativism occurred in 1840 when the Rev. William Deive wrote to Melbourne to urge that Palestine should be restored to the Jews and the prophecies thus be fulfilled. Melbourne, who could never resist entering into argument with a crank, duly replied:

With respect to the Prophecies of the Holy Scripture, Divine Providence either has fulfilled or will fulfill them by its own means and at its own season. Man has neither the knowledge nor the power which can enable him either to hasten or to hinder their completion, and it appears to me to be almost as presumptuous to attempt the one as the other . . .

The Jews, I believe, form at present the smallest portion of the population of Syria; they form the most despised and most oppressed portion. By the Mahometans they are more detested even than the Christians, and any attempt to establish them as the rulers of the country would, as far as we can see, only have the effect of bringing down upon them more bitter persecution and possibly utter extirpation.[36]

It is impossible to deny the author of this letter a certain prescience. There are always excellent reasons for not doing something in the Middle East. And yet if there had been less people like Melbourne to pour cold water on every proposition it is at least conceivable that the area today would not be in so hideous a mess.

'In general,' wrote Melbourne, with that disarming frankness which made him so attractive a man, if not always so proficient a politician, 'nobody is so much for shuffling over differences of opinion and getting over matters as well as possible, as I am.'[37] Any successful politician must be to some extent a shuffler; the arts of evasion, of compromise, of conciliation are essential weapons in his armoury. The weakness of Melbourne was that he used these arts not as a means to an end, but as a substitute for a policy. He shuffled, not to aid his progress, but so as to avoid the necessity for making any movement. It was one of the more ironical twists of history that he first gained cabinet office in a government dedicated to a programme of radical reform.

CHAPTER 9

Captain Swing

FOR A RICH MAN of conservative temperament the composition of Grey's first government must have been reassuring. Melbourne found most of his colleagues congenial enough. In the blueness of their blood and the extensiveness of their estates they were as well endowed as any eighteenth-century government, certainly more aristocratic than their Tory predecessors. The new cabinet, reported Princess Lieven, 'will be liberal – but very temperately, and I even exaggerate in saying so'.[1]

If guarantee were needed that this would be so, it could have been found in the character of its leader. 'Dismiss from your mind the idea . . . that Lord Grey is a liberal,' urged the Princess. 'He is so near to becoming the very opposite that only yesterday he told me that his only wish was to be dictator for six months.'[2] One cannot escape the suspicion that if Grey had achieved office twenty years before and expended his reforming energies when still comparatively young, he would by 1830 have been a monument of reaction. Instead he found himself the champion of a programme for which he had lost much of his enthusiasm. He was sixty-six years old, he pined for the tranquillity of his beloved home in Northumberland, his distaste for the techniques of political skirmishing was only equalled by his disdain for the mob. He was to prove an awkward premier: partly from his irritating habit of resigning whenever the pressures became too great, partly from what Brougham described as 'his royal dislike of the truth being told him'. His nepotism too was extravagant even by the standards of the age. His son-in-law was in the cabinet; his son at the Colonial Office; a cousin in charge of Woods and Forests; a brother-in-law at the Treasury. In 1832 it was calculated that he bestowed patronage worth £18,000 on his not-particularly grateful family. Yet with all this he was a great parliamentarian and a man of grandeur and nobility, un-questioned leader of his party and probably the only one who could have held it together under the stresses of the next few years.[3]

Lord Althorp was to be Grey's Chancellor of the Exchequer – though the idea filled him with dismay – right-hand man and designated successor. He was an abominable speaker – 'a more miserable figure was never cut . . .' remarked Greville after one of his speeches; his knowledge of economics was rudimentary and he was almost unique among politicians in being genuinely without ambition. That he succeeded in spite of these handicaps, almost against his will, was a tribute to his decency and integrity. In a debate on the Reform Bill Croker made a skilful speech most destructive of the Whig case. Althorp rose to reply but merely remarked 'that he had made some calculations which he considered as entirely conclusive in refutation of the Right Honourable Gentleman's arguments; but unfortunately he had mislaid them, so that he could only say that if the House would be guided by his advice they would reject the amendment'. The House did as he suggested. As Sir Henry Hardinge somewhat wistfully observed, 'There was no standing against such influence as this'.[4]

There could hardly have been a more striking contrast than that between Althorp and Henry Brougham. Brougham was a man of prodigious talents; the best brain in parliament allied to spectacular oratory and a capacity for hard work which would have killed weaker men. Yet he was marred by vanity and arrogance and veered erratically from position to position to suit the whim of the moment – 'tossed about', as Melbourne put it, 'in permanent caprice'.[5] He was adored by the people and indispensable to any Whig administration. Grey and the King between them manoeuvred him into the office of Lord Chancellor and in the House of Lords he found that he was as Samson shorn of his locks, with his strength departed. Melbourne distrusted his principles and deplored his practice, but he could never escape the attraction of that brilliant and forceful personality. They quarrelled ferociously, but Melbourne was always at pains to make it up again and after his death, to the consternation of his family, it was found that Brougham was one of the two men whom he had nominated to act as his executors.

The two younger members of the government, who were to be carried to fame by their role in formulating and passing the Great Reform Bill, were Lord John Russell, a younger son of the Duke of Bedford, and Lord Durham. It was easy to admire John Russell for his courage, his pertinacity, his industry; more difficult to like him.

Creevey, claiming he spoke for Grey as well, wrote that Russell 'has an over-weening conceit of himself, is very obstinate, very pert, and can be very rude', while Disraeli called him, 'Cold, inanimate, with a weak voice and a mincing manner'.[6] He had all the Russell arrogance and found it hard to suffer even clever men gladly, fools were beneath his view. Melbourne on the whole worked well with him and respected his abilities but even he occasionally found him hard to endure, particularly when Russell, through impatience or insensitivity, involved his party in a quarrel which could easily have been avoided. 'Johnny can be quiet about nothing,' wrote Melbourne in exasperation on one such occasion, 'and will give us a great deal of trouble. He is in my opinion . . . worse than Durham.'[7]

The provocation must indeed have been great for it was not often that Melbourne would concede that anybody could be worse than Durham. 'His carbonic Majesty', as Frederick Lamb called him in tribute both to his great wealth based on coal mines and his sulphurous temper, was Grey's son-in-law but owed his position to his own talents. These were great and he had a noble vision which enabled him to propound plans of a breadth and daring none of his colleagues except perhaps Brougham could rival. But he was egocentric and self-seeking, tormented by physical pain and family misfortunes. Melbourne could not appreciate his qualities and was acutely alive to his defects. 'His temper is his least fault,' he told Russell. 'He is dishonest and unprincipled. There is no opinion nor person he will not sacrifice to further his immediate end.'[8]

For the rest Holland and Lansdowne were old friends, elder statesmen of the party destined to play a background role. The Duke of Richmond was an ultra-Tory. He found himself allied with the Whigs for little reason except a mutual disapproval of Wellington but now that he was in their camp he was ready to stick by them loyally. Melbourne called him 'sharp and quick', an opinion that may have owed something to the number of issues on which their views were similar. Stanley, the Chief Secretary for Ireland, was said to have great potential but was as yet largely untried. Of the other Canningites, Charles Grant was at the Board of Control and Palmerston at the Foreign Office. Palmerston was closer to Melbourne than anybody else in the government yet the two followed different paths. Melbourne contrived so to modulate his conservative convictions that he seemed at home in a Whig government; Palmerston was if anything closer to the Whigs on the central pillars of their policy, yet remained obstinately out of place and indulged in angry confrontations with his more liberal colleagues. Melbourne the radicals disapproved of but tolerated, Palmerston they could not endure. It was a distinction which was to assume importance when Grey resigned four years later.

The primary function of a Home Secretary in the early nineteenth century – perhaps indeed at any other time – was to maintain law and order. There was a range of other duties – certain church preferments, trade-licences, regulations covering aliens, some ill-defined responsibilities for Ireland and the Channel Islands – but by the security of the citizen the reputation of the Home Secretary stood or fell. It was, of course, possible for a minister who so desired to do far more. Robert Peel, Melbourne's immediate predecessor and one of the most creative of Home Secretaries, had been responsible for major reforms in the legal system and the development of the Metropolitan Police. Even Melbourne himself, averse as he was to innovation, was involved in new initiatives of some importance. For the most part, however, and particularly in the first few months, he was almost exclusively preoccupied with curbing disorder and averting what seemed at the time alarmingly close to a full-blooded revolution.

'I cannot look upon my intended appointment as a fit subject of congratulation,' Peel had observed gloomily nine years before.[9] Melbourne had good reason to echo the remark. In the autumn and winter of 1830 rural England, in particular the south and east, was swept by a wave of disorder so violent that it seemed to threaten the very fabric of society. No one factor can be said to have caused this turmoil. Gradually over the preceding fifty years the status of the agricultural labourer had been eroded, both economically and socially. The open fields and commons whose use he had traditionally enjoyed were now largely barred to him by enclosures. The delicate balance of loyalties and responsibilities between squire and peasant, which had endured, for better or worse, over several hundred years, had finally crumbled, to be replaced by a new nexus between employer and employed, a relationship which neither party properly understood and which the peasant, in particular, was unable to manipulate to his advantage.[10]

In periods of dramatic social change it is always likely that the weakest will go to the wall. It was inevitable that the lot of the rural labourer at this period would be disagreeable, in the 1820s a combination of circumstances conspired to make it intolerable. The boom that had accompanied the Napoleonic Wars collapsed into deflation and a flood of demobilized soldiers and sailors who returned in search of work that was no longer there. Threshing machinery was widely introduced, taking away the winter work from those who had been fortunate enough to find employment in the summer. A bad harvest in 1828 was followed by disaster in 1829; by the time spring came in 1830 the prospect of another winter of such fearful deprivation must have seemed past enduring. Word of the new revolution in France fell on the ears of men who felt that their own social system could produce nothing but suffering and injustice. Local discontents – an influx of Irish harvesters, a brutal cut-back in poor-law relief – were matches tossed into a can of petrol. By the time Melbourne entered the Home Office as Secretary of State, the south of England was ablaze.

There was not much in his immediate surroundings to reassure him. Some twenty years previously *The Times* had denounced the Home Office as 'the sink of all the imbecility attached to every ministry for the last thirty years'.[11] Under the long reigns of Sidmouth and Peel there had been improvements, both in the quality and the numbers of its officials, but its reputation was still far from brilliant. The Permanent Under Secretary, Samuel March Phillipps, was sage, prudent and experienced; as unlikely to venture any striking initiative as his new minister was to expect one. As Parliamentary Under Secretary, to speak for the department in the House of Commons, Melbourne brought in his own brother George. George Lamb was no fool; he was affable, conciliatory and capable of spasmodic bursts of hard work; but he was already a sick man and at no time would he have been fit for the sustained drudgery which was needed if his functions were to be properly performed. Besides these dignitaries there were fourteen regular clerks and one extra clerk responsible only for criminal business: a meagre team barely able to deal with the day to day transaction of business, let alone handle something close to a civil war. 'A most alarming and responsible office . . .' wrote George Lamb gloomily, describing his new position to the Duke of Devonshire.[12] He can not be accused of exaggeration.

Nor were the weapons at the disposal of the Home Secretary throughout the country much more impressive. With his creation of a proper metropolitan police force Peel had done much to improve the situation in London but no other city enjoyed a comparable service and in the countryside Constables Dogberry and Verges were still at work, fit perhaps to deal with the occasional drunk or poacher but alarmingly inadequate to confront the present conflagration. Yet in spite of the obvious deficiencies of the present body Melbourne shrank from drastic measures to reinforce or refashion it. A 'new and general system of police . . . for the whole of the country', would, he felt, be inexpedient and 'legislating beyond the demands of the occasion'. The most that could be done was to extend Peel's system to a few of the larger cities, and even this only in cases where the magistrates requested it and the citizens were ready to foot the bill. The whole question, he concluded, was very difficult and called for 'full and mature deliberation' before any plan was submitted to parliament.[13]

With the aid of this vestigial force, the Justices of the Peace and above them the Lords Lieutenant were broadly responsible for keeping the countryside at peace. The Lords Lieutenant, normally the grandest of local grandees, were also major figures on the London stage and when hunting and shooting did not lure them to their rural palaces were more often to be found at court than on their estates. There were exceptions, like the Duke of Wellington, who took their duties with exemplary seriousness, but on the whole the local magistrates were left to their own devices and to whatever guidance they could procure from the Home Office. There were about five thousand of these, a little army of worthy if limited gentlemen on whose energy, courage and good judgement depended the welfare of the nation. Their powers were wide and, once appointed, only the most outrageous misconduct could lead to their dismissal. They were almost entirely responsible for local defence; the militia and yeomanry could only be called out at their behest; they could proclaim states of riot, enrol constables and, as a last resort, call for the help of regular troops. An apathetic justice could allow his district to drift swiftly into chaos, his over-eager neighbour might conjure up a crisis where none existed. Fortunately most of them were men of common sense who steered a middle course; if they had not been, the already dangerous situation could soon have slipped into catastrophe.

If the authority of the local constable and the power of the magistrate's eye proved insufficient to quell a tumult, then the first recourse was to the yeomanry. Melbourne always distrusted this body, believing that it was subject to the twin risks of turning into a vigilante patrol of vengeful land-owners who would chop up the peasantry with improper zest, or falling into still more dangerous sympathy with their victims and rallying to the insurgents. Some use, he accepted, must be made of them, but as little as possible. 'A certain number of yeomanry corps *well* and *safely* composed and officered by gentlemen of weight and influence would I think be of great service; but I do not wish a great number of such corps to start up at once under the influence of alarm, indiscriminately brought together and perhaps commanded by individuals of doubtful trustworthiness and respectability.'[14]

The ultimate weapon at the disposal of the civil power was the regular army. Though now little over a hundred thousand strong, of which half were overseas, this was an efficient and well-disciplined force and the one most likely to put down tumult with a minimum of bloodshed. Nevertheless its use was repugnant to the great mass of the population; only with the consent of the Home Secretary could troops go into action against civilians and such consent was rarely forthcoming. Indeed Melbourne was quickly to discover that among the most important of his functions was curbing the exuberance of those magistrates who saw in every burnt hay-stack a sign of bloody revolution and would happily have called in the dragoons to confront a couple of hapless peasants suspected of poaching their landlord's game.

Within twelve days of taking over, Melbourne had received panic-stricken messages from Rickmansworth and Ramsbury, Sutton and Sevenoaks, Fordingbridge, Romsey, Devizes, Orpington and Bromley, Blandford and Dorchester, Lymington and Lyme Regis and many other tranquil rural centres. All told the same story: the labourers were on the march. Armed with sticks and sledge-hammers, scythes and pitch-forks, they swarmed along the lanes of southern England, descending on isolated farmhouses and smashing the threshing machines with which they linked their misery, firing ricks, demanding larger wages or reduced tithes, sacking ale houses, bellowing fearsome war-cries: 'Bread or Blood!' 'Reduce the Taxes and Rents!' 'Blood for Blood!' Starting mainly in south-east England, spreading through the home counties and the midlands, Hampshire and the west country, East Anglia and the north, it seemed that the exiguous forces of law and order must be overwhelmed by this great tide of revolt. Behind it lurked the shadow figure of 'Captain Swing', as much a myth as his predecessor Ned Ludd but lending his name to a multitude of outrages and none the less fearsome for being a man of mystery.

It is easy to conclude in retrospect that the labourers were not concerned with bloody revolution, all they wanted was regular work and a wage on which they could live. A few old scores were paid off along the way but in only a handful of cases was the fury of the mob not swiftly appeased by the concession of even part of what it wanted. Yet many revolutions have started with such modest ends, only to conclude in the complete reversal of the social order. To Melbourne, sequestered in Whitehall and dependent for his information on frequently alarmist magistrates, it was not surprising that things looked black. No one can read the endless reports in the Home Office archives or among Melbourne's own papers without understanding how immense the menace must have seemed. Panic and vanity led the justices to exaggerate their problems. Crimes seemed always to be committed 'at midnight by a desperate gang amounting to upwards of 200 persons',[15] when in fact a score of peasants had gathered together after supper to smash the threshing machines of an unpopular farmer. Incidents never happened in isolation, but were always part of a deep-laid conspiracy which only the superior acumen of the magistrate had enabled him to penetrate. In their masterly analysis of these disorders Hobsbawm and Rudé have established the existence of well over a thousand more or less serious incidents occurring between the spring of 1830 and the autumn of 1831.[16] When one considers the lurid terms in which such affairs were usually reported George Lamb can hardly be blamed for viewing his duties with gloom and apprehension.

The pressure on Melbourne to react to this violence with panic measures of repression can hardly be overstated. It must have seemed to him at times as if every landowner in the affected areas was clamouring for a squadron of dragoons to hold his villainous tenants at bay. Lord Byron demanded that spring guns should be used to deter would-be arsonists, Colonel Whitelands called for martial law with summary execution of any rioter caught with weapons in his hands. The King was constantly appealing for stronger measures and swifter action. He urged that all those involved in the disturbances should be brought to trial with a minimum of delay and that after they had been convicted – as he took it for granted they would be – they should at once be transported to Australia.[17]

It is to Melbourne's credit that he did not make many concessions to such appeals. In particular he stood firm against those zealots who would have covered the countryside with private armies dedicated to stamping out disorder. He applied for advice to the Duke of Wellington, who, with all the prudence of the professional soldier, responded: 'You cannot be too cautious in issuing arms and equipment. None ought to be issued excepting to persons regularly authorized by the King to carry them . . .' Melbourne could not have received more welcome counsel. It was his contention that, in almost every case, the regular forces of law and order, if properly used, were fit to deal with any possible trouble. Justices who clamoured for the support of troops or wanted to raise a local militia were nuisances who deserved discouragement. To the timorous Mr William Dickinson of Sherborne he answered unsympathetically: 'If you apprehend tumult swear in special constables, divide them into sections, put one or two chief constables at the head of every section, arm them as you think proper, and thus put the district in the way of maintaining its own tranquillity, which may be easily done by a little energy and exertion.'[18]

Melbourne was not wholly without understanding of the causes which underlay the agrarian troubles. When Lady Portman complained about the disaffection of the peasants in Dorset he retorted bluntly that it was the fault of the landlords for paying such inadequate wages. He agreed heartily with Poulett Scrope that the practice of keeping wages artificially low and relying on the poor rate to avert starvation was pernicious, since it defrauded workers of 'their just share of the produce of the land, by a conspiracy between farmers, overseers and landlords . . .'[19] But it would be rash indeed to deduce from such remarks that he felt there was anything fundamentally wrong with the state of rural society, still less that it was a proper function of government to seek to rectify it. That the rich man would remain in his castle and the poor man at his gate was inevitable – whether or not it was also desirable was an empty speculation with which he saw no need to concern himself. The God which had ordered their estate would no doubt arrange some suitable compensation in the after life; meanwhile the most that could be expected of ministers was that they should ensure the rules of society were not abused in favour of its richer and more powerful members. In this belief he was as one with almost all his peers, Whig or Tory, reactionary or reformer. Melbourne was a child of his age and it would be futile to search among his actions for any evidence of especial enlightenment or a willingness to challenge the *mores* that governed his society.

Nor could he ever accept that violence should be met by concessions, since this would be to condone it. To magistrates who had recommended that the use of threshing machinery should be discontinued, at least until the worst of the depression was overcome, he retorted that machines were as much entitled to the protection of the law as any other form of property. To surrender to blackmail in such a case was 'to connive at, or rather assist in the establishment of a tyranny of the most oppressive character'. The landlord who yielded to threats and granted higher wages rather than see his ricks burned was almost as much at fault in his encouragement of disorder as those who had originally created it.[20]

Any Home Secretary must think the preservation of peace and order of paramount importance; Melbourne was temperamentally disposed to feel it virtually the only thing that mattered. About rural violence he spoke in the House of Lords with almost incoherent indignation, denouncing it as arising 'from the most pure, and unmixed, and diabolical feeling of senseless malignity'. Outbursts of this kind did him little good with the radicals of his day, nor indeed with the liberals of posterity. They were also uncharacteristic, in that he rarely expressed himself on any subject with such lack of moderation. How far he translated immoderate words into extravagant deeds is another matter. To G. M. Trevelyan, latter day guardian at the temple of Foxite Whiggery, there was no room for doubt. Melbourne stained the reputation of his party 'by cruelties which history, now that she knows the facts, can pardon as little as Peterloo'. There are, however, facts and facts, and even the most eminent historian is not always above selecting those which most conveniently fit his theory. [21]

It is a fact that Melbourne, on 8 December 1830, issued a circular to all magistrates calling on them to act with vigour and to reject out of hand any suggestion that concessions might be made to the disaffected. It is a fact that the day after he took up his post he issued a proclamation offering rewards of £500 – a massive sum for those days – to anyone who brought rioters or incendiaries to justice. It is true that military intervention under Melbourne, though still a rarity, occurred more often than in the early days of the risings under Peel. It is true that a Special Commission was set up to try some of the 1900 or so prisoners who had been involved in the disturbances, that the laws which they applied were harsh, and that the penalties were hideous. All this testifies to the Home Secretary's resolve to stamp out disorder, at whatever the cost.

But it proves no more than that. The Special Commission, whatever the radical propagandists may have maintained, was not a replay of the Bloody Assizes, turning the English law into a mockery. 'We do not come here,' said Mr Justice Alderson, 'to inquire into grievances. We come here to decide law.' It was a chilly doctrine; but for a judge it was also the only correct one. Nor was it always applied with inhumanity. As Alderson's colleague Mr Justice Park declared: 'I beg you to understand that every prisoner who cannot afford to employ counsel is my client . . .' [22]

Of the 992 prisoners tried before these commissions, 387 were acquitted, 227 were sentenced to death: a horrifying figure, yet of these only eleven were committed for execution by the judges and in the end only three were not reprieved by the recommendation of the Home Secretary. Three too many, perhaps, and the imagination can scarcely comprehend the misery caused by the four or five hundred transportations to Australasia which followed these and similar trials. Yet the law was applied no more brutally than at other periods and it is not necessary to search far in the world today to find instances where still more feeble threats to the existing order have been stamped out with greater ferocity and indifference to human rights.

As Home Secretary Melbourne believed that the law must run its course. He would maintain this with equal determination when it worked to his disadvantage but it would be foolish to deny that he could have done more to mitigate its savagery. He did not: partly because he believed that to overrule by reprieves the sentences imposed by the judges would undermine their authority; still more because he thought England would be a better country if rid for ever of arsonists and rioters. As for their wives and children, the criminals should have thought of them before they indulged in their activities. It was hardly a charitable outlook, yet one may doubt whether anything substantially different would have been met with from other members of the cabinet.

Within these somewhat rigid limits, Melbourne played fair. He was several times urged to agree to the use of spies who would ingratiate themselves into the confidence of the labourers and then denounce them. Always he refused. To Henry Drummond he wrote: 'The danger of employing spies and accomplices has always been found to be that in order to further their own ends, satisfy their employers . . . and maintain their credit, they are too apt, first to bring forward false accusations; secondly, to excite and encourage the commission of crimes . . .' Drummond then urged that the spy should be used to gather information on condition that he did not give evidence in court. Melbourne rejected even this modified proposal.[23]

He also made intermittent, if hardly sustained efforts to achieve an understanding of working class aspirations and even to deal with them in a way which, though it stopped far short of real negotiations, still showed some readiness to consider their point of view. For this his favourite instrument was Francis Place, a radical breeches-maker whom Melbourne had encountered during various Westminster elections and who was one of the few people of his world ready and able to exchange words with members of the ruling classes. Perhaps for this very reason his influence with his fellow radicals was not as great as Melbourne imagined, certainly not anything like as great as Place himself supposed, but he still was listened to and was a valuable channel for passing on offers or warnings. In November 1830 the Home Secretary sent his brother George to ask Place to 'write two or three papers to the working people, and especially the agricultural labourers, to persuade them to desist from the enormities they were committing . .' Place was not prepared to lend himself to any blanket denunciation of people with whose aims he so closely identified himself, but he did in the end come up with a pamphlet pointing out the futility of burning ricks.[24]

Place found George Lamb ill-informed and irritatingly vague. For future contacts Melbourne preferred to use his worldly-wise if also raffish private secretary, Tom Young. Young, the son of a Nairn farmer, had been to sea and rose to be purser on the Duke of Devonshire's yacht. The Duke turned him into a kind of confidential secretary, charged in particular with cultivating good relations with the Press. Shrewd, unscrupulous and with a curious sensitivity, he had a chameleon-like capacity for adapting himself to his surroundings and ingratiating himself with the object of his attentions. 'You never quit him without having a better opinion of yourself,' commented Denis le Marchant, who had observed him holding his own in 'the highest society in London'. His combination of cheek, obsequiousness and vulgarity indeed proved irresistible to many of the grandees. As he moved down the social scale, so his oddity became less marked and his charms faded. Place, not surprisingly, was unimpressed. Young, he said, was 'a cleverish sort of fellow, with a vulgar air of frankness which may at times put people off their guard . . .' and then, with all the hauteur of a good breeches-maker, 'but he is not at all the right sort of man to be private secretary and spy for the Home Secretary'.[25]

Melbourne was loyal to his egregious subaltern and constantly tried to procure him a permanent job under the government, a keepership of the records or some such function.[26] But he did not trust him very far. 'Through him,' the Home Secretary was supposed to have said, in words so patronizing that one feels they must have been correctly quoted, 'I am able to look down below; which for me is more important than all I can learn from all the fine gentleman clerks about me.'[27] Melbourne did indeed seek to look down below; but if ever a vision was through a glass darkly and never face to face, it was Melbourne's of the lower classes. Like many aristocrats he suffered from the illusion that he enjoyed a special *rapport* with the lower orders of society. 'I don't like the middle classes,' he told Victoria. 'They say that the upper and lower classes are very much like each other in this country; the middle classes are bad; the higher and lower classes there's some good in, but the middle classes are all affectation and conceit and pretence and concealment.'[28] Above all, one suspects, they did not know their places; while decent gamekeepers and peasants were content to pull forelocks and doff bonnets until eternity. It took events like those of 1830 and 1831 to reveal the chasm of incomprehension which divided him from those whom he professed to understand.

And yet the groping gestures which he made in their direction were those of a decent if sorely puzzled man. In June 1831, what Melbourne described to Anglesey as 'a devil of an uproar' occurred at Merthyr Tydfil. There was widespread rioting, the 93rd Highlanders were called in, their commanding officer was injured, fire was opened and at least fourteen of the rioters were killed on the spot. The final death toll was probably over twenty. William IV, rampant in defence of his troops, was at once eager to write an open letter congratulating them on their conduct. Melbourne remonstrated with him. The army had indeed behaved with moderation, but the affray 'was a civil riot, in its nature the greatest misfortune which can befall a country, in which the blood of Englishmen was necessarily, but unhappily, shed by the hands of their own countrymen; and in times of civil contest it is believed to have been customary . . . to abstain from everything which could by possibility be misconstrued into expressions of triumph or exultation'.[29]

By the end of 1831 the worst of the agrarian troubles was over. A good harvest and modest concessions on pay and the use of machinery took some of the sting out of the revolt, harsh repression stamped out whatever will to resist survived. Though the prisoner rotting in the hulks as he awaited transportation, the sullen labourer still desperately short of work or food, would hardly have agreed, most people whose opinion has been recorded felt Melbourne had deserved well of his country. There had been considerable doubt when his appointment had first been announced. 'It will be an agreeable surprise to us,' pronounced the *Manchester Guardian*, 'if he should make an industrious or efficient public officer.' It was commonly held that he was an agreeable play-boy, incapable of addressing himself to any task. Littleton recorded in a letter to Wellesley a 'great outcry against Melbourne and George Lamb in the Home Department . . . they are denounced as idle. But without any evidence that I know of. Surely an Irish Secretary out of place has a right to lay on his sofa and read a romance – if not to cuckold Ld Branden.'[30]

Greville was typical of those who deplored the appointment but within a few weeks changed their tune. His first reaction was that Melbourne was too idle to make a success of it, yet by the middle of December he was describing in amazement the 'sudden display of activity and vigour, rapid and diligent transaction of business, for which nobody was prepared'. Melbourne was showing himself a competent administrator and an excellent minister: ready to listen to advice from any quarter, sound in judgement, quick to make up his mind, resolute when he had done so. Innovations in policy there were none, but his colleagues did not want them. What they looked for was the assurance that the Home Office was in the hands of someone of calm, efficiency and determination. Brougham, that most critical of statesmen, told the Duke of Devonshire that, 'W. Lamb's department is the hardest worked and no man *can* do the work better'. Recollecting the period of tranquillity many years later he concluded that the Admiralty, the Foreign Office and the Home Office were the three best administered departments.[31]

Not everyone was equally impressed. He is said to have offended the worthy Harriet Martineau by blowing a feather around the top of his desk while she was expounding some tricky point of social policy. He would irritate deputations of manufacturers by professing total ignorance of their problems, even though in fact he had read them up conscientiously the night before. A visiting small boy who asked for some sealing-wax was offered pens as well – 'All these things belong to the public', was the minister's avuncular advice, 'and your business must always be to get out of the public as much as you can'. Such anecdotes were probably exaggerated or apocryphal and anyway prove little except his perennial desire to be considered a casually brilliant amateur rather than a serious professional. To some however they seemed more significant. In September 1831 Grey contemplated moving Melbourne to the Privy Seal and giving Richmond the Home Office. His reason was Melbourne's alleged idleness. Holland, whom Grey consulted, was dismayed by the proposal. He noted in his journal: '. . . a dislike to meddling legislation and his careless nonchalance might give him the character of an indolent man with the unobservant but those who had business with the office did not find him so. He did uncommonly well there and I strongly deprecated his removal . . .'[32]

Grey was convinced: indeed his doubts can never have been serious since on every other occasion he seemed well satisfied with Melbourne's conduct of affairs. Holland certainly spoke for most of his colleagues. By the autumn of 1831 Melbourne was deemed an unequivocal success. He had always been considered a safe man, now he was known as a strong one too.

CHAPTER 10

The Years of the Reform Bill

IN JUNE 1831 Melbourne wrote in gloom to Grey about serious riots in the Forest of Dean. 'I expect we shall have them wherever there are real or imaginary grievances, and that is everywhere. However it appears perfectly clear that neither reform nor any other political feeling has anything to do with it . . . Perhaps I am weakened by illness, but I feel as if internal affairs were in a very perplexing and alarming state.'[1] It was Melbourne's misfortune that he was a leading member of a government whose *raison d'être* was a substantial measure of parliamentary reform, yet believed in his heart that such reform was unnecessary and futile. He was also in a position of some embarrassment in that in the past he had been one of the most vociferous enemies of reform, while now he had to display himself, even though *sotto voce*, as its champion.

Temperamentally he was well adapted to emerge unscathed from this predicament. Never, in any field, was he a fundamentalist. The corollary of his belief that nothing would do much good was an equally firm conviction that nothing would do much harm. This enabled him to accept philosophically decisions that he might have been expected to find intolerable. If the Bill did not really matter, still less did its precise contents. Melbourne felt that the government's conduct while drafting and passing it should be governed by two complementary considerations: it must be sufficiently extensive to satisfy those who wanted it; yet any amendment was permissible if it made it more likely to pass through parliament without serious conflict. The fact that, because of the obstinacy of extremists on both sides, these considerations might prove to be not so much complementary as contradictory, was something Melbourne was disinclined to contemplate.

What was wanted was a Bill which would appear revolutionary to the radicals and moderate to the opposition. Melbourne's attitude towards the Bill was always ambivalent. Those responsible for drafting it – Althorp, Durham and Russell – viewed him with suspicion. He and Palmerston, complained Russell were 'very slack' about the measure. Yet when the details were discussed in cabinet Melbourne seems to have played little part, certainly not to have taken the lead in opposing the more daring provisions. On the problem of what financial or other qualifications were needed before a man might vote, he was indeed inclined to radicalism. 'Unless we have a large basis to work upon,' he would propound, 'we shall do nothing.'[2]

He made his most serious attempt to define his position in the House of Lords in October 1831 when, with what Professor Gash has well described as 'melancholy eloquence', he put forward the practical arguments for accepting the Bill. He admitted frankly that he had always opposed reform in the past and would have liked to have gone on doing so. 'If ever there was an individual . . . more anxious than another that the affairs of the country might have gone on without our being forced to incur the hazard and responsibility which must result from so great and fundamental a change in the House of Commons, I am that person.' But when an institution no longer enjoyed the respect of the country, it must be modified; '. . . although it may be our duty to resist the will of the people for a time, is it possible to resist it for ever?' He pleaded that 'when the wishes of the people are founded on reason and justice, and when they are consistent with the fundamental principles of the constitution . . . the legislature and executive must yield to the popular voice or be annihilated'.[3]

The Reform Bill introduced into the Commons by John Russell on 1 March 1831 abolished 60 boroughs altogether and removed one member from a further 47: a total by far exceeding the hopes of even the most radical members. It was believed by many that if Peel had immediately challenged the government and divided the House, the Bill might have been strangled at birth. If so he missed his chance. Melbourne was dining with Brougham that night and regular bulletins arrived, reporting the progress of the debate. When the final note arrived all glasses were refilled to stiffen the nerves of the diners. As soon as Brougham read that Russell had sat down and that the debate was continuing he waved the sheet of paper exultantly around his head and shouted 'Victory!'[4]

It is doubtful whether Melbourne would have joined in the cry, even after the triumph of 22 March when the second reading was carried by a single vote. He suspected what troubles lay ahead. When the Bill was defeated in committee the choice was between throwing in the towel and recommending to the King that the House of Commons should be dissolved. Melbourne made no contribution to the debate in cabinet until the very end; then tersely asked, 'Can we dissolve?' 'Yes.' 'Dissolve then.'* The King grumpily agreed. He became grumpier still when the Lord Mayor chose to celebrate the royal decision by circulating handbills which invited citizens to illuminate their houses, and the mob joined in the fun by breaking the windows of those who failed to accept the invitation. Melbourne was caught between the outrage of the King, who threatened to cancel a scheduled visit to the city, and the chagrin of the mayor, who felt that he had done no more than his duty as a good Whig and, anyway, denied responsibility for the offending handbills. Eventually he achieved an uneasy truce by which the King accepted the mayor's assurances, renewed his promise to visit the city and then suffered a convenient attack of gout which prevented him doing so. Melbourne defended the Lord Mayor halfheartedly in the House of Lords but privately he must have been on the side of the King: illuminations always led 'to violence among the lower orders' and should be avoided, like anything else liable to foment excitement.[5]

The elections were a triumph for the Whigs and by the autumn of 1831 the battle for reform moved to the House of Lords. With a massive Tory majority among the peers confrontation between the two Houses was inevitable. What would the Whigs then do? Abandon their bill? Resign, in spite of their majority? Or seek to overcome the resistance of the Lords? Opinions varied: from that of Lord Essex, who wanted the King to stop at the first stand of hackney carriages in Piccadilly and ennoble every coachman in succession until there were enough safe new votes to overwhelm the recalcitrants; to the Duke of Richmond, who felt that the decision of the upper house was sacrosanct and the creation of more peers unconstitutional. Melbourne was generally believed to favour the second school but he avoided committing himself. In cabinet he lay low until the conversation turned to the question of those individuals who might be made peers if the need arose, then intervened to protest strongly against the inclusion of the diplomatist Bagot. 'Damme', he told Lord Holland afterwards, 'I

* Or so Stanley told Arbuthnot. One wonders what the cabinet had been discussing during the meeting if this somewhat crucial question remained undecided at the end.

should have been plagued to death about my brother Frederick if Bagot had got a peerage.'[6]

In October 1831 the House of Lords defeated the Second Reform Bill by a majority of 42, which included the votes of 21 bishops.[7] The people of Bristol quickly made evident their view of the proceedings. It had seemed obvious to Melbourne that the forthcoming visit to the city on a Gaol Delivery of the highly unpopular Recorder, the ultra-Tory Sir Charles Wetherell, was likely to spark off considerable trouble. The local magistrates urged postponement but the eventual decision was that the visit should continue and the authority of the law be strengthened by some support from the regular cavalry. By 26 October, well in advance of the Recorder, Lt.-Col. Brereton with three troops comprising 93 mounted men arrived at Bristol.[8] Sir Charles packed his bags in the reasonable confidence that his visit would be a peaceful one.

What followed demonstrated partly the fecklessness of the senior citizenry, partly the ineptness of Colonel Brereton, but most of all the passionate resentment of the average man in the street at the way in which he had been deprived at the last minute of what he had learnt to think of as his salvation. Riots began soon after Wetherell's arrival, the Mansion House was sacked and Colonel Brereton, dissatisfied with the support offered him by the magistrates, concluded there was not much he could do to help and pulled his troops out of the city. The bishop's nephew wrote in horror to Melbourne from the Palace reporting that, even as the cavalry withdrew, he could see the rioters begin to gather again in the adjoining square.[9] Within a few hours the Palace and much of the centre of Bristol was left in gutted ruins.

Melbourne thought Brereton's action of very doubtful prudence, 'or rather not doubtful at all',[10] but he resisted with spirit any attempt to shuffle off on the military the full responsibility for the disaster. In answer to a memorial from the citizens of Bristol complaining that proper precautions had not been taken, he replied with hauteur that he was not surprised they should be 'anxious to take the earliest opportunity . . . of relieving themselves from the imputation of having either encouraged or permitted such lawless outrage or violence'. He agreed investigation was called for, but 'into the conduct both of the civil and military authorities, and of all the householders and other inhabitants of the city'.[11] Everyone, it seemed to him, had come badly out of the affair; not least his own colleague Brougham who tried to play down the riots as 'a groaning and hissing match . . . almost made a rebellion by dint of corporation magistrates'. The most alarming consideration was that the same thing might happen in any other city of the realm.

Party feeling, he told Grey, was so bad that people were 'far more gratified at seeing their neighbours' property burning than they are alarmed at the consequent danger to their own'.[12]

For the next two or three weeks, while the intentions of the government for their benighted Reform Bill remained uncertain, England was as close as at any time in the nineteenth century to bloody revolution. In Birmingham the Political Union announced that, since the government seemed unable to organize the city's proper protection, it would take it on itself. It needed little imagination to envisage how a national guard created to defend the people's property could grow into a militia to defend the people's rights. They were planning, Attwood told ministers, against the danger of Grey's fall. In London the National Political Union called a monster meeting at the traditional rallying ground of White Conduit Fields, participants to be armed with twenty-inch staves. A police informer reported a general instruction to all workmen 'to arm themselves and form by their union a guard to themselves'. From Dublin, Mr Lawless wrote in alarm of a secret society now 'at full play in London'. The most desperate and determined of villains were being 'patronized, encouraged and employed by men whose rank and station in life should shield them even from suspicion of being in the most remote degree connected with . . . so Hell-born a scheme'. Given only a few more days, Mr Lawless promised, and the Home Secretary would witness a nation in its final convulsions. It is hardly surprising that Holland found Melbourne on 11 November 'deeply impressed not to say alarmed, at the state of the country, thinks some convulsion must happen, but notes with some pleasantry that neither Bristol nor White Conduit Lane nor the innumerable informations he has received make him half so gloomy as a hour's conversation with Abercrombie*, who is . . . fully convinced that a week's delay in passing the bill, or the change of a vote will subvert the whole frame of constitution and throw the whole island into confusion'.[13]

Things were perhaps not so perilous as they seemed. When Melbourne passed word to Attwood that the government considered his private army 'unconstitutional and illegal' he was assured that the idea had been adjourned. A proclamation on 21 November banning political unions organized on a basis which would allow them recourse to arms was accepted with almost disconcerting meekness.[14] The meeting at White Conduit Fields was postponed without protest when the leaders were told that otherwise they would be prosecuted for treason. But Melbourne was satisfied that serious trouble could only be averted if

* James Abercromby, at that time Chief Baron of the Exchequer of Scotland.

the people were persuaded that the government were still determined to carry through their Bill. For this reason he felt that the speediest possible meeting of parliament was called for, with some dramatic re-affirmation of the government's determination. The issue was debated for five hours on 19 November in cabinet. Grey, Palmerston and the other, more conservative members of the cabinet were anxious to postpone a meeting of parliament for as long as possible so as to allow time for negotiations with the moderates among the Tory Lords. Brougham, Durham and the other thunderers demanded that the Commons should meet immediately to confront the Upper House squarely with its iniquities. Melbourne was dismayed as much by his allies as by his adversaries but he stuck to his view and 'gave his somewhat reluctant but decided opinion that (the publick mind) would be aggravated very materially by postponement'.[15] His opinions swung the day, to the outrage of Palmerston who was convinced that only a few more days' negotiation were needed to produce a Reform Bill magically acceptable to left and right alike.

Between the defeat of the Reform Bill in the Lords in October 1831 and its final passage in May 1832, the Whig cabinet was deeply divided on two critical issues: whether enough peers should be created to force the Bill through the Lords and what concessions, if any, should be offered to Tory moderates in an effort to win their votes. All divided cabinets must be disagreeable to sit in; the nature of the issues and, still more, of the personalities involved ensured that this one was of almost unique unpleasantness. Hardly a meeting went by without some fiery row: threats of resignation; accusations of treachery; the vulgarest and most unstatesmanlike abuse. Chief offender was Durham, the always frail guard on his temper now worn to nothing by ill health and family troubles. Though he would often attack Melbourne or Palmerston, his father-in-law Grey was his favourite target and he would explode with diatribes of a violence so hideous as to reduce the rest of the cabinet to an embarrassed silence and, on one occasion at least, the Prime Minister to tears. 'If I had been Lord Grey,' Melbourne told Greville after this last outburst, 'I would have knocked him arse-over-head.'[16]

Melbourne did not feel passionately committed over the creation of new peers and he played a small part in the discussions. His inclination was to take the conservative side yet his over-riding preoccupation to avoid a disastrous split ensured that, in the last resort, he would always support that section of the cabinet which seemed most likely to rally a decisive majority behind it. He was, as Lady Cowper described him, 'tossed backwards and forwards between opposite sentiments and feelings'. On 1 January he told Brougham he had almost come round to his point of view; the following day in cabinet he 'urged the danger of the precedent, considered it was a much more violent and permanent measure in its results than a dissolution, and exaggerated the magnitude, importance and danger of so extraordinary an expedient'. Yet even this, apparently conclusive, opinion he managed to cloak with some measure of uncertainty; Melbourne, noted Graham, was 'more hesitating than I ever saw him . . .'[17]

His attitude was equally irresolute over negotiations with the moderate Tories. A group of Tory peers, usually referred to as 'The Waverers', took it on themselves to put forward certain modifications to the Bill which, if accepted, might swing enough Tories behind it to make its passage certain. The trouble was that they could never state with confidence what votes they controlled. Though the Whigs might have given away a lot in the interests of a quick solution they were not prepared to be generous if this merely led to fresh negotiations and a demand for still further concessions. Palmerston, nevertheless, was convinced that a settlement of this kind was the best, if not the only hope and Melbourne was ready to go along with him. The difference between them was, however, fundamental. Palmerston was ready to push his view to the point of a breach with the rest of the cabinet; Melbourne shrank from any such extremism.

> I am most anxious (he wrote to Palmerston) that you should if possible suppress the expression of any difference of opinion in tonight's debate. Only consider the consequences. The breaking up of the government would, I verily believe, be followed by a general convulsion, which their keeping together will undoubtedly prevent at present. Any appearance of hesitation or change now in one, who has hitherto gone along with the Bill, will induce immediately in the public mind a suspicion or rather a conviction of treachery and will counteract the very object you have in view . . .[18]

A curious snapshot of his attitude at this time is provided by Greville, who spoke to him at a ball at the French Embassy on 29 March. Melbourne volunteered the view that 'there was no strong feeling in the country for the measure'. Greville agreed. 'Why then,' speculated the Home Secretary, 'might it not be thrown out?' Greville suggested that Melbourne's own colleagues provided an obvious reason, whereupon his companion moved on into a dirge for the departed rotten boroughs. 'I do not see how the government is to be carried on without them. Some means may be found . . . but I am not aware of any, and I do not see how any government can be carried on when these are swept away.' Lord David Cecil has suggested that in so speaking Melbourne was 'teasing Greville by a display of cynicism'. It is hard to decide which would have been more irresponsible: for a senior minister to speak thus to the Clerk of the Council in complete sincerity or as an obscure joke. The most simple explanation is surely that he spoke with the honesty of a tired, ill-tempered and possibly rather drunken man. Certainly what he said to Greville reflected his private views, a useful reminder of the gap between him and most of his colleagues and of the constant effort he had to make in order not to commit the crime, unforgivable in his eyes, of rocking the boat.[19]

On 14 April the Bill passed its second reading in the House of Lords. Hobhouse congratulated Melbourne on the narrow victory. 'He said it had been a most nervous moment. He did not think that all was over yet.'[20] His judgement was quickly justified. The opposition, it soon transpired, planned only to substitute the death of a thousand cuts for more summary execution and to dismember the Bill leisurely in committee. Once more there was confrontation, but now all doubts were over. Either the King must back his ministers by pledging himself to create however many peers were necessary, or he must find himself a new government. Only the Duke of Richmond among the cabinet could not bring himself to sign the memorandum to the King. William IV thrashed about in his efforts to avoid complete surrender, called in the Tories to pass a modified Bill, tried to bargain with all and sundry. In the end he gave way and in face of his threat to create peers all resistance collapsed. The Reform Bill was passed on 18 May 1832, to be greeted by an explosion of national joy.

Melbourne felt no joy, at the most relief that the affair had passed off without violent uprising. In the last few days, when it had seemed possible that the Duke of Wellington might assume the government, the nation had appeared on the verge of taking to the barricades. 'I have never till within these 48 hours,' wrote Lady Holland on 18 May, 'been seriously alarmed at the state of the country, always ascribing much to exaggeration and vapouring. But now it really appears there is, bona fide, an organization of the people amounting to a national guard, all ready equipped, disciplined, and as *yet* obedient to their leaders.'[21] In Birmingham soldiers were rumoured to be joining the Political Union. There was a threatening run on the banks. Francis

Place placarded London with the sinister instruction: 'To Stop the Duke Go for Gold!' There was little enough that the Home Secretary could do. He confined the London garrison to barracks, battened down the hatches and awaited the hurricane. Now, in the nick of time, the hurricane had been called off. An absence of hurricanes, though certainly a reason for relief, need not necessarily appear a source of joy. An ill-contrived and unnecessary measure had been passed without disaster – that was all. Now it remained to work out the consequences. To govern a reformed Britain was not a prospect that fired Melbourne with enthusiasm. The past two years might have been stormy but, he confidently predicted, the future would be considerably worse.

CHAPTER 11

The Irish and the Unions

CATHOLIC EMANCIPATION had signally failed to cure the ills of Ireland. 'What all the wise men promised has not happened,' commented Melbourne gloomily, 'and what all the damned fools said would happen has come to pass.' Once emancipation was granted, Irish protest gradually shifted to a demand that the Union of 1800 be repealed; other grievances and cries there were in plenty but repeal became the standard under which all of them were gathered. In face of such a crusade Melbourne's prescription was that the government should be fair but firm. In this he was better than those of his compatriots who believed that firmness alone was enough, but it could still hardly be called a forward-looking policy. Unfortunately, he despised the Irish and believed that they could always be bullied into subjection: '. . . the most conspiring people on the face of the earth', he described them, 'a very violent and a very noisy people . . . but not a very courageous people, particularly not morally courageous'.[1]

Responsibility for the government of Ireland rested uneasily between the Lord Lieutenant in Dublin, the Home Secretary in London and the Chief Secretary between the two. The Home Secretary's role was the least defined of the three; if the other two knew their jobs and were determined to do them then his responsibilities might be no more than shadowy. Anglesey, the Lord Lieutenant, certainly knew his job or at least had clear ideas about what it ought to be. He was a cavalry officer by training and temperament: vigorous, impetuous, filled with generous schemes and radical proposals, but neither a tactful nor a subtle man. 'I cannot persuade people I am clever for I am not,' he told Holland rather wistfully, 'but they know I am honest.' Melbourne liked and respected him, though he could have wished him less active and better trained in the running of an office. Several times he was led to protest when Anglesey conducted business according to his own idea of what was proper. 'There is no official correspondence between the Lord Lieutenant of Ireland and any department of the state, other than this office,' he wrote sharply. 'Letters written to any other person are merely of a private and confidential character.'[2]

Stanley, the Chief Secretary, was another matter. The best debater in the party; quick, intelligent and resolute; a man of the most forceful disposition; he was nevertheless moody and inconstant, at his best formidable, at his worst a menace. Melbourne had the highest opinion of him, described him to Disraeli as 'a young eagle' and said he could not fail to succeed Grey as Prime Minister. He was more than happy to leave the Irish business in the hands of such a man. Unfortunately the Irish were less satisfied. To O'Connell the Chief Secretary's talents appeared negligible and 'the snappish, impertinent, overbearing, high church Mr Stanley' was one of the principal obstacles to harmonious government.[3] Indeed, to certain genuinely liberal ideas Stanley allied a belief in strong government and exaggerated tenderness towards the privileges and possessions of the Anglican church in Ireland: a prescription not likely to appear seductive to the angry young radicals of the repealist lobby.

The government's policy in Ireland, Melbourne told Anglesey in his official instructions, was not only 'to maintain the public peace' but 'to do their utmost for the alleviation of the evils which exist in that country'.[4] That sounded well and was certainly well-meant, but as so often in Ireland good intentions gave way to an urgent necessity to maintain the peace. Until the publication of the details of the Reform Bill convinced O'Connell that it was in the best interests of the Irish to back the Whigs, Anglesey found himself confronted by mounting disorder. Melbourne was in no doubts where to turn: 'With respect to the protestants of the north, I have always felt that it is to them that the government must look for support in circumstances of difficulty'. Now was the time for all who were well affected to rally in defence of the realm. He told Stanley that it would be necessary not only to maintain the existing coercive laws but to strengthen them, in particular so far as public meetings were concerned. 'I am well aware that it will be no easy matter to reconcile such a law with the constitutional right of discussion and petition . . . but I trust means may be found for repressing turbulence and sedition without interfering with these important privileges.' The suspension of *habeas corpus*, he rather wistfully noted, was a temporary measure only to be resorted to in times of crisis but no such objection could arise in the case of a seditious meetings bill, which ought, indeed, 'to form a part of the perpetual rule of every people who wished to live in peace and security'.[5]

Unfortunately Melbourne was less ready a coadjutor when it came to improving the lot of the Irish Catholic. He agreed with Stanley that in principle it would be an excellent thing to pay Roman Catholic priests, but felt that the time was hardly propitious; he accepted the need for an Irish Poor Law, but considered a great deal of deliberation would first be needed.[6] When it was a question of urgently needed famine relief he saw only the objections: the risk of fraud, the chances that the food would fall into the wrong hands, the damage done to the people's morale.[7] Meanwhile the Irish starved. Almost the only issue on which he urged immediate action was the arrest of O'Connell in March 1831. Yet even on something so close to his heart he did not feel bound to take any initiative. 'It is always my strong feeling and opinion that persons actually upon the spot form a more correct judgement upon the state of circumstances and the effects of events, than those who are at a distance.'[8] Few would dispute the truth of this, but there was a curious quality in the Irish air which ensured that those who breathed it were as prone to confusion on the local issues as those who surveyed them from afar. It might have been no bad thing if Melbourne had waived his detachment and involved himself more actively in the day-to-day business of Irish affairs.

With the Reform Bill at last out of the way, the Whigs were able to devote themselves to reform in Ireland. In the summer of 1832 some modest proposals were put forward. The tithe system was to be adjusted, a few Irish bishoprics suppressed, the fatter livings taxed and the resultant income devoted to the building of churches and improved stipends for the poorer clergy. As is usually the case, such palliatives pleased nobody. O'Connell and his friends were wholly dissatisfied, especially when their favourite clause, a provision that in certain circumstances church funds might be diverted to lay purposes, was shelved as being too controversial. On the other hand the champions of the Irish church were outraged at what seemed to them a barefaced assault on the sacred rights of property. Since Anglesey subscribed generally to the first school of thought and Stanley the second it is hardly surprising that some ill-temper crept into the administration of Irish affairs; for Melbourne as good a reason as any for keeping out of them.

By the autumn agrarian troubles, particularly in the south, had got out of control. 'The murders, outrages etc. are dreadful,' Melbourne told Lansdowne, 'and will unfortunately sooner or later compel the adoption of measures stronger than the ordinary laws. I have long foreseen this but such measures must not be prematurely proposed. You must carry along with you the public feeling.' The cabinet was divided between those who called for harsh coercive measures and those who wanted to satisfy the grievances of the Irish by immediate reform. At a critical meeting at Grey's house in East Sheen on 19 October, Althorp, Durham and Russell argued that O'Connell should be conciliated while Melbourne, Stanley and the Prime Minister were for repression. The latter carried the day. Shortly after this Melbourne was threatened with far more direct involvement in Irish affairs. The relationship between Anglesey and Stanley had now become impossible. Grey's first instinct was to appeal to Wellington – 'I believe that the iron hand of the Duke . . . would be the most effectual government for Ireland' – but he regretfully concluded that such a solution would not work. As a second best he considered that Melbourne's combination of firmness and good-fellowship qualified him to replace the Lord Lieutenant. 'Melbourne is as certain to agree as your name is Grey,' Brougham announced firmly, offering to fix the matter himself if a go-between of authority was needed. But Melbourne proved recalcitrant. He brooded for a couple of days, then turned down the offer, 'upon various grounds, private and personal, public and political, which it is superfluous to detail'. The deteriorating state of his son's health must have been a factor, probably too a disinclination to leave a London adorned by the singular bright light of Mrs Norton. In any case the grandiose pomposity of viceregal life would hardly have appealed to him. Instead Anglesey and Stanley struggled on together for another few months. The bedraggled figure of Lord Wellesley was then dusted down and sent to Dublin while in March 1833 Wellesley's son-in-law, the busy and self-important Littleton, took the place of Stanley.[9]

By the beginning of 1833 arrears in tithes amounted to £1.2m and the impossibility of collecting them became ever more apparent. It was an ironic commentary on the hopes raised by the great Reform Bill that the first major measure considered in the reformed parliament was one of the most drastic measures against civil disturbance ever framed by a British government. Palmerston called it 'a real *tour de force*, but then it is to be followed by remedial measures, and there is the difference between us and Metternich and the Pope'. Melbourne's main preoccupation was that the new restrictions should fall as harshly on Protestant as Catholic. In particular he deplored the activities of the Orange Lodges, cells of fanatics under the patronage of the Duke of

Cumberland whose aim was to protect the protestant hegemony by any means, fair or foul. He urged Grey to consider banning them as illegal assemblies under the terms of the Coercion Act. Such a step '. . . would probably offend the Protestants even more than anything that has been done yet, but still it appears to me almost impossible to submit to the existence of societies which break the law in a manner so open and audacious'. The leaders of the Lodges, who were never short of accurate information about the intentions of ministers, acted with rather more restraint over the next few months, and the scare died down.[10]

One letter from Anglesey to Melbourne at this period is particularly poignant to the biographer. Melbourne had written to order the transfer of a regiment of infantry. 'It must be acknowledged that your 50s and your 80s are fatally alike', replied Anglesey. 'However, I soon discovered my error . . . and the 50th, instead of the 80th is upon the move.' Only those who have studied Lord Melbourne's later correspondence can realize just how little Anglesey had to complain about. 'I used to write a very ugly hand,' Melbourne told Queen Victoria, 'but it used to be a very legible hand; and now I've got to write a hand that almost nobody can read; what I judge from is, that when I've read it over myself I can't read it, and so I think if I can't read it, nobody else can.' He was right. By 1833 deterioration had already set in, by the later years of his ministry he had attained something close to complete illegibility. Members of his government would pass his letters from hand to hand, speculating about this word or that as if it were some diabolic crossword puzzle. 'I have given you in pencil the benefit of my partial decipher,' wrote Clarendon to John Russell, '– a long and laborious operation.' What must have made the labour still more galling was the suspicion that Melbourne took a certain pride in his frailty, viewing it, like Mr Bingley of *Pride and Prejudice*, as proceeding from a rapidity of thought and carelessness of execution which, if not actually praiseworthy, was at least highly interesting.[11]

By May 1834 the different attitudes towards Ireland in the cabinet could no longer be reconciled. Althorp's bill for the reform of the Irish church had finally been enacted the previous year, leaving undecided the question of whether surplus church funds could ever be appropriated for lay purposes such as education. Now this prickly issue was revived. John Russell agreed in cabinet that the matter should be played as quietly as possible, then was stung into a rousing affirmation in the House of Commons that 'in justice to Ireland', such appropriation must be permitted. 'John Russell has upset the coach', scribbled Stanley in a note to Graham, and promptly proceeded to tumble off it himself, taking with him in his resignation three other conservative-minded members of the ministry. Melbourne deplored their parting because on most matters he agreed with them but on this particular issue he felt no urge to take their side. He did not care two-pence about the appropriation of church funds and considered both Russell and Stanley asses for taking the matter so much to heart, but regretfully he accepted that the government were committed to some such course.

Stanley's resignation left the government more homogeneous and as such certainly no weaker. As a debater and administrator, however, he was a severe loss. To Melbourne, who had envisaged him as Grey's successor, his disappearance seemed particularly grave. It is unlikely that the idea even fleetingly occurred to him that a rival might have been cleared from his path. Nevertheless the absence of Stanley was to be a matter of the highest significance when the next crisis over Ireland shook the cabinet only six weeks later.

Since the repeal of the Combination Acts in 1824 successive govern-ments had been preoccupied by the various unions in which members of the working class banded together to achieve social, political or economic ends. Melbourne's views were simple and clear-cut. It was the duty of those in authority to govern and of the rest of society to be governed. Any body which sought to interpose itself between one class and the other was superfluous and usually mischievous. This was true whether the body consisted of prosperous Anglo-Irish landlords banded together in an Orange Lodge or of indigent lace-workers or brass founders. The one might prove more well-conducted or amenable than the other, but both sought to interfere with the proper role of government. As such they were to be deplored and, if possible, dis-banded.

It did not follow from this, however, that Melbourne was anxious to introduce new legislation which would make all such combinations illegal. On the contrary, he accepted that they were evils to be lived with, that people had a right to unite and that government could only properly seek to curb them if they were acting in some way subversive to the state. To Lord Derby he denounced the 'democratic tyranny' of the unions but at the same time denied the need for new laws. In his denunciation he was no more immoderate than most of his colleagues:

it was Brougham who stated that unions were *'conspiracies* of the worst kind, their existence a blot upon a system such as no government ought to suffer'.[12]

There must however be a point at which a grouping of citizens becomes a threat to the security of the state and Melbourne was always alive to the need to act if such a point were in his view reached. The threat was obviously at its most potent whenever working class bodies concerned with wages or working conditions were inspired by the socialist ideas of men such as Robert Owen to widen their movement to embrace social and political objectives. Asa Briggs speaks of a pendulum which swung between 'economic action through trade unions and political action through Chartism'. In good times the former seemed predominant, in bad times the latter.[13] In the years before the Reform Bill became law political panaceas were particularly favoured. In December 1829 Thomas Attwood set up in Birmingham a 'Political Union of the Lower and Middle Classes of the People', whose objects were defined in their first great meeting as being 'to collect and organize the moral power of the country for the restoration of the people's rights, to conciliate the passions, the prejudices, and the interests of all, and to bring all to unite in one common bond of union together'.[14] To Melbourne such aspirations seemed vague and ridiculous, but also dangerous; whatever 'rights' the people might merit they enjoyed already. Once the 'moral power' of the nation was harnessed to increase them then only the most naive Home Secretary would not anticipate physical power being brought into the issue as well.

At the end of 1830 Melbourne took the advice of the law officers on whether the unions were acting outside the law. 'In the meantime,' he told Grey, 'I will obtain all the information I possibly can upon the nature and working of these combinations as a ground for considering whether it is possible to frame any new measures . . . The question really is whether it is wiser to suffer a union and conspiracy to form and consolidate itself until it menaces the peace of the country . . . or to take measures which shall prevent its ever arriving at such a height.' As a first step he asked Nassau Senior, the professor of political economy at Oxford, to investigate the activities of the unions and suggest possible counter-measures. The professor did a shabby job, confining his researches to chats with a few senior employers and arriving rapidly at his conclusion that the powers of the unions should be rigorously circumscribed and their funds confiscated. In the best tradition of British government Melbourne wholly ignored the expert

The 1st Viscount Melbourne.
From the painting
The Milbankes and the Melbournes *by Stubbs.*

Lady Melbourne with her father,
Sir Ralph Milbanke, by Stubbs.

William Lamb with a dog, and (BOTTOM) *George Lamb
as the infant Bacchus with lion cubs,
both by Maria Cosway.*

William Lamb at Eton in Montem dress, by Hoppner.

OPPOSITE TOP:

Emily Lamb (later Lady Cowper
and Lady Palmerston), by Hoppner.

OPPOSITE BOTTOM:

Lady Caroline Lamb.
From a mezzotint at Melbourne Hall.

Brocket Hall, Hertfordshire.

Melbourne Hall, Derbyshire.

William, Augustus, and Caroline Lamb,
a sketch by Caroline Lamb.

Mrs. Norton, by Stone.

William Lamb aged about 35, by Lawrence.

OPPOSITE TOP:

Receiving the Fatal News!
*Lord Melbourne tells the Cabinet of their dismissal
in July, 1834.* CLOCKWISE FROM MELBOURNE: *Duncannon, Russell,
Brougham, Holland, Spring Rice, Auckland* (AT FAR REAR),
Hobhouse, Palmerston, and Grant.

OPPOSITE BOTTOM:

The Galley Slaves. *O'Connell leads Melbourne, Russell,
Spring Rice, and Hobhouse in chains behind him.*

Lord Palmerston, by Partridge, circa 1844.

OPPOSITE TOP:

Lord Grey, after Lawrence, circa 1828.

OPPOSITE BOTTOM:

Lord Brougham, by Lonsdale.

Lord John Russell, by Grant, circa 1853.

OPPOSITE TOP:

The First Council, *by Wilkie.*

OPPOSITE BOTTOM:

*Melbourne riding with the Queen
at Windsor, by Grant.*

Frederick Lamb in 1846, by Partridge.

The Diner-Out:
*Lord Melbourne stands pensively with a royal
invitation to dinner in his hand as Victoria
and Albert watch sorrowfully from above.
From* Punch, *September 1841.*

Lord Melbourne in old age, by Landseer.
A sketch at Broadlands for the portrait
now hanging in 10 Downing Street.

opinion which he had previously solicited and all ideas for new laws were temporarily abandoned.[15]

In the autumn of 1831, however, the trouble was exacerbated. With the rejection of the Reform Bill by the House of Lords a lively possibility, those people who rightly or wrongly felt that they would be its beneficiaries betrayed a disconcerting determination to take the protection of their interests into their own hands. William IV, always the first to scent incipient revolution, wrote in high alarm to report that the unions in the manufacturing towns were plotting mischief, a refusal to pay rates and taxes was to be followed by recourse to violence. Sadly Melbourne wrote to admit that much of what the King said was true. 'The political unions, as far as I can learn, are undoubtedly extending themselves, increasing their numbers, and completing their arrangements. They are not so numerous as the unions for the purpose of raising wages and regulating trade, from which they are as yet separate and distinct, but in both cases much communication and cooperation takes place.' If the unions held to their intention of withholding taxes it would be 'a blow levelled at the very existence of all our institutions . . . attended with the most disastrous circumstances'.[16] The rejection of the Bill in the House of Lords was immediately followed by the foundation in London of the National Political Union. Melbourne tried to persuade Burdett not to accept the Union's presidency but was too late; he could however take some comfort from the fact that the movement seemed formidably respectable, composed largely of artisans and small tradesmen and giving no countenance to such wild radical chimeras as annual elections or universal suffrage.[17]

The same could not be said of Attwood's Birmingham Union. Early in November it was rumoured that the Union was buying large quantities of arms and organizing itself on a para-military basis. Cross-examined, Attwood denied the charge but admitted to a local magistrate, Francis Lawley, that they were preparing to deal with a possible insurrection by the 'lowest people' and to protect themselves from any sort of outside threat. 'I believe,' Lawley concluded hopefully, 'there is no need to apprehend evil from their proceedings at present.' Gloomily Melbourne underlined the words 'at present'. 'You will observe,' he replied, 'that this body is by its name, by its rules, by its speeches and all its proceedings, avowedly formed with political objects and for political purposes. Now political objects should be carried by reason, by persuasion, by civil means and legal proceedings. For these what need is there of organization, of divisions into tens, into hundreds, into thousands? It is unnecessary that a deliberative body should be arrayed, and an arrayed body is entirely unfit for deliberations.' To the King he described the activities of the Birmingham Union with distaste tinged with alarm, calling it 'a conspiracy to supersede and assume the power of the state'.[18]

His problems were made no easier by the fact that while, as Home Secretary and a conservative, he deplored the existence of the political unions almost as much as the King himself, as a minister in the government responsible for the Reform Bill he had to admit that their hearts were in the right place. Some at least of his colleagues thought that the unions were doing an excellent job by reminding the King and the House of Lords that the Whigs spoke with the voice of the people and that it would be perilous to ignore them. Nevertheless some step had to be taken, if only to satisfy the King at a time when his support over the Reform Bill was more than ever essential. On 21 November 1831 a proclamation banned all political unions organized on a basis which equipped them for rapid recourse to arms.[19] The order was received almost without protest, indeed with a certain relief by some of the movement's leaders who suspected that they might have created a monster which could easily escape their control. Certainly the political unions might have experienced a formidable revival if things had gone differently in the final stages of the Reform Bill's passage but at the beginning of 1832 the Home Secretary could view with some satisfaction the apparent extinction of what, only three months before, had seemed to bear all the marks of a powerful and potentially explosive force.

To the King the proclamation did not go far enough in that it made no attempt to strike at the trades unions proper. Melbourne felt some sympathy for this point of view but was more struck by their folly than their malevolence. Trades unions could not last because they were 'inconsistent and impossible and contradictory to the laws of nature'. With exquisite logic he demonstrated their absurdity to the King. Some workmen had refused 25s. a week and stood out for 30s. 'Now if a man under these circumstances remains twelve weeks out of work he loses £15. If at the end of the twelve weeks he is obliged to submit ... his loss is irretrievable. If he succeeds, he must still labour for more than a year to make up his loss – 5s. a week for 52 weeks amounting only to £13. This is so clearly a losing game that its disadvantages must in time become obvious to the most vulgar understanding.'[20]

Given this happy confidence that the movement was doomed, Melbourne did not feel the same urge to restrict it by new legislation as did some of his colleagues. To Lord Sandon he deplored the inability of the law to touch the 'gross injustice and blind tyranny' practised by the unions but pointed out that, since the M.P.s from the manufacturing towns would be too cowardly to support any new bill, it would be impossible to secure its passage. They must simply soldier on as best they could. When Howick joined Melbourne at the Home Office he was relieved to find the Secretary of State 'decidedly against any new laws against the trade unions'. The same was equally true when the evil spread from the industrial towns to the rural areas; it went against the grain to sit back and watch the corruption of a whole society but there was nothing to be done except to encourage farmers to dismiss any employee who joined a union and enforce vigorously such laws as *did* exist against conspiracy and the taking of illegal oaths.[21]

In a long letter to Lord Lyttelton, Melbourne set out his views on the whole problem. Lyttelton had complained that, far from dying away as the Home Secretary had predicted, the unions seemed to be gathering strength. Melbourne replied on 29 March 1834:

'Altho' I certainly do anticipate the decay and natural death of the trade unions, I have never expected such results to take place immediately, nor without the unions spreading much more extensively . . . nor without much contest, inconvenience and loss, nor without much menace, much alarm and possibly actual commotion. In the end I am convinced that they must fail, but I am well aware that in their progress they may inflict serious evil upon the commerce and prosperity of the country'. The best hope lay in the lack of any real community of interest or cohesion between unionists. 'The brass founders are apprehensive of violating the law, the button burnishers have been intimidated by the firmness of their masters, the needle makers fear the competition of machinery; and I have no doubt if other trades were accurately enquired into, there would be found many other discrepancies in their condition and consequently in the conduct which may be expected from them'. But this overall weakness did not mitigate the damage unionists might do in individual industries. 'The case of the master builders . . . is a very hard one. The workmen employ against them the most formidable weapon which circumstances have placed in their hands, and the power of wielding which renders the contest between them and their masters so entirely unfair and unequal. The principal advantages possessed by the workmen appear to be two: 1st Their numbers and their superiority of physical force . . . – and 2nd Their power of withholding their labour at a moment when the master is bound by a contract which he must either fulfil or be ruined . . . I am well aware', Melbourne concluded, 'of the obstinate fidelity with which the lower classes cling to one another . . . at the same time I trust that the convictions which have lately taken place in Dorsetshire will have some effect in proving to them the illegality of their combinations.'[22]

The convictions in Dorsetshire arose from what was certainly the most notorious and probably the least creditable episode during Melbourne's sojourn at the Home Office. The Friendly Society of Agricultural Labourers in the little Dorset village of Tolpuddle was a group of sedate and serious peasants, anxious to improve their lot but equally anxious to observe the law.[23] Their standards were high – no swearing, no obscenity, above all no violence – but some mumbo jumbo of secret oaths was gone through by new members as they stood in front of a painting of an old gentleman variously reported to represent either Death or Father Time. This proved their undoing. On 31 January 1834 Melbourne had recommended to magistrates that, where agricultural unions were involved, they might have recourse to 57 Geo III of 1817, a statute under which a society became illegal if its members took an oath 'not recognized or authorized by law'.[24] This statute had originally been devised to prevent the seduction from their loyalty of soldiers or sailors but there seemed no reason why it should not serve well in the present case. In February six members of the Society were arrested. At their trial the judge claimed that their activities were 'calculated to shake the foundations of society' and made it clear that their punishment was intended not only to fit the crime but also to offer 'an example and a warning' to other would-be offenders. A savage sentence of seven years' transportation was imposed and the Tolpuddle Martyrs were born.

Melbourne was already acquainted with the case through his brother-in-law, William Ponsonby, who lived in the area and who had been foreman of the grand jury which had found the original indictment valid. He did not become officially involved, however, until 27 March when he wrote to James Frampton, the local magistrate, asking for information about the six men so as to prepare himself for what was likely to prove some hostile questioning in parliament. Frampton replied with a damning indictment of these 'saucy', 'idle' and discontented men – an account which, while recognizably referring to the accused, was still a travesty of the truth. Melbourne was very ready to accept so convenient an account; a petition was dismissed by the King and the accused were hustled abroad with indecent speed. This merely stirred up the indignation of the radicals: even newspapers habitually on the side of ministers denounced the brutal sentences and said that the unions, deplorable though they might be, should not be attacked 'by a side-wind'. Young told Place that the cabinet had decided to carry out the sentence 'lest it should be inferred that they had remitted it through fear', an attitude which seemed to Place the basest kind of 'narrow-minded cowardice'.[25]

On 21 April a monster demonstration met under the patronage of Robert Owen at Copenhagen Fields near King's Cross. The plan was to march to Whitehall, present a petition in favour of the Martyrs at the Home Office; then proceed over Westminster Bridge and disperse in Lambeth. Melbourne, with some reluctance, agreed that the march could take place and undertook to be in the Home Office the entire day – a Sunday – but shortly before the demonstration began he made it clear to its leaders that he would not be prepared to receive any deputation backed by an army of supporters. Detachments of the Lancers, the Queen's Bays, the Royals from Croydon, eight infantry battalions and 29 pieces of ordnance from Woolwich were ordered to stand by, discreetly out of sight, while Melbourne stood ostentatiously by a front window of the Home Office and Howick dismissed the deputation politely but decisively. The great procession, 35,000 strong, filed quietly by and dispersed without any serious incident. After the event ministers were energetic in denying that they had ever felt alarm. 'All sorts of absurd rumours were afloat as to these poor people', wrote Hobhouse. 'A near connection of mine told me that 15,000 of them carried stilettoes; I did not believe that 15,000 stilettoes could be found in all England – no, nor in all Europe.'[26] Yet there is no doubt that on the day of the demonstration the government were ready for serious disorder and would not have been surprised to see it spread beyond the metropolis to other industrial centres and even to the countryside.

Whether the demonstration was a success or failure depended on the point of view of the observer. To Princess Lieven the march failed because 'the *canaille* here are cowardly and the classes are courageous'; to *The Pioneer* it was a triumphant display of well-ordered unity, the day 'labour put its hat upon its head and walked towards the throne'. Nor was there any more agreement about whether the sentences on the six men of Tolpuddle had had a salutary effect upon the national scene. Melbourne assured the King that the clamour raised by the unions arose from 'their consciousness of the mortal blow which it strikes at the root of the whole of their proceedings'. Francis Place was equally sure that the government's action had saved the movement: 'We are now on our legs again . . . Had a proclamation been issued declaring the law and the determination henceforth to enforce it . . ., an end would have been, at once, put to all trades unions.' Given the subsequent development of the Labour movement and the shining role played by the Tolpuddle Martyrs in socialist hagiography, it is not difficult to decide today who showed the sounder judgement. Nor was the martyrdom long protracted; in 1836, in spite of some opposition from Melbourne, a free pardon was given to the six labourers and they returned home in triumph. Yet in the days that followed the march from Copenhagen Fields few conservatives would have doubted that a heavy blow had been struck at the unions and that Lord Melbourne deserved well of his country.[27]

A few days after the great march Haydon found Melbourne looking 'fagged and ill'.[28] In the circumstances this was perhaps hardly surprising yet there are many accounts of the period which show him in high spirits and obviously enjoying life to the full. At dinner with Lord Lansdowne, laughing *more* and *at less* than ever'; with John Russell, where he 'spluttered, spoke loud, and swilled wine, as usual, very jovially'; mocking an earnest literary gathering at Holland House – ' "I see there is a new edition of Crabbe coming out; it is a good thing when these authors die, for then one gets their works and has done with them!" Though this sounds insolent when written, it was said with so joyous and jovial an air, followed by that scarcely human though cheerful laugh . . ., with his ejaculations "Eh! Eh!" interposed at every burst, that it was impossible not to enjoy it as much as himself.'[29] The fact is that for a man of energy, organizing ability, a tranquil temperament and limited imagination, the Home Office provided most congenial occupation. Melbourne enjoyed the work, enjoyed the flow of humanity that passed through his office, enjoyed the consequence and the feeling that he was on top of his job. Though occasionally he professed boredom or fatigue he left his colleagues in no doubt that he was prepared to soldier on indefinitely.

By his subordinates he was liked and respected, and he stood up for them nobly. When the Duke of Newcastle complained that his enquiries had not been dealt with properly by Home Office officials Melbourne battered away at him until the Duke admitted that his complaint was unjustified and made a grovelling apology. He always defended the independence of the courts, even when he disapproved of their verdicts. When certain members of parliament agitated for the mitigation of a libel sentence against a newspaper editor he commented with asperity: 'If such a course should be successful there is an end to the complete and impartial administration of justice in this country, and if they address the King to grant a pardon to Coker, another Secretary of State must be found to sign it.' That traditional bugbear of Home Secretaries, the death penalty, did not trouble him deeply though he was always conscientious in considering the case for a reprieve; sometimes spending four or five hours discussing every detail with the Chief Justice. Greville described his embarrassment when called upon to defend the execution of a half-wit peasant charged with bestiality; and yet it would be surprising if such macabre follies ever cost Melbourne a sleepless night or caused him to question the merits of the legal system for which he was in part responsible.[30]

Like several of his colleagues he had grave doubts whether the House of Commons would be manageable after the Reform Bill.

'I do not myself much like the complexion of the public meetings of constituents of which I read in the newspapers,' he told his brother Fred. 'They seem to me to be very violent . . . and to be demanding pledges in a very positive manner which are given rather too readily. The real thing to be feared is the presence [?] of the blackguard interest in parliament and I fear there will be no inconsiderable portion of members of that description . . . It is quite evident that when the new parliament meets we shall be pressed to go further in reform . . . There is no knowing to what one may be led by circumstances, but at present I am determined to make my stand here and not to advance any further.'[31]

In the event pressure for further reform proved less intense than he had expected and the new House of Commons looked disconcertingly like its predecessors. Melbourne was soon fortified in his original conviction that the Reform Bill was as irrelevant to the needs of the people as any other piece of legislation and that things could be relied on to continue much as they had before.

The feverish energy and limitless ambitions of Brougham spared the Home Secretary much uncongenial labour. Brougham, for instance, took charge of the new Poor Law, a well-intentioned piece of legislation which probably contributed more to the sum of human unhappiness than any other single measure of the nineteenth century. Melbourne refused to become involved in the minutiae of what he suspected to be a distasteful measure. Mr Denison tried to lobby him about some proposed changes to the bill and Melbourne brusquely referred him to his brother George. 'I have been with him', complained Denison, 'but he damned me, and damned the bill, and damned the paupers!' 'Well, damn it, what more could he do?' enquired Lord Melbourne. The main purport of this legislation was to relieve the admittedly crippling burden on the parishes by ending outdoor relief and sending all paupers to workhouses for men or for women. The suffering likely to be caused to families broken up to suit this rigid system had not, it seems, occurred to Melbourne; indeed one of his principal objections to the previous system had been that it favoured the family by giving greater relief to the married than to the single man.[32]

On penal reform he was equally happy to leave the initiative to the Lord Chancellor. His views on crime and punishment, even by the standards of the time, can hardly be called progressive. 'No man,' he propounded, 'could know anything of the mind of another, except what he derived from conjectures founded on the knowledge of his own mind.' Only another criminal, therefore, could hope to understand those who 'had already got over all sense of moral rectitude . . . all sense of shame . . . all regard for the opinions of friends and relations, or for their own characters and respectability'. The only thing that could deter such lost souls was the fear of punishment, and even this 'could not be expected to exercise a very powerful influence over those who had already leaped over higher barriers and more forcible restraints'. He went on to ponder the merits of education as a means of raising the lower orders above these criminal urges. His conclusions were predictable and dispiriting. 'If the education was such as to inspire the lower orders with opinions above their situation and to impart to them a distaste for labour, it would be the most fatal and destructive gift which could be presented to them . . . But if the education given to them were such as to teach them the necessity of labour, and of conforming themselves to their situations in life, he could have no doubt that it . . . would be productive of the most advantageous results.'[33]

In certain fields his views were less illiberal. He championed the emancipation of the Jews, 'on the principles of justice, humanity and common-sense'. He sponsored a bill prohibiting the employment of children under nine, and regulating the conditions under which they might work between the ages of nine and eleven. He disliked the gutter Press as furiously as any statesman of either party but consistently sought to block any official prosecution of offending journals. It is true that his motives were more the difficulties in the way of prosecution and the trouble which such trials always stirred up than any respect for the freedom of the Press, but in general he felt that people should be allowed to do whatever they wanted and only interfered with if they became an intolerable nuisance to society. It was not particularly idealistic but equally not a bad point of view for a Home Secretary to hold.[34]

At the beginning of 1834 George Lamb, Melbourne's brother and Under Secretary, died, allegedly of gout aggravated by constant overdoses of calcium. His long illness and extreme suffering had saddened Melbourne. Though Lamb had not been particularly efficient as a subordinate he had still been somebody in whom the Home Secretary could have complete trust and who looked at every issue in the same way. On the night before Lamb died, Ellice visited Melbourne and asked that the almost-vacant post might be given to Lord Howick, the Prime Minister's son. Melbourne, wrote Emily Eden, 'has such an aversion to Lord Howick that it would not surprise me to find he had made a stand against him', but Melbourne was in no mood to make a stand over any issue. He wrote to Grey to say that the Prime Minister should fix the matter as he thought best, but stressing that whoever did fill the post would have to be prepared fully to back the official line on every issue: 'I hope also he is not infected with any of these wild notions . . . respecting the awfulness [?] of inflicting capital punishment. If he is, it surely is a decisive objection to his accepting the place.'[35]

Grey showed the letter to Howick who took it with unusual good temper. Melbourne, he commented, obviously considered him 'an impracticable, headstrong sort of person whom it will be necessary to keep under the strictest control. However, though certainly not flattering to me, I do not dislike his letter as it is written in a frank and manly tone.' He was still anxious to have the job, though apprehensive how he would find it after three years of having things all his own way under the insignificant Goderich: 'I see clearly that I must be a great deal more cautious in my way of acting than I formerly was.' Grey assured Melbourne that his son would be loyal to his superior, and that, while he would wish to limit cases of capital punishment to the minimum possible, 'he has none of that morbid sentiment that would reject them altogether'. Melbourne suppressed whatever misgivings he felt and accepted the appointment with good grace.[36]

It was just as well that they were only to have six months together. Howick was energetic, ambitious, filled with ideas and astonishingly tactless: a combination of characteristics which made up the antithesis of Melbourne's ideal assistant. Howick was filled with interesting ideas on secondary punishment. Melbourne urged him to write a paper on it. Howick did so, and Melbourne dismissed it as far too radical. Howick re-wrote it, only to find Melbourne so preoccupied with Irish Tithes that he could not even find time to discuss it. It took two months and the intervention of Grey before Melbourne could be induced to pay attention and even then he was no more than cautiously helpful and anxious to pass the responsibility for any action on to the Lord Chancellor.[37] The same pattern was repeated on other matters, the two men grew steadily more irritated with each other and only the collapse of the government prevented what might have been an embittered imbroglio.

Meanwhile Melbourne had become an acceptable and trusted figure at Windsor. Since the passage of the Reform Bill, William IV's disenchantment with the Whigs had become almost complete. Grey he could still accept but Durham, Brougham, Russell, even Althorp were all anathema and he longed for the day when he could send them packing and revert to the Tories. Melbourne, however, was an exception. The King enjoyed his company and thought his judgement sound. He had the good sense to steer clear of the ferociously pro-Tory Queen and thus avoid the rows into which several of his fellow ministers were trapped: 'I used never to go near her', he told Queen Victoria, 'but used to talk to the maids of honour; she complained of that, but it was much better . . .'[38] William said he was a gentleman, and knew no higher form of praise. Melbourne attached no particular importance to this royal approval, except in so far as it made his work as Home Secretary a little easier. Certainly he can never have stopped to think, as he made himself affable amid the stuffy splendour of the court, that the favour of the King might shortly prove a decisive factor in his career.

CHAPTER 12

Prime Minister

IN THE LAST few months of 1833 Lord Grey had been almost constantly in a resigning mood and 1834 showed no change of heart. In January he almost brought it off when the cabinet split over the question of intervention in Portugal. Grey, backed by his Foreign Secretary and three others, was strongly for sending troops to help the government; Melbourne and the other members over-ruled any such adventure. Princess Lieven presents Melbourne as the leader of the opposition group, Howick claims that Althorp was the prime mover and the Home Secretary no more than a lukewarm supporter. Since both got their information from Grey the discrepancy is curious. Probably Howick was nearer the mark but at all events Grey bitterly resented this mutiny and had to be cajoled into remaining in office.[1]

Grey's view at this time was that Althorp should go to the Lords to succeed him and Stanley take over in the Commons. Then came Stanley's resignation with 'his bottle-holders . . . pig-head Richmond and canting Graham'. Grey was as unhappy as anyone over what Greville described as the 'paltry patching-up' of the government that followed, and once again threatened instant resignation. The *Morning Post* announced that Palmerston was to follow Stanley, but was quickly proved wrong. Mackworth Praed hymned the news in terms that echoed the deep distrust in which Palmerston was now held by the more liberal wing of the Whig party:

> England has commerce yet to lose,
> And friendships yet to cast away.
> Dead are her laurels, dim her fame,
> But destiny has yet behind
> A darker doom, a fouler shame;
> Lord Palmerston has not resigned![2]

Once again the government prepared to limp along under its present leadership. To Tavistock, John Russell's elder brother, it seemed that the only alternative was a coalition under Peel; Melbourne still fancied Stanley would return to lead the party; Althorp remained the general favourite; some spoke of Lansdowne, Durham, even Brougham. Then came the final crash. 'A foolish dispute . . . about some Irish job', was Campbell's crisp summary of the crisis,[3] and indeed it was little more significant. The Irish Coercion Act was about to lapse and Wellesley urged its renewal, including the stringent provisions against public meetings. Grey accepted the advice and committed himself fully to it. Meanwhile Brougham, working hand in glove with the Irish Secretary, Littleton, decided that O'Connell could only be managed if some concessions were made and in particular the three most offensive clauses in the Act were abandoned. He urged Wellesley to change his mind, which the Lord Lieutenant obligingly did, telling Grey on 21 June that he considered these clauses no longer essential. Encouraged by this Littleton, with Althorp's approval, told O'Connell that he could count on the Act being amended. Grey, however, was not prepared to change his mind with the same alacrity as the Lord Lieutenant and insisted that the clauses must be retained. When this was announced in the House of Commons O'Connell rose in rage to reveal how he had been betrayed. 'There, now the pig's killed', whispered Althorp to John Russell. Littleton resigned, Althorp resigned, with ill-concealed relief Grey resigned as well. The government was in ruins.

It was a curious story from which no one emerged with credit. Brougham, though he probably had not plotted Grey's destruction as many contemporaries believed, had certainly been devious and mischievous. Wellesley had shown himself vacillating, Littleton inept, Althorp imprudent. Melbourne's role is remarkable for its insignificance. He complained that Wellesley had sent his crucial letter to the Prime Minister rather than to him but Wellesley retorted that it was the Home Secretary's fault since he had never bothered to reply to the Lord Lieutenant's earlier letter on the subject: '*You* were the culprit and you made *me* the villain.' The accusation can not be proven but Melbourne never directly denied it and it would have been in character for him to ignore Wellesley's effort to re-open a subject which he felt to be already satisfactorily settled.[4] He considered that the Lord Lieutenant had mishandled things deplorably while Brougham and Littleton had been both foolish and irresponsible. 'Littleton's informing O'Connell of such a secret as the Ld Lieutenant's change of opinion upon so important a subject', he wrote to Palmerston, 'which change of opinion had only been communicated to the Prime Minister in a secret and confidential letter, was an act sufficient to destroy twenty men like Littleton, and could not do otherwise than seriously endanger the government . . .'[5]

The government had disintegrated, that much was clear; but little was clear besides. 'Of course the government is at an end', Grey told Lansdowne, but did his resignation inevitably involve that of his cabinet? The Duchess of Dino, niece and hostess to the French Ambassador, found the courage to put this question to Grey himself. 'In theory, yes; but in fact, no', he replied helpfully.[6] Privately he did not believe that any Whig ministry could survive without him. It was a point of view that most of his colleagues shared, as late as 12 July Melbourne was telling Palmerston that the only hope lay in persuading Grey to return and sponsor the truncated Coercion Bill. But Grey's pride made such a dénouement impossible. If the Whigs could not find another leader acceptable to the King then they were out of office.

The problem was to select their leader. It was by no means certain that Althorp could be coaxed back into the government, there was no possibility that he would profit by the crisis which he had helped create by himself replacing the Prime Minister. If Brougham had ever been in the running his conduct in the last few weeks had ruled him out. Palmerston was unacceptable to the left and even centre of the party. Stanley and Durham had temporarily left the race. Lansdowne stated categorically that he was not interested. If only by default Melbourne was the obvious choice. Yet in fact there was more in his favour than that. His popularity was his strongest card. Some months before at a dinner party a group of politicians were discussing who could succeed Grey. 'Melbourne is the only man to be Prime Minister', pronounced Durham, 'because he is the only one of whom none of us would be jealous.'[7] At the Home Office he had won the respect of his colleagues as a man of strength and resolution; yet somehow had contrived to remain acceptable to, if far from loved by the radicals.

Most important of all he was agreeable to the King. Grey in the past had suggested to William IV that Melbourne might be a possible alternative to Althorp as his successor, so the idea did not come as a shock to that unimaginative monarch. The Queen was abroad at the time, a fortunate chance since she thought Melbourne's sense of humour improper and his principles worse. William himself was shrewd enough to realize that, as Holland put it: 'Melbourne was neither in church nor state a reformer by choice, that on the contrary it was in his nature to lament the necessity of it, but it was in his understanding to perceive it and not to impair the grace of unavoidable boons by too slow, niggardly or ungracious compliance with them.' Though far less intelligent and flexible, the King himself groped uncertainly in the same direction. He recognized a fellow conservative at heart and put his confidence in the man rather than the party label.[8]

The way therefore was relatively clear; but even though it had been set with pitfalls Brougham would have laboured to push the candidate of his choice along it. The Lord Chancellor took Grey's resignation as a personal affront as well as a blow at the security of the realm. 'As all this unintelligible proceeding', he told Melbourne, ' – tho' well enough calculated to spare the trouble and, for anything I know, to save the honour of one or two individuals, leaves the *country* as much unconsidered as if it were Japan or San Domingo – I think it very fitting that someone should cast a single look upon that subject . . .' A Tory government would be disastrous, a coalition impracticable. All that was left was 'reforming our ministry under you. This could be done without any difficulty if you had a House of Commons leader – and on the whole I don't see any great harm in Althorp keeping his place and the three clauses being struck out of the bill.'[9] Brougham convinced himself that it was his intervention with the King that had overcome the loathing of Melbourne House which William had inherited from George III and that he alone had prevented the appointment of a Tory ministry. This characteristic *folie de grandeur* had little foundation of truth; the King's distrust of Brougham was so profound that he was likely to reject a Prime Minister whom the Lord Chancellor recommended on that ground alone. Yet Brougham's energy and ceaseless battering did at least help to overcome the forces of inertia and to propel Melbourne towards a height he might never have reached under his own power.

The King's first summons to Melbourne stressed his title of Home Secretary, a broad hint that the matter of the succession was by no means settled. Nevertheless, Melbourne knew that, barring some unpredictable disaster, he would be the next Prime Minister. It must have been on this occasion that he turned to his private secretary and said that he thought it a damned bore, he was in many minds what he should do. 'Why, damn it', Young is supposed to have replied, 'such a position never was occupied by any Greek or Roman, and, if it only lasts two months, it is well worth while to have been Prime Minister of England.' 'By God that's true', said Melbourne. 'I'll go.'[10] The dialogue is wholly convincing but it would be naive indeed to imagine that these were Melbourne's real thoughts. He could justly say that he had had office thrust upon him; yet, the opportunity once offered, he was quick to accept it. If Prime Ministers can be divided into professionals and amateurs, Melbourne was the professional *par excellence*, and like many good professionals, he knew that an attitude of casual indifference would make his performance more acceptable.

The first obstacle to overcome was the King's conviction, revived throughout his reign, that a coalition of all that was most talented and patriotic was the perfect solution to the nation's ills. Melbourne was politely sceptical but promised to go through the motions of inviting Peel and Wellington to join his government. If ever a question was patently prefixed by the celebrated '*num*', expecting the answer no, it was his letter to the Tory statesmen. It got the expected response; as Wellington said with lapidary finality: 'It must be obvious that a union of public men in your Majesty's councils who appear not to concur in any one principle or policy . . . cannot promote your Majesty's service, cannot conciliate the confidence of the public, or acquire the support of parliament, and must lead to the most disastrous results.'[11]

Grey gloomily concluded that William's response to this rejection would be to instruct Peel or Wellington to form a ministry. Such indeed may have been the King's private wish, but he had too much common sense to suppose that a Tory government could be thrust on the House of Commons in present circumstances. He abandoned all idea of calling on Peel or the Duke and, as one Tory back-bencher put it, 'gave Ld Melbourne full power to reconstruct his radical government'. But full power was one thing Melbourne knew he did not possess. He had inherited Grey's administration by kind permission of its former leader and his preoccupation must be to keep change to a minimum. The first essential was to persuade Althorp to resume his former position. On 14 July he told the House of Lords that he had no intention of trying to form an administration without Althorp's co-operation and Grey's 'sanction and approbation'.[12] He knew well that many members of the House of Commons felt Althorp should be Prime Minister, saw no reason why he should not become so in a few months and would prove restive if anybody else tried to run the party in the Lower House.[13] 'The tortoise on which the world now rests', Melbourne described him, and though the phrase may not seem particularly flattering it still reflects the rock-like solidity which Althorp represented for the Whigs. The price for retaining him proved high. Melbourne would dearly have liked to shed some of those whom he considered especially culpable in the recent troubles, yet Althorp said that he was as much to blame as anyone and that if Littleton, in particular, were asked to go, then in honour he would have to follow.[14] If even the arch-bungler Littleton had to stay, how much less could his father-in-law Wellesley be abandoned?

It was also obvious that Althorp could not return unless the three offending clauses were dropped from the Coercion Bill. 'In justice to my own character', Melbourne had written proudly to Holland on 10 July, 'in justice to Grey, and in justice to Ireland, I could not acquiesce in passing this Coercion Bill in any other form, than that in which it has been introduced.' Character and Ireland could quickly be put out of mind but Grey was harder to forget. A week later in the House of Lords Melbourne withdrew the clauses, 'very unwillingly' and, as he freely admitted, because he would otherwise not be able to form a government. Gleefully Buckingham seized the chance to make mischief. Melbourne might imagine that 'he had buried the noble earl lately at the head of the government, but he was mistaken . . . The noble earl's spirit would arise and . . . would disturb the noble viscount in his slumbers . . .' Though Melbourne was reasonably confident that Grey's ghost would not trouble him so rapidly he must still have felt some apprehension about the reactions of that volatile veteran. In the event all went well. Grey, Brougham reported with relief, 'almost exceeded himself in generous and honourable support of our government and said had he been in our place he would have *taken our course*'. But Melbourne knew that this support would not necessarily last. Ten days later Wellington challenged the omission of the three clauses in the Lords. Melbourne begged Grey to attend and defend the government. Grey refused. 'I think it will be better for me to be absent. You know I am pledged over head and ears in favour of the omitted clauses . . .' It was a portent of what lay ahead.[15]

With Althorp's co-operation secured it was relatively easy to cobble together the rest of Grey's administration.* When Melbourne selected his own brother-in-law, Lord Duncannon, as Home Secretary, there were complaints of nepotism but in fact Duncannon was capable enough and enjoyed the sovereign advantage of getting on well with O'Connell. Hobhouse, a lapsed radical, was offered Woods and Forests with a seat in the cabinet: 'God bless you, and thank you sincerely', said Melbourne after Hobhouse accepted the post, gratitude which might have come better from the in-coming minister. Melbourne was anxious to keep Howick in the government as evidence of Grey's continued support. Grey advised his son to stay in but without much enthusiasm and made no effort to hide his pleasure when Howick at

* See Appendix I for Melbourne's first cabinet.

first decided to resign. 'On Melbourne's own judgment and on his wish to promote the real good of the country I have considerable reliance', wrote Howick loftily in his journal, 'but I know that he has no very nice sense of political rectitude nor very high standard of morality . . .' Howick's own political rectitude was not so strong as to lead him to refuse the post of Secretary for War and all the other important posts remained unchanged.[16]

William IV was not pleased by the appointments of Duncannon and Hobhouse but swallowed them without too much protest. On 13 July he had presented his putative Prime Minister with a daunting memorandum in which he expanded on his political philosophy and concluded that all 'reasonable minds' must agree that there could be no case for 'changes and innovations' within the British Isles. Melbourne consulted with his colleagues. He was far too canny to enter into any general debate on the desirability of further reforms but he could not let the King's extravagant conservatism pass unchallenged. His government, he said, would 'be conducted upon the principle of firmly maintaining the civil and religious establishment of the country, subject to such prudent and well-considered but effectual reformation as may render them more suited to their own purposes, more commensurate with their objects, as may be dictated by sound policy, and as are called for by a majority of the respectable part of the community'. These dulcet phrases provided little to which the King could object while leaving freedom of action to his ministers. In the end it came down to a question of whether the King trusted Melbourne, and whether he had any other recourse if he did not. Since the answer to the second question was probably *no*, the King persuaded himself without too much difficulty that the answer to the first must undoubtedly be *yes*.[17]

Nevertheless the royal confidence was not enough to dispel the doubts of many of Melbourne's contemporaries. How, asked Princess Lieven, 'can the wretched remaining dregs get on without Grey? Melbourne is a man of honour – a gentleman – but why is he so suddenly endowed with energy?' From within the government Lansdowne said that he was 'far from satisfied with the changes'; only the certainty that he would destroy the government had prevented him from retiring to sulk in his palatial tent at Bowood. Palmerston, in many ways Melbourne's stoutest ally, showed marked doubts about the chances of the administration surviving more than a few weeks. Most significant of all was the scepticism and even distaste of Grey. First he did not think the King would accept Melbourne, then he believed it would be impossible to form a government, finally he convinced himself that the new ministry could not stand. His doubts were those of the man who believes himself indispensable, but were not unreasonable. The government cannot exist, mocked *The Times*, 'because cutting a man's head off involves the death of the body. Decapitation is death.'[18]

Brougham, with all the venomous objectivity of a man who considered he would far better fill the role of Prime Minister himself, summed up Melbourne's strengths and weaknesses. 'I felt all the evils of Melbourne's unpopularity; and of all the former known parts of his public life – his ratting from Grey, his support of the Six Acts and Manchester massacre, his opposing reform till it became lucrative, his joining the Tories . . . I also felt the evils of his bad personal habits as a man of business, his inefficiency in debate, his careless temper . . . Then I also knew that Melbourne had many valuable and brilliant qualities, and I hoped that both would become unfolded to the world . . .'[19] Brougham fancied himself as king-maker, the man who had decided that 'Lamb should be at the Treasury'. If these were the words of Melbourne's champion then who can feel surprise if there were doubts among his enemies?

Melbourne's first government was not in any proper sense *his* government at all. So said the King, who declared that Melbourne 'had no position either at home or abroad to be compared with Lord Grey, and that, as to the rest of the government, they were *nobody*'. So said Lansdowne, who 'considered Lord Melbourne's government only as a continuation of Lord Grey's'. So, most important of all, said Melbourne himself when in a debate on foreign affairs he excused himself from stating government policy on the grounds that his 'was not in any respect a new government, it was in fact only the renewal of the old government, with the loss of one member, whose loss all must deplore'. The administration lived in the shadow of its former master; it was generally assumed that it stood only by Grey's favour and would crumble if he withdrew the light of his countenance. Melbourne's prime preoccupation was to woo his late leader, every appointment of importance was submitted to Grey for prior approval, every matter of policy referred to him.[20]

With his ministers imposed upon him and his policies laid down by the previous government, Melbourne was left with the most limited freedom of manoeuvre. No doubt he would gradually have liberated himself from the thrall of his predecessor even if the King had not done the job for him by abruptly bringing his government to an end. For these few months, however, he acted as and was generally considered a caretaker, an inadequate deutero-Grey shuffling nervously in shoes that were patently several sizes too big for him. He made no attempt to impose his own style of government on his alien team and was content to remain in office and let events take their course.

Yet even in this period a new tendency could be detected. O'Connell, who took to himself the credit for destroying Grey's ministry, summed it up shrewdly. 'We are,' he wrote, 'on the way from a half Whig, half Tory government to one half Radical, half Whig, without the slightest admixture of Toryism.' From July 1834 the radicals, who since the passage of the Reform Bill had been often the most vociferous section of the opposition, in general supported the Whig government. Hobhouse and Duncannon, though far from revolutionaries, did represent some reinforcement to the liberal wing of the party. From now on there was to be less effort made to conciliate the Lords; as Althorp wrote contentedly to his father, Lord Spencer, Melbourne agreed with the majority of ministers that measures should be aimed at pleasing the House of Commons and that the views of the Lords should not be heeded 'so much as Lord Grey has hitherto attended to them'.[21]

It would be wrong to make too much of this. There were many among the radicals who felt that the Whig oligarchy offered no prospects for the future. 'You had better give up the idea of vamping up the old rogues', wrote Mrs Grote, the formidable wife of the historian and radical George Grote, to Joseph Parkes. Durham might make a possible leader: 'The people surely are more likely to espouse this than the Melbourne cause.' Nor was Melbourne himself more enthusiastic about a radical alliance. After the collapse of his government in December he wrote in some indignation to Lytton about an article in *The Examiner* which called for union between Whigs and radicals. 'Pray tell Mr Fonblanque from me that a little steady support of a minister, when he is in office, is worth a ream of panegyric after he has retired from it. By steady support I mean support in difficult emergencies and upon unpopular questions. Support upon popular questions is not worth a damn! Those will support themselves.' But little affection though they might have for each other, Whigs and radicals found themselves forced inexorably into alliance as the Whig party grew weaker and the threat of a Tory return to power seemed more urgent. It was diverting for the radicals to make mischief with the ultra-Tories when the Whig majority seemed secure, but even the rabid Mrs Grote must wonder whether the destruction of Melbourne could be sensible if it was to be followed by the return of Peel and Wellington.[22]

Melbourne himself was more disposed to look towards the right for reinforcements. His private wish was that Stanley and his followers should be brought back into the government. In September, at dinner with Palmerston, he had a long and friendly conversation with Graham in which he was remarkably frank about the weaknesses of his ministry and his determination to be master in his own camp. His message seemed to be, reported Graham: 'Let us continue friends. You and those with whom you act differ less from me than many of those with whom I am now associated. I may have to fall back on you; do not be impatient.' Graham was clearly hearing what he wanted to hear but there is no reason to suppose that Melbourne was seriously misinterpreted.[23]

For Melbourne there were two main groups of problems during these first precarious months: those posed by the House of Lords and those caused by his own colleagues. Of the two, the latter proved far the more vexatious. It was bad enough that he should have to put up with the continued presence of Wellesley and Littleton but when as well as this he had to endure the tantrums of Lansdowne and Abercromby, who threatened resignation with the same energy as Wellesley refused it, he began to find the life of a Prime Minister troublesome indeed.

Brougham was worse than any of these. He was convinced that Melbourne was his puppet; that he was himself the real commander; worse still, as Campbell noted, like Bottom in *Midsummer Night's Dream*, he wished to play every part himself. 'The universal feeling seems to be that Brougham is, in fact, first minister', wrote Wharncliffe, and at times Melbourne felt so overborne that he almost subscribed to the report himself. Haydon was sketching Melbourne in his house in South Street when Brougham burst in without even waiting to be announced. 'Lord Melbourne, evidently embarrassed at such a contempt of all decorum and of all that was due to a nobleman in his own house, looked really quite awkward. He was evidently shocked, as if his nose had been pulled.' Haydon left the house speculating whether Melbourne was merely acting as *locum tenens* for the Lord Chancellor. Brougham insisted on going his own way without reference to other ministers, opposing the government line over a tax on newspapers and tabling a bill to reform procedure in the House of Lords without any prior consultation in cabinet. Melbourne gloomily predicted that Brougham would 'end some day by blowing up both us and himself'.[24]

The worst damage done by Brougham was to the government's relations with the King. In the summer of 1834 the Lord Chancellor packed up the great seal and set off for Scotland, drunk with self-esteem and occasionally whisky toddy. The only things more extravagant than his speeches were the letters he wrote to the King reporting his triumphs and extolling all he had done to boost the standing of the monarchy. 'There could not indeed be a more revolting spectacle', pontificated *The Times*, 'than for the highest law officer of the empire to be travelling about like a quack doctor through the provinces, puffing himself and his little nostrums, and committing and degrading the government of which he had the honour to be a member.' Melbourne wrote to warn him that the King was seriously displeased. Brougham's reply was reasonable in tone but betrayed an astonishing inability to sense the feelings either of his Prime Minister or his monarch. William IV concluded not only that the Lord Chancellor was insane but that Melbourne was incapable of controlling the members of his cabinet.[25]

Yet Melbourne's worst troubles were those caused by his predecessor. Grey was jealously on the look-out in case any word was said which implied Melbourne's handling of affairs might be superior to that of the previous administration. He demanded not merely that the record of his government should not be criticized but that it should be the subject of constant praise. Nothing that Melbourne did was ever right: 'He never was contented for a moment with his own government', commented the new minister, 'and cannot therefore reasonably be expected to be so with that of anyone else.' Grey quickly convinced himself that the government was likely to sell out to O'Connell and the radicals. Its chief object ought to be to maintain authority against 'the violence of democratic faction. Will the present administration so conduct itself as to insure this result? I must fairly say, *J'en doute*.' As time wore on his attitude hardened. In October he was said to be '*peu édifié*' by the conduct of the ministry; by November he was bluntly telling Lord John Russell that he would not support the government unless it mended its ways and dealt firmly with the radicals. Grey's prestige was still massive, the government was believed to exist by his authority, his overt opposition could have proved a deadly blow.[26]

Compared with the activities of his friends, Melbourne's political opponents could hardly trouble him. Nevertheless the House of Lords made a good try. In the four months of Melbourne's first government they rejected every bill of importance which was put forward. To the surprise of the bishops Melbourne showed himself an 'able and learned adversary' on matters of theology and ecclesiastical policy but apart from this personal hobby-horse he showed little inclination to join in major battles.[27] Though he denied that the government had pro-crastinated on other, more crucial issues such as the reform of municipal corporations it is certainly true that the somewhat leisurely examination of the facts which he initiated gave no impression of great urgency. His preoccupation seemed to be more the avoidance than the solution of problems; he opposed the idea of civil marriages not on any grounds of principle but from doubts 'what . . . the Methodists and the Wesleyans particularly (would) say to such a proposition'.[28]

He showed himself no more adventurous when the contumacy of the Lords led to a revival of proposals that there should be a creation of new peers sufficient to crush the Tory majority. Brougham took the lead and even Palmerston felt sufficiently disturbed to propose that a limited number should be created. Melbourne at once saw all the difficulties. 'A nugatory step', he described it, 'productive of much evil by the number of persons it will offend and of the claims it will produce . . . Upon the whole I doubt whether making eight or ten might not weaken rather than assist us.'[29]

And yet Melbourne contrived to enjoy his labours with characteristic gusto. Benjamin Haydon, as superb a diarist as he was inadequate a painter, visited Melbourne frequently at this time and left a vivid im-pression of what he saw.[30] Haydon was a resolute champion of official patronage for art, a cause which amused Melbourne but left him wholly unmoved. 'What d'ye want?' he asked Haydon. ' "£2000 a year!" "Ah", said Lord Melbourne, shaking his head and looking with his arch eyes. "God help the minister that meddles with art." "Why, my Lord?" "He will get the whole academy on his back." Then Lord Melbourne turned round, full of fun, and said, "Drawing is no use, it is an obstruction to genius. Correggio could not draw, Reynolds could not draw." '

With the destruction of the House of Commons by fire, Haydon was filled with rosy visions of covering the walls of the new chamber with vast historical paintings. Melbourne was enchanted by the absurdity of the idea. He asked who could paint the pictures. ' "Myself, Hilton and Etty!" "Etty? Why he paints old whores!" ' Haydon asked whether Melbourne intended to give up his house in South Street and move to Downing Street, no doubt planning to place a few historical paintings in the state rooms there. 'He said "No" with hesitation. I fear he fears his lease, but he is a man fond of his leisure, and by keeping his house he is out of the way of bore till business hours.' Finally came direct confrontation. 'Is there any prospect', asked

Haydon, 'of the House of Lords being ornamented by pictures?' ' "No", he thundered out, and began to laugh. "What is the use of painting a room of deliberation?" ' It may have been some consolation to Haydon to know that Melbourne was quite as disinclined to rally the state to the aid of other artists or savants. Haydon found him one day 'lounging over the *Edinburgh Review*. He began instantly, "Why, here are a set of fellows too who want money for scientific purposes, as well as you for painting; they are a set of ragamuffins". He roared with laughter and rubbed his hands.' It was characteristic of him that over the same period as he was thus dashing Haydon's hopes, Melbourne showed great generosity in lending the painter money without any expectation of seeing a penny of it back again.

His informal style was generally approved. He received Haydon in his dressing gown having only just got out of bed and would proudly cite as an example of his eagerness to save time his habit of holding a kind of levée for distinguished visitors while being shaved or dressing. Thomas Moore observed him at dinner with the Hollands, '. . . a scene that would rather have alarmed, I think, a Tory of the full dress school. There was the Chancellor in his black frock coat, black cravat, while upon the sofa stretched the Prime Minister, also in frock and boots, and with his legs cocked upon one of Lady Holland's fine chairs.' Lord Holland sat beside them while Lady Holland chatted to Prince Talleyrand, the French Ambassador, in the far corner, in case he might otherwise pay too much attention to this impromptu cabinet committee. 'Lord Melbourne is in the highest state of spirits,' reported Emily Eden in October, 'which seems to me odd for the Prime Minister of the country.' But then Lord Melbourne was in some ways a very odd Prime Minister.[31]

In October 1834 the Houses of Parliament were destroyed by fire. Melbourne walked round the ruins with Hobhouse, apparently little moved, cracking jokes and laughing heartily when one of the helpers, mindful of Hobhouse's radical past, proudly assured the minister that he had been able to save King Charles's death warrant. But he was still annoyed by the waste and inefficiency. To Grey he described it as 'one of the greatest instances of stupidity upon record. I have no doubt it had been burning the whole day. No private house would have been destroyed in such circumstances.' The capital buzzed with rumours of sabotage and Melbourne thought it worth calling the Chancellor back to London and setting up a committee of the Privy Council to establish who was at fault.[32]

One by-product of this disaster was a peevish dispute with the King. William loathed the pomposity of Buckingham Palace and had already tried to persuade his government that it would make an excellent barracks. Now, with parliament in ruins, he proposed that the palace should be converted for the use of the legislature. 'It would be the finest thing in Europe', he promised. 'Mind, I mean Buckingham Palace as a permanent gift. Mind that!' Melbourne, dismayed at this prospect, hurriedly asked the architect Blore for a report and was relieved to be able to tell the King that the project was impracticable. William was less gratified and angrily retorted that it was the royal prerogative to appoint the place at which parliament should meet. Melbourne was determined not to concede the point but had no wish to offend the King. The House of Commons, he suggested, was most unreasonably suspicious about royal intentions. If William stuck to his point, members might retaliate with irritating proposals for St James's Palace and Marlborough House. Dexterously he argued the perils of transferring parliament to a more roomy site: 'it will be very difficult to avoid providing much larger accommodation for spectators as well as members, and Lord Melbourne need not recall to your Majesty's mind the fatal effects which large galleries filled with the multitude have had upon the deliberations of public assemblies.'[33]

The King gave way but he did not pretend that he was convinced by Melbourne's excuses. Superficially all seemed smooth that autumn between him and his ministers. 'The King is . . . perfectly satisfied and well pleased . . . ' wrote Palmerston complacently. No alternative government was even a possibility. Melbourne would not have been so naive. He told Victoria that, though civil, the King 'wasn't at all open' with him; he suspected that there was little affection and less loyalty concealed beneath that bluff exterior. Still, in August all seemed well. For the first time the King asked his ministers to dinner. Cynically Disraeli noted that this proved he was about to dismiss them since he did not wish it said that, during the whole administration, he had never once invited them to the royal table. In this he was being over subtle. William IV was not the man to lull his adversaries into tranquillity before he slew them and he was genuinely anxious to get on well with his ministers provided he was satisfied that they deserved well by him and by the country. Even Melbourne felt that he was treading on firmer ground. A few days later it crumbled abruptly under his feet.[34]

——◆◆◆——

CHAPTER 13

Peel's Hundred Days

LORD SPENCER died on 10 November 1834. Rarely can the passing of an aged and decrepit peer, long past his years of usefulness, have caused greater consternation. Lord Althorp was now translated to the Lords. It had become accepted that he was indispensable to the party as Leader of the House of Commons. It was Grey who had told the King that the loss of Althorp 'would be, of itself, a sufficient reason for breaking up his administration', and since then events had seemed only to enhance the stature of that most unassuming statesman. Melbourne made no attempt to hide the gravity of what had happened in the letter that he addressed to the King on 12 November. 'Your Majesty will recollect,' he ventured, 'that the government in its present form was mainly founded upon the personal weight and influence possessed by Earl Spencer in the House of Commons . . .' With that influence lost it was obvious that the King would need to reconsider the position. 'Viscount Melbourne will never abandon your Majesty . . . but earnestly entreats that no personal consideration for him may prevent your Majesty from taking any measures or seeking any other advice which your Majesty may think more likely to conduce to . . . the advantage of the country.'[1]

This handsome invitation was not one which the Prime Minister thought likely to be accepted. The government still enjoyed a substantial majority in the Commons and, though some reorganization would be called for, only the most pessimistic believed that it would prove impossible to overcome the difficulty. With Lord Spencer on his deathbed, Melbourne was discussing with Holland the next step to take and agreeing that John Russell was the obvious man to replace Althorp in the Commons. Lady Cowper saw the event as meaning little more than some extra work for her brother. Melbourne, she felt, 'has really been most unfortunate – from the moment of his premiership there has been a succession of deaths and accidents – fire not excluded – an evil spirit has pursued him. Nevertheless', she concluded with a burst of optimism, 'affairs of state are proceeding well, and he enjoys the people's confidence. I believe that there has never been a minister of whom so little ill has been spoken.'[2]

Melbourne was less confident when he went to Brighton for his audience but still did not expect much worse than some fairly severe grumbling. The first setback came when the King objected strongly to the promotion of Lord John Russell. William had always disliked Russell, whom he found arrogant, offensive and too clever for his own good – 'as for that young man', he would snort, 'I don't understand what he means'.[3] But he also identified Russell with the policy which he disliked most of all – the appropriation of the funds of the Irish church for lay purposes. He felt Russell should be dismissed, certainly not made Leader. With dwindling enthusiasm Melbourne put forward the names of Abercromby, Spring Rice, even Hobhouse. The King's distaste seemed to grow with each new name – fortunately, perhaps, since both Abercromby and Spring Rice had said they did not want the job.

The King then switched to the attack. Was it not true that the cabinet was split over the Irish church; that Lansdowne and Spring Rice would resign if Russell had his way? There was indeed enough disunity in the cabinet to make Melbourne sensitive on this point, but he always maintained that it would never have been pursued to the point of resignations. Later history suggested that he was right. The King was unconvinced however. He turned to a denunciation of the government's plans. Was it not true that Irish church revenues were to be despoiled? Melbourne expounded his policy. 'I will never listen to such a proposition', the King is supposed to have replied.[4] In fact he was less explicit, concluding the interview with a few harsh words about the latest antics of Lord Brougham, but his opinion must have been abundantly clear. At dinner that night Lady Brownlow noticed that the King was in high spirits, laughing heartily at the jokes of his bastard son, Lord Adolphus FitzClarence. The Prime Minister, however, seemed 'less talkative and agreeable than usual'.[5]

Next morning the King handed Melbourne his formal letter of dismissal. He restated his arguments of the night before and concluded that it would not 'be acting *fairly* or *honourably*' to maintain his Prime Minister in so precarious a position.[6] Melbourne accepted the news affably and then went to take leave of the King's private secretary, Sir

Herbert Taylor, who, with something less than perfect tact, asked the departing minister to carry with him to London the letter summoning Wellington for an audience. The Duke subsequently claimed that Melbourne's readiness to do this implied approval of the contents; a charge that Melbourne angrily dismissed, saying it would have been 'the most captious, churlish, ungracious conduct' to have refused Taylor such a favour. On his way into London he called on Palmerston. 'Have you brought any news?' asked the Foreign Secretary. 'By God I have', replied Melbourne, producing his letter of dismissal.[7]

On 15 November, before most of the ministers had heard the news, *The Times* carried a paragraph reporting that the ministry was at an end and concluding 'The Queen has done it all'. Edward Ellice was probably responsible for the leak but Brougham was generally blamed. To Melbourne it was yet another charge to lay to the Chancellor's account. 'I only tell you', he wrote accusingly, 'which I hear from all quarters, that the articles in the newspapers . . . are doing all of us, and more particularly you, mischief in public opinion.' In his own crabbed and arthritic hand William IV wrote his ex-Prime Minister a sentimental letter praising the latter's 'honourably disinterested conduct' and assuring him of his continued esteem. Melbourne was offered an earldom and the Garter, honours which were to be pressed on him several times in his career and which were always refused with equal alacrity.[8]

The Whigs were generally outraged. Brougham, though excessive as usual, still reflected the opinion of most of his colleagues when he omitted to hand over the great seal in person but instead sent it back to William IV wrapped up in a bag 'exactly as a fishmonger might have sent a salmon for the King's dinner'. Lady Holland, in uncharacteristically genteel terms, referred to the dismissal as 'most offensive in the mode, so abrupt, so unlike anything gentleman-like'. It was indeed the suddenness and unexpectedness of their downfall which caused most chagrin to the victims. Ministers had to sit up all night burning their papers while Spring Rice was called on to surrender his keys a mere two hours after the Duke of Wellington kissed hands, thus losing touch with all his private letters and not getting them back until his successor was appointed a week later.[9]

But not all the Whigs felt the same. Grey told Holland that the King's decision was 'a very natural one in the circumstances', and that he was 'not at all sure, everything considered, that it is not the best'. To Melbourne he expressed himself little less firmly, obligingly pointing out that, since the government would have stood no chance of surviving, it was better that it should be ended in this way than destroyed in parliament. Melbourne himself showed few signs of discomfiture. 'I hate to be considered ill-used', he told Emily Eden. 'I have always thought complaints of ill-usage contemptible, whether from a seduced, disappointed girl, or a turned-out Prime Minister.'[10] To Grey he set out his thoughts with striking generosity:

> I am not surprised at his decision, nor do I know that I can entirely condemn it. You know the motives which have led him to form it as well as I do. His great distrust of the majority of the members of the present cabinet; his particular dislike to John Russell . . . ; the recent conduct of the Chancellor . . . ; his lively apprehension of the measures which he expected to be proposed to him with respect to the church . . . these considerations . . . have led him to this conclusion; and it is impossible to say . . . that all these feelings are unreasonable and unfounded. It is almost superfluous to state to you that towards me personally the King's conduct has been most fair, honourable and kind . . .[11]

Indeed, it seemed as if Melbourne was the man least disturbed by his own dismissal. He was observed at the theatre the night after his return from Brighton, watching a play called *The Regent* in which there was much talk about turning out a minister. He laughed heartily, rubbed his hands together and seemed delighted by the performance. 'He does not care a button about *office*, whatever he may do about power', commented Greville. Melbourne himself summed up his feelings rather more acutely. 'I hardly ever felt so much relaxed or in better spirits in my life,' he told Holland. 'I know by experience that after a time one gets tired of being out and longs for office, but at first nothing can be more delightful.'[12]

To some people it seemed that Melbourne had put up too little fight; that in fact he had not so much been dismissed as had resigned. Brougham was sufficiently alarmed by the rumours to urge Melbourne to set out his own side of the story without delay.[13] Melbourne appealed to the King who responded handsomely. During the interview between William IV and his Prime Minister, said Herbert Taylor in a letter of 19 November:

> not a word fell from you . . . which could justify the assertion in the *Standard* that you 'had said to the King that the government must necessarily fall to pieces in consequence of its own differences before the meeting of parliament'. The King has ordered me to be thus

explicit that your Lordship may possess a document of which you may make such use as your own good judgment and discretion shall prescribe. No man is more desirous than is his Majesty that justice should be done to your conduct.[14]

Formally, therefore, Melbourne can be cleared of the charge of suicide. There is an important distinction between wilful self-destruction and neglect to take proper measures of self-defence. Yet of the latter charge it is hard not to find Melbourne guilty. The emphasis that he laid on the essential role of Althorp, the explicit suggestion in his letter to the King that a change of government might be desirable, the failure to justify with energy his administration's policies and composition: all these contribute to a picture of a man who was not merely ready to accept dismissal but positively welcomed it.

Indeed, he had good reason for doing so. No one benefited by the events of November 1834 so much as Melbourne. He knew that it was highly unlikely that any Tory government put in by favour of the King would be allowed a long life by the House of Commons. In exchange for a few months out of office he was offered freedom from the ugly heritage of Grey's government. When he came back it would be to an immeasurably strengthened position, master in his own house, free to pick the ministers he wanted and to exclude those he loathed. The King would know that he was there to stay, not the puppet head of a temporary administration. 'This is a new point of departure', he wrote triumphantly to Grey in January. 'I consider myself now free, entirely free, to choose both the principles upon which, and the men with whom, I will consent to engage either in government or in opposition.'[15] It would be an over-simplification to state that Melbourne courted dismissal because he knew such freedom would be his eventual reward, but the knowledge that he had lost little and might gain much must have comforted him on the drive back from Brighton. It is perhaps not surprising that he looked conspicuously cheerful over the next few weeks.

Rejoicing at his liberation Melbourne set off for the north, to Melbourne Hall in Derbyshire, the family home which he had hardly visited in the last ten years. But he could not escape from politics. On 26 November the citizens of Melbourne presented an address to which he replied in the most placid tones, stressing that he felt no personal grievance against the King. 'No man could have acted more like a gentleman and a man of honour than Melbourne did', said the Duke of Wellington, a commendation that, if widely published, would have reinforced the suspicion of liberals and radicals that their leader was taking an unduly pacific line.[16]

Duncannon was particularly incensed at so mealy-mouthed a declaration and urged Melbourne to say something quickly which might restore the morale of the rank and file. Melbourne took the advice; a week later at Derby he made a speech which, while still moderate, included a vigorous rebuttal of suggestions that the government had been on the point of collapse under its own momentum. 'The consequence is', wrote Hobhouse, 'that the conservative journals begin to find that Lord Melbourne is not the very superior, superfine gentleman which they have hitherto represented him to be.' The speech did something to appease Melbourne's critics from his own party, it satisfied everybody and extinguished discussion according to Holland, but a residue of doubt was left, not merely among the radicals but also among Whigs who would not usually have been thought of as extremists.[17]

Meanwhile in London Wellington, awaiting the return of Peel from Rome to take over the government, cheerfully took the oath as Lord Treasurer, Home Secretary, Foreign Secretary and Secretary for War. 'His highness the dictator', Grey angrily styled him. 'Nothing could be more unconstitutional, or more dangerous as a precedent.' Melbourne found it difficult to take the complaint seriously. He knew that the Duke had made no improper use of his extravagant powers, nor had ever thought of doing so, and considered that it would be both silly and hypocritical to make a fuss about the matter in the House of Lords. His view prevailed, but once again he gave little satisfaction to his more firebrand followers.

Peel returned and set to work piecing together a government. One unexpected volunteer was the former Chancellor, Lord Brougham, who offered to serve as Chief Baron of the Exchequer for a mere £1000 a year plus his pension instead of the usual £6000. He was astounded at the uproar which his proposal caused and complained to Melbourne of the 'utterly inconceivable and most ridiculous clamour against me'. He would have been more bitter still if he had read Melbourne's letter to Lansdowne in which his conduct was described as proving 'a greater want of judgment and a grosser ignorance of his own situation', than any of his earlier follies.[18]

For Peel, the crucial question was whether Stanley and his followers could be induced to join. It is a curious tribute both to Stanley's personality and to his evasiveness that on both sides the moderates considered him not merely indispensable to their success but actually likely to rally to their ranks. Holland told Melbourne categorically that 'the accession or the hopes of the accession of Stanley to your party can alone enable you to form a ministry with the slightest prospect of stability . . .'[19] and the words might have been echoed by Peel or half a dozen other leading Tories. Peel made his overture but Stanley was too prudent to commit himself to so rickety an enterprise. He promised his neutrality would be benevolent but would go no further. If he had come in it is conceivable that some of the right-wing Whigs might have been lured away to join him. William Percival pressed Rice to act in this way: 'Where is the Whig party? Is it with Stanley? Is it with Lord Grey? . . . Is Peel a Tory? Does he covet the name? Parties have been so split and resplit that they ought to signify nothing . . .'[20] Deprived of the temptation by Stanley's abstention the right wing Whigs stayed loyal in opposition, a relief to Melbourne who was already having more than enough trouble with his radicals.

Peel made a valiant effort to save his government. He dissolved the strongly Whig House of Commons and went to the country, a step which Melbourne knew to be both proper and inevitable but denounced in rather perfunctory terms as an invitation to disorder. Then, in his great speech at Tamworth, Peel laid the foundations of a new conservatism intended to meet the needs of the nineteenth century. He was aided in the election by the disorder among the opposition. The election committee run by Edward Ellice had a strongly radical-liberal tinge and was viewed with distaste by its own leader. In many constituencies radicals opposed Whigs, indeed considered them the chief enemies. 'The Whigs are cold, selfish, factioning men as a party', stormed Parkes to Durham. 'I can't make *time* and *money* for them.' Grey was gloomily convinced that the radicals would be the only winners, the Whigs the great losers; a view which contrasted sharply with the official party estimate that Melbourne and his followers would have a majority of 130 to 150.[21]

In the event everyone was disappointed. Party labels were often meaningless and any calculation was made more difficult by uncertainty about the likely behaviour of O'Connell's Irish party but it was clear that the Tories had gained, were the largest single party, but could command nothing approaching a majority in the House of Commons. If Whigs and radicals united and O'Connell either supported them or remained neutral then Peel's government could be defeated on any issue.[22] But should it be defeated, if to do so would be to substitute a government based on such a rag-bag of supporters? When he wrote to Grey on 23 January Melbourne was doubtful. '. . . am I justified in declaring a decided opposition to the present government, unless we see a reasonable prospect of being able to form another in case we are successful . . . ?' For the first time he stated his determination to have nothing to do with Brougham, Durham or O'Connell, let alone 'minor difficulties' like Wellesley and Littleton. To Holland he bewailed the number of new members who seemed to be committed to extravagances like the secret ballot and triennial parliaments. How could he contemplate forming a government based on the support of such extremists? In such circumstances, 'is it not a serious question for a man to decide whether he shall . . . engage in a political warfare with the crown, with the decided majority of the House of Peers, with almost the whole of the clergy, and I do not overstate when I add, with three parts at least of the gentlemen of the country?'[23]*

Today such squeamishness appears exaggerated, yet to many people of the time the idea of forcing on the King a government which he had so recently rejected seemed repugnant and perhaps even unconstitutional. Hobhouse, a former minister with some pretensions to radicalism, considered such action unthinkable. The Whigs could not look the King in the face again, nor he them. Littleton thought that the King's honour would prevent him sending for Melbourne; his conclusion was that the former Prime Minister, though 'the shrewdest of men', was not the right person to lead the party back to power and should be shelved in favour of Lord Spencer.[24]

Melbourne's chief fear, shared to the point of paranoia by Lord Grey, was that the radicals would take over the party and he would find himself compelled to buy their support by unwise concessions. He admitted that they were temporarily behaving 'with judgment and moderation', but could this last? How long would the alliance endure? His fears were not baseless but as Duncannon and Russell argued, without the radical alliance there would never be a Whig government at all. Besides, they were quite as averse to Tory rule as any Whig could be, and there was no more reason to expect the Whigs to become the prisoners of the radicals, than the radicals of the Whigs. Duncannon in particular urged a close link between the two groups and was ready to espouse various liberal reforms so as to make the marriage seem more attractive to the smaller party. In fact the true radicals never numbered more than seventy who usually split into several feuding groups, so they did not present as formidable a threat as Melbourne feared. Durham was the only man who could have welded radicals and

* A formula he evidently fancied since he repeated it almost verbatim in a letter to Spencer some two months later.

liberals into a serious challenge to the Whig leadership and he was too impatient and egocentric to take advantage of his opportunities. But he was always a bugbear in the minds of the traditionalists. Palmerston urged Melbourne to come back to London: 'You ought to be looking after your stray sheep. That wolf Durham is prowling about the fold.'[25]

Co-operation with O'Connell's Irishmen presented still more perplexing problems. John Russell's declaration that he would support lay appropriation of Irish church funds had won the hearts of the Irish members. In an engagingly honest letter to Russell, Melbourne implied that he would underwrite the policy. 'You are quite right to be explicit about the Irish church', he wrote on 12 February. 'You know that in general nobody is so much for shuffling over differences of opinion and getting over matters . . . as I am. I was always exhorting the different sections of Grey's government to this course, which was very often followed. But this is really an important moment, and a fresh start, and it is nonsense now not to understand one another at least upon matters so important and so urgent.'[26] But to accept the inevitability of this feature of Whig policy was one thing; to court the embraces of O'Connell was another, more distasteful. Left to himself Melbourne might never have brought himself to do so. But in these months of opposition, he rarely *was* left to himself. He bore the appearance of a man carried along on the flood-tide of his subordinates' determination, impelled not altogether against his will perhaps but certainly with limited enthusiasm.

Russell and Duncannon were convinced that the Irish votes were needed, and that O'Connell was ready to provide them. 'I think I may promise that the Irish members of the popular party will avoid all topics on which they may differ with you . . .', O'Connell told Russell. 'We will be steady allies without any mutiny in your camp.'[27] The implications of this attitude and of Melbourne's acceptance of the Irish church as the critical battlefield between Whig and Tory, were to be far reaching. Grey, of course, believed it a crucial error; closing the door to any reconciliation with Stanley and thus dooming the government to be dragged behind the chariot wheels of its radical and Irish allies.[28] It is equally legitimate to regard it as a clever coup by which the Irish were tricked into supporting a party which was certainly unable and probably unwilling to give them what they wanted. In either case, it made inevitable a future conflict with the House of Lords and set the pattern for Whig politics over the next six or seven years.[29]

On 18 February Whigs, radicals and Irish repealers from the House of Commons met at Lichfield House to discuss a common policy. The invitation to O'Connell seems to have been sent by mistake, though no doubt it was one of those mistakes which were tacitly endorsed in advance by someone in high places. Melbourne disliked the whole idea and told Russell that it would lead to disunity and the encouragement of a strong radical block.[30] Russell professed to share these doubts but pointed out that the meeting would be a lot more mischievous unless a few people like him went along to control it. In fact those present concerned themselves mainly with tactics, no pledges were given and the celebrated 'Lichfield House Compact' can not be said to have existed in any formal sense. Nevertheless, at the end of the day, radicals and repealers stood broadly committed to help the Whigs in the coming parliamentary struggle and the Whigs had given precious little in return. Even the sceptical Melbourne had to admit that things might have turned out worse.

It remained to decide how to use this blank cheque. The concept that the function of an opposition was to oppose, though not totally a novelty, was still far from taken for granted. To Melbourne the idea that he should attack the King's government merely because he disapproved of its composition and without reference to its actions, was shocking if not wholly unacceptable. He conceded that he must move an amendment to the address on Irish appropriation, but he did so with little zest and felt that, having done so, his bolt was shot. At a meeting at John Russell's after the debate he urged that there should be a period of inactivity during which Peel could be given a chance to define his position. Rather grudgingly the others agreed, but so sure was Russell that the Tory government would swiftly be destroyed that he set up what was in effect a 'shadow cabinet' which met every Sunday and followed the course of events with vigilant disapproval.[31]

In fact the Whigs were already involved in what was to be the first and in some ways the most ferocious battle of Peel's hundred days. Manners-Sutton had been a competent and reasonably impartial Speaker of the House of Commons. He had, however, played a prominent part in the constitutional *coup d'état* of November and the more activist Whigs were determined to frustrate his re-election as Speaker; both as an act of vengeance and to prove at once the frailty of Peel's administration. 'How the devil does John Russell make out the question of the Speakership to be one of principle?' asked Grey indignantly. 'Nobody can be more thoroughly of opinion than I am that the attempt is most inexpedient.' Melbourne was less decided. A month before he had agreed with Russell that Sutton's conduct had made him unfit for the chair, and now he defended the decision to oppose him. But typically, he hedged his views. 'It might, however, as you say, have been more prudent to have acquiesced', he admitted to Grey, 'but I was informed on all sides that this was a resolution which it was impossible to adopt.' If the attempt failed, he suggested hopefully, 'it will check the eager and induce prudence and moderation . . .' In other words, he supported the opposition to Sutton because his followers insisted and he thought that, with luck, it would anyway fail.[32]

At least everyone agreed that the Whigs must put forward their strongest candidate. Melbourne's personal choice would have been the conservative, Rice. He felt less enthusiastic about the other front runner, Abercromby, a dour, selfish man who had come to prominence by keeping the accounts of the Duke of Devonshire. His prejudice was reinforced by the fact that Rice passionately coveted the Speakership while Abercromby viewed the prospect with distaste. Unfortunately Rice was disliked by the Irish and radicals while Abercromby's selection would ensure their support. Melbourne, therefore, found himself having to plead with a man he disliked to accept the candidature while enraging his own favourite by refusing him the chance of the job.[33]

The critical vote came on 18 February. Thomas Moore was dining at Brooks's that night and observed: 'Immense anxiety, and reports of the progress of the debate coming in from time to time . . . a young fellow . . . came running breathless into the room and cried out, "Won it by ten! Won it by ten!" He was soon encircled, and questioned, and pulled about by one and another, while the whole party hurrahed and shook hands, and were as uproarious as a party of schoolboys.' Elation at Brooks's was matched by gloom and indignation among the Tories. Peel had claimed a fortnight before that he would consider defeat on the Speakership 'a mere fleabite', but he would have been naive indeed if he had not privately believed this flea could kill. The Duke of Wellington was more prescient when he ordered his private secretary to get ready to quit the Foreign Office. 'The vile Whigs have won by a majority of ten . . .' stormed Lady Wharncliffe. 'It is the most disgraceful act ever committed by any party. I am *boiling over with indignation.*'[34]

Melbourne's pleasure was qualified. Now there would be no checking the hot-heads of his party. To him the most unpleasant feature was the Tory *canard* that Abercromby's selection had been dictated by O'Connell. Of course it was not true but 'it was impossible to feel quite certain what communications may have taken place between some of our friends and O'Connell. They worship him as the savages do the evil demon. They consider his power too great to be resisted and that all necessary must be done to deprecate his wrath. I am of the contrary opinion.'[35]

At least O'Connell had no hand in delivering the next blow at Peel's administration. Wellington had unwisely selected a grotesque reactionary, Lord Londonderry, to go as Ambassador to Russia. Melbourne was against opposing the choice: 'he hated these personal questions, . . .' he said, and added cautiously, 'every government was obliged to make some very bad appointments which it would be very inconvenient to establish the practice of discussing'.[36] His party, however, was beyond such cool reasoning. The appointment was condemned in the House of Commons and even Stanley voted with the opposition. Londonderry renounced his embassy.

It was now only a question of when Peel would surrender, or rather when the King would allow him to do so. As defeat followed defeat in the House of Commons William IV brought himself to accept the humiliation of calling back the Whigs. Early in April 1835, he finally yielded.

He turned, however, not to Lord Melbourne, but to Grey. On 11 April he instructed his last Prime Minister but one to approach his last Prime Minister but two, so as to establish whether the latter would be ready to form a government. Melbourne accepted this curious mission with good grace and on the same day joined with Lansdowne, Holland, Palmerston and Rice in sending Grey a plea that he should return to them, if not as Prime Minister then at least as Foreign Secretary. If he found it humiliating thus to subscribe to such implicit doubts in his capacity to lead the government he showed no signs of it. No doubt he considered the approach a tiresome formality that must be gone through before his own claims would become paramount. That it was only a formality seemed certain, and sure enough Grey's reply was an unequivocal refusal: 'I should sink under a burden which I have not strength to maintain.' Instead Grey recommended the King to send for Melbourne and Lansdowne, offering to attend the meeting himself and help ease what might otherwise prove a somewhat sticky interview. The King had no recourse but to accept the advice. The details still had to be settled but in effect Melbourne was once more Prime Minister.[37]

———— ◆◆ ————

CHAPTER 14

Master in His Own House

OVER THE LAST three months Melbourne had given an impression of striking irresolution, even feebleness. Not merely had he left it to others to make the running, he had appeared hardly aware that a race was on. Partly he shrank from the role of intemperate opposition, partly he was determined that when power was offered him again he should be able to say that he had never sought it. He had lived long enough in the shadow of Lord Grey; if he was to take office again it would be on his own terms and as head of his own ministry. From 11 April 1835 he behaved with new resolution and authority. The doubting, *fainéant* figure of opposition was transformed into a man who knew what he wanted and was determined to get it. The change was, of course, more apparent than real, more one of presentation than of substance, but it was little less remarkable for that. Melbourne for the first time felt himself truly in command. It was a sensation which he relished and an opportunity which he did not intend to waste.

The first obstacle to tackle was the King. Politely but firmly Melbourne laid down his conditions. Under Lord Grey officers of the royal household had spoken and voted against the government. In future this would not be tolerated. If the King supported his ministers then his flunkeys must do the same, anything else would be a denial of royal confidence. Furthermore, the King must demonstrate his confidence by an immediate creation of peers. To both these points William assented, only stressing that he would never agree to a creation of peers on the scale suggested in 1832. Since Melbourne had never contemplated such a proposal, this issue did not seem to him one on which he need do battle.

Next came the 'principle of exclusion'. The King had announced that he reserved the right to veto certain names if they were put forward. To this Melbourne could not agree, 'he can neither admire nor acquiesce in any general or particular exclusions and . . . must reserve to himself the power of recommending for employment any one of your Majesty's subjects who is qualified by law to serve your Majesty'. But Melbourne was always one to temper principle with pragmatism. He knew that the King's most violent objections were to the Irishmen, O'Connell, and Sheil and to the radical, Hume. Since he had no intention of including any of the trio in his government he contrived to pass this information through Lord Grey to the royal ears. The 'principle of exclusion' slipped quietly from the agenda.

The Irish church was less easily disposed of. The King had got it into his head that the Whig proposal to appropriate surplus church revenues for lay purposes would in some way violate his coronation oath. Melbourne stated flatly that he was not prepared to form any government unless the King would undertake not to oppose this measure. William now came up with the curious suggestion that he should refer the question to a panel of the fifteen judges. 'Highly inexpedient', retorted Melbourne, especially as it was 'a question, not of law but of conscience.' Against his better judgement he eventually conceded that the King might bare his heart to the outgoing Chancellor, Lord Lyndhurst. He had little cause for concern. Lyndhurst was quick to scent possible embarrassment. He pleaded total ignorance of the Bill and consequently of the royal dilemma. 'The Lord Chancellor positively declines giving any opinion *whatsoever* to the King', reported William indignantly. Driven from his last line of defence he now abruptly concluded that the issue was not, after all, as severe a strain on his conscience as he had previously imagined. With his capitulation Melbourne had gained all he needed.[1]

There remained the formation of a government. For Melbourne, who was left out was even more important than who stayed in. He had told Grey that he would never serve again with Durham or Littleton, Wellesley or Brougham. Grey had entered a plea for the retention of Brougham and John Russell had taken the same line: 'his merits are great and conspicuous, his demerits vexatious but not vital'.[2] Melbourne listened politely to their views, offered no contradiction and bided his time. Now the time had come.

Durham presented little problem. He had not had a seat in Melbourne's last cabinet, was generally held to be more radical than Whig, and would have been surprised if offered a place. He would need conciliating but not at the price of enduring his termagant presence at the cabinet table. Littleton was small fry, who had now lost the protection which he had enjoyed at the time of his great gaffe the previous year. Incredibly, he expected to be offered a seat in the cabinet, a belief which demonstrated as well as anything his lack of political intelligence. Melbourne left him for nearly a week in tormented expectation, then summoned him to South Street. Littleton found him 'lying on his sofa on his back, with four candles on a table before him, saying he was confoundedly tired'. Melbourne blandly remarked that, given Littleton's standing in the country, he assumed his ultimate goal must be a peerage. Littleton admitted that this was so, whereupon Melbourne announced: 'Well, that being the case, it will afford me great pleasure to submit your name to the King'. Littleton was disconcerted but on the whole gratified, accepting the offer as a proper tribute to his services.[3]

It would have taken the offer of a dukedom similarly to satisfy Littleton's father-in-law, the Marquis Wellesley. Wellesley considered that he should be Prime Minister and took it for granted that he would be sent back as Lord Lieutenant to Ireland. He was disconcerted when he found himself fobbed off with an office in the royal household; after what happened the year before, Melbourne explained, he did not think the Irish government could be reconstituted without a complete shuffle of the senior personnel. Wellesley replied in polite enough terms, however, accepting the post of Lord Chamberlain – not, as he later insisted, because he wanted the job but so as to spare the government the embarrassment of losing a minister of his eminence. Then it was announced that Mulgrave, a lightweight of liberal tendencies, was to go to Dublin in his stead. Brougham hastened to make mischief, writing to Wellesley with relish of 'the *impossible* transmutation of our *theatrical* and excellent friend Mulgrave into a Viceroy, and yourself into a superintendent of stage plays. It is a feat of our harlequin friend Melbourne's which diverts and surprises rather than pleases me.'[4] But it did not take any extra heat from Brougham to set the pot of Wellesley's indignation bubbling. On the day Mulgrave's appointment was announced he erupted to his son-in-law:

Am I a man to be treated with disrespect? I who have spent a long life in the service of the country, who for my services have received high rank – I, who have added millions to the empire? Am I to be treated with contumely or indifference by this puppy, this damned scoundrel? Sir, the offence can only be expiated by blood! I'll send instantly for my respected and gallant friend, Lord Howden. He shall arrange a meeting between us tomorrow!

Littleton talked him out of his blackest fury but within a month Wellesley had resigned. Melbourne did not meet him face to face to discuss their differences until early in 1836. Wellesley left a somewhat one-sided account of the interview in which he claimed to have reduced Melbourne to 'much faltering and confusion' and a virtual admission of guilt. He asked the Prime Minister why he had not been restored as Lord Lieutenant. Melbourne 'immediately answered (in a very rough and vulgar manner, and in such language as I believe never was applied before by a person of his station to a person of mine), "You wrote an imprudent letter to Lord Grey, the moment I read that letter I determined that, on the reconstruction of the government of Ireland, there must be a *general sweep*".' Wellesley taxed Melbourne with barbarous cruelty, injustice and above all a betrayal of honour in that he had for so long planned to destroy his innocent colleague without breathing a word of his intention. 'Did you ever know such a resolution to be communicated to the object of it?' asked Melbourne, a query so characteristically frank that one feels this part of the conversation at least has been accurately recorded. The two men were never fully reconciled and Wellesley's summing up represented the nearest he could bring himself to charity. Melbourne's conduct, he concluded, arose 'more from habitual indolence, carelessness, imbecility and utter ineptitude for serious business, than from positive depravity'.[5]

Last and mightiest victim was to be Lord Brougham. Melbourne was well aware what a dangerous enemy the former Chancellor could prove but his experience over the last twelve months had satisfied him that Brougham was still more lethal as a colleague. 'The more I think of it', he told Russell, 'the more I am convinced that, whatever may happen with respect to Brougham, it can never be safe to place him, as you suggest, in an important executive or administrative office. Recollect as Chancellor he could do nothing. He could talk, God knows, and meddle and write, but he could do no act. If he were Secretary of State you would find things done without your privity, which you could neither amend nor recall, nor condemn him for having done.'[6] Even Russell, almost Brougham's last champion within the Whig leadership, had to accept that life would be more peaceful without him.

It was one thing to decide to dispense with Brougham, another and harder one to break the news to him. The operation fell into two parts.

First, in February 1835, Brougham returned from abroad, indignant that the former government had not done more to defend him from attacks in the newspapers and demanding an explanation. Melbourne obliged in two of the most brutal letters that can ever have been written by an ex-Prime Minister to a former colleague. Anyone who conceives him as a pliable and easy-going gentleman, too decent and too detached to indulge in the coarser kinds of political in-fighting, should study them with care. Melbourne, indeed, valued his tranquillity, yet in defence of it he could fight with a ruthlessness that may not command admiration but certainly inspires awe.

It is a very disagreeable task [wrote Melbourne] to have to say to a statesman that his character is injured in the public estimation; it is still more unpleasant to have to add that you consider this his own fault, and it is idle to expect to be able to convince almost any man, and more particularly a man of very superior abilities and of un-bounded confidence in those abilities, that this is the truth. I must however state plainly that your conduct was one of the principal causes of the dismissal of the late ministry, and that it forms the most popular justification of that step.

Brougham pressed for particulars and was answered by a further broadside. As Chancellor, he was told, he 'had committed errors and imprudences of such a magnitude as greatly to impair the vast and almost unparalleled powers which you possess of rendering service'. His antics in Scotland had given 'very great and general offence'. In the government 'you domineered too much, you interfered too much with other departments, you encroached upon the province of the Prime Minister, you worked, as I believe, with the press in a manner unbecoming the dignity of your station, and you formed political views of your own and pursued them by means which were unfair towards your colleagues'. His behaviour in connection with the downfall of Lord Grey was indefensible. 'Few things have given me more concern than this correspondence', concluded Melbourne, 'and I am anxious to close it. I should do so with something more like satisfaction if I could only hope that it would not leave any bitterness or acrimony behind it.'[7]

This must have seemed a faint hope, but Brougham in fact accepted his stunning rebuke with remarkable good humour and even humility. 'As to *domineering*, it is probably true', he wrote wistfully to Spencer. 'I am of a hasty and violent, at least vehement nature, and not bred in courts or offices, and never was a subaltern . . . However, I meant no harm.' Incredibly, he continued to take it for granted that, when the next Whig government was formed, he would again be Lord Chancellor. On 13 April Melbourne went round in person to Brougham's house in Berkeley Square to break the news of his exclusion. It was a long and painful interview. 'Am I mad?' shouted Brougham repeatedly. 'Am I mad, do you think?' Melbourne soothed him down and emphasized that it was above all the King who was responsible for Brougham's disgrace – an argument of doubtful honesty since William had told Grey that he was ready to accept Brougham though he would think the worse of Melbourne for including him. He would not be replaced but instead the office of Chancellor would be put into commission. Brougham was left with the impression that his exile was only temporary; as soon as William IV's indignation had died down he would be reinstated. If Melbourne even hinted that this was so then he was being less than scrupulous since he knew that under no circumstances would he allow Brougham into his ministry again. Whether he did deliberately foster this impression or whether Brougham merely heard what he wanted to hear will never be known, but it seems clear that Melbourne allowed his anxiety to avoid an open clash to lead him into something near duplicity. Even so the interview ended tempestuously; according to Brougham Melbourne's last words were: 'God damn you, I tell you I can't give you the great seal, and there's an end of it!'[8]

'Neutrality – armed or unarmed – is not in my way', was Brougham's menacing message a few days after the interview, but he ended on a note of personal friendship. 'For you I have an affection and true attachment which will survive even the grave. Nothing you can do, however weak – or however strong – can alter that.' He was almost certainly sincere. Brougham was genuinely fond of Melbourne, as Melbourne was of Brougham, and even when their political feud was at its height they found attraction in each other's company. To Brougham, Melbourne wrote a friendly letter urging him not to believe the various malicious rumours which were circulating, telling that one person or another had been responsible for his downfall. It had always been Brougham's weakness to believe that he was surrounded by hidden enemies. 'Depend upon it, you are doing the same now. If anyone has wronged you, it is I who have done it and no one else'.[9]

In the short term at least Melbourne seemed to have convinced Brougham that the government deserved his support. Less than a week after their meeting in Berkeley Square, Alvanley rose in the House of Lords to ask the Prime Minister a searching question about the price he had paid for O'Connell's support. Brougham leapt up and tried to answer the question himself. 'I did not address the question to the noble and learned Lord', protested Alvanley. 'No, and it is precisely for that very reason that I rise to answer it', replied Brougham. Uproar followed and Melbourne eventually dealt with the question himself. It was said that Brougham, having ceased to be Lord Chancellor, now aspired to the still loftier duties of Lord Protector. The job was not one which he was to fill for long.[10]

So much for the hatchet work. It remained to form a government. There were plenty of doubters, among his friends as well as the opposition, who believed the task would be beyond his powers. Rice was pondering his chances of a good job under Stanley or even Peel. Howick said no Whig government could stand without Lord Grey in it. Lord Grey concurred. Melbourne himself was hesitant and evidently wrote to Palmerston suggesting he was disinclined to carry on. 'I am not prepared', replied Palmerston robustly, 'to acquiesce in your position, that in the present state of affairs, . . . it would be better to give up the attempt, rather than undertake a task, encompassed by difficulties *apparently* insurmountable. Those who turn out one government are surely bound to set up another in its place.' Melbourne did not take much persuading, indeed it seems doubtful if he was ever quite so reluctant as Palmerston imagined. He defined his position to Ellice in a letter written at almost exactly the same time. Never again, he said, would he place himself at the head of a government 'made up in a scrambling manner or of which the constitution was evidently unstable or transient'.[11] Having successfully eliminated the main elements of instability, he now proceeded at a dignified, unscrambling pace to choose his ministers.*

Russell must lead in the Commons and be Home Secretary, that was the first requirement. Lansdowne and Holland were found roles of empty dignity as President of the Council and Chancellor of the Duchy of Lancaster. Duncannon came in as Privy Seal to keep the radicals in order. Rice grumblingly accepted the Exchequer, Charles Poulett Thomson continued his reign at the Board of Trade. Since Grey would not serve it was essential that Howick should stand witness to the great man's continued support. He too took up his old post as Secretary of War; thus, to the disgust of his wife, 'embarking with this most crazy government, many of whose members differ from him most widely in their principles and want of principles'.[12] Up to the last

* See Appendix II for Melbourne's second Cabinet.

moment Rice and Lansdowne doubted whether it would be proper for them to join a ministry so tainted by radical influence. 'Oh for some masculine mind to save us from the councils of these small-beer statesmen!' wrote Ellice angrily.[13]

Palmerston had no such scruples but he was anathema to the left wing of the party and Grey too pleaded urgently that he should not be returned to the Foreign Office. He was, said Grey, personally offensive to all the foreign ministers of Europe and our foreign policy could only suffer by his presence. Reluctantly Melbourne summoned Palmerston and suggested that he might feel more at home in the Colonial Office. There were strong objections within the government to his serving again as foreign minister – 'That is to say by a knot of intriguers headed by Ed^d Ellice' – Palmerston added in an angry marginal comment on the letter from Grey which Melbourne had somewhat unwisely passed on to the subject of its strictures. Either he got the Foreign Office, he stated bluntly, or he stayed outside the government; 'I consider myself to have conducted our foreign relations with great success, during four years of excessive labour'.[14]

Melbourne was in considerable doubt. Even at home he was torn in two directions, with his sister Emily pleading her lover's cause and Fred Lamb urging his exclusion. Personally, Melbourne would have liked to retain him but he shrank from offending Grey and many of his future colleagues. In the event it seems that the Austrian and Prussian Ambassadors may have saved the day for Palmerston by forming up to warn Melbourne that relations between their countries would suffer unless a change were made. As Metternich realized as soon as he heard of his Ambassador's action, this could only drive any self-respecting Prime Minister into doing the opposite of what he was asked. Sure enough, Palmerston's appointment to the Foreign Office was quickly confirmed.[15]

The man whose help Melbourne most wanted remained obstinately unavailable. Melbourne pleaded with Spencer to return to the public service: 'we have fearful odds to bear up against', he announced. '. . . if this attempt on the part of the Whig and Liberal party should fail, that party will most probably sink into insignificance.' But having once escaped the trammels of office, Spencer was not to be recaptured. He pleaded that his first duty must be to his family and the estate which had been sadly neglected over the last decade. 'I have every reason to be assured', he added obligingly, 'that an administration of which you are the head will be one of whose measures I shall approve and in whose principles I shall have entire confidence.' This was cold comfort but with it Melbourne had to rest content.[16]

He was even more concerned to keep O'Connell out than to get Spencer in, but fortunately this task proved easier. The importance of the Irish vote was such that O'Connell could have made it almost impossible to form a stable government. Many people took it for granted that he would do so unless offered a congenial post.[17] They reckoned without his common sense. He knew that the Irish had more to hope for from Whigs than Tories and that for him to force his way into office would be to produce a disastrous conflict with the King and the old guard of the party. He sacrificed his immediate ambitions in the interest of his country. This simple explanation was not good enough for Greville. O'Connell had been suborned by 'underhand management or persuasion', it was all a nefarious juggle. The *Morning Post* was even able to tell its readers the exact extent of the bribe which had been paid. O'Connell was to nominate the Irish law officers and to have the right of veto on the Lord Lieutenant, while the qualification for the vote in Ireland was to be lowered. Melbourne found himself forced to deny the stories in the House of Lords: no terms had been negotiated with O'Connell, no terms would be negotiated with O'Connell and the Prime Minister had not the remotest idea about O'Connell's intentions in the House of Commons.[18]

Literally there is no doubt that he was speaking the truth. No formal deal was struck with O'Connell; either by Melbourne or by one of his juniors. Equally Melbourne was determined to set up a government in Dublin which could work with the repealers and with luck convert them to a more amenable state of mind. There were plenty of well-wishers delighted to act as go-betweens and to ensure discreetly that the Prime Minister's proposals were likely to prove acceptable to his uncomfortable allies. It can have been no surprise to O'Connell when Mulgrave was appointed Lord Lieutenant, nor was Morpeth, gentle, kindly and liberal, a Chief Secretary whose appointment was likely to offend even the most rampant of Irish nationalists. The deciding moment came when the pro-Catholic Louis Perrin was named as Attorney General. In an allegedly 'spontaneous' gesture, O'Connell and his followers trooped across the floor of the House of Commons to sit with ministers.

A 'meagre' triumph, Greville described the formation of the government; a frail body likely to fall to bits in the first storm that struck it. Melbourne felt he had reason for modest satisfaction. He had selected a ministry in which only Glenelg at the Colonies was demonstrably inadequate. He had eliminated most of the trouble-makers who had made Grey's cabinets a cacophanous inferno. He had struck a balance between left and right, so that to the King his mixture seemed dangerously flavoured with revolution while to Hobhouse it was noticeably less liberal than its predecessor. With the reasonable certainty of radical and Irish support he was assured a comfortable majority in the House of Commons, while he was no weaker than his predecessor in the House of Lords. The King was hostile, but the King had burnt his fingers badly and was unlikely to risk doing so again for some time at least. The political barometer was hardly set fair, but there was reason to hope for clement weather.[19]

Few spectacles are sadder than that of a great reforming ministry which has run out of steam. In fact the Whig administration of 1835 still had some life left in it. In the reform of municipal corporations, in particular, it was to introduce legislation little if at all less important than the Great Reform Bill itself. Yet this was a legacy from its predecessors, the fruit of a commission set up three years before. Few striking new initiatives could be expected from the present leadership; nor indeed would they have been acceptable to parliament, or that part of the people who enjoyed the right to vote. It was no hidebound conservative but John Stuart Mill who wrote of 'the ten years of inevitable reaction' after the passage of the Reform Bill and the introduction of 'the few legislative improvements which the public really cared for'.[20] The Whigs were in a dilemma. As the Tory opposition grew in strength and confidence, so the government was under pressure to react by adopting more popular courses. Yet the narrow electoral base meant that the popularity in the country which they might win by such measures could not be translated into parliamentary support. All that a Whig government could do if it were to survive was to cast occasional sops to its left wing while in fact devoting its real energies to the delicate political art of standing still.

For such a role Melbourne was admirably qualified. The policy favoured by most Tories was far more to his taste than the views of three-quarters of his own supporters. He considered reform a measure to be resorted to only when it was demonstrably true that an institution would otherwise invite its own destruction. If the Whigs were to survive, however, they had to preserve the fiction that they were the natural leaders of liberal opinion. Melbourne was prepared to do his bit to achieve this end, but about its fundamental unreality he had no illusions. In his attitude he corresponded far more closely to the great majority of his predecessors than had Lord Grey. The concept that each government would arrive in office brandishing an imposing array of new laws which it proposed to implement evolved slowly over the nineteenth century. The eighteenth century idea of government was rather that it should concern itself only with defence, foreign policy and the administration of the country. New laws were only needed to meet specific crises. In subscribing to this view Melbourne spoke for the majority of political leaders, Whig or Tory. Russell and Peel were the men of the future: Melbourne, Holland, Lansdowne, Palmerston, for the Whigs; Wellington, Aberdeen, Lyndhurst for the Tories; reflected the traditional wisdom of the past.

In theory Grey had been a proponent of government by departments. If only to emphasize how remote he was from the autocratic Wellington he had made much play with his resolution to appoint the best ministers and then allow them to get on with their task. The cabinet was to be a true council, the Prime Minister no more than *primus inter pares*. Unfortunately his unyielding disposition, strong convictions and tendency to treat all opposition as a personal affront, meant that his principles were more extolled than applied: rows in cabinet were frequent but only those ministers who relished hurricanes habitually maintained their views when they knew that the Prime Minister differed from them. Melbourne practised what Grey preached. It was nearly thirty years since he had discussed the selection of a minister and concluded, 'when appointed the utmost confidence should be reposed in him, and the more he acts upon his single opinion with respect to the general plan, the more likely, I believe, will his enterprise be to succeed.'[21] Now he had a chance to put his ideas into effect. His lack of strong convictions and readiness to take an approving interest in his critics ensured that he would treat the cabinet as a committee with himself as its chairman. His function as he saw it was not to impose his view, not even necessarily to *have* a view, but to establish a consensus. When an issue divided his ministers he rarely sought to make up his mind on the rights or wrongs involved but instead asked himself which course was supported by the more numerous, powerful and vociferous partisans. This once decided, his course was to urge concessions on the stronger and surrender on the weaker. To come to an agreed conclusion was the first pre-occupation, the nature of the conclusion a secondary consideration.

Within this somewhat restricted interpretation of his role Melbourne was to prove remarkably successful. He used to manage meetings, said Hatherton (as Littleton had now become), with 'remarkable sagacity and prudence, and that extraordinary mixture of good humour with quick sensibility which was said to be one of his peculiar characteristics'. Howick complained of the time wasted, the 'indolence and inefficiency', the endless discussions of detail before any principle was established, but this was all part of Melbourne's technique. He did not like time-wasting any more than Howick did, but if allowing a discussion to drag on, letting the principle at stake sink into a sea of detail, made it easier to avoid confrontations and to paper over differences, then the extra hours would be well spent. As the discussion grew more heated so he would grow more detached and urbane. 'Nothing induces a man to keep his own temper,' he once remarked, 'so much as the observation that others either have lost or are likely to lose theirs.'[22]

To his colleagues his conduct often seemed like weakness. Foreign affairs provide a typical example. Ponsonby, British Ambassador in Constantinople, was behaving with a recklessness that seemed likely to lead to war with Russia. Howick pleaded that he be checked and the cabinet generally agreed with him, but, as Howick noted in his diary: '. . . as Palmerston dissented I fear that this will not be of much use unless Ld Melbourne can be prevailed upon firmly to exercise his authority, and *insist* upon the adoption of a quite different tone'. Melbourne, of course, could not, failing even to express an opinion on the subject. But this was not so much because he was afraid to tackle Palmerston as because he believed that, on the whole, Palmerston was a good Foreign Secretary and he did not intend to interfere with him unless forced to do so. Nor did he feel himself competent to meddle except on the broadest issues. In this humility he seems to have been well justified. Both Esterhazy and Hummelauer complained to Metternich about the futility of discussing foreign affairs with the Prime Minister, since he never knew what was going on.[23]

Yet Melbourne could be tough. To him loyalty and cohesion were paramount. In an age when cabinet unity was still far from taken for granted, he treated it as an essential element of successful government. At his first cabinet meeting Howick was intrigued and slightly surprised to note that 'Lord Melbourne gave Sir J. Hobhouse an amazing snub with a stern look', in relation to some speech which Hobhouse had made in defiance of the party line. Loyalty to party should be absolute and preclude criticism of particular aspects of its policy. He had no time for men of discriminating conscience who could swallow the Whig camel and then strain at some gnat like the secret ballot or triennial parliaments. 'You must take a ministry attitude and support it', he told Ellice. 'You must not take objection to particular departments.' Judge the whole. 'If more of the departments in your opinion are bad than good, the ministry is a bad one', if the other way round, then it was good and should be supported. 'These are *truisms* (what by the way does truism mean?), but many people act as if they were not true, or as if they did not know them to be so. Adieu my good fellow and be not irascible.'[24]

One can tell much about a prime minister by his attitude to patronage. Melbourne was no leveller and would have regarded the doctrine of equality of opportunity as the most consummate balderdash. He believed, however, that when a job was to be done, the man best qualified for it should be appointed. Bishops were different, they had a vote in the House of Lords and, therefore, inevitably, other considerations came into account. For the more humdrum posts, however, it was merit that counted. '. . . his feelings about patronage appear perfect', wrote Althorp in wonder. 'I am extremely glad that he has agreed to appoint the treasury clerks by examination.' The selection of public servants was indeed one of the few issues which betrayed Melbourne into excessive zeal. At a dinner at Holland House he was pressed by one or two of the guests to appoint only those who were known to be sympathetic to Whig politics. Melbourne 'broke out into an abrupt, violent and extravagant fury . . . He clenched his fist, stamped with his foot, gnashed his teeth, crying "Let's hear no more of it! Now have done with it! I will not hear of it, so by God say no more on the subject!" and similar ejaculations with angry gesticulations ensued.'[25] Melbourne ended with a laugh and five minutes later was in his usual benign form, but the incident impressed hearers greatly.

Sir Hussey Vivian tried Melbourne deeply over such issues. Over the course of three years he asked that he should be created Head Warden of the Stannaries, Master of St Catherine's, Lord Lieutenant of Cornwall, Colonel-in-Chief of the Life Guards and, on at least eight occasions, a peer. He wished his son to be an Auditor of the Duchy, Secretary to the Master General of the Ordnance, a royal Equerry, a Clerk of the Ordnance, a Groom of the Chamber and a Lord of the Treasury. All this Melbourne endured with resignation but he finally exploded when Vivian pulled every string within reach to prevent the transfer of the packet or mail station from Falmouth to Dartmouth. 'In this matter of the packets', he stormed, 'all that is said of justice and injustice, claim and right, appears to me to be just so much nonsense. No post nor county, nor part of the county has any peculiar claim whatever. The only question is which is best for the service and for the general advantage . . . There is too much canvass and solicitation and county interest about this matter, a great deal too much.'[26]

He worked on the premise that all politicians tended to be partial in their distribution of favours; all men, indeed, since he did not believe politicians to be conspicuously worse than anybody else. He had no more faith in his own party than any other, less indeed: 'I believe no ministry ever before so completely excluded their enemies and promoted their friends as ours has done . . .' he wrote two months after becoming Prime Minister for the first time. 'The fact is that our people are more violent, more greedy, more exclusive than their opponents and consider their accession to power as a decisive party triumph, of which they are to enjoy all the advantage and all the superiority.'[27]

Such lofty disdain for the frailty of his colleagues did not preclude some prejudices on his own part, but he showed readiness to reconsider them when challenged. John Russell was infuriated because he had put forward the names of two men suitable to serve as magistrates in one of the big cities, only to have them vetoed by the Lord Lieutenant on the ground that the candidates were in trade. If they were unfit to judge in cases that might involve questions of business, argued Russell, then country gentlemen should not judge matters involving hares or pheasants. Melbourne was inclined to support the Lord Lieutenant. He had always been against traders, he said. There was perhaps no reason to expect better things of the gentry, 'but after all, country gentlemen have held, and still do hold, a higher character than master manufacturers'. On the contrary, retorted Russell, the landed gentry 'are certainly the class in this country most ignorant, prejudiced and narrow-minded of any. The uneducated labourers beat them hollow in intelligence.' Melbourne was struck by the force of this. 'I am inclined to agree with you about your magistrates', he conceded. 'I think some manufacturers and persons in business should be admitted.'[28]

Titles and decorations Melbourne considered to be gew-gaws which some men were idiots enough to want and which could therefore be useful as bribes. Pensions were more serious, but the right people never seemed to want them. At one moment he listed the present applicants: 'Leigh Hunt, distinguished writer of seditious and treasonable libels; Colonel Napier, historian of the war in Spain, conceited and dogmatic radical . . .; Mr Cary, translator of Dante, madman . . .' His awards were idiosyncratic but almost always sensible. A pension was asked for on behalf of the sons of the poet, Thomas Moore. Melbourne thought Moore an overrated hack but was happy to grant *him* a pension. His sons were a different matter, however; young men had a way to make in life and nothing should be done which would divert them from it. The worshippers of Wordsworth wanted the same favour for their hero. Melbourne concurred, but only on condition that the grant stated specifically that this was not done because Wordsworth was the leading poet of the age.[29]

As much as any Prime Minister, Melbourne imposed his style upon the office. It was not to everyone's taste. The prudish were offended, the formal outraged, his enemies saw in it many sticks with which to beat him. It was hopeless to expect, wrote Disraeli, that Melbourne should 'cease to saunter over the destinies of a nation, and lounge away the glory of an empire'. What more could be expected from 'the sleekest swine in Epicurus' sty'? Sauntering and lounging were epithets often applied to him, whose use he was at pains to justify. 'Sleek' was less apt. On the contrary a bluntness, almost roughness, marked his everyday performance. It was not often that, as on 5 August 1835, he came back to the Lords after dinner at Syon House and 'made a speech in a state of great excitement, being very drunk', but whenever he was present there was the hope that something unexpected, possibly shocking, might be said or done. He could be guilty of what, to his more orthodox colleagues, seemed appalling frankness, as when he admitted to Stanley at the dinner table that he had 'concurred in all the great liberal measures of late years not from choice but from necessity'. When put upon, his bluntness could become rudeness. Plagued by John Russell and the Duke of Bedford to offer preferment to their brother Wrio he dismissed him as 'a snivelling Methodist and a foolish fellow'. Nobody, he commented sadly, 'has the least sense where their own connections are concerned, and a large family is a greater impediment than riches to entry into the Kingdom of Heaven'. And yet even at his most brusque he rarely gave offence; patent honesty and good-will robbed his words of the power to hurt. Creevey summed it up as well as anybody: 'Altho', as old Talleyrand observed, 'Melbourne may be *trop camarade* for a Prime Minister in some things, yet it is this very familiar, unguarded manner, when it is backed by perfect integrity and quite sufficient talent, that makes him perfectly invaluable and invulnerable'. It was an unusual prescription for a man in his position but, at first at least, it seemed to work quite well.[30]

CHAPTER 15

Church and State

ALMOST EVERY ministry inherits from its period of opposition some doctrine which seemed irresistibly attractive when propounded but gradually loses its delights as the difficulties of putting it into practice become more evident. In Melbourne's case it was the reform of the Irish church and, in particular, the appropriation of its surplus funds for use in lay education. Not only was this one of the most conspicuous planks in the party platform, it was the issue on which the King had dismissed the Whigs in 1834 and which he had been forced to swallow when they came back to power. There is no commitment that cannot be shuffled off but it was going to be exceptionally difficult for Melbourne to escape from this one.

Not at first that he wished to. Melbourne felt for the plight of the Roman Catholics in Ireland an indignant sympathy rare in this most temperate of men. The Protestant church in that country seemed to him to symbolize all the greed, the selfishness, the intolerance, which had made hideous the life of the majority of the people. 'Religious establishment is eminently for population, not for property', he wrote to William IV. 'Its existence is for the benefit of the poor and the needy, not of the opulent.' He pushed forward the bill with something as near to zest as his character permitted. 'The question of the Irish church can neither be avoided nor postponed', he told Lansdowne. 'It must therefore be attempted to be solved.'[1]

The debate in the House of Commons was the first serious test of the government since its return to power. Its majority of 37, though less than some had hoped, was generous enough to satisfy both ministers and opposition that there was still no opening for a Tory government. In August 1835 the Bill was debated in the Lords. Melbourne chose the occasion to make one of his most important speeches, enlarging not only on the system of tithes, but on his attitude towards the Roman Catholic church and the future of Ireland. It was a vigorous and, for him, unusually impassioned plea for religious tolerance and a proper respect for one's fellow human beings. Quoting Herodotus he argued: 'those who are anxious to establish their influence in any country, ought not to begin by offending the religion of the majority of the community.' The role of the protestant clergyman in Ireland was an anomalous one. He was not a pastor in any proper sense of the word since as often as not he had no flock. Still less was he a missionary sent to convert the heathen. And yet at times he behaved as if this were his role. 'It is not fitting', said Melbourne, 'to treat the Roman Catholics with insult, as if they were worshippers of Juggernaut, or the votaries of any other barbarous superstition.' He admitted that the present legislation would be a blow to the protestant establishment and a triumph for its adversaries, but such ill effects would not be long-lasting. The future happiness of Ireland must depend upon its peoples living in harmony together, and this could only happen if the injustices and humiliations at present imposed upon the great majority of its inhabitants were speedily removed.[2]

His speech stung the die-hard defenders of the protestant establishment into a paroxysm of fury. That 'gospel-vilifying, Jehovah-defying statesman', one pamphleteer described him, with his 'ignorance and blind hostility to religion'. To Disraeli, whose concern for the Irish church can hardly have run deep, he seemed insolent and audacious – shame and misery, he reported, were stamped upon Melbourne's suffering countenance when he rose 'to propose the second reading of the Irish Church Spoliation Bill'. Nobody else detected such emotions and most felt that he was at his best. But his eloquence was not enough to sway the Tory mass. The appropriation clause was defeated by a large majority and Melbourne abandoned the bill altogether. 'Unspeakably wicked', Greville described this action; a sacrifice of the national interest to the needs of party. Nothing could have proved more clearly the domination of the Whig party by O'Connell and the radicals. It is true that, even shorn of its most controversial clause, the Tithes Bill was well worth passing but it is hard to see how Melbourne could have abandoned at the first challenge the principle under whose banner he had come to power.[3]

Nevertheless it is possible to detect a distinct loss of zeal in the months between the defeat in the Lords and the opening of the new session. For one thing it was becoming more and more evident that,

unless conditions in Ireland improved dramatically, there was unlikely to be any surplus of church funds to appropriate. To court defeat
for the sake of a principle seemed less attractive when it appeared that
nothing was to be gained by victory. 'I am much rejoiced to hear that
you have some notions respecting the Irish church', wrote Melbourne
drily to John Russell, 'but you must be a clever fellow, if you can hit
upon a plan, with which the Tories will agree, and which will be in
any respect satisfactory to our supporters.' Week by week he viewed
the commitment with less enthusiasm. In a cabinet towards the end of
November Lansdowne spoke out for the old brigade when he proposed
that a new bill be prepared making no direct reference to appropriation.
Howick in consternation asked, if they now abandoned the principle,
what right they could have had to turn Peel out. 'Oh, that's done!' said
Melbourne. It was to be another three years before everyone would
admit it but, effectively, with those words appropriation died.[4]

It was fortunate for the government that the Prime Minister's dwindling
fervour was not known to his Irish supporters. O'Connell's men proved
considerably more loyal than their radical allies. Repeal was put into
cold storage and uniform support given to every governmental project.
They had, indeed, good reason to be satisfied. Mulgrave, Morpeth and,
perhaps most of all, the new Under-Secretary, Thomas Drummond,
proved anxious to meet all the more moderate Irish aspirations. Liberal
appointments were made among the judges and magistrates, many
more Roman Catholics were given posts under the government,
legislation was introduced to reform the municipal corporations, the
constabulary, the Poor Law. 'The old gang were cleared out of the
Castle', and gradually the more rabid Orangemen were eliminated
from the police.

However, it was Mulgrave's more flamboyant gestures which caused
the Irish the greatest pleasure. He made his first entry into Dublin
with an escort of enthusiasts carrying banners urging repeal and the
abolition of tithes. They were, of course, not there by invitation of the
Lord Lieutenant, but he did nothing to discourage them. Melbourne
found himself called on to defend the incident in the Lords and did so
with marked distaste. He told Mulgrave that some had thought his
attitude 'too low' but that he had no intention of encouraging such
displays in future by pretending to an enthusiasm he did not feel.
Worse, or perhaps better was to follow when, in October, the Lord
Lieutenant invited O'Connell to dinner at Dublin Castle. This gesture

caused much distress not only to Grey, who was determined to be distressed about something, but also to party stalwarts like Lord Dacre who insisted that Mulgrave should be reprimanded for thus fêting a criminal. This time Melbourne was more whole-hearted in his Lord Lieutenant's defence. The responsibility, he said, was quite as much his as Mulgrave's. O'Connell had been treated with no special honour but like any other member of the House of Commons. To slight him and thus repudiate his support would be 'little short of madness . . . As a popular government . . . we must get on as we can, and avail ourselves of the assistance that offers itself, without scrutinizing too closely the grounds upon which it is given.'[5]

More serious was the effect of Mulgrave's action on the King. William IV complained that it was only a few months since, in the speech from the throne, he had been required to denounce O'Connell as a disturber of the public peace. It seemed now inconsistent that his personal representative should entertain him in Dublin. What was worse, he had heard Mulgrave wanted to make O'Connell a privy councillor. This at least Melbourne could deny; no such proposal had been made, he said, nor would it be entertained if it had been.[6]

This was only one of a series of issues on which the King did battle with his ministers. What Londonderry called 'his sovereign ill-humour and disgust' poisoned his relationship with the government so that the most trifling aberration on the part of ministers became a major grievance; any real offence almost a cause for war. Reluctantly convinced of his own impotence William IV was still unable to come to terms with reality and worked off his bile in a protracted guerrilla campaign against his conquerors. In June 1835, for instance, ministers conceived the happy idea of ridding themselves of Durham by sending him as Ambassador to St Petersburg. Unfortunately Palmerston sounded out the Russians before consulting the King. William IV could not decide whether he was more outraged by the impropriety of the original proposal or the insolence of Palmerston in thus by-passing his sovereign. 'There is the devil to pay about this appointment of Durham's', wrote Melbourne ruefully. The King's censure of Palmerston was 'so violent that I know not how I can acquiesce in it'. The Prime Minister answered by defending Durham's nomination and taking on himself the blame for not first of all approaching the King. William still held that Durham was unsuitable but gave way with some grace: 'If the great autocrat has made up his mind to receive Lord Durham, His Majesty will not withhold his acquiescence, especially as he is quite ready to admit that this country and its government, under any circumstances, will be benefited by the absence of Lord Durham.' Palmerston's conduct he could not condone but the Prime Minister gained credit for 'the handsome and manly manner in which Viscount Melbourne takes upon himself a full share of the proceeding'.[7]

Another cause for quarrel was a proposal that the militia staff should be reduced. The King, who was constantly anticipating attack by either French or Russians, sometimes by both at once, exploded with indignation at a meeting of the Council. 'My Lords', he told them, 'I am an old man – older than any of your Lordships – I therefore know more than any of you.' He would never agree to the destruction of the militia and would have them restored in the next session – adding menacingly, 'whoever may be, and whoever are, ministers'. Melbourne, according to Hobhouse, looked 'very black and very haughty', but kept quiet and let the King simmer down. The same pained calm was maintained when the King berated Lord Gosford, newly appointed Governor of Canada, whom he suspected had been given instructions which would permit the alienation of certain crown lands. He would rather turn out ten ministers than sanction the dismemberment of the empire. 'Mind me, my Lord, the cabinet is not my cabinet; they had better take care or, by God, I will have them impeached!' Melbourne duly reported this outburst to his colleagues but all agreed that the best solution was to lie low and pretend nothing had been said.[8]

Such restraint could not apply, however, when the King denounced the Colonial Secretary in front of Sir Charles Grey, a newly appointed member of the Canadian Commission, and criticized the instructions that Grey had received. '. . . a mass of muddle and impropriety such as never probably was equalled before', commented Melbourne with some irritation. He put the matter before the cabinet who drafted a solemn remonstrance to the King, condemning the royal practise of criticizing ministers in front of third parties. Melbourne called on the King who 'heard me with great patience and attention . . . he admitted the full force of my observations, and felt that he had said more than he ought to have said'. For a little time his penitence seems to have been real. A week or so later he proudly told his Prime Minister that 'he had received Glenelg graciously' and that in future he would only seek to regulate official instructions on the advice of the minister concerned. Melbourne 'coldly assented with a bow' and pointed out that the instructions to which the King had taken exception were in fact almost identical to those drafted by Aberdeen for the last government and already approved by William IV. This cool response to the royal sackcloth and ashes may seem churlish but Melbourne's scepticism proved justified the following year when the King was at it again, condemning Glenelg as 'vacillating and procrastinating' and provoking another reproachful letter from his Prime Minister.[9]

Beneath the huffing and the puffing, however, the relationship between King and Prime Minister remained remarkably stable. When Melbourne called on William for his first audience he said that he hoped the King would give him his confidence. 'Good God!' was the reply, 'I wouldn't have sent for you if I didn't mean to do so.' He meant it then and he never changed his mind. Though he detested John Russell and had serious doubts about several other ministers, Melbourne he always liked and trusted. He spoke to him with often alarming frankness and took it for granted – usually correctly – that the Prime Minister viewed the more radical elements of his party and his programme with as much distaste as did the monarch himself. Melbourne for his part well deserved Hobhouse's tribute: 'It was clear to me that, if we continued in the government, it would be entirely owing to the good sense and good manners of our chief, who knows how to deal with his master as well as with his colleagues, and never, that I saw, made a mistake in regard to either . . .'[10]

Nevertheless, the King's hostility was a constant worry. It is never restful to live on the slopes of an active volcano, even though the lava may not be as destructive as it first appears. By the end of the session in August 1835 Lansdowne found that Melbourne seemed tired and harassed while Hatherton noticed his unusual irritability. The strain of holding his supporters together must have contributed as much to this as the vagaries of the King. An opposition, Walter Scott remarked, 'like a wave of the sea, forms indeed but a single body, when it is rolling towards the shore, but dashes into foam and dispersion the instant it reaches its object'. Melbourne was now on the beach amidst the foam, worse still half deafened by the melancholy, long, withdrawing roar of his majority ebbing away from him. As early as April he had told Holland that he expected the discontent of the radicals to pare his majority down to thirty or so and lead to 'defeat and discomfiture'. Though occasionally discomfited he had survived the session without defeat except in the Lords where it could be taken for granted. So far so good, but he had little confidence that his luck could hold. In October he wrote gloomily to Brougham:

The Tories are in fact the strongest party in the country – strong in property, strong in station, strong in prejudice, strong in union . . . When our administration was formed in 1830 it was clear it could not have stood without the Reform Bill which gave us a transient, phrenetic and epileptic strength. When that ceased we were again left in a state of feebleness increased by the attacks of our discontented friends and of O'Connell.

At the moment their dislike of the Tories meant that the more moderate radicals were anxious to convince themselves that Melbourne's government was more worthy of support than Grey's. Evidence was hard to find, however, and it seemed only too likely that soon they would tire of the quest.[11]

Yet in fact on the most important battlefield of 1835 the government had been remarkably successful. The passage of the Municipal Corporations Bill is of particular interest, not merely because of its intrinsic importance but because it provides the only occasion on which we see Melbourne whole-heartedly behind a major piece of reforming legislation and leading his troops vigorously in its defence. The Bill was designed to remedy the situation whereby great cities like Manchester and Birmingham were still controlled by a 'Lord of the manor'. Even where councils existed new members were habitually co-opted by those already in office rather than elected by the citizenry. Incompetence and corruption were the norm and no responsibility was admitted for lighting, sewage, schooling or other essentials of urban life.

It had been drafted by a Royal Commission of which Joseph Parkes was secretary and which was dominated by a massive radical majority.[12] Its terms were correspondingly emphatic. 'We clear the roost from top to bottom', wrote Parkes exultantly. 'Town clerk and all . . . give a simple town council . . . It is a smasher – a grand point to get household suffrage and a thorough purge of the existing corporations.' But it was one thing to draft a radical report, another to sell it to a Whig cabinet. Ellice and Parkes undertook to approach Melbourne but did so in pessimism and with some alarm. To their delight he accepted their ideas in full and undertook to convert the cabinet, a task he performed so well that the only change introduced there was to *reduce* the qualification to vote. This almost drove Spring Rice to resignation and stirred the King to protest. In his reply Melbourne admitted that he often found himself putting forward proposals in which he had little faith but on municipal corporations 'it has always been his own strong and sincere opinion that a thorough reformation of them was required'.[13]

Peel concurred, so the bill sailed through the Commons. The Lords, however, proved a doughtier lot. Battle was joined in July and August. Melbourne pleaded that for the Tory peers to oppose the Bill in defiance of public opinion and the views of their own leaders in the Commons would be tantamount to suicide. Unimpressed, the Lords called for further evidence. As a result of this blocking device a stream of town clerks appeared before the House, each, of course, extolling the singular merits of his own corporation. Melbourne showed his opinion of these proceedings by sitting 'surrounded by his boxes and papers, transacting his own business'.[14]

On 12 August the real debate was resumed. The question, said Melbourne, concerned the middle orders – a body, it is fair to say, for which he had not hitherto shown himself well qualified to speak. 'They feel it more, and consequently they understand it much better than your Lordships. There may be questions upon which your Lordships may be able to form a better judgment than the bulk of the people; but upon this question the people are much better judges than you are.'[15] This less than conciliatory approach failed to appease the Lords who responded by fighting each clause in committee and depriving the Bill of almost all its potency. A fortnight later it was returned, emasculated, to the House of Commons.

Behind the scenes Parkes vigorously encouraged the Prime Minister to stand firm. On 14 August he wrote enthusiastically to Durham: 'I am just come out of Lord Melbourne's drawing room who is full of resolution of character and acuteness. I believe his resolution added to his stature has alone successfully held the helm'. But though ready to remain at the helm as long as needed, Melbourne had no intention of running on to the rocks. If a disastrous clash with the Lords could be avoided then he would do so, even at the cost of certain concessions and the scorn of the hot-heads like Howick who talked of the Lords being 'swept away like chaff'. Fortunately there were moderates too on the other side. Peel hastened back to London, resolved to call his lordly mavericks to order, while in the Lords itself men like Aberdeen reflected that the Bill was extremely popular in the country and the Tories would be fools to oppose it.[16]

In the event it did not prove difficult to thrash out a compromise which Wellington undertook would be accepted. The powers of the new councils were somewhat limited, the rights of existing freemen were preserved, but the essential elements of the scheme survived. The radicals deplored the changes but only Hume stood out for the whole bill or nothing. '. . . looking at our governors, that Melbourne is the only good contriver', wrote Parkes regretfully, 'I am advising our rads to accept.' They would indeed have been foolish not to do so. Almost without meaning it, Melbourne had secured the passage of a Bill as revolutionary in its consequences as the Great Reform Bill and with far more immediate impact on the lives of the people. 'It marshals all the middle classes in all the towns of England in the ranks of reform', wrote Creevey exultantly; 'aye, and gives them monstrous power too.' To Melbourne the Bill was still more significant for the power which it put into the hands of the dissenters. Almost overnight a new political force had been created which was going rapidly to make its strength felt not merely on local but on national issues. 'Depend upon it', said Melbourne darkly, 'it is the established church, not the hereditary peerage, that has need to set its house in order.'[17]

The established church pre-occupied Melbourne at that moment. His feelings about it were ambivalent. What he wanted was a sedate and tranquil church, one that would act as a calming influence in a distressingly turbulent world. When, driving back from an ostentatiously splendid dinner with the Archbishop of Canterbury, he told Howick that 'he was all for a *rich* and *lazy* church, against a *poor* and *active* one', he was no more than half joking. He disliked the more flamboyant forms of service because he found them inconsistent with 'calm and right devotion', yet he was equally against any puritan excesses. He took a perverse pleasure in travelling on a Sunday, 'being averse to the Sabbitarian heresy which prevails in the country'. When asked to define his personal belief he said that he sought to be a quietist: 'so perfect that you are exempted from all external ordinances, and are always living in God'. The church had got no business to meddle with him, nor indeed with the business of the state. The state, however, provided it did not overdo it, had a perfect right to interfere with the church. Melbourne was a good, if temperate Erastian: 'I do not know how I could reconcile it to my conscience to take the part of any church or of anything ecclesiastical anywhere in opposition to the law, which is and ought to be the supreme government of every country.'[18]

The Church of England seemed to him on the whole an admirable body. It was rich, it was established, excessive zeal was not often encountered in its upper reaches. No institution did more to stifle protest. The trouble was that it had done its job too wholeheartedly. The wit who described it as 'the Tory party at prayer' did no more than justice to the partisan bias which had made it, in Professor Gash's phrase, 'politically unpopular, socially exclusive, and administratively corrupt'.[19] Its opulence, ostentation and complacency, its growing irrelevance to the problems of the nineteenth century, had turned it from a discreet and temperate brake on social advance into a goad to extreme radicalism. Melbourne would not himself have initiated reform but he was equally disinclined to defend the church against what he accepted to be an attack based on rational and well justified grounds. Such an attitude came as no surprise to those who knew him: as Sydney Smith put it, 'Viscount Melbourne declares himself quite satisfied with the church as it is; but if the public had any desire to alter it, they might do as they pleased.'

Even this modest enthusiasm for reform was limited in its practical application. Though he exhibited a lively interest in the more recondite works of sixteenth- and seventeenth-century theologians, the minutiae of church government in the nineteenth century frankly bored him. There was quite enough dull detail to be mastered in connection with municipal corporations or Irish tithes without having to bother about the number of canons at St Paul's or the stipend of the Bishop of Barchester. No one, he told Archbishop Whately with a weary sigh, had any notion what a deal of trouble it was, reforming a church.[20] His object, anyway, was not to revolutionize but to provide a face lift; to overhaul the machinery so that it worked more smoothly, not to adapt it for a different task. As Professor Chadwick put it in his majestic and entertaining study of the Victorian Church, the aim was to defend by tinkering. It was not a promising outlook for those few churchmen who were convinced of the need for drastic renovation. Yet the fact remained that Melbourne was aware of the need for change. 'Human affairs never stand still, particularly not religious affairs', he told Cowper. 'They are always moving, forward, backward, laterally, up, down, straight, crooked, in some direction or another.'[21]

Fortunately for Melbourne the ideal instrument for tinkering, probably in a lateral direction, existed in the Ecclesiastical Commission. This Commission, with five bishops among its thirteen members, had been set up by Peel to recommend reforms to the Church of England. When Melbourne renewed the Commission in April 1835, Archbishop Howley looked askance at Whig ministers – even a stalwart like Lansdowne – taking the places of their safer Tory predecessors. He refused to serve until he had extracted a promise from Melbourne that, apart from the inevitable appropriation and the abolition of church rates in England, no bills concerning the church would be introduced without the approval of the bishops. His misgivings proved unfounded.

The Whig ministers rarely bothered to attend meetings and when they did, to judge by the number of Melbourne's letters which bore the superscription of 'Ecclesiastical Commission', mainly occupied themselves with their more pressing lay concerns. The Commission continued on its placid way; recommending reforms of minor, though often real significance, but never occupying itself with what to others seemed the crucial issues of the day.

It was the dissenters rather than the anglican reformists who benefited from Melbourne's favours. He was an improbable champion for their cause. Dissent to him was, by definition, undesirable. He can rarely have known a dissenter personally but suspected they were sanctimonious, self-assertive and ill-adapted to the social frame-work in which they had their being. But this did not seem to him reason to deny them rights which did not conflict with the interests of the nation. He was not prepared to disestablish the Church of England or revise the 39 articles, but when it came to allowing the civil registration or celebration of their marriages rather than subjecting them to the humiliation of using the parish churches of the anglicans, he saw no reason why they should not be gratified. Nor was he less ready to abolish the church rate, which compelled the dissenter to subscribe to the upkeep of this same detested parish church. With the Municipal Corporation Act his government had done much to strengthen the position of the dissenter in local government. In 1836 the Whigs removed their most vexatious grievance when the Dissenters' Marriage Bill became law. For the abolition of church rate they would have longer to wait but the good intentions of ministers were made clear. Benevolence earned a political bonus; Melbourne was the more ready to redress the wrongs of the dissenters because they offered the prospect of substantial electoral support over the coming years.

Neither civil marriage nor church rate, however, provoked the sharpest confrontation between Melbourne and the hierarchy. Bishops voted in the House of Lords and, therefore, every Prime Minister wanted to appoint bishops who would support him. In 1835 a massive majority of the bishops were Tory. This both made it more desirable for Melbourne to appoint Whigs and more difficult for him to find candidates who would be acceptable to their colleagues. He was accused of selecting bishops solely on political grounds. An imaginary dialogue, described in a speech in the House of Commons, had him asking:

'Is he a good man?'

'An excellent man; he is a most accomplished theologian, an exemplary clergyman, and is truly beloved throughout his district . . .'

'Aye, aye, I understand all that; but is he a *good* man – is he a good Whig – will he vote for the Irish Corporations Bill?'

The satire was not wholly fair. On at least one occasion he rejected a candidate of impeccable political qualifications on the grounds that he would make a rotten bishop. But he certainly paid at least due attention to their party loyalties. Indeed the only other consideration which seemed to weigh as much with him was their education. A surprising number of his bishops came from his own college of Trinity, Cambridge. But then, as he pointed out when questioned: 'Trinity College produces ten able men when any other seminary produces one'.[22]

It was, however, not his appointments to the bench of bishops, but to the office of regius professor of divinity at Oxford, traditionally a Tory stronghold, that set the prelates buzzing like angry bees around his ears. When the incumbent died in January 1836, the Archbishop put forward various names for a replacement. Melbourne ignored them and instead offered the post to Dr Hampden, 'an ugly, solid, dull man with a heavy manner and a harsh voice', who was nevertheless a formidable churchman and theologian and had only not been made a bishop before because of his somewhat *outré* views on the 39 articles.[23] The King, unsuspecting, agreed to the appointment, but in Oxford a ferocious opposition built up. 'We had to give the alarm and cry fire', explained Pusey, and with him, Newman and Keble to the fore, the tocsin was soon sounding all over England. Hampden, they declared, was unorthodox, heretical, anathema.

Melbourne faltered dangerously before confirming the appointment and gave Hampden's enemies time to recruit the King. William IV now said that he had given his consent prematurely, he had assumed the Archbishop of Canterbury had been consulted, the appointment must be reconsidered. The temptation to surrender was considerable, since the proposal had never been made public and no face would have been lost. Melbourne, however, decided that his honour was pledged. The arguments against Hampden were 'mere clamour and outcry', the sort of hubbub to be expected from the universities, in which bodies there was 'as much bitterness, as much faction, as much violence, as much prejudice as there ever was in any public assembly or popular club . . .' Though the storm blew on there was no further question of the appointment being cancelled. 'I know very little about Dr Hampden's works', Melbourne told the archbishops tartly, 'but I know infinitely more than the right reverend prelates.'[24]

It proved a Pyrrhic victory. The furore, which lasted long after Hampden was securely installed, forced Melbourne to be prudent in his selection of future bishops. Henceforward they tended to be dull, donnish and conservative. Dr Arnold, headmaster of Rugby and by liberal standards an obvious candidate for the bench, was a victim of this attitude; though Melbourne would personally have liked to promote him he could not face the uproar it would provoke. The field from which he could make his choice was thus still more restricted; especially since tradition dictated that Oxford and Cambridge must be drawn on in rotation and to find an Oxonian Whig was notoriously difficult. 'Damn it, another bishop dead! they do it to vex me', is the cry with which he is supposed to have greeted the news of a fresh ecclesiastical vacancy.[25] He had burnt his fingers once and did not propose to run the risk again.

Meanwhile the politicians whom he had butchered when he made his government rose from their graves to trouble him. On 11 May, after less than a month in office, Wellesley resigned as Lord Chamberlain. Three days later he was cornered by the Duke of Cumberland at a royal drawing-room and pressed for details. On 15 May *The Times* published the story; he had resigned because 'the government of Ireland had been delegated by Lord Melbourne, or some *irresponsible* colleague of the noble Lord, into the hands of Mr O'Connell'. A hectic triangular correspondence now ensued; Wellesley denying he had spoken these words, Cumberland sticking to his guns and Melbourne grumbling impartially at both of them. But however many denials, no one doubted that Wellesley's real feelings had been revealed. In the House of Lords ten days later, when Lord Harrowby attacked the government's Irish policy, Wellesley was observed '*cheering* him all the time'. He remained technically a Whig but could never forgive Melbourne for what, four years later, he was still describing as an 'injust, treacherous and cruel act'. The final blow was struck in March 1839: 'Although your Lordship may probably deem this communication unimportant, I think it proper to inform you, that my vote in the House of Lords can no longer be given in support of your Lordship's administration.'[26]

Melbourne did indeed deem Wellesley's defection of slight importance, but Brougham could not be treated so lightly. For the first few months, the former Lord Chancellor was on his best behaviour. Over the Municipal Corporations Bill he fought valiantly, 'like a tiger in a jungle', wrote Parkes, 'dealing out death where'er he fixed his prodigious claws'.[27] He was given his head over primary education, in which field his ideas were so far ahead of his time that it was another 35 years before they were realized. Melbourne supported them with a tepid enthusiasm that hardly concealed his scepticism but was enough to satisfy Brougham. But he knew that, in the end, he would have to appoint a new Chancellor and that it would be then that the prodigious claws might be turned on him.

By the end of 1835 the clamour of the legal profession and their frustrated customers convinced him that the time had come. He reached the conclusion with reluctance. It did not seem to him that the Lord Chancellor performed any very useful function and when Campbell complained of the growing arrears in the Court of Chancery, he replied cheerfully, 'the groans of the suitors do not disturb my rest'. The groans of his law-officers, however, did. But before a new Chancellor could be selected the old one must be prepared for and, if possible, reconciled to the new development. 'It would be dishonourable to leave Brougham under the impression that he had a chance of the situation', wrote Melbourne to Russell. 'Whatever we do with him we must deal with him fairly. He appreciates such conduct and it to a certain degree awes him, whereas he is naturally incensed by the contrary and most powerful in taking advantage of it.' A week later Brougham took the initiative himself. In a generous letter he said that, if Melbourne thought the government would be the stronger for his absence, then he wished to be put out of the question.[28]

Emboldened by this unexpected self-sacrifice, Melbourne called together the cabinet to discuss whom to appoint. Campbell, in some ways the strongest candidate, was ruled out as not being an equity lawyer. Melbourne was for Pepys, a decent, safe, honourable man. Howick suggested the more brilliant but also more volatile Bickersteth. It was generally felt that the latter was unsound. 'Nothing', wrote Howick angrily, 'ever gave me a stronger impression of the fatal mediocrity of the majority of the cabinet . . .' Pepys therefore it was: 'I'm like a man who has broken for good with a termagant mistress, and married the best of cooks', remarked Melbourne with profound satisfaction. He wrote to Brougham in rather different terms. 'I flatter myself that this selection will be more agreeable to you than any other that could have been made, and I can assure you that this consideration has had no small share in inducing me to come to this determination.'[29]

Brougham took the news admirably. He professed a great respect for Pepys, with some reservations about his value when the battle in the

Lords grew hot, and promised his continued support. Six months later he was equally benign, suppressing certain doubts he had about a bill 'from the sincere desire of doing nothing in the least injurious to the government'. But these letters were written from the south of France, where ill-health, real or alleged, kept him throughout 1836. Would his charitable mood survive his return; the sight of others enjoying the delights of office and the temptation to reassert himself by making mischief? Melbourne doubted it but was grateful for the breathing-space which the absence of his turbulent colleague ensured him.[30]

'Had I been as hostile to the government as Lord Grey is well known to be on all occasions privately, and publicly, too ...,' wrote Brougham in June, 'I verily believe that my opinions would have had far more weight . . .' The mute sulkiness of Grey, watching events from his fastness in Northumberland and grumbling to his family about the inadequacy, the inefficiency, the ingratitude of the present ministers, caused Melbourne more concern that the overt hatred of Wellesley or the distant threat of Brougham. 'He is still very sore', the Prime Minister explained to Hatherton, '. . . and perhaps a little jealous of our present success.' Grey constantly brooded over the speeches of ministers or their supporters in search of phrases critical of his own administration. With the Irish and the radicals justifying their support for the present government by denouncing the last one, he did not have far to look. Melbourne was in a quandary. He could not afford to reject those who offered him support – 'it is not for us to quarrel with the grounds upon which it is given or to dictate those upon which it should be given' – but equally, as he remarked after a particularly violent speech by O'Connell, 'we are not so superdamnably strong as to insult Grey, Anglesey, *and* Stanley'.[31]

Open conflict was averted but Melbourne was left in no doubt that he could not afford to take his predecessor's support for granted. When he wrote early in 1836 to give Melbourne his proxy for the coming session Grey added the somewhat sinister rider that, if he needed to, he could always write to stop him using it. He had two points to make, he said. Appropriation, which he had never liked, should now be written off. He would not promise to support it if it were revived. And he would come out in the most determined opposition if any new measure of parliamentary reform was introduced such as the secret ballot, a larger suffrage or shorter periods between elections. It would not even be acceptable if Melbourne trimmed in the hope of conciliating his radical supporters: 'Any uncertain and temporizing conduct over these vital subjects would compel me, however unwillingly, to express publickly my difference from it.'[32]

Grey was obsessed by the belief that Melbourne was a weak man, fatally under the influence of the repealers and the radicals. It was a view many others shared: '. . . these poor Melbourne people', wrote Carlyle, 'will be obliged to walk on at a much quicker pace than formerly (considerably against their will, I believe), with the radical bayonets pricking them behind'. And yet, in the first eighteen months at least, it is hard to see much evidence that Melbourne's ministry was indeed prisoner of its extremists. On the contrary, it is easier to identify symptoms of what Professor Gash has described as 'the progressive emasculation' of the parliamentary radicals. In June 1835 they were filled with bluster and bravado. When the ballot was debated in the Commons Molesworth exultantly told his mother that the young radicals had shone mightily. 'We have damaged the Whigs, and some of them had better look to their seats . . . There is but one opinion with regard to the present administration; they are the miserablest brutes that God almighty ever put guts into.' But the more responsible radicals knew that they could not afford such triumphs. 'We do not want to be split off from the Whigs', explained Charles Villiers.[33]

It was on the issue of the secret ballot that Melbourne found himself most perplexed between the radical Scylla and Charybdis Grey. It is hard today, when it is taken for granted that a man shall vote in privacy, to recapture the emotions stirred by the ballot in the 1830s. To the Whigs, however, it seemed unmanly, un-English, that a voter should be afraid to proclaim his loyalties; more practically, it would weaken the power of the landlord to control his tenants' voting. There was also the somewhat paradoxical argument that the ballot would in fact work against democracy. In a system whereby the majority of Englishmen had no vote, the only way in which they could make their voices heard was by bringing pressure on the enfranchized minority. Let the latter vote in secret and all control over them would be lost. Melbourne's attitude was easily predictable. He was against the secret ballot but did not think it would have the effects expected of it and was not disposed to make much of a fight against it if it seemed that the weight of opinion in the party and the country had swung against him. He was later to expound his views to Queen Victoria in a way which displayed either his own confusion or, more probably, the Queen's inability to follow his arguments. ' "Now everything is certainty" ', he told her, ' "and then it would be uncertainty"; and he said there would be great fraud exercised in carrying it into execution; because, if a man asks a man, For whom are you going to vote? He answers, I

can't say; then the other says, Oh! I know you are going to vote
against me; upon which the man says, Oh! no; thereby telling a false-
hood, very probably; and Lord M continued, you can't then win any
election, because you don't know who voted.' Equally, he went on, he
understood the arguments on the other side and saw their force: 'therefore, I don't wonder at *their* wishing to try it'. He knew that eventually
he would have at least to admit the ballot as an open question on which
ministers could vote according to their conscience but was determined
to postpone the decision as long as possible: 'It will divide the ministry
into two parties; one of which will be considered liberal; the other
illiberal; the one party acting with the Tories; the other with the
radicals, and both more in unison with their enemies than their friends'.
When the question was voted on in the Commons he told Poulett
Thomson to avoid discussing the principle or the future and to base his
vote 'solely upon the present time being inopportune'.[34]

His tactics worked. Grey remained overtly in support whatever his
private views; the radicals grew restive but not to the point of outright
war. Their weakness was demonstrated early in 1836 when Hume,
Place and others demanded that the stamp duty on newspapers be removed. A month later the stamp duty was indeed lowered but simultaneously harsher penalties were proclaimed for those newspapers
which failed to pay it. To the radicals this was worse than what had
gone before, and yet they were powerless to prevent it since on such an
issue the Tories would certainly support ministers. They could only
defeat Melbourne's government by making common cause with the
opposition; and much though they disapproved of the Whigs they did
not yet hate them so much that they were ready to destroy them to make
way for the Tories. Even more were they terrified lest, by affronting the
Whigs, they might drive them into alliance with the moderate Tories;
with Stanley, perhaps even with Peel. A strong party of the centre-
right, possessing a vast majority of votes in the Commons and probably
also in the Lords, was a chilling prospect for the radicals. Better to
soldier on with the devil you know than to risk such a painful meta-
morphosis.

The end of the session found the uneasy equilibrium surviving. The
Irish Corporations Bill had been destroyed in the House of Lords.
O'Connell and the radicals clamoured for revenge, Howick and Russell
called for a creation of peers. Melbourne stood firm and said that any
such step would be inexpedient. Angrily Howick railed at the 'total

want of energy and courage which is constantly shown in the cabinet',
with greater bitterness the radicals complained that they had been betrayed. Still they forbore to strike. But Melbourne knew that it could
not go on indefinitely. In July Parkes wrote to Durham saying that
unless there were some concessions, particularly on the ballot and
triennial parliaments, then 'the whole concern must go to pieces'.
Melbourne knew that, before parliament met again in November, he
would probably be faced by a revolt. The prospect worried him but
less than it might have done at another time. In the summer of 1836
he had other, still more pressing problems on his mind.[35]

CHAPTER 16

'The Threat of Passion'

RIDING WITH Lord Melbourne in the park one morning in July 1832, Littleton asked him whether the rumour was true that he was going to be married to a beautiful widow. Melbourne laughed heartily and at once said: 'Oh, I know whom they mean – Lady Branden'.[1] Littleton was shocked at what he took to be unbecoming frankness but in fact Melbourne was being disingenuous. It was already more than six months since he had been attracted to and almost wholly preoccupied by the beautiful wife of a former Tory member of parliament, Caroline Norton.

Caroline was the daughter of Tom Sheridan, granddaughter of the great Richard Brinsley. It is said that, at the age of three, she was paraded on a table before her grandfather. He stared at her thoughtfully for a few minutes, then observed: 'Well, that is not a child I would care to meet in a dark wood.'[2] Since then she had grown more cultivated, but had never lost the faint scent of the wild animal which hangs about some people even after a lifetime in civilization. Her father died when she was only three and she was brought up in the well-ordered precincts of Hampton Court. The three daughters – Helen, who became Mrs Blackwood and subsequently Lady Dufferin; Caroline; and Georgie, who married the Duke of Somerset – were devoted to each other and must have made an imposing trio. 'Georgie's the beauty', Mrs Blackwood used to say plaintively, 'and Carrie's the wit, and I ought to be the good one, but then I am not.'[3] Almost before she left the nursery Caroline was engaged to George Norton, younger brother of Lord Grantley, a handsome, apparently affable barrister who, in 1826, added to his allure by becoming member for Guildford. Caroline was uncertain whether she loved him but knew that it was her business to get married as soon as possible and thus ease the straitened family finances. She acted accordingly in July 1827, being then nineteen years old.

Caroline Norton was supremely articulate, commanded the sympathy of those around her, and never hesitated to proclaim it loudly if she felt that she was being misused. Her husband was a louche and lowering creature and his intimates tended to be as uncommunicative as himself. The portrait of their marriage comes, therefore, almost entirely from Caroline's side and is no doubt thoroughly unfair. But though there is no reason to accept that George Norton was indeed the monstrous Caliban he has been painted, it seems at least sure that he was insensitive and unintelligent, incapable of dealing with a high-spirited and exhaustingly temperamental wife. The marriage was a failure from the start, and when Norton lost his seat and only occupation in the election at the end of 1830, it grew worse. Jealousy was now added to the other elements of dissension, since Mrs Norton had scored a considerable success with a volume of poetry while her husband's career was foundering. From the little house in Storey's Gate, just off St James's Park, where they had settled, Caroline pleaded with all her influential Whig acquaintances to find her husband a job; not so much from consideration of his feelings as to raise some badly-needed money. By the time Melbourne, alerted by such an appeal, dropped in at the house to see at closer quarters this radiant poetess who was so much spoken of, husband and wife had already drifted far apart.

Mrs Norton was twenty-two in 1831. Her face was perhaps beautiful but never pretty; the pronounced cheek-bones and strong chin, the sternly regular features, could make it seem heavy in repose, even sometimes coarse. Repose, however, was not her characteristic attitude; more an intense, sometimes feverish animation. At such times her huge black eyes blazed with life: 'There is something tropical in her look', noted a visiting American, 'it is so intensely bright and burning, with large dark eyes, dark hair and Italian complexion.' 'Radiant', is the adjective most often applied to her; she looked as if she were made of precious stones, said Fanny Kemble. To Haydon, who surveyed her with the eyes of a would-be lover as well as a portrait painter, she was 'like a bit of Greek sculpture, just breaking into life'. In noting this he put his finger on an important weapon in Mrs Norton's battery of charms. Galatea to a bevy of Pygmalions, she would visibly come to life when a man engaged her interest, and to every man she could give the impression – fleetingly at least – that he alone possessed the power of conjuring animation into her stony beauty. It is fair to say that to those who disliked her she could look very different. 'You have the damdest skin woman was ever cursed with', declared one victim of her wit, 'your upper lip is that of a negress, your under an animal. Your hands are those of a porter and your feet like a dray-horse. And as to your talent, it is a damned humbug!' Mrs Norton not unreasonably burst into tears.[4]

Her talent was not humbug, though by no means as considerable as she and her more ardent admirers believed. She had a quick mind, a lively imagination, and wrote fluently both in prose and verse. Born into another class she might have been an actress of quality. Her education had been much better than that offered to most girls of the period and her excellent memory ensured that she could display it to advantage. But her real gift was for conversation. She was, as her sister said, the wit of the family, but there was also a spontaneous gaiety, a gift for vivid imagery, above all a capacity to listen. Yet always below the froth of warm good-humour there was a hint of toughness, a reminder that, neither intellectually nor emotionally, was she to be taken lightly. 'Her conversation', said her American admirer, 'is so pleasant and powerful without being masculine; or rather it is masculine without being mannish, there is the grace and ease of the woman, with a strength and skill of which any man might well be proud.'

Women disliked her. Emily Eden had her own reasons for resenting her relationship with Melbourne but there is a ring of truth about her astringent comment: 'What a woman Mrs Norton is! As beautiful I think as it is possible to be . . . but tiresome society, never natural for one moment, and affecting to be so much more wicked than there is the slightest call for.' Affectation was the most common charge against her. She was smooth as glass, kept her sharp tongue under control when with those who could harm her, but was rarely trusted. 'Mrs Norton is so nice', wrote Harriet Granville cryptically, 'it is a pity she is not quite nice, for if she were quite nice she would be so very nice.' 'Not quite nice', that elusive but damning judgement, catches exactly the feeling that there was something wrong about her; a falsity, a flashiness which disqualified her for the politer reaches of society. Yet Emily Eden's adjective 'tiresome' was still more to the point. To anyone not attracted by Mrs Norton she must have seemed maddening in her whims, her postures, her constant clamour for attention. Even for those who loved her she could be too much of a good thing. One evening at the Duke of Devonshire's Mrs Norton was urging Melbourne to do her some favour. She took his hand and said cajolingly: 'Now *do*, my dear Lord Melbourne, *do*!' 'Do let go of my hand', replied Melbourne coolly. 'I want to scratch my nose.' For him the most vexatious thing about Mrs Norton was her unpredictability. She might at any moment take offence, sulk, rage, make a scene, then with equal speed display affection as exaggerated and as embarrassing as what had gone before. '. . . most passionate, giddy, imprudent and dangerous', he much later described her to Stockmar. It was a harsh but not unreasonable verdict.[5]

He would certainly not have said anything so uncharitable early in 1831 when he first called on Caroline in Storey's Gate. Though willing to help her husband, he told her, he had nothing immediate to suggest. Nor had he; yet so satisfied was he by his reception that he addressed himself vigorously to the problem and, within a few months, had secured George Norton a judgeship in the Metropolitan Police Courts at a useful stipend of £1000. For this reason alone Mrs Norton would have been anxious to please him, but Melbourne had far more to offer. He had power, wealth, rank, the mature good looks of a distinguished fifty-year-old, the glamour of a man who has suffered a dramatically unhappy marriage. She found him as attractive as he found her. Melbourne formed the habit of dropping in almost every day to gossip about politics, personalities, the latest book or play.

Their friendship must have ripened rapidly. Fanny Kemble, a young actress and noted beauty, met Melbourne early in March, was 'charmed with his face, voice, and manners' and flattered to be asked to dinner the following week. She went there with vague plans to captivate him but found him wholly absorbed by Mrs Norton, so briskly fell out of love again.[6] When Mrs Norton left London in August, leaving Melbourne trapped by the duties of the session, they wrote to each other every two or three days, not in terms of passion but with intimate, teasing affection. Caroline evidently taxed him with some disloyalty and was amused to find him in his reply, 'so agitated in your attempt to contradict my suspicions and soothe my fury respecting the fair maid of Windsor' that he misdated the letter.[7]

The inevitable theme of flagellation crept in. Melbourne had evidently extolled the virtues of whipping. Caroline replied that she had always bitten the whipper and rushed off to commit the crime again, 'which proves that it was good for you to be whipped and bad for me'. George Norton not only knew about and condoned the relationship but actively encouraged it. Caroline half-jokingly asked her husband whether she ought to accept a present of a horse from Melbourne. Norton replied that he had so high an opinion of Melbourne's merits that he felt any present would be acceptable. He cautiously added that Caroline had perhaps better enquire the age of the filly first. Soon Melbourne had advanced from 'Dear Lord' to 'Dearest Lord'. Georgia, the Norton's elder daughter, used to refer to him as her mother's 'pet Lamb' and wish that she could have one too. Inevitably Melbourne lagged behind in the correspondence and Caroline shrewdly appealed to that didactic side which was always so evident in his relationships with women. 'I did imagine I had coaxed you into writing by asking you that information for my poem. You always say you are glad to teach me things and supply me with scraps of knowledge.'[8]

And so the *ménage à trois* prospered, to the satisfaction of all parties. People gossiped occasionally about them but the affair was now largely taken for granted. One of the few exceptions was Benjamin Haydon who was convinced that Mrs Norton was secretly in love with him and only wanted an opportunity to slip away both from her husband and Lord Melbourne and join him in doubly illicit ecstasy. Mrs Norton went to Antwerp with her sister and Haydon commented crossly: 'What an artful devil she must be – absolutely making *** to me, while *he* believes she dotes on *him* only!' Whether she did absolutely make *** to Haydon is doubtful, but she could never resist encouraging any personable man and the painter may well have amused and even attracted her. One Sunday Haydon called on Melbourne at his house in South Street and was ushered into his bedroom where he found him reading the Acts in a quarto Greek testament that had belonged to Samuel Johnson. Beside his bed was a sketch of Mrs Norton which Haydon had done and given him, 'and he was fancying he could appease his God by reading the bible on Sunday!'[9]

So things might have continued if only the Nortons had contrived to remain on tolerably good terms with each other. Unfortunately they did not, their quarrels became more ferocious, their estrangement more evident. For a few weeks Caroline actually fled her husband's house and took refuge with a sister. Simultaneously her relationship with Melbourne, now Prime Minister, took on a new stridency. It was as if she had decided to abandon discretion. At a party given by the French Ambassador in May 1835, 'she talked in a most extraordinary manner, and kicked Lord Melbourne's hat over her head'. The diplomatic corps tut-tutted and society began to speculate about the future. Even the King talked darkly about Melbourne's 'profligacy about women' and commented, with a curious knowingness about his Prime Minister's habits, 'I imagine he is far less condescending in his amours than he used to be'. By the end of the year the Nortons were regularly appearing again in public as a couple but, as James Stuart Wortley noted when he went with them to a theatre, Melbourne and Caroline 'appeared better friends than I should have liked if I had been Norton'. Worse still, there grew a mood of marked disapproval among the more upright members of the establishment. The cardinal rule of polite society was being broken: that you may sin to your heart's content but must always do so unobtrusively. Even within the government there were murmurings. 'It is not very right', Lord Howick told his diary, 'that Mrs Norton should be asked everywhere to meet Ld M. I think even *he* must be shocked at it.'[10]

Early in 1836 the Nortons were apart again, this time with a greater air of permanence about their separation. 'The fact is', Melbourne told Holland, 'he is a stupid brute and she had not temper nor dissimulation enough to enable her to manage him.' He urged Mrs Norton to be tranquil and not give way to passion: 'You know that I have always counselled you to bear everything and remain to the last'. In repeated letters he argued the case for reconciliation, the dangers to her if the separation continued, the damage that would be done to the children. But, whatever happened, he would be loyal. 'You describe me very truly when you say that I am always more annoyed that there is a row than sorry for the persons engaged in it. But, after all, you know that you can count upon me.'[11]

At this point it does not seem to have occurred to Melbourne that he might be involved in the scandal. It is hard to be sure what led Norton to emulate Lord Branden and bring a civil suit for damages against the Prime Minister. In part he no doubt tired of being treated as a complaisant cuckold by his acquaintances; in part he may have despaired of further patronage from Lord Melbourne and have concluded that there was nothing to be gained by tolerating further a humiliating situation. Mrs George Lamb maintained that the action was a put-up job, arranged by Lord Wynford and certain others of the more malign Tories who used Norton 'as a political engine' to destroy an enemy. Whatever the reasons, Melbourne was surprised and shocked. His first reaction was to treat the charge as almost too ridiculous to require answer, and even after he had realized that a case could be brought against him he remained convinced that it would be dismissed by any right-minded man. 'Whatever is alleged', he wrote to Caroline, 'is utterly false, and what is false can rarely be made to appear true.'[12]

But a sense of rectitude is not necessarily enough to dispel disquiet. Melbourne's worry showed itself in unaccustomed bad temper. 'All

my vexations had their *key stone* put on by the irritability of Ld M',
complained Mrs Norton. 'I suppose it is in human – at least in *man's*
nature always to resent being in this sort of scrape.' By the second week
in May – to the cost of the Whigs in the House of Lords where the
Irish Corporation Bill was being debated – he fretted himself into a
quite serious illness. For nearly two weeks he did not leave his bed,
for another month after that he was constantly crying off dinners or
cabinet meetings at the last moment on the plea of sickness. '. . . since
I first heard I was proceeded against', he told Mrs Norton, 'I have
suffered more intensely than I ever did in my life. I had neither sleep
nor appetite, and I attributed the whole of my illness (at least the
severity of it) to the uneasiness of my mind.'[13]

The main cause of his distress, he assured her, was his fear that her
character might be unfairly damaged by the proceedings. But he was
also worried about his own position, in particular over the possible
fate of his letters to Mrs Norton which it was feared were in the
possession of her husband. Over the last few years he must have
written her several hundred. Looking back Caroline Norton described
'their length, the playful eloquence, the interest in *little* things that
interested me, the feeling and the beauty that runs through them all'.
Few of these letters seem to have survived but it would be extraordinary
if they had not contained much which would have damaged Melbourne
gravely if published: not because they would have borne on his guilt or
innocence but because of the indiscretions about political figures.
Rumours were all over London about the sort of things that would be
read out in court: 'That he was going to that old fool the King – That
he had got rid of that *calf* Mulgrave by sending him to Ireland – Remarks upon flirtations of Lord Lansdowne, etc.' Probably there was
much exaggeration in all this but Young, who knew as much as any
man what was in Melbourne's mind, implied to Creevey that it was
above all this correspondence which was disquieting his master.[14]

And yet, when the celebrated letters were read out in court they
proved to be of such triviality that they were greeted with laughter.
The young Charles Dickens was in court covering the case for the
Morning Chronicle. He listened entranced as Sir William Follett expounded, for the benefit of those too obtuse to grasp the point, the
sinister nature of Melbourne's correspondence: The three letters which
were before the court, said Follett,

> . . . relate only to his hours of calling on Mrs Norton, nothing more;
> but there is something in the style even of these trivial notes to lead

to something like suspicion. Here is one of them: 'I will call about ½ past 4 or 5 o'clock. Yours, Melbourne.' There is no regular beginning of the letters; they don't commence with 'My dear Mrs Norton', or anything of that sort, as is usual in this country when a gentleman writes to a lady. Here is another . . . 'How are you?' Again there is no beginning, as you see. 'How are you? I shall not be able to call today, but probably shall tomorrow. Yours, Melbourne.' This is not the note of a gentleman to a lady with whom he may be acquainted. The third runs: 'There is no house today. I shall call after the levée, about 4 or ½ past. If you wish it later let me know. I shall then explain to you about going to Vauxhall. Yours, Melbourne.' They seem to import much more than the words convey. They are written cautiously, I admit – there is no profession of love in them, they are not love-letters, but they are not written in the ordinary style of correspondence usually adopted . . . between intimate friends.

It is hard to be sure which was the more grotesque: Sir William's valiant effort to make bricks without straw or the still more celebrated speech which he directly inspired, that of Sergeant Buzfuz in the case of *Bardell v Pickwick*. Norton's case, indeed, largely foundered on his inability to produce any documentary evidence for his contention that Melbourne's relationship with his wife was one of more than friendship. Charles Arbuthnot claimed to know for a fact that the letters had been stolen from Norton shortly before the trial by a friend of Caroline.[15] If this is the case, it is hard to see why Norton did not make more of a fuss about it. It seems unlikely, however, that he would have gone so far with his action if he had not had at one time evidence more substantial than that produced in court.

As it was, the trial was something of a farce. Even before proceedings began the betting was five to one on Melbourne's acquittal. So much, indeed, was the prosecution's case dismissed as a farrago of absurdity that it comes as a surprise, when reading the transcript of the trial, to find how much evidence there was that Mrs Norton and her putative lover had behaved with indiscretion and in a way that might have stirred even the mildest husband to indignation. The weakness of Norton's case was that none of his witnesses could say that they had actually *seen* anything and that those who claimed to have got nearest to it usually turned out to have been discharged by Mrs Norton for dishonesty or drunkenness. Where more reliable witnesses were called, as for instance the local clergyman, the tactic misfired since this most proper gentleman admitted that he habitually used the 'private door', which the prosecution suggested would only have been resorted to by a would-be philanderer like Lord Melbourne. William Cowper, who was covering the case for the family and reporting by note at hourly intervals, wrote with relief: 'There is no attempt at proof, only circumstantial evidence'. The other, decisive, factor was that Norton had condoned the relationship for so long. His counsel, the former Tory solicitor-general Sir William Follett, is said to have asked him whether it was true that he had sometimes walked with his wife to Lord Melbourne's house and left her there. Norton admitted that that was the case, whereupon Follett told him that there was an end of his action. Campbell did not even bother to call the defence witnesses, though this confidence did not stop him making a speech of six hours himself.[16]

For Melbourne, odds of five to one or not, the trial had been a gruelling ordeal. He hated lawyers – 'All the attorneys I have ever seen have the same manner: hard, cold, incredulous, distrustful, sarcastic, sneering'. To be thrust into daily contact with them, to be forced to expose his private life to their prying eyes, was a torment. He knew too that his friends and relations were, at the best, sceptical about his innocence. 'Don't let Wm think himself invulnerable for having got off again this time', was his brother's comment; 'no man's luck can go farther.' Granville was still more incredulous: '. . . we none of us I think can doubt what passed in the numerous visits which were reciprocally made in South St and at Storey's Gate.' The derision of his friends was translated into ferocious invective in the opposition Press. The *Standard* commented that the Prime Minister must indeed be in a bad way if 'not to be convicted of adultery' was deemed a triumph. We see nothing in his conduct, the paper trumpeted, except 'evidence of a passion most improper in anyone . . . and most preposterous in an old man . . .' Mrs Norton's resistance made his advances more ridiculous but no less criminal. *The Times* sympathized with Mrs Norton for having had to pay for her husband's new job by enduring visits which she found 'a grievous, if not a degrading affliction', compelling her to listen to 'the twaddling gossip of a vain man of 53'. Melbourne had cultivated a fine disdain for what the papers said but he can hardly have relished publicity like this.[17]

'The low Tories, the herd, exult . . .' wrote Greville in May and Princess Lieven announced that Melbourne's position as Prime Minister should now be untenable. He had indeed talked of resignation but had been persuaded without much difficulty by his colleagues that such a step would be politically disastrous and interpreted as an admission of guilt. The King growled that it was all 'an under plot' when the Duke of Cumberland suggested that it was high time Melbourne went and, when told that such a man was not fit to be Prime Minister, retorted pertinently 'Then I am not fit to be King'. The verdict brought with it a wave of popular sympathy: half the nation being delighted that he was innocent, and the other half that he had diddled the lawyers and the vengeful husband. The sharpest criticism was that of the elderly Tory who remarked that Melbourne had no cause for triumph since 'it had been proved that he had had more opportunities than any man ever had before, and had made no use of them'. Or, as Haydon put it more tersely, if they were truly innocent, then 'she is an unfeeling hypocrite, and he a smuggering fool'.[18]

Were they truly innocent? The fact that many contemporaries believed them guilty, though relevant, is far from conclusive: the capacity of people to believe the worst of their friends was no less marked in 1836 than it is today. Melbourne himself asserted categorically that the charges were false. He gave Serjeant Wilde 'his word of honour as a gentleman' that he was innocent, and told his counsel, Campbell: 'I wish it to be stated in the most clear, distinct and emphatic manner that I have never committed adultery with Mrs Norton . . .'[19] It is a curious commentary on upper-class morality that, though both Wilde and Campbell were perfectly ready to believe that Melbourne would have perjured himself in court if he had been called as a witness, they accepted without question that such a statement made to them privately could only be true. In his letters to Mrs Norton he consistently referred to the accusation as being totally unfounded and it is said that he left with his will a letter* to his brother reiterating that he had told Campbell the entire truth.[20] Against this there is a somewhat ambiguous letter from Mrs Norton whose mother had written to her in terms that made it clear she doubted her daughter's virtue. 'Nothing can vex me, more than I am vexed, and I knew she disbelieved me all along, so it makes little difference; and in the sight of heaven my crime is the same as if I had been yr mistress these five years – so I don't wonder or complain.' A possible interpretation of this is certainly that they had made love, if only rarely, but Mrs Norton was given to extravagant expressions and she may well have meant no more than that she had been indiscreet, or paid insufficient attention to her children.

But the most convincing reason for believing them innocent is that this would have been in keeping with both their characters. Mrs Norton

---

* There is no trace of this letter but a copy of another farewell letter to Fred Lamb dated 22 May 1845 survives among the Panshanger MSS. (Box 58) and contains no reference to Mrs Norton.

was an *allumeuse*, one more anxious to fire men with desire than to gratify it once enflamed, and Melbourne would have been content to accept what she was prepared to offer. With Caroline Norton as with Lady Branden a protracted flirtation, combining all the joys of companionship with the agreeable trimmings of a romantic liaison, was his ideal relationship. It was not Mrs Norton's body that he wanted but the idea of her body and the reality of her company. He may have made love to her but if he did it would not have been a particularly important part of their life together. When he said that there was no such episode he was probably telling the truth.

Caroline Norton was the real victim. Her marriage was broken and she seemed likely to lose her children. Her reputation, admittedly never her strongest point, had suffered gravely. Those hostesses who would have been happy to receive Lord Melbourne even though he had been found guilty, looked askance at her in spite of her being declared innocent. 'I thought people good-natured about him', wrote the Duke of Devonshire, describing how the result of the trial became known during a concert in Bridgewater House, 'but not about her. She is far from popular . . .' Her standing in London society was never fully to recover.[21]

Worst of all, it seemed as if she might lose Lord Melbourne. In two sad, almost tragic letters, one of which must have been written shortly before the trial began, the other after its end, she wrote of her sense of loss and isolation. 'You need not fear my writing to you if you think it *commits you*', she told him. 'I *struggle* to think over all the fortuitous circumstances which make *your* position seem of more consequence than *mine*. I will not deny that among all the bitterness of this hour, what strikes me *most* is the thought of *you* – of the expression of your eye the day I told it you at Downing St – the *shrinking* from me and my burdensome and embarrassing distress. God forgive you, for I do believe no one, young or old, ever loved another better than I have loved you . . .' The image of Lord Melbourne, recoiling in dismay at the thought of being involved in anything so unsavoury as a court case, is not an attractive one. But it is not unconvincing. In moments of danger or stress his instinct always was to run for cover and to consider from that vantage point whether there was any battle to be fought. Certainly he did not mean to be cruel but his whole future was at stake. If his defence might be rendered more difficult by further contact with Caroline, then it would be in the interests of both of them that such contacts should cease. Not surprisingly Caroline could not see things in so rational a light. She bemoaned her inability to attach people to her. For nine years she had been a 'legal mistress to her husband; never more':

> But *you*! I was of no comfort or service to you because I have never been in a position to tender either – but my life has been divided (in my eyes) into the days I saw you and the days I did not. Nothing else seemed of importance but you; your opinions, even your fancies (for you *have* had them) have been law to me. Yet you are not *attached* to me. That is not a reproach – at least it is not meant as such. As time wears on, and sobers me, I shall perhaps do you more justice and condemn my own wild expectations, rather than any part of your conduct towards me. I was not two and twenty when you first visited me and I thought merrily and carelessly about you. I am six years older and I think sadly – perhaps something more! The time shall doubtless arrive when I shall think *calmly and contentedly*. Would it were come!

The trial passed, and now there was fresh offence. Melbourne did not call on her to wish her joy of the result, he did not even write her a word of sympathy or congratulation. 'There is no woman, *however strict*, who has not appeared to take it for granted I have seen you', yet in fact there had been only silence. What to him seemed the most elementary prudence, to her was betrayal. Edward Ellice, a man often used by Melbourne where negotiations were likely to be delicate, acted as a go-between but his task was a hard one. Caroline Norton's wish was that things should return to what they had been, Melbourne knew that this could never be. Angrily she railed at him, 'now safe from all risk and sitting in triumph in South St'. By now Melbourne had begun to write to her again but the letters were formal and chilly compared with what had gone before. 'What have I ever done to you that you should grind me too? Have you *always* so preserved the inequality of age and understanding between us that you should talk to me like God delivering the tablets of law to Moses?' At one moment she seems to have threatened to publish Melbourne's letters, then hurriedly withdrew and said that she had never really meant to, had only wanted to remind him that she *could*. Her final cry can hardly have failed to move him:

> Others (perhaps more unhappy) have preceded me – others as unhappy may succeed me – but no one either in the past or the future will have loved you more earnestly, more completely, and I may say more steadily than the woman whose threat of passion you pretend to fear – and who has been made to appear a painted prostitute

in a public court . . . for the sake of an acquaintance with one who did not think it worthwhile to ask after her the next morning!

After this turbulence the relationship settled down, but it was never to recover its former ease or ardour. Caroline Norton's remark about 'the threat of passion you pretend to fear' had been to the point. Melbourne was frightened, not so much of scandal as of an emotional involvement which he did not feel himself able to sustain. He shrank back into distant amiability. This Mrs Norton might have accepted but it was harder for her to hear of him enjoying himself in London society, shining in drawing-rooms to which she was not invited, flirting with women who would not even deign to be introduced to her. 'Now you run about to Stanhopes, Litchfield, Fox Lane's . . . with the buoyancy of a boy, and the carelessness of a greyhound (the only dog beside yourself who cannot attach himself *to any one person*, but to the cushion where he habitually rests and the house where he is accustomed to be fed).'

The bitterness of the jibe is accounted for by the reference to the Stanhopes. Lady Stanhope, beautiful, witty, notoriously on bad terms with her husband, almost certainly a former mistress of Frederick Lamb, was eminently well suited to the sort of discreet yet public flirtation that Melbourne favoured. Lady Holland described her as 'very amusing, gay and original, not of the best polish, but still very sprightly, . . . and highly coloured in her stories'.[22] There is no reason to believe that either of them felt real affection for the other but both enjoyed the game of producing a superfluity of smoke from the smallest possible fire. This was more than enough for Mrs Norton. Shortly after Victoria's accession she wrote in rage that everyone was describing Lady Stanhope 'as your mistress and wonders at your thrusting her on the Queen'. Don't think that I will put up with this, she stormed. 'I will proclaim what this woman is, who is so fortunately protected and who sins without observation. The visits to you which in me were *crime*, I presume even in her case are scarcely proper.'

What hurt most of all was that Lady Stanhope should be invited to court while she was not. Melbourne's failure to do anything for her beloved brother Seymour or to lay before the Queen a pamphlet dealing with the problems she was having with her husband over the custody of their children, was a perpetual source of offence, but the real sting came from his inclusion of Lady Stanhope in what Mrs Norton described as 'a little family reunion of you, the Queen, and the woman you never made any doubt has been your brother's mistress (if she has not also been yours)'. Nor was she the only person who felt this improper. In July 1838 Lady Howick deplored the Queen's habit of including Lady Stanhope in 'her most intimate gatherings'.[23] To Mrs Norton it seemed that Melbourne delighted in spending his evenings with people who notoriously detested her. 'Heartless and cold blooded', she described his conduct. 'You are also much mistaken if you think the circle of flattery and intrigue in which you pass your time, adds to your political importance and stability. There is not a day in which some incautious or uncertain speech of yours is not reported – a fact which I dare say you utterly disbelieve and will continue to disbelieve till the *necessity* which checks the wavering and discontented portion of your supporters passes away, and you perceive as an individual, what you refused to see as a minister . . . Someone may make a leap past you as well as past Ld Grey.'

This baleful note marked the nadir of their relationship. Lady Stanhope faded from a scene on which she had never played a role half as significant as that imagined by her rival. It became clear to Mrs Norton that Melbourne was almost exclusively preoccupied with the young Victoria. Of any other woman one could be jealous but in the case of the Queen it hardly seemed worth while. She continued to grumble that Melbourne neglected her, but resigned affection became the prevailing attitude. If he would not change, then she could only make the best of what he was. But their friendship never became what it had been before. Until he ceased to be Prime Minister Melbourne had neither the time nor the energy for vigorous flirtation; when he retired he was too old and ill. Her passion simmered down into a quiet affection, a companionship which was to give him much relief in his last years. It was, perhaps, more than he deserved.

As, when re-reading *Mansfield Park*, one each time wishes that Fanny Price would dispose of her priggish cousin and marry the less suitable but far more entertaining Mr Crawford; so one constantly regrets that Melbourne could not have dispensed with his tempestuous mistresses and married the one woman who might really have made him happy. Emily Eden was one of the most delightful women of her age. She was intelligent, witty, kind, gentle, with a tranquil gaiety that infected all around her. Her elder brother, Lord Auckland, was a political associate and friend of Melbourne's. She wrote two novels of unassuming charm, was well read enough in theology to join Melbourne in his musings and described her life in India with humour and a brilliant eye for detail both in her letters and in a book which she published in 1844.

When Caroline Lamb died, Emily Eden was thirty-one. Many people thought what a suitable match she would make for the new widower and they were much thrown together. 'I hear Lord Melbourne flirts immensely with Emily Eden', reported Lady Granville with satisfaction. In 1832 Lady Cowper decided to take the matter in hand. She invited Miss Eden to Panshanger and sought more or less to confine her there until she arrived at some understanding with her brother. The effort was well meant but unavailing. 'I can derive but little vanity from Lord Melbourne's admiration', Miss Eden wrote. 'I stand very low in the list of loves, and as for his thinking well of my principles, it would be rather hard if he did not, considering the society he lives in.' Nor was she at all sure that she really liked him: 'I do not think him half so pleasant as Sir Frederick . . . and probably just as wicked, and he frightens me, and bewilders me, and he swears too much. However, we ended by being very good friends . . .'[24]

Very good friends they remained. She was a constant recourse in times of stress, sharing his background and interests, enthusiastically his supporter in all his doings, offering him friendship without cloying sentiment or demands for attention. That she wished for something more can hardly be doubted but the very serenity which made her precious to him ruled her out in his mind for anything more than close companionship. She was, perhaps, too much like him; to stir his passions called for a nature more turbulent, more demanding, most of all, no doubt, less suitable.

In September 1835, Melbourne despatched Lord Auckland as Governor General to India. With regret and trepidation his sister agreed to accompany him. She urged Melbourne not to come to the boat to see them off. 'There is no use in it, and I am unhappy enough as it is. You said you would give me some little book which you have read and marked. I do not care what it is – only let your name be written in it.' Please write to me, she concluded. 'For so many years I have been used to listen to your confidences – good and bad – that I cannot bear to lose them altogether . . .' She can hardly have expected that her injunction not to come to the boat would be obeyed but Melbourne was ever ready to avoid the unpleasant duty. 'My mother always used to say that I was very selfish, both boy and man', he replied, 'and I believe she was right – at least I know that I am always anxious to escape from anything of a painful nature, and find every excuse for doing so. Very few events could be more painful to me than your going, and therefore I am not unwilling to avoid wishing you goodbye. Then God bless you . . .' His parting present was a copy of Milton which he had owned for many years and often read in. Perhaps she found some consolation during her journey in poring over *Paradise Lost* and reflecting on

> . . . that forbidden tree, whose mortal taste
> brought death into the world, and all our woe,
> with loss of Eden.[25]

There were other things to worry Melbourne at this time. He was beginning to display the excessive preoccupation with his personal finances that so marred his old age. He had made a somewhat rash investment in the Nottingham railway and feared that he was going to lose his money. What was worse, as he confessed to Victoria some years later, he disliked railways anyway, thought they were 'bad for the country as they brought such a shocking set of people who commit every horror'. For a man so apparently insouciant he had all his life been curiously concerned about money and his own fortune. He inscribed in his Commonplace Book improving adages on the subject: if you estimate that your expenses will equal, or almost equal your income then you are 'an embarrassed, if not a ruined man'; wealth 'is so much the greatest good that fortune has to bestow that in the Latin and English languages it has usurped her name'. Yet it is hard to see that he had any need to worry. His maximum loss from the railway investment was £1000 yet his annual income, he told Hatherton, was exactly £21,000 a year. It is true that of this sum some £10,000 a year was paid away in various charges on the estate but he was still left with £11,000 to meet expenses of about £10,000. When in office, of course, the situation was even healthier. Theoretically at least, as Prime Minister he was saving £6000 a year.[26]

His health caused him more real concern. The gout, which had troubled him for many years, was now striking more fiercely and more often, particularly to the right knee. Sometimes he was crippled and immobile for a week at a time. More than this, he found himself often bilious and lethargic, sleeping badly at the times when sleep would have been in order and finding it hard to keep awake at moments when anything else smacked of incivility. To Russell he complained of 'langour and despondency'. With striking bluntness the latter replied that this was the price of eating and drinking too much and taking no exercise; one of these might be supportable but the two together could only be disastrous. The accusation was a fair one. Melbourne habitually ate and drank enormously. Two years later Lady Lyttelton observed that nothing could remove him from office, 'unless he contrives to displace himself by dint of consommées, truffles, pears, ices, and anchovies, which he does his best to revolutionize his stomach with every day'. In 1836 his constitution could still stand it but already it was feeling the strain. The irregular hours of parliamentary life and the stress of office combined to help the transformation of a man of conspicuous health into a fretful invalid.[27]

From this time too Melbourne's habit of talking to himself became more apparent. At Brooks's he was overheard to mutter 'I'll be hanged if I do it for you, my lord!' – part, no doubt, of an imaginary dialogue in which he opposed the pretensions of one of his supporters to a Lord Lieutenancy or promotion in the peerage. 'That's smoking', he remarked to himself in apparent awe when he first saw the Duke of Sussex smoking a cigar. The trick was an amiable eccentricity yet it indicated some erosion of self-control. Even when he knew he was speaking aloud he seemed sometimes to be following some hidden seam of speculation of which a part had suddenly emerged into the light of day. Mrs Norton referred to his habit of 'roosting', slipping into a post-prandial torpor in which it was impossible to say whether he was taking in anything around him. From one such trance he suddenly rounded on Lady Clarendon and demanded: 'Do you love your neighbour as yourself?' A few moments before she had noticed him smiling and laughing to himself, as if he were having some particularly amusing thought.[28]

For more than twenty years his son, Augustus, had lingered on the frontiers of infantilism. He had grown into a gentle and quite good-looking man who varied tracts of almost vegetable existence with sudden bursts of ferocious joy or rage. He could never be left unattended and his existence was a cause of constant worry and little joy to his troubled father. Mrs Norton described how Melbourne would stop in the middle of the most animated conversation and strain his ears in case some noise from Augustus heralded a fresh outbreak. It was one more of the personal worries which tried him harshly in the summer and autumn of 1836.

It was not to last much longer. On 26 November 1836 he cancelled a visit to Panshanger because his son had suddenly become extremely ill. That evening he was working with Augustus, as he thought, dozing on a sofa beside him. Suddenly the invalid looked up and quietly asked: 'I wish you would give me some franks, that I may write and thank people who have been kind in their inquiries'. The pen dropped from Melbourne's hand 'as if I had been struck; for the words and the manner were as clear and thoughtful as if no cloud had ever hung heavily over him. I cannot give any notion of what I felt; for I believed it to be as it proved the lightning before death. In a few hours he was gone.' When the doctors opened Augustus's skull they found that the bones were unusually thick and the substance of the brain so dense that a knife could hardly be forced through it.[29]

The cabinet on 28 November was held in Lansdowne House rather than the Prime Minister's house in South Street. 'Melbourne did not affect any grief', noted Hobhouse, 'but went on with our business.'[30] Augustus's life had not been such that much joy was lost with the ending of it and the memories which he provoked of wife and marriage can not have been happy ones. But he still provided a focal point for a life that otherwise was socially and emotionally diffuse. Wherever Augustus was, was home: not much of a home, perhaps, but still the symbol of that web of loves, hopes and responsibilities that makes up a family. With his departure there was nothing. Melbourne was deeply attached to his brother and sister. He was soon to replace Mrs Norton by the young Queen as the most intimate of his confidantes. He had many friends and innumerable acquaintances. He rarely needed to be alone. Yet at the very centre there was a void. Cheerful, sociable, yet curiously desolate, Melbourne faced the future in solitude.

CHAPTER 17

'Fretted by Opposition'

AT THE END of the session, in August 1836, Lord Lyndhurst launched a ferocious assault on the Whig government, denouncing their policies and their principles, deriding their ministers and accusing them of being mere puppets of their radical and Irish masters. The speech, reported *The Times* gleefully, 'fell upon the ranks of the government like a Congreve rocket ... No words can describe the outrageous irritability of Lord Melbourne or the blank rage of Lord Holland ... Lord Melbourne writhed like a scotched snake, Lord Holland gambolled like an excited elephant ...' Unaware that he had been scotched, Melbourne replied with what Campbell considered the best speech he had ever made. He admitted that much of the government's legislative programme had been aborted but put the blame for this entirely on the House of Lords. The irresponsible nihilism of the Tory peers had made good government impossible and put in peril the status, if not the very existence, of the upper house. If retaliation followed they would only have themselves to blame. In so saying Melbourne sketched out what was to be the principal battlefield of the next twelve months. It was perhaps symbolic of the fact that both he and Lyndhurst suspected the battle would produce more noise than casualties that Lyndhurst, directly the debate was over, walked over to Melbourne and sat down beside him. 'They laughed and joked together, both pleased with themselves, thinking that in this *rencontre* each had tilted to the admiration of the bystanders.'[1]

In his peroration Lyndhurst had challenged the Prime Minister to accept the fact of his impotence and leave the field to someone capable of wielding the powers of government. 'As to holding office', replied Melbourne, 'I have only to say that I conscientiously believe that the well-being of the country requires that I should hold it – and hold it I will – till I am removed.' They were brave words, yet in private he spoke a different language. The strain of having to fight almost single-handed in the Lords was beginning to tell, and the fact that some of the most arduous debates coincided with the scandal of the Norton trial and the final illness of Augustus did nothing to relieve the pressure. 'I feel my temper giving way', he told Russell. 'To have two or three great points to fight would be nothing, but to be fretted by opposition on every little matter is intolerable.' At one point in August the government's majority in the Commons slipped to 26. The radicals seemed to be gaining strength on one wing, the Tories on the other. In cabinet Melbourne speculated whether it could be 'right and becoming' to go on with the government in the teeth of the court, the Lords, and it now seemed the English constituencies. 'Lord Melbourne said a man must have the patience of an ass to stand against such odds.' There was no shortage of pessimists to share his view: Lansdowne said he would resign if the Tories passed a vote of censure in the Lords, Howick predicted that the government would be out before the next session started.[2]

In the country as well as in parliament things seemed to be going badly. It was already clear that the harvest of 1836 was going to be the worst for several years and that substantial quantities of corn would have to be imported. This was particularly unfortunate at a time when the bullion reserves of the Bank of England were already under strain. Bank rate rose to an unprecedented 4% and industry, forced to borrow on such usurious terms, found itself in difficulty. Bankruptcies were in the air and Melbourne sent an SOS to his Chancellor, Rice, who was holidaying in Ireland. 'I do not mind the railing or the abuse', he explained, 'but I think it would be awkward if half-a-dozen houses were to come tumbling about our ears in your absence.' Business-men, he had noticed, showed an ungentlemanlike tendency to protest if their interests were assailed: 'inconveniencing and discontenting the moneyed men creates a clamour as shrill and as unappeasable as does the killing of a pig. Nothing is as violent as a moneyed interest in difficulties, nothing so loud . . .'[3] Rice hastened back, a rescue operation was mounted, and the squeals of the moneyed men were at least temporarily stilled. But the drying up of orders from America and the consequential unemployment promised a troubled winter.

And yet, in spite of these difficulties, Melbourne's own reputation stood higher at the end of 1836 than ever before. Lord Holland, certainly not an unprejudiced but still a shrewd and by no means blindly partisan observer, summed it up well in his diary for September:

> On the whole, Ld Melbourne rose as a speaker as well as a minister
> on the session of this year. Though his language is good, his manner
> and voice fine and his knowledge and learning extensive, yet there
> is a want of parliamentary aptitude and ready apprehension and
> logick that always leaves one something to desiderate in his speeches.
> But on the other hand, his admissions, though apparently imprudent,
> give an air of frankness and candour, and his sudden and sometimes
> unprovoked bursts of passion imply such fearlessness of character
> and such singleness of purpose that they in a great degree disarm his
> enemies, endear him to his friends and above all ingratiate him with
> the publick, with whom he becomes not only politically but personally
> too a real favourite.[4]

He was to need all the fearlessness at his command in the forthcoming session. He had enemies on every side. Most dangerous, if also
least predictable, were the radicals. The Tory peers could only block
his legislation, the radicals could destroy him with a single vote.
Melbourne was anxious to avoid a direct confrontation, but daily his
manoeuvres became more difficult. Howick visited him at Brocket in
October and found him almost in despair. The radicals were getting
tired of a situation in which they were called on to make the sacrifices
while the Whigs took the profits; it was only a question of time before
it would be 'no longer possible for us to stand as we have done between
the two extreme parties'.[5]

The only hope seemed that the radicals would remain as widely
divided as they had been in the past. Parkes admirably exemplified their
schizophrenia: telling Durham in October that the lesser evil might be
'to let the Tories in, and begin *de novo*', and assuring Ellice less than
two months later that it would be arrant folly 'to play such a suicidal
game when we are the only country in Europe enjoying a *practical*
republic daily improving'.[6] It was from people of such infirmity of
purpose that fanatics like Roebuck and 'Mother' Grote – Madame
Defarge designate of the English Revolution – longed to wrest the
dagger. Once they succeeded, the 'feeble and conservative' Lord
Melbourne would be the first to feel the taste of steel.

'However strongly you may feel against our bills, you need not be
uneasy lest they should become law', wrote Melbourne to Brougham in
the summer of 1836. 'The Lords will certainly dispose of them.'[7] This

wry remark was no joke. The House of Lords were relishing revenge for their humiliation over the Reform Bill in 1832. Under the skilful leadership of Lyndhurst the Tory peers enjoyed not only a massive advantage in numbers but also superiority in debate. In Henry Phillpotts, the redoubtable and reactionary Bishop of Exeter, they possessed a Mrs Grote of the ultra-Tories who was distrusted by many of his fellow bishops but still had great influence when it came to whipping them into line on a crucial vote. Together these worthies treated their party leaders in the Commons with disdain: 'Peel? What is Peel to me? Damn Peel!' Lyndhurst is supposed to have retorted when it was pointed out to him that he was acting flatly against the wishes of his former Prime Minister. Occasionally the Duke of Wellington might call his troops to order but even he interfered with diffidence. Usually Lyndhurst was left to conduct his campaigns as he thought best.

In 1836 the Tory peers so badly mauled the Irish Tithes Bill, the Irish Corporations Bill and the English Municipal Corporations Bill, that all were withdrawn. These excesses, coming on top of the havoc which the Lords had made of the legislative programme the previous year, seemed to many supporters of the government to be intolerable. The will of the nation was being flouted by a handful of irresponsible die-hards. '. . . there is, in my opinion', wrote Macaulay to Spring Rice, 'a question compared with which the Ballot and everything else sinks into insignificance. I mean the question of the hereditary peerage. I do not see how it is possible to avoid a final collision between the two Houses.'[8]

Melbourne's reaction was predictably more philosophical. He refused even to contemplate a final, or even a preliminary collision between the Houses. When the Whigs were beaten in the Lords on the Irish Corporations Bill he remarked in cabinet that normally a government would resign in such a case but that, as they had taken office in spite of the declared opposition of the peers, 'we know nothing now that we did not know before, and our resignations would not be justifiable'. The only thing to do, he suggested, was to 'go on quietly, and try a new measure next session'. The truth was that he did not think the point at issue worth a major row. There seemed to him a great deal to be said on both sides. Sometimes the Lords had even been quite useful. When they were attacked for interfering with the Municipal Corporations Bill he told Brougham that he thought the outcry 'most unreasonable. The fact is they did the Municipal Bill little harm. They adopted the most essential parts of it, and in some respects they improved it'.[9]

This anaemic approach to party warfare was not well received by all Melbourne's supporters. In the winter of 1835 O'Connell toured Scotland and North England, preaching the radical reform of the House of Lords. 'Nothing can be more absurd than all the plans proposed for the reformation of the House of Lords except O'Connell's', wrote Melbourne, 'and that is pure democracy.' By the following summer the conviction that something must be done was more widespread. John Russell drafted a memorandum for the cabinet, arguing that the Lords should be coerced by the immediate creation of eight, ten or twelve peers and the threat to do the same every time an important piece of legislation was unreasonably blocked. He sent the draft to Melbourne and asked his views. 'It is a very serious step', replied the Prime Minister, 'and, there is no doubt, if taken, will lead to the resignation of the government and the attempt to form another . . .' Russell's initiative withered in the face of this determined lack of enthusiasm. Melbourne was ready to extract extra peerages from a reluctant King whenever an opportunity offered but shrank from creating them as part of a deliberate policy. There was an endearing vagueness about him when it came to selecting those to be honoured. In December 1836 he told Lansdowne that Rosebery would be an excellent candidate since he would vacate no seat in the House of Commons. In this he was quite correct. Rosebery had been a peer of the United Kingdom since 1828.[10]

Melbourne had some reason for avoiding a confrontation with the Lords. With reform of the constitution and the corporations safely behind them, the Whig government was left with no important piece of legislation which did not relate primarily to Ireland. There was therefore no battlefield on which the Lords could be attacked with a guarantee of popular support. The slogan of 'Peers against People' could prove a dangerous one if it turned out that peers and people were in fact united against an unpopular government. Melbourne preferred to temper his policies so that they would be acceptable to the Tory moderates. Donald Southgate was perhaps going too far when he wrote of 'a half-conscious coalition with Peel', but Melbourne's bias towards the dictates of conservatism was too evident to be denied.[11]

One issue on which he was in no doubt that the Lords would block his legislation was the old one of appropriation. By the beginning of 1837 Melbourne was heartily sick of this troublesome irrelevance which, by its unpopularity with the Tories, made impossible the passage of the Tithes Bill of which it was a part. 'I should be very glad to extricate myself and colleagues from the difficulty in which we are placed', he confessed to Grey, 'and to get rid of the resolution of 1835 by burying it in a larger and more effectual proposal.' Russell was of the same mind and made a speech hinting broadly that this was his intention. The Prime Minister was alarmed: it would be necessary first to get the consent of the cabinet and 'I rather fear the wrong-headedness of some of them'. Wrong-headed or right-minded, it quickly became clear that a hard core of irreconcilables, including Hobhouse, Glenelg and Melbourne's brother-in-law Duncannon, were prepared to stick to their principles whatever the cost. A decision on appropriation was put off until the policy of the Lords on other issues had been established.[12]

On Church rates it was already clear. The Whig plans to abolish them were met with outrage by the Archbishop of Canterbury and his acolytes and denounced as part of an all-out assault on the church. Melbourne was genuinely distressed by such an accusation:

I am for an established church [he told Grey]. . . . An established church appears to me to be necessary for the instruction of the public and for the maintenance of the national purity of religious doctrine. I think, there is so much of the truth of the gospel, mixed I daresay with errors, in the Church of England form, in the Roman Catholic form and in the Presbyterian form of Christianity, as to justify a Christian in acquiescing in the establishment of any one of them. If my lot were now to be cast by any chance in a Roman Catholic country, as a citizen, I should certainly not conform to that religion, but I should not think myself justified in attempting to subvert it.[13]

He answered the Archbishop with greater anger than was habitual. The object of the bill, he said, was to promote peace and harmony – something for which he would have expected the church hierarchy to feel at least some sympathy. The bishops were unimpressed and the Bill perished.

Fresh troubles arose when the reform of the Irish municipalities was mooted. Melbourne was for some reason convinced that the bill, which had been maimed by the Lords the year before, would this time be suffered to pass substantially unscathed. He was quickly proved wrong. The talk was now of resignation. The only considerations which held him back, Melbourne told Russell, were a dislike of letting down his friends and fear that he might bring about a situation in which it would be impossible for anyone to form a government. This last anxiety, he admitted, might well be chimerical, but, 'not having quite the confidence in the stability of popular and constitutional forms of government which others have, and thinking them very likely to break up of themselves, I cannot feel quite free from it'. He was pitching his altruism a little high. Melbourne, in common with most of his ministers, would have done his best to hold on to office even though a perfectly adequate alternative had existed. The lot of a Whig Prime Minister in 1837 might not be a particularly happy one, but it was still better than the humiliation of defeat. Peel gleefully told Croker that the government, harassed by the radicals whom they could only control with Tory help, was 'dying to die, and looking out for the rope by which they might most gracefully terminate their existence'. The rope which Melbourne was looking for was one by which he might escape from the present impasse with the Lords.[14]

By May it seemed as if he might have found one. In the face of hints that the Lords would pass the Irish Municipal Corporations Bill if the appropriation clause were dropped from the Tithes Bill, resistance in the cabinet crumbled. O'Connell had anyway made the purists look foolish when he indicated that his followers would not be particularly distressed if the clause vanished. By May Melbourne felt able to tell Wharncliffe that he did not foresee any real difficulty in burying appropriation for ever. Things, he said hopefully if a little vaguely, were 'soothing down'.[15] His optimism was not put to the test. In mid-May 1837 the political situation was transformed by what seemed likely to prove the fatal illness of the King. What the future under Queen Victoria might hold no one dared predict but at least, from the point of view of the Whigs, things could hardly get any worse.

Relations between the King and his ministers had improved little since the Whigs had forced their way back into power. The furore over Lord Glenelg had hardly died down before another, potentially far more dangerous quarrel broke out over policy towards Spain. Melbourne never took much interest in foreign affairs. He saw his role mainly as a mediatory one; intervening only to act as a brake on Palmerston's exuberance or to patch up a compromise between him and the King or other members of the cabinet. In the main he was loyal to Palmerston; briskly rejecting an attempt by the Austrian Ambassador to deal directly with him on the grounds that it would be improper for him to abet the by-passing of his Foreign Secretary. But he was not above by-passing Palmerston himself from time to time. On one occasion Palmerston wrote Metternich a 'clever and insolent' despatch. Melbourne disapproved of it but let it go. When it got to Vienna, however, the British Ambassador suppressed it. 'Very judicious', said Melbourne approvingly. Greville saw this as an illustration of Melbourne's feebleness. He should have vetoed the despatch himself; 'But he is only Prime Minister in name, and has no authority'. It is easier, however, to see the somewhat peremptory conduct of the envoy as evidence of collusion between the Prime Minister and his Ambassador – who was, after all, his own brother Fred.[16]

Melbourne's principles in foreign affairs were as pragmatic as in any other sphere. Almost nothing, he believed, could justify a war. In maintaining this view he had to counter not only the sabre-rattlers in his cabinet but also the bellicose and ultra-patriotic William IV. Warn Metternich, he instructed his brother Fred, that though all the ministers wished for peace, 'Kings of England like war, which they wage in comparative security, and which offers them nothing but pleasurable excitement, and commands and promotions to give and to make'. Though all systems of government devised by man were fallible, a constitutional monarchy offered the best chance of success. It was therefore reasonable to offer limited encouragement to regimes progressing in the right direction. But such encouragement must stop short of active interference. Nothing could be more absurd than to risk serious involvement abroad so as to set up a new government which might be as bad or worse than the last one 'All these chambers and free presses in other countries are very fine things', Melbourne warned Palmerston, 'but depend upon it, they are fully as hostile to England as the old governments.'[17]

Over Europe his views were in the classical British tradition. The greatest danger, he told Grey, was 'a close alliance between Russia and France, in which the latter should say to the former, take your course in the east and let me take mine in my neighbourhood. If Russia could by any means carry Prussia along with her in this policy there would remain no sufficient check to the power of such a combination.' This, he went on, had been the problem which Britain faced under the Bourbons. The July Revolution had broken the pattern and produced a situation in which we were France's natural ally. This was something which our national interest demanded that we should foster. Though not a fanatical francophile in the mould of Lansdowne, Holland and the other Foxite Whigs Melbourne was always disposed to work with the French if this proved possible. When he first took office he sent the King of the French a personal message to assure him that there was 'no man in England more deeply impressed with the advantage of such an alliance and mutual good understanding between England and

France, as is consistent with the honour and interest of both parties'. In general he proved true to his words. When the King and the press united in their condemnation of Louis Philippe in the autumn of 1836 he urged that something be done to induce a better tone, at least in the ministerial papers. Complete estrangement between Britain and France must otherwise follow – this might be inevitable, 'but it does not seem to me to be our business to hurry it'.[18]

If Melbourne had been his own Foreign Secretary things would have gone more smoothly between Downing Street and Windsor. Palmerston, however, more activist, ambitious and impatient, was constantly involved in clashes with his royal master; leaving Melbourne, whose views were usually somewhere between the two, trying to soften the impact when they collided and to pick up the bits after the accident had taken place. The controversy over Spain illustrated his role. For several years a civil war had been dragging on between the legitimate government under the Queen Regent and her infant daughter and the Carlists under the Queen's reactionary uncle, Don Carlos. Russia and Austria supported Don Carlos, England and France the Queen. In 1835, when the Queen's cause seemed on the point of foundering, there was much pressure for direct intervention in her support. Melbourne was against sending troops, though ready to countenance such action by the French; the British Ambassador in Madrid and Foreign Secretary in London clamoured for an expeditionary force; William IV was against any such step and indeed felt our prime preoccupation should not be to support the Queen but rather to frustrate the French. Clearly it was impossible to satisfy everyone but the compromise adopted inspired universal distaste. A 'British Legion' of volunteers was to be raised which would fight the Queen's cause without involving the government in London. With well-justified doubts the King and Melbourne acquiesced in this proposal; Melbourne being particularly anxious lest we should recruit in Ireland and thus lay ourselves open to the charge of seeking to get rid of the Roman Catholic population.[19]

By the spring of 1836 the question of French intervention had become a major bone of contention. Melbourne warned Palmerston: 'The King is deeply impressed with the notion that Louis Philippe has acted falsely, and he is also persuaded that the entry of French troops into Spain would be the signal for war being made upon her by Austria and Russia'. Palmerston was convinced that, if we could not send an army to support the Queen, we should at least offer her a massive loan. He found little support for the idea in cabinet but did not allow this to check his enthusiasm. Melbourne told one of his colleagues that he was so uneasy about the whole affair that he could not sleep at night for thinking of it. Since the crisis coincided with the early days of the Norton scandal other factors may also have contributed to his insomnia.[20]

In the summer of 1836 a *coup d'état* in Spain forced the Queen Regent to accept a liberal constitution. Palmerston was delighted, William outraged. When in August Melbourne submitted to him a draft Speech from the Throne which contained a modestly optimistic passage about the chances of the royalist cause, he indignantly struck it out. 'He has not the least confidence in the Queen's government', he retorted, 'no opinion of the patriotism of the Spanish nation . . .'[21] What was worse, he insisted that the new constitution relieved us of all our treaty obligations towards Spain; a point of view from which no amount of argument could shift him. Palmerston bore the brunt of his displeasure but Melbourne found both exhausting and unprofitable the hours which he had to devote to the role of peace-maker.

That autumn things got abruptly better. When Melbourne wrote to propose a day for the meeting of parliament, the King replied benignly: 'He hopes that everybody will dine with him after the council, and drink two bottles of wine a man . . .'[22] In part, at least, his affability indicated his anxiety to enlist Melbourne on his side in the battle he was waging against the mother of the future Queen Victoria, the Duchess of Kent. The Duchess, egged on by her malevolent toady, Sir John Conroy, not only acted with all the ostentation of a future regent, but frequently conducted herself as if the role was already hers. She kept the young Princess jealously secluded and, if she had dared, would have cut her off altogether from any contact with her uncle. William IV responded by doing all he could to frustrate her and finally insulted her publicly at a banquet in the summer of 1836.

Melbourne's main preoccupation was to keep out of the firing-line, and in this he showed his usual dexterity. When the question of Victoria's marriage began to be mooted, however, the issue became too serious to be ignored. Various names had been suggested: notably William's candidate, the Prince of Orange, and the Duchess's, Albert of Saxe-Coburg. In April 1836 William formally enquired of his Lord Chancellor whether he could forbid the Duchess to invite Albert to stay. The Chancellor thought not, but felt that he could refuse Albert permission to see Victoria. Alarmed at what could quickly blossom into a most embarrassing imbroglio, Melbourne hastened off to talk some sense into the King:

> An heiress of the crown of England seventeen years of age is a troublesome commodity [he told Palmerston]. If the King tries to regulate her marriage by authority, he will probably fail. Chance makes marriages, even royal ones, and perhaps better than policy.
>
> I do not like the Duke of Coburg. We have Coburgs enough. The Duchess of Kent mother of the Queen and her nephew husband of the Queen would be a strong family coalition.
>
> I do not like the Prince of Orange. The connection is a bad one and may lead to perplexities. But she must marry somebody. Why not the Prince of Cambridge? After all, he has been educated here and we know him . . . If the King sets himself against the Duke of Coburg, he will give him a great advantage.[23]

In May 1837 Melbourne became directly involved in the warfare between King and Duchess. The problem arose of what sort of an establishment Victoria should have when she reached the age of eighteen. William would have liked to separate her entirely from her mother. Melbourne realized the impossibility of such a course. As he pointed out to the King, even after she had become eighteen the Princess would still be a minor, 'like any other infant, in all respects and for all purposes except succeeding to the throne'. He urged 'the quietest and easiest course' of increasing the present grant, perhaps taking some precautions to prevent Conroy and the Duchess laying their hands on all the extra money.[24] Grudgingly the King agreed but insisted that the Princess should have her own privy purse and financial comptroller. For this task he nominated Sir Benjamin Stephenson, whom he knew to be totally unacceptable to his sister-in-law.

The Duchess of Kent's reaction was predictable. She told Melbourne that she hoped parliament would reject the grant. 'Passed over, wounded on every occasion that circumstances will allow, I still know what is due to my station and rank and to my maternal duties, supported by the tears of my child, who has, of her own free will, told the King, that she desires nothing but to be left as heretofore with her mother.' Melbourne posted back to the King with a plea for further concessions. 'It is to be observed', he added apprehensively, 'how determined her Royal Highness is to fix me with the responsibility of what has been done, which shows that she contemplates publicity and parliamentary discussion.' William stuck to his guns. He would surrender Sir Benjamin, but not the separate privy purse – any retreat from that position would be humiliating. Melbourne later maintained that, if he had suspected the sort of pressure which the unfortunate Victoria was under from her mother and John Conroy, he would have supported the King to the hilt. As it was he assumed mother and child spoke more or less as one. To the King he insisted that the cabinet must be consulted before he went back to the Duchess. He succeeded in extracting one further concession: the original £10,000 a year proposed for Victoria should be split up, with £6000 going to the mother and only £4000 directly to the child. Even this was rejected and deadlock followed.[25]

Though he had gone further than the King liked in arguing the Duchess's case Melbourne had still left no doubt that his heart was in the right place. 'It is an ill wind that blows nobody good', wrote Holland in his diary, 'and this fracas with Kensington seems to have brought H.M. to a sense of the merits of his ministers – for he complimented Melbourne on his honour and high-mindedness, apologized for having brought him and his colleagues into contact with "low and vulgar upstarts" . . . and even spoke kindly of John Russell.'[26]

His favour was not to be enjoyed for long. Even when Holland wrote these words the King's life was guttering out. Early in the morning of 20 June he died. Into his place stepped an eighteen-year-old princess about whom nothing was known beyond the conspicuous facts of her youth and inexperience. Whether she would prove Whig or Tory, progressive or reactionary, obstinate or amenable, only time would tell. Melbourne looked forward to their first interview with some apprehension, much interest and a high degree of hope.

CHAPTER 18

Protector Somerset

THE RELATIONSHIP between Queen Victoria and her first Prime
Minister has been described *ad* and sometimes beyond *nauseam*. Customarily it is painted in pastel shades: the twilight romance of the wise,
grizzled, old statesman whose life had known such sadness and who
now found in the little Queen the consolation of the daughter whom
he had never had; the relief and joy of a girl of eighteen so happily
discovering in her Prime Minister the love and gentle tutelage of the
father whom she too had lacked. Other accounts are less sympathetic:
the seduction – emotional and intellectual if not physical – of an
innocent girl by a hardened sinner who sought to fix her for ever under
his control. Yet others are more coolly analytical. The throne, though
shorn of much of its consequence, was still the repository of immense
power. Victoria had no conception of how this power should be employed. Whoever undertook her political education would inevitably
be in a position of privilege; able to ensure immense advantage for their
party and policies. The peculiar fascination of the relationship is that
all these are part of the truth. Melbourne and Victoria were indeed
bound by ties too strong and too disinterested to be denied the name
of love yet the Prime Minister never forgot that he had a political case
to argue and a party whose interests must be furthered. All intimate
associations are made up of a web of complex strands. Those linking
Melbourne and Victoria were no more strange than can be found elsewhere; it was the fact that one was Prime Minister, the other Queen,
which rendered the relationship unique.

Their first formal interview took place a few hours after the old King's death. According to Lord Holland, Victoria had already been in touch with Melbourne a few days before and had asked him to prepare her accession speech.[1] This seems unlikely, especially given the fact that up till that moment she had been virtually the prisoner of her mother and Sir John Conroy.[2] The Prime Minister was, however, left in no doubt about the sovereign's intentions. She told him that she had long meant to confirm him in office and that the government could not be in better hands. 'Nothing could be more proper and feeling than her behaviour', a gratified Melbourne wrote to Lansdowne. At eleven the same morning she held her first council. It would have been a hardened cynic indeed who did not feel some emotion at the dignity and self-possession with which this slight girl in black took charge of the destinies of the nation. 'Everyone appeared touched with her manner', noted Hobhouse, 'particularly the Duke of Wellington and Lord Melbourne. I saw some tears in the eyes of the latter.'[3]

To read Queen Victoria's journal is sometimes to get the impression that her Prime Minister was almost permanently on the edge of crying. As seems often to be the case with those who find difficulty in making any deep commitment to another human being, Melbourne was a man of quick sentimentality. Tears would well into his eyes whenever the future of the Queen was under discussion; when speaking of the speech from the throne he 'became touched to tears'; he had tears in his eyes when he told Victoria that the Duchess of Kent's annuity had been approved by parliament; his eyes 'filled with tears in speaking of England's glories; he *loves* his country *truly*'; he even had tears in his eyes when he remarked that the Duke of Wellington was in a good humour and an excellent man to do business with. A Whig politician who would shed tears over the virtues of the Duke of Wellington was, indeed, unusual. And when, at the coronation, poor old Lord Rolle, becoming entangled in his robes, bounced down the steps to the bottom and the Queen stepped down from the throne to accept his homage from where he had landed – my goodness, how Lord Melbourne cried.

To the Queen this was but one more proof of his warmth and kindness. Her conviction of his perfections was quickly formed. In the first three weeks of their acquaintance she described him in her journal as: 'very straightforward, honest, clever and good'; 'very honest, good and kind hearted, as well as very clever'; 'good, honest, kind hearted and clever'; 'a most truly honest, straight forward and noble-minded man'; 'good and honest'; and 'honest, good and kind hearted'.[4] The emphasis on his honesty is revealing. Almost the only man whom she had hitherto known well was Sir John Conroy, whom she had, with good reason, distrusted. Melbourne, with his lack of guile and patent dedication to her service, seemed almost a being from another world. After Duncannon had called on her she noted that he was agreeable and amusing, but that neither he nor other ministers had 'that kindness, mildness and open frankness, and *agreeability* which I find in my kind friend Lord Melbourne; he *alone* inspires me with that feeling of great confidence and I may say *security*, for I feel *so safe* when he speaks to me and is with me . . .'

She was, of course, in a sense in love with him. To her Miranda he was both Prospero and Ferdinand.[5] At fifty-eight Melbourne was still an exceptionally handsome man. He was witty, urbane, sophisticated; he could make her laugh, could fascinate her with stories about her ancestors. She longed to be taught, and Melbourne had always enjoyed teaching: 'he has *such* stores of knowledge; such a wonderful memory; he knows about everybody and everything; *who* they were and *what* they did; . . . it does me a *world* of good; and his conversations always *improve* one greatly'. Her attitude, said Hobhouse, was that of a child to a parent. He was easy but respectful, and behaved as became himself and his sovereign.[6] He fussed about her health, urged her to be vaccinated: 'Do! Think if you were to have it . . . think of the scrape you'd get us all into'. She countered in kind, telling him that diet was the best physician for him. 'He said laughing, he drank too much *champagne*, and I added, mixed too many wines; at which he laughed a good deal.'

There were those who saw more in the relationship. The Queen's feelings, wrote Greville, 'are sexual though she does not know it'. In a sense he was right. Victoria was intensely conscious of the fact that Melbourne was a man and she a woman, but on the sexual level her feeling for him can never have been more than a schoolgirl crush. Nor can he have found her physically attractive. 'Ld Melbourne', said Princess Lieven, '*a auprès d'elle un air d'amour, de contentement, de vanité même* . . .' Loving he was, indeed, and he was certainly contented with his position, but even in the gutter Press there were few accusations that his affection went beyond the parental. 'I hope you are amused at the report of Lord Melbourne being likely to marry the Queen . . .' wrote Lady Grey to Creevey. The fact that this singularly upright and well-informed lady thought the matter one for joking, shows how innocent the relationship must have been. It was Greville, once again, who put Melbourne's feeling most surely into perspective:

I have no doubt he is passionately fond of her as he might be of his daughter if he had one; and the more because he is a man with a capacity for loving without having anything in the world to love. It is become his province to educate, instruct and form the most interesting mind and character in the world.[7]

That he did not love her blindly is shown by a conversation which he had with Lord Holland two months after the accession. He was, he said, much struck by her sagacity and by her calm determination. He was pleased 'on the whole with her feelings but not without misgivings that her aversion to Conroy and her estrangement from her mother . . . may break out in some way harsh and unamiable and injurious to her character'. Already there were signs that she could form strong opinions and hold them in the face of any opposition. 'Her family complexion and blood, her period of life and her inordinate love of musick all . . . indicate the germs of a warm constitution.'[8] He seemed to regard her as the proud owner of a tiger cub might consider his pet: playful, affectionate and docile but already capable of giving a nasty scratch and potentially lethal.

There was no sign of these doubts in his manner when he spoke to her. His conversation was delightful; to the Queen, from her cribbed background and starved as she had been of the company of people of wit or wisdom, it was almost intoxicating. He rambled on: sometimes flippant, sometimes irreverent, always gay and entertaining, usually with some little nugget of information or advice lurking beneath the surface frivolity. Eagerly she rushed off to inscribe his words in her journal; often betraying in her artless entries a total failure to understand what her hero had told her.

He would frequently talk of books. *Hamlet* and *Macbeth* were Shakespeare's best plays, though to read *As You Like It* was to spend an hour or two in a forest of fairyland. He preferred French books to English: 'They write shortly and clearly, and very concise, with a good deal of *nettété*'. English books were too long and prosing while the Germans were misty and obscure. 'No woman ever wrote a really good book; no sterling book.' They had too much passion and too little sense, though he made an exception for Mme de Sévigné and admitted that, in general, women wrote the better letters. Mme de Staël was the best living female writer and very clever, but 'a great humbug'. He was fond of novels but had little time to read them; Scott had some good things but also some very bad ones and he anyway preferred his poetry.

On painting he found little good in Murillo and Rubens, preferring the Italian masters. His favourite pictures were of the Holy Family: 'After all a woman and child is the most beautiful subject one can have'. Reynolds, he thought, was the greatest painter England had ever produced, but in general he advised the Queen to keep clear of artists, '. . . they're a waspish set of people'. On music Victoria for once reduced him to silence, by observing she thought *Don Giovanni* old-fashioned. Melbourne merely 'clasped his hands and looked up in astonishment'. On the other hand the sentimental and fashionable ballads of Tom Moore sent him to sleep. He was sceptical about the value of education: '. . . none of the Pagets can read or write and they get on well enough.' Nor were his views on religion those likely to have been put forward by her more orthodox teachers. It mattered little to what church one belonged; the Church of England was probably the best because it was 'the least meddling'. It was important not to waste too much time considering theological conundrums like the true nature of Christ, 'for that isn't comprehensible. The Trinity isn't comprehensible.' He was often in trouble for not attending church and pleaded it was a matter of generations. 'My father and mother never went. People didn't use to go so much formerly; it wasn't the fashion.' He conceded handsomely that it was 'a right thing to do' but showed no signs of amending his practice accordingly. 'I'm afraid to go to church for fear of hearing something very extraordinary', he pleaded on another occasion. The Queen laughed and said that he usually pretended to be ill.

There seemed no subject on which he was not prepared to express a concise and usually heterodox opinion. On procrastination: 'If a thing is very urgent you can always find time for it; but if a thing can be put off, why then you put it off'. On the world of philanthropists and their works: 'I hate societies. I think they always lead to mischief, they are always for the benefit of the banker and the treasurer'. On Bishop Heber drowning in his bath: 'He was a blustering, awkward fellow. Everything is awkwardness . . . *c'est les maladroits qui sont malheureux*'. On wife beating: 'Why, it is almost worthwhile for a woman to be beat, considering the exceeding pity she excites'. On the country: 'Everything does better in London; London beats the country hollow in flowers . . . All gardens are dull, a garden is a dull thing.' It seemed nothing could discompose him. When the Queen and he were hissed at Ascot by two women, Wellington remarked that such conduct was unladylike. 'If you mean by *unladylike*, that it is unlike what a lady *ought* to do, I quite agree with you; but if you mean that it is unlike what ladies *do* do, I cannot agree.' Safely back at Windsor, the Queen eagerly transcribed the aphorism with all the others in her journal.

On the whole there is no doubt that his influence was beneficial. A solid code of conduct underpinned the superficial flippancy. '. . . truly excellent and moral', Victoria described him, 'and has such a strong feeling against immorality and wickedness.' Certainly she never recorded any remark of Melbourne's which would seem improper to any but the most censorious and Holland even noticed the Prime Minister checking her in 'a little harmless and playful disposition to mimicking'. He was relentless in the cause of duty. 'A queen's life is very laborious . . . hardly any leisure', he told her. When it seemed that parliament might have to open as early as 9 January she said that, in that case, she would *not* open it herself. ' "Oh, you must", he said. "That would never do." I wouldn't, I said, and always wished to get out of that [sic]. "You mustn't do that", he said kindly and gently. After dinner . . . I again teased him about not opening parliament in person. "Oh! you will do it", he said earnestly, with his good kind face expressing anxiety I should.' She did, of course, and relished the stern voice of her conscience. In Wellington's words, he taught her 'to preside over the destinies of this great country'. She would anyway have learnt the lesson yet otherwise she could hardly have hoped to do it so painlessly, so pleasantly or so fast.[9]

But a most important lesson he signally failed to inculcate. Though the Queen could accept the position intellectually, it took her many years to behave as the ruler of a nation and not a party. Melbourne was her dearest friend; his allies, therefore, must be her allies; still more – for she was a formidable hater – his enemies her enemies. He would argue that really there was nothing to choose between the parties, she would assume that he was joking. When Lord Lyndhurst was being particularly outrageous in the House of Lords, Victoria declared that he was a bad man and she disliked him. 'Do you dislike all bad men?' asked Lord Melbourne. 'For that comprises a large number.' He went on to say 'that Lyndhurst was a very agreeable man, which I denied'. The Duke of Bedford remarked that Melbourne did all he could to mitigate her hatred of the Tories and not let reasonable disapproval of a few zealots extend to blanket condemnation of a party. So far did he go that once, when the Queen was roundly denouncing the conduct of the Tories to some trusted hearer, she naively added: 'It is very odd, but I cannot get Lord Melbourne to see it in that light.'[10]

And here the limitations of Melbourne's tutelage became most clear. Try though he might to alleviate it, her dependence on him was absolute. She refused to discuss important matters with other ministers on the ground that 'she don't like to talk . . . about politics of a general character to anybody but Lord Melbourne'. She accepted uncritically almost anything he cared to tell her, while usually missing the note of questioning scepticism which gave his words their special value. When he was not there she pined for him; in the evenings the chair in which he usually sat stood empty as if Banquo's ghost might enter at any moment to take possession of it; his room was reserved for him at Windsor and it only needed a word of his coming for the roaring fires which he found necessary in summer and winter alike to be lit for his coming. 'The part she at present plays', wrote Creevey, 'is putting herself unreservedly into the exclusive management of Melbourne, without apparently thinking of anyone else.' It was hardly surprising that the Tories were reduced to anger or despair. 'It is a most grievous state of things', complained Charles Arbuthnot. '. . . with the young foolish Queen against us we can have but little hope. She seems to be full of power for evil – and to be full of weakness for good.'[11]

In one way at least the 'weakness for good' can be laid to Melbourne's charge. The Prime Minister's, not mere indifference to, but wilful determination to ignore the social condition of the people has already been remarked. He did not consciously set out to instruct Victoria along the same lines, but his insensibility, his urbane and comfortable scoffing, inevitably had this result. Few people indeed *want* to be confronted by unpleasant reality when it is far more agreeable to ramble along the primrose paths of indifference. As Lady Longford put it: 'Melbourne did not dry up the wells of her pity . . . but he did blunt her social conscience by starting the evil legend that all discontent was due to a handful of agitators.' His refusal to read *Oliver Twist* – 'It's all among workhouses, and coffin-makers, and pickpockets. I don't like that low, debasing style . . .' – was typical of his attitude on a hundred issues. Victoria tried to defend the book. 'I don't *like* those things. I wish to avoid them; I don't like them in *reality*, and therefore I don't wish to see them represented.' On the fate of the evicted Irish peasantry, he remarked blithely: 'They become *absorbed* somehow or other', and added, 'they ate too much and there was not enough for them and you.' 'You had better try to do no good, and then you'll get into no scrapes', is a pleasantly harmless piece of nonsense which becomes dangerous when preached by precept and example to an impressionable girl who is in a position to do much good if she feels so inclined. Wellington, as so often, put his finger on it when he said he was sure Melbourne was the best minister the Queen could have and that he had given her very good advice, 'but I'm afraid he jokes too much with her, and makes her treat things too lightly, which are very serious'. Melbourne's response when told of the Duke's remark was equally characteristic; he thought there might well be something in it, 'it shows the shrewdness of the man'.[12]

For Melbourne the situation was not entirely without thorns. For a man whose idea of a pleasant evening was dalliance with Mrs Norton or racy gossip around the table at Holland House, Buckingham Palace and Windsor offered limited attractions. The latter, in particular, must have palled. Shilling whist with the Duchess of Kent, six hours a day of tête-à-tête with the Queen, a perpetual check on swearing and loose talk. Mackworth Praed indulged himself on the subject:

> . . . More safely now
> The Minister shall buzz and bow
> In regions where no comment rude
> From lip or pen shall e'er intrude.
> There he, the fond and favoured guest,
> Shall look his liveliest, gloze his best,
> On everything or nothing chatter,
> And smoothly fawn and softly flatter . . .[13]

It must indeed have seemed stultifying, sometimes almost unendurably so. At such times he would break out. December 1838 found him lingering in London when the Queen urgently required his presence in Windsor. 'Lord Melbourne assures your Majesty that he would not delay in London, if he did not feel it to be absolutely necessary for your Majesty's service', yet there was not much going on and the previous night he had supped and been to the theatre with the Normanbys. But such occasions were rare. Night after night would find him patiently in attendance.

It was worth it to him. Quite apart from the pleasure which he found in her company and her instruction, Victoria for Melbourne represented power. His virtual monopoly of her attention guaranteed him an inestimable political advantage. Lord Aberdeen, not usually a man to express himself extravagantly, summed it up admirably when he told Princess Lieven:

> . . . no minister in this country, since the days of Protector Somerset, ever was placed in such a situation . . . He has a young and inexperienced infant in his hands, whose whole conduct and opinions must necessarily be in complete subservience to his views. I do him

the justice to believe that he has some feeling for his situation . . . but in the nature of things, this power must be absolute, at least at court.[14]

Croker believed – or professed to believe – that the Prime Minister deliberately thrust unnecessary papers on Victoria so as to sicken her with work and ensure that all the decisions were left to him. '. . . his situation is certainly the most dictatorial, the most despotic, that the world has ever seen. Wolsey and Walpole were in strait waistcoats compared to him.'[15] It was, of course, natural that the Tories should stress the autocratic nature of Melbourne's position. In fact, if Croker had known a little more about the helpless child in Buckingham Palace he would have realized that she was very capable of looking after herself and that, though Melbourne's influence was indeed enormous, it had to be used with constant tact and discretion. Overt bullying would have swiftly ended his rule: Queen Victoria did not intend to have two Conroys.

That Melbourne relished his position is certain. This was not because he wished to accumulate wealth or honours for himself. Shortly after her accession the Queen, through Baron Stockmar, asked the Prime Minister whether he would accept the Garter, ultimate accolade of royal favour. Melbourne replied: 'I don't care a sixpence for any order, and I will not take it either now or ever. The reason why the Queen must not offer it to me, is that if I were to have it, everybody would say, Ld Melbourne has taken unfair advantage of the Queen's youth and inexperience, and his first act has been to make her give him the Garter.' This is not the language of a self-seeker. But though he would not use his power for selfish purposes he still rejoiced in it. Hobhouse noticed how in cabinet the Prime Minister, who had previously envisaged the possibility of resignation with equanimity, was now determined to fight on even though his majority fell to one. 'I attributed this to the partiality manifested by the Queen for Lord Melbourne's administration and general management.' The next few years were to show the value of the Queen's partiality and the strength of Melbourne's determination.[16]

It is remarkable how even those Tories who inveighed most hotly against Melbourne's favour generally conceded that he made little improper use of it. Like Warren Hastings, he had a right to be astounded at his own moderation. It was a former Tory minister who remarked that, in another country, Melbourne's position would have caused his opponents to despair. 'Here, it does not signify a single farthing.' In saying this he exaggerated, and knew it. Melbourne's relationship with the Queen was worth many farthings to the Whigs and was to keep them in office long after they would otherwise have perished. But it could have been worth far more; in the hands of an unscrupulous man it could have been used to gain the Whigs massive advantage which it might have taken twenty years to erode. In July 1837 Wellington told the Queen that he was sure she would find 'Ld Melbourne an honourable man and one in whom her Majesty might put confidence, that he was a man apt to treat too lightly or, as he expressed it, *"poco curante"*, but in the main an honest and an honourable man'. Opinions may differ about the Duke's performance as a statesman but few would deny that on honesty and honour he was a considerable authority. Nor did he change his views. When, in August 1839, the Duchess of Kent attacked Melbourne's conduct towards the Queen, Wellington defended him whole-heartedly, saying that he had done nothing but his duty. In his position, said the Duke, 'I should not only have done the same, but have done more than he has done'.[17]

CHAPTER 19

The Queen's First Minister

MELBOURNE'S FIRST TASK was to dispose of Sir John Conroy. The Duchess of Kent's counsellor had abetted his employer in her efforts to impose her will on the young Victoria and had made himself so loathed in the process that the Queen was literally not prepared to be in the same room as him. The Duchess was equally passionate in her loyalty. Baron Stockmar, most confidential agent of Victoria's uncle, King Leopold of Belgium, who had been despatched to her as a sort of accession present, met Melbourne after the first council meeting and gave him a note of the terms on which Conroy would retire quietly from the royal service. The most important elements were a pension of £3000 a year and a peerage. 'This is really too bad! Have you ever heard such impudence?' exclaimed the Prime Minister.[1] But it was worth paying a lot to eliminate this sly and dangerous man. The pension and a baronetcy were conceded, an Irish peerage would follow when one became available. The latter promise was never honoured and Conroy lingered on, to prove a potent source of mischief in the future.

What Conroy wanted was the post of private secretary to the Queen. Melbourne had no intention of gratifying this ambition, or indeed of letting anyone else enjoy the same privileges. It was more than thirty years since he had argued against the employment of McMahon as private secretary to King George III – 'an indolent monarch', he protested, would soon let such a figure 'usurp the peculiar functions of the chief magistrate' – and now that he might be the victim of such a usurpation he saw the force of his argument still more strongly. It seemed to him, he told Russell, 'highly to be desired upon constitutional grounds', that nobody should come between monarch and minister. Even the impeccably honourable Sir Herbert Taylor, with a master who knew his own mind, had sometimes seemed an impediment to communication rather than an aid. A man of greater ambition, working for the inexperienced Queen, could quickly make himself master of the palace. But if such a function were to be dispensed with it would be 'absolutely required that the minister should be always near her'. He would, himself, in effect act as Victoria's private secretary.[2]

The flaw in this proposition, which was quickly to become apparent, was that the task of private secretary should be full-time. The office of Prime Minister also made certain demands on the time and energy of its incumbent. To fill the two jobs at once called not merely for superhuman industry but the capacity to be almost permanently in two places at the same time. In the first flush of confidence, however, Melbourne took on the duties blithely. So did Victoria. When Melbourne asked her whether she was sure she could endure all the fatigue of the signature and arrangement of the papers, she 'answered sprightlily "I don't know but I will try" '. How could she have said anything else when the reward for her assiduity would be an undisturbed relationship with her beloved minister. '. . . take care Victoria you know your prerogative!' came the baleful warning of the Duchess of Kent – a reminder which her own activities might reasonably have been thought to have made superfluous. 'Take care that Lord Melbourne is not King . . .'[3]

After Conroy the Duchess was, indeed, the greatest of Melbourne's problems at court. She had moved with her daughter to Buckingham Palace, to act as duenna in the royal household, but found her interpretation of the role very different from Victoria's. Inevitably Melbourne was forced to arbitrate. He told Holland that, though he considered the Duchess of Kent a foolish, even stupid woman, governed by the malignant Conroy, he was still anxious to avoid any breach between mother and daughter. Few things would have been more damaging to the Queen's reputation than the departure of the Duchess from the palace; extracting, as she would have, every drop of pathos from the role of forlorn widow. But though Melbourne saw what was necessary he proved surprisingly inept at bringing it about. Sometimes, indeed, it seemed as if he were more anxious to exacerbate the relationship than to heal it, so vigorously did he take the Queen's part and encourage her into intransigence.[4]

The Duchess could be exceptionally annoying. Having risked some political unpopularity by pushing through an increase in her annuity by £8000 to £30,000 a year, Melbourne was dismayed to discover that she was £70,000 in debt. The Duchess took it for granted that the Queen or the government would find the money and was deeply offended at their reluctance. 'The Duchess of Kent', Melbourne told Ellice, 'has undertaken in a very high tone to pay these debts herself. Let her do so . . . I entirely object to the Queen being subjected to any expense or charge.' Her resolution did not last long and within a few days she was pestering her daughter once more. Melbourne advised the Queen to say that she would do as much as her ministers proposed, but could do nothing for herself. He much regretted that she should be thus 'subjected to so much annoyance and importunity from a quarter in which your Majesty ought only to find assistance and affection'. The comment was justified, but hardly appropriate from a man out to restore harmony to a troubled relationship.[5]

The Duchess considered Melbourne her enemy and took little trouble to conceal her view. Relations, however, though strained, were never broken, and the Prime Minister was regularly plagued by applications for jobs or pensions for her hangers-on. Once, for instance, she asked that Dr Card, vicar of Great Malvern, should be made Dean of Durham. She received a tactful reply to the effect that this was a senior post and one for which the applicant was hardly qualified. Very well, replied the Duchess, but she hoped that other preferment would soon be found. Melbourne's patience ran thin. It would raise false hopes to promise anything. 'Dr Card', he stated bluntly, 'is incessant in his applications, and aspires to advancement to which he appears to me to have insufficient claims.' Not in the least abashed, the Duchess tried another tack. The worthy priest, it seemed, had a son called William. Now, a place in the Navy would suit him very well . . .[6]

In the meantime there was a coronation to be organized. Melbourne felt personally responsible for its success; indeed at times he seemed to consider all other business, domestic or international, as being of secondary importance to this cumbrous ceremony. There were certainly plenty of problems to preoccupy him. The date proved unexpectedly difficult. The original proposal had been for 26 June 1838, but then some Tory journalist recollected that this was the day on which George IV had died and cried scandal at such an insult to the departed monarch. Cumberland, always glad to cause trouble, affected great displeasure and the Duchess of Kent made little secret of her satisfaction at the imbroglio. Conroy would never have made so naive a gaffe. Victoria was for sticking to the date and defying opinion but Melbourne, more wisely, saw that nothing would be gained by obstinacy and talked the Queen into accepting a postponement of two days.[7]

Melbourne was all for keeping the ceremony as short as possible. At the council to discuss the arrangements he muttered discontentedly – apparently under the impression that he was musing to himself alone – 'The fellows now never preach less than an hour and a half'. As the Bishop of London rather sourly commented, this showed how rarely the Prime Minister went to church. Then there was the question of whether the peers should all kiss the Queen. Melbourne felt that this was more than flesh and blood could stand. Greville reassured him. The peers had only made-believe to kiss Queen Anne and, anyway, this part of the ceremony could well be omitted. She would, however, have to go through with it in the case of the bishops. There was the question of who should be asked to the various balls and banquets – Melbourne thought the behaviour of those who clamoured for invitations 'very pushing and very degrading' – and the difficulty posed by the French who suggested that the King's son, the Duc de Nemours, should represent his father. 'The presence of a young Roman Catholic foreign prince upon such an occasion', felt Melbourne, 'would be objectionable, would produce observation and excite alarm.'[8]

So the great day came, and was generally agreed to have passed off well. The congregation greeted the more exalted guests with partisan zeal. Marshal Soult, who had taken the place of the dangerously dashing Duc de Nemours, was met with loud applause; O'Connell was hissed. According to Lord Aberdeen the 'spontaneous and universal burst of applause' which greeted the homage of the Duke of Wellington, contrasted strikingly with 'the feeble attempt to treat Lord Melbourne with the same honours'.[9] The Queen, however, was satisfied that Melbourne was cheered loudly.

'Melbourne looked very awkward and uncouth', noted Disraeli, 'with his coronet cocked over his nose, his robes under his feet, and holding the great sword of state like a butcher.' Lady Lyttelton thought that he was looking 'picturesquely old' and even Victoria noticed that he seemed to be finding the sword of state excessively heavy. In fact he must have been in almost intolerable discomfort. He had had violent diarrhoea the day before and had checked it with lavish doses of laudanum and brandy. By the time the ceremony was over he was so exhausted that he took a strong draught of calomel and did not attend cabinet for a week.[10]

No one can have doubted that Melbourne's main concern in all these doings was to protect the Queen. He saw it as his function to shield her from hostile criticism and to provide a cocoon in which she need have no contact with the harsh realities of everyday life. Sometimes this proved difficult, as when Lord Palmerston, by then his brother-in-law, tried to rape one of the ladies-in-waiting whilst at Windsor Castle. He arrived, possibly by mistake, in the bedroom of Mrs Susan Brand, locked one door, blockaded the other and advanced lecherously on the lady's bed. His attempt cannot have been forced home with great conviction since Mrs Brand escaped and appealed to Stockmar for protection. Stockmar, in his turn, appealed to Melbourne, who was 'shocked beyond measure at this atrocious attempt. He said in all his experience he had *never* attempted any woman against her will . . . He thought it could not escape detection, and the result would be much damage to the character of the court and even the Queen, and the immediate break-up of the administration.' He sent a note to Palmerston insisting that he at once write an apology to Mrs Brand. Palmerston complied, the apology was accepted and the scandal hushed up. According to Greville word got to the Queen who was in high indignation but allowed Melbourne to talk her out of taking any action.[11]

On one occasion the Prime Minister found himself in trouble for failing to protect the Queen. Robert Owen, industrialist and utopian, wished to present a petition to Victoria pleading that certain measures be taken to combat ignorance and pauperism among the lower classes. Melbourne thought the petition nonsensical but harmless and agreed to present Owen at a levée. On 26 June 1839, be-wigged and sworded, the great philanthropist laid his petition before her Majesty. That, Melbourne supposed, was the end of the matter. He reckoned without the clergy. Did he not realize, asked the Rev. Thomas Tragett, that the person he was introducing into 'the presence of our beloved, pure and maiden Queen was the organ of a society which under the specious name of "Rational Religionists" repudiated the revealed word of Almighty God' and systematically disseminated works of the most disgusting obscenity? Whether Melbourne was wicked or merely criminally negligent was the problem that concerned the Rev. Mr Giles.[12]

The question was even raised in the House of Lords where the Bishop of Exeter remarked that Melbourne must have been ignorant of Owen's character and activities, on which Wellington commented how remiss it was to present to the sovereign someone with whom one was not personally acquainted. Somewhat defensively Melbourne argued that to present someone at a levée was not to endorse their views. He himself thought Owen's ideas wild, even dangerous, though rendered less so by their 'mitigating character of extreme absurdity'. Nor did he think his opinions any less mischievous because they came 'clothed in the disguise of philanthropy'. On the contrary, 'those who professed and appeared to feel the deepest regard for their species, and the widest sentiments of humanity, often became in the course of events the most reckless and merciless'. But Owen was as much a subject of the Queen as anyone else, convicted of no crime, guilty of no immorality. He had a right to put forward his views and no harm had been done. Nor, alas, had it. It seems unlikely that Victoria even glanced at the memorandum; certainly she remained uncontaminated by its contents.

The scandal of Lady Flora Hastings was altogether more serious. Lady Flora was one of the Queen's ladies-in-waiting; a pious, self-contained, chilly woman of thirty-two. She came from a rampantly Tory family and was viewed by Victoria as a spy placed in her camp by her mother and Sir John Conroy. Early in 1839 she found herself suffering from prolonged and painful stomach-aches and protuberance of the belly. The Queen had already begun to speculate about a possible liaison between Conroy and Lady Flora – regrettably encouraged in this by the tittle-tattle of Lord Melbourne – and it only needed some casual reference to her distended stomach to start the gossip going. Sir James Clark, the Queen's doctor, admitted that he had his suspicions. Lady Tavistock, senior Lady-of-the-bedchamber, was called in to protect the purity of her charges. She in turn appealed to Melbourne who concluded that the only thing to do was to wait and see.

His conclusion could hardly have been more dangerous. Delay could only let gossip spread and fester. The obvious course was for the Queen to speak to her mother and the latter to have a quiet word with Lady Flora. Unfortunately relations between the two households were now so strained that anything straightforward was out of the question. The affair was allowed to drag on for another three weeks; then Sir James Clark, his suspicions hardened into near certainty, was encouraged to insist upon a medical examination. Lady Flora was outraged but eventually agreed and, in the event, was found blameless. That, with a few grovelling apologies and some common sense all round, could still have been the end of the affair. Unfortunately, however, in spite of his having signed a certificate attesting to his patient's illness, Clark still had his doubts and did not hesitate in communicating them to Melbourne, to Lady Portman, who had now succeeded Lady Tavistock, and even to the Queen. As Lord William Russell observed, Melbourne had properly chosen the most chaste Whig ladies to place around the Queen but 'forgot good sense, good feelings, and other little virtues which adorn the female character'. The sanctimonious harpies of Buckingham Palace did not hesitate to believe the worst and Lady Flora, officially innocent, found herself looked at chillingly askance.[13]

Now the Hastings family roared into the fray. Shortly after the first examination the Chancellor, Lord Cottenham, was sent by Melbourne to interview Lady Flora's brother, the Marquess, and try to smooth things over. Ominously he reported '. . . much more excitement than before, general demands for reparation'.[14] The family, partly to further Tory interests but mainly, no doubt, from genuine concern for Lady Flora's honour, were out for blood. Who, they repeatedly demanded, had been responsible for the original rumour? Was it Sir James Clark? Was it the Queen's beloved governess and confidante, Baroness Lehzen? The old dowager-marchioness wrote to Melbourne to demand Clark's dismissal. Her letter was peremptory and offensive but the Hastings family had been the victims in the affair and she deserved better than the cold rebuff which she received. In this Melbourne described her letter as so 'unprecedented and objectionable' that he could not bring himself to do more than acknowledge it.[15]

Lord Hastings, after three months cogitation, now took up the quarrel. He had been unable to find the person responsible for the foul slander on his sister, he said, but at least he had to hand the Prime Minister's 'offensive and insulting' letter to his mother. For this he demanded a full apology. Melbourne's reply was modestly conciliatory. He could not see anything in the least objectionable in his letter but was happy to assure the injured marchioness that 'nothing was further from my intention than to offer her ladyship any offence'. Hastings had to make do with this somewhat mildewed olive branch. On reflection Melbourne felt that here too he had blundered. He should have told Lady Hastings bluntly: 'I'll give no explanation, but I'm responsible for it all'. If he had he would certainly have provoked Lord Hastings to still noisier blustering but he would at least have spared the women of the palace much tribulation and brought a touch of honesty into an otherwise discreditable business.[16]

Meanwhile a palace scandal had become, first the talk of London society, then, as the Hastings family published pamphlets and sent letters to the newspapers, an affair of national interest. In a way they over-played their hand: their determination to damage the court and wreck the government became so evident that it forfeited some of the sympathy they had won for their real grievance. On the government side there was a demand for an official statement but Melbourne, backed by the Duke of Wellington, stoutly opposed it. 'If the Holy Ghost were to publish one', remarked Fred Lamb, 'it would only serve as aliment for the vile press.' The policy of silence would no doubt have succeeded and the scandal died down if the unfortunate Lady Flora had not predeceased it. In July 1839 she died in great pain – the post-mortem revealing that the illness and swelling had been caused by a tumour on the liver. Her death caused a fresh upsurge of public sympathy and of indignation against the Queen and her advisers. Stones were thrown at the royal carriage as it accompanied Lady Flora's funeral procession, Melbourne and Victoria were insulted when they rode together in Hyde Park and the Duchess of Montrose even hissed the Queen and called out 'Mrs Melbourne', when the royal party appeared on the balcony at Ascot.[17]

It seemed as if Victoria's name had been irretrievably tarnished and though time was to show that the public memory was no more reliable on this issue than on any other, in the summer of 1839 things looked black. To none did they seem blacker than to Melbourne who held himself largely responsible for the mess. In this he was correct. It was not so much that he had done the wrong thing as that he had conspicuously failed to do the right. As Greville sensibly commented: 'There may be objections to Melbourne's extraordinary domiciliation in the palace; but the compensation ought to be found in his good sense and experience preventing the possibility of such transactions and *tracasseries* as these'.[18] If he had acted decisively when he had first heard of the affair he could at once have checked it. Instead he dithered and let the scandal blaze out of control. It was to be a long time before the Queen regained her confidence.

Summing up, Lord Holland called the affair 'an ugly offspring of prudery, tittle-tattle and folly'. Viewing it from the cabinet chamber rather than the palace, he deplored the extent to which it had distracted Melbourne from his duties as Prime Minister. 'These court dissensions harass Ld Melbourne and engross his mind too much . . . constant intercourse with her has warped his judgment.'[19] While the Prime Minister had been mismanaging matters in the palace, catastrophe had overtaken his party and the Queen was faced with a new danger. 'All, ALL my happiness gone!' she wrote in her journal on 7 May 1839. 'That happy peaceful life destroyed, that dearest kind Lord Melbourne no more my minister.'

CHAPTER 20

The 'Stationary System'

WHILE MELBOURNE'S position at court had become ever more impregnable, his support in the country was steadily being eroded. The Whigs went into the general election of August 1837 in optimistic mood, basking in the overt approval of the Queen. Even when it became clear that it was going to be a close-run thing they remained sure that their royal talisman would win them the day: 'When I hear of Lord Melbourne looking very ill and worn', wrote Lady Granville, 'and see how neck-and-neck the election runs, I feel as if our great dependence was in her grace and favour.' Melbourne himself was always more sceptical about the value of the Queen's favour than were his followers. He wrote gloomily to Howick when less than half the results were in: 'The elections seem to be passing in such a manner as may probably relieve us from the responsibility of our present situation . . .' He was perplexed to explain their setback. He felt the hostility of the clergy must be partly to blame but they could hardly have been more active than they had been in 1835.[1]

Certainly the rancour of the Church of England against a government which had meddled in its affairs was one of the factors responsible for the result. So too was the highly unpopular poor law. 'Either is sufficient to turn a nearly balanced election', Melbourne told Russell, 'and all was now nearly balanced.' More partisan observers insisted the damage was done by Tory sharp practice, or, more charitably, their better organization. There was something in all these arguments. But fundamentally, the voter had turned against a party which seemed to have no cause at heart except that of the Roman Catholics in Ireland. It is arguable that no programme of reform would have swept the country in 1837, that Britain had relapsed into that period of apathy and consolidation which traditionally follows years of innovation. Be that as it may, it is certain that a reforming ministry with no reforms to propose – offering instability without the hope of progress – has little chance of winning popular support. 'If the matter had been looked at dispassionately', Melbourne confessed to Lady Holland, 'we had no reason to expect otherwise.'[2]

Though everyone agreed that the government had done badly, there was less certainty about how badly it had done and who had been the victors. The most systematic study of the election suggests that the government's overall majority – on the most generous definition of its supporters – had been whittled down to 24. The radicals had been the main victims, though their losses had occurred as much in defections over the preceding twelve months as actually at the election itself.[3] Hume and Roebuck were among their defeated leaders; the latter roundly denounced the delinquent voters: 'Let them servilely worship their rising sun; let them crawl before his Lordship and sycophantically adore him. I have done with them!' The Tories exultantly assumed that ministers must now abandon their former trimming and depend on conservative support: a Whig government pursuing moderate Tory policies against an opposition of ultras and radicals seemed to them the likely outcome.[4]

Melbourne was less certain. The essentials of the situation had not changed. The Tories still could not form a viable government, the Whigs were still dependent on Irish and radical votes, the Irish still thought there were richer pickings to be got from the Whigs than any other party, the radicals still shrank from defeating their lesser enemies to promote their greater. 'Have we lost in the late elections by being too radical or by being too little radical?' mused Melbourne. If the latter, then ballot should be made an open question, if the former then any such step would be disastrous. In the meantime the only thing to do was to wait and see. Russell suggested tentatively that some steps forward might be taken in at least one of the fields in which the Whigs were supposed to favour activity; if not the ballot, then perhaps education or the reform of the War Office. The Prime Minister saw no virtue in such proposals. 'It is most impolitic', he stated firmly, 'to begin making changes of this magnitude at the present moment.' He could not contemplate any serious modification of the *status quo,* whether in the way of innovation or reaction. 'I think our principle should be to hold the ground which we have taken, but not to occupy new ground rashly.'[5]

A policy of negation when adopted by the party of progress will inevitably appear more outrageous to the left than to the right. Melbourne was prepared to accept the consequences. 'To approach nearer the Rads', he told Russell, 'is not a cure for evils which have come upon us because we were already too close to them.'[6] The next two years were to witness Melbourne's attempt to govern, not without radical support, since that would have been impossible, but without paying the radicals the danegeld which they might reasonably have expected. Danes without danegeld are notoriously unruly. The remarkable thing is not that the radicals revolted when they did but that they waited so long before doing so.

Russell, once he had made his half-hearted plea for further reform, rallied to his Prime Minister with embarrassing fervour. Goaded by the radicals in the first debate of the new parliament he turned on them and pledged his colleagues to systematic opposition to all further parliamentary reform, not only in the present session but at any time in the foreseeable future. The legend of 'Finality Jack' was born. Melbourne was dismayed. There was nothing in the speech with which he disagreed but a great deal which he would have preferred not to hear spelt out so lucidly in the House of Commons. The radicals were predictably enraged, *The Times* as predictably delighted with this new 'quasi-conservatism'. Russell himself never doubted that he had been guilty of a serious blunder, and that his influence in the Commons was much diminished. Constantly he offered to resign as Leader, so as to make way for a man less committed to a policy distasteful to many members of the party. With equal regularity Melbourne refused the offer. 'I told him that would never do', the Prime Minister explained to Victoria, 'it would never do for me to give the government a more radical character.'[7]

Howick, the member of the cabinet who more than any other was to find the inactivity of the next two years distasteful, summed up his leader's political philosophy in a letter to his father. Lord Melbourne, he said, adhered to:

> the 'stationary system', cannot bear adopting any new measures unless he is absolutely compelled to do so, and thinks it quite enough to deal with the difficulties which immediately press upon him without looking forward to those which are likely to arise hereafter.[8]

The system could only work so long as Tories hungry for office and radicals for vengeance did not unite. At the end of 1837 Melbourne could not see the uneasy equilibrium lasting much longer. 'My anxiety', he told Abercromby, 'is that the government, if it is to fall, should fall in the open light, and not be dissolved by embarrassments arising within itself.'⁹ Pending such relief there was nothing to be done but to endure the punishment that would be meted out to them in parliament with as good a grace as possible.

That punishment was likely to be most severe in the House of Lords. Not only was there a massive Tory majority led by the skilful and unscrupulous Lord Lyndhurst, but Lord Brougham had now joined them in making the life of ministers intolerable. The death of William IV had finally cured Brougham of his illusion that only royal disfavour kept him out of office. Even before this, however, he had been making overtures towards the radicals, urging Grote and Place into more overt hostility to the government and – at least according to Melbourne – 'evidently intending to offer himself to the Radicals for the place at their head'.¹⁰ By the time the royal finances were debated in the House of Lords, in August 1837, relations with his former colleagues were strained. In his speech he referred to the Duchess of Kent as Queen Mother. Melbourne sprang up to point out that this was a mistake. Fairly or not, Brougham took this as a sneer. 'On a point of this sort I humble myself before my noble friend', he replied offensively. 'I have no courtier-like cultivation. I am rude of speech. The tongue of my noble friend is so well hung, and so well-attuned to courtly airs, that I cannot compete with him for the prize which he is now so eagerly. struggling to win. Not being given to glozing and flattery, I may say that the Duchess of Kent (whether to be called Queen Mother or mother of the Queen) is nearly connected with the throne.' Melbourne lost his temper and retorted with a schoolboy *tu quoque*. 'I know no man in this country who can more gloze and flatter and bend the knee than the noble and learned Lord himself – not one!' The two men glowered at each other and did not speak after the debate was over.

Melbourne regretted the row but he was acutely sensitive about his role at court and resentful of the fact that to some his behaviour seemed ridiculous – 'chief counsellor and mutton-chop consumer . . .' as one contemporary *Private Eye* described him, 'an old, stupid, lame, toothless foozle . . . bordering close on his hundredth year, and fitted, in many respects, to be her majesty's grandmother.' It was notable that nothing would sting him more quickly to anger than a suggestion that he was neglecting his duties to dance attendance at the palace, or gaining political advantage by fawning on the Queen. This explains both the sharpness of his original correction and the anger of his later report. He told Russell that the fracas was quite unnecessary and 'originated in a mistake . . . I entirely disclaim having intended to assume anything of an offensive or contemptuous tone . . .'[11]

It was too late for regrets. After years of affectionate intimacy, Brougham's next letter to Melbourne began formally: 'My Lord' and concluded 'I remain, my Lord, your Lordship's faithful and obedient servant'. The estrangement did not last more than eighteen months or so. By the middle of 1839 he was omitting any prefix and ending 'Yours Ever'; by the end of that year it was 'My dear Melbourne' and 'Yours' once more. 'I may flatter myself but I think he likes me', Melbourne told the Queen. 'I haven't the slightest animosity against Brougham.' But in the interval much damage was done, nor indeed did their personal reconciliation noticeably soften Brougham's attacks on the ministry. 'Nothing can equal Lord Brougham's hatred and contempt of the government, which he now shows on every occasion', reported Aberdeen. 'He is determined at all hazards to do his utmost to turn them out.'[12]

It should have been possible to redress the balance of power in the Lords, in debating skills if not in numbers, by recruiting a few of the more eligible Whigs from the Commons or outside. In practice this posed problems, however. To take members from the Commons meant by-elections, and it soon became clear that such contests were likely to result in a seat lost to the opposition. Nor was there a plethora of willing and suitable candidates. All he wanted, Melbourne told Russell, was that they should be 'a creditable set of fellows with clean shirts', but when it came to the point even these modest requirements seemed hard to meet. The pity of it was that the most unsuitable people were always the most importunate. 'What you want in a peer', he explained more seriously, 'is what you want in everybody else: prudence, probity, right-feeling etc. These will make a man rich upon two thousand a year. The contrary ensures his poverty upon fifty.'[13]

What saved the government was not its debating skills in the Lords or its majority in the Commons but the moderation of Wellington in the one and the 'Fabian System' of Peel in the other. Peel considered that, until he was in a position to form his own government, he should supervise the activities of the Whigs, accepting their policies when they seemed to deserve it, revising them when they did not, in the confidence that the Lords would curb any attempt on the part of ministers to strike out on an independent line. To depend thus on Tory charity was unsatisfactory, some might even have thought degrading, but Melbourne was not concerned about his dignity provided he got what he wanted. In 1837 and 1838 he wanted to remain in office. 'The only thing that might have made the Whigs break-up', wrote Lady Carlisle,

' – Lord Melbourne's weariness and discouragement – [is] no longer possible. His situation is of such unexampled interest as well as his duty, that he will never give up, but be more riveted to it.'[14]

It was the old bugbear of Irish tithes and the appropriation of some part of them for lay purposes which Melbourne felt was the issue most likely to destroy the government. In February 1838 he made his final surrender to the radicals when he agreed to a modified appropriation clause being once more included in the Bill. Warily he told Russell that he supposed they must go through the motions of putting the matter to the new parliament but that they should agree that, once they met with their inevitable defeat, they should abandon appropriation and settle the tithes question without it.[15] The rest of the cabinet regretfully concurred. When it came to a vote in the Commons, 47 members, mainly radicals but with a few Irish among them, stuck to their guns and voted for the re-introduction of the clause but the rest of the party contested themselves with a hollow affirmation that the tithes question could never be finally settled without appropriation being an element of it. It was almost total victory for the Tories, and the fact that the prize was not one which Melbourne thought worth fighting for made his humiliation little less painful.

In practical terms the most important question was how this would affect the Irish and their support for the government. If Melbourne had had any doubts they would have been quietened shortly before the crucial debate when O'Connell wrote to him to urge that under no circumstances should the government resign. 'You know how deep has been and still is the conviction of the Irish people that the dominion of England works only for mischief. *Your* Ministry is the first to lessen that conviction, and it only requires time and a perseverance in the present course to obliterate it for ever.'[16] So long as they continued to enjoy a monopoly of Irish patronage and Mulgrave ran the government of Ireland upon pro-Catholic lines, then the Prime Minister knew that he could count on a legion of loyal Irish votes.

In June 1838 an opportunity occurred to bind O'Connell still more strongly to the government by offering him the job of Master of the Rolls in Ireland. Melbourne raised the question in cabinet and found that he was almost the only minister to have serious doubts. What, he wondered, would be the reaction in the country? Someone said it would only cause a short clamour. 'But are we in a situation to stand a clamour?' asked Melbourne. 'I know nothing worse than a clamour.'[17]

In the event O'Connell refused the offer but amicably. However, his sweet reasonableness at Westminster was not accompanied by equal restraint in Ireland. So as to keep up the pressure on his Whig allies and revive enthusiasm among his disillusioned followers, O'Connell in August founded the 'Precursor Society', a body of uncertain objects and inconstant membership, whose attitude towards repeal was never clearly defined but which was felt in London to represent a vague but substantial menace. Melbourne would have been optimistic indeed if he had not assumed that, before the end of the year, something rather worse than mere clamour might be expected from the Queen's Irish subjects.

The cabinet at this time was not a happy or harmonious body. Spring Rice complained of Howick, Howick abused Glenelg; Russell was criticized for being too reactionary, Duncannon for being too liberal; Holland and Lansdowne said Palmerston was outrageous in his European policy, Palmerston retorted that his colleagues systematically betrayed him. The Queen once asked Melbourne whether he did not find the House of Lords very tiring. 'It is not the House of Lords', he replied. 'There's some fun in that; I like that . . . it's those internal dissensions that vex me.' As a body ministers felt the same sort of apathetic despair as sailors who are adrift, know there are rocks ahead, yet have no means of propulsion left to them. Howick was 'beyond measure provoked by the desultory do-nothing way in which the business was gone through; Lord Glenelg making a most wretched figure and Lord Melbourne, who was partly engaged with the newspaper, now and then putting in a few of his sceptical remarks'. The fact was, however, that there were no new measures to discuss and the issues occupying the cabinet were exactly those sterile and electorally unrewarding topics which were least likely to produce enlightened discussion.[18]

If there could be no new measures there might at least be some new faces. By the autumn of 1838 it seemed that almost every member of the cabinet was eager to see sweeping changes; each one, of course, with the implicit proviso that their department alone was satisfactorily administered. Rice, Glenelg and Minto were the three ministers most generally favoured for extinction, but the Duke of Bedford was not alone in thinking that three-quarters of the cabinet could advantageously be disposed of.[19] Melbourne had no intention of consenting to anything so comprehensive. Any changes would mean not only unpleasantness with those dispossessed but also dissension between those who wanted to replace them. He played for time. Glenelg, he agreed, must go, but some other place must be found for him, he must first be sounded out, it would be dangerous to retire him while he was under attack from the opposition. If Rice replaced him then the exchequer would need to be filled. There were objections to Howick, to Thomson, to Baring. 'These are all matters which, with many others, require consideration.'[20] It was to be nearly twelve months before he was forced by resignations to refashion the cabinet as his colleagues wanted.

However, there were troubles ahead. Ireland and Canada seemed on the verge of eruption. The harvest was poor, the trade recession worsening. 'Your Majesty is too well acquainted with the nature of human affairs', he wrote in late October, 'not to be well aware that they cannot very well go on even as quietly as they have gone on during the last sixteen months.' The most urgent problem was provided by the radicals. 'They are the same sour roundheads of other times', reported Ellice from the Reform Club, 'little alive to generous feelings, but are still to be managed to scrape you through the session.'[21] Yet Russell's obdurate refusal to tolerate any colleague unless he would accept the party line on the ballot effectively blocked promotion for even the most responsible members of the left wing. When a new solicitor-general was needed Melbourne ruefully told Spring Rice that all the suitable lawyers in the House of Commons were 'ballot men'.[22]

The sharpest conflict between radicals and ministers came not over domestic issues but in the field of colonial policy. Canada was divided into two provinces: the Upper, which was mainly Scottish and Protestant; the lower, French and Catholic.[23] In both the elected representatives were in conflict with the nominated legislative councils. Both were in revolt by the end of 1837 against the rigid refusal of the Whig government to allow any move towards responsible government. The risings were crushed without too much difficulty but the problem of what to do next now posed itself. As Melbourne complained some time later: '. . . how these provinces are to be settled with anything like security, I do not see. The French population entirely hostile and ready to rise whenever called upon, the frontier thronged with refugees, the Americans always exciting and ready to assist rebellion, and the English population loyal according to their own fancy, and upon condition that they have their own way in everything.'[24]

The radicals seized upon Whig policy as illustrating all that they disliked most about the government: stubborn, reactionary, deaf to the voices of reason and enlightenment. Many of the more orthodox Whigs also had qualms. With some exasperation Melbourne urged Fitzwilliam to get it into his head that, 'the present Canada affair has nothing to do with your old American recollections nor with your dislike of war. One must defend oneself. Don't let the lamp of history blind you . . .' The Foxite Whigs and their heirs, however, were concerned about what seemed to them the legitimate aspirations of the Canadians. There were ferocious rows within the cabinet: all agreeing that the uprisings must be crushed but Howick in particular insisting that this must be followed by 'measures of amendment and conciliation'. Glenelg, he argued, was patently inadequate to cope with the crisis. In a letter unusual as coming to a Prime Minister from a relatively junior member of the cabinet he urged Melbourne to take up the task himself:

> You must excuse my saying that in my opinion you ought much sooner to have given your serious attention to the affairs of this colony, in conducting which you must be aware that hitherto you have given no real assistance to Glenelg. There is no man more capable than yourself of forming a correct judgement as to what ought to be done . . . and of acting firmly upon that judgement, but in order to do this you must in the first place have an accurate knowledge of the real state of things, and from what I have observed I cannot be mistaken in concluding that you have not taken the pains necessary for acquiring this knowledge.[25]

Melbourne seems to have taken this reprimand in good part, and he endured Howick's insistent battering in cabinet with the same equanimity. 'I can never think any man unreasonable who presses his opinion, when he considers it to be of so much importance that he cannot depart from it', he wrote after a stormy session in January. 'I only wished to recall to your recollection how much had been conceded for the sake of agreement.' When the question was debated in the Lords and the Whigs proposed that the constitution of Lower Canada be suspended, Brougham attacked the government record with vigour and venom. 'I never saw anything more beaten than Melbourne in his reply', was Wharncliffe's no doubt partisan comment. The government was saved by Wellington who pronounced that, all things considered, they had done very well and that if he had been Prime Minister he would have pursued an almost identical policy. In the Commons the government would have fared even worse if it had not been for the news that Lord Durham, 'Radical Jack', hero of the Reform Bill, darling of the progressives, was to replace Lord Gosford as Governor in Canada.[26]

In July 1837 Russell had suggested that it might be wise to bring this tormented spirit back into the fold. Melbourne refused flatly: to do so would destroy any chance of harmony within the cabinet and give that body an undesirably radical tinge. On the other hand he conceded that Durham had intelligence, energy and imagination and that he would be a danger so long as he remained in England. The possibility of sending him to Canada was mooted in August, dropped when Durham showed little interest, then revived in the crisis of late autumn. '. . . now was the time', Melbourne told the cabinet, 'to disprove the accusation of the advocates of despotism, that our constitutional governments did very well for fair weather and peaceable times, but would not work well in days of difficulties and war.' Now was the time, he might have said, to perform the well-known conjuring trick of sending a man of notoriously liberal views to enact a repressive role. Durham himself held few illusions. 'He knew he was sent abroad', wrote Hobhouse, 'in order to be got rid of, and that, excepting myself, there was not a man in the cabinet who cared a farthing for him.' Armed, however, with the promise of a free hand, a short term of office, and 'unstinted appointment of all civil officers', Durham concluded that the game was worth the candle. In mid-January 1838 he accepted the assignment. 'As far as I am concerned,' said Melbourne, in words that were to echo in his ears in the months to come, '. . . you will receive the firmest and most unflinching support.'27

It was the proviso about the civil officers which was to cause the greatest trouble. Durham wanted to take with him as legal adviser Thomas Turton, a highly competent lawyer who had worked with him on the Reform Bill. Unfortunately, Turton had a skeleton in his cupboard. Melbourne's initial reaction was to let it moulder unheeded. 'Turton is a man of great abilities . . .' he told Russell. 'Sixteen years ago he was divorced from his wife on account of an affair with her sister. This was bad, but since then he has been at the head of the bar at Calcutta, has married another wife and has a large family of children – and nothing else upon his reputation. Surely there should be some time of limitation for affairs of this sort?' Russell, however, did not agree and Melbourne regretfully accepted that Turton's appointment should be prevented. It was too late, said Durham; to retract would mean ruin for this unfortunate lawyer. 'The fact is', commented Melbourne, 'this mission is the greatest scrape we have yet got into and the greatest blunder we have committed.'28

A compromise was reached. Turton was not to receive any appointment from the government but was to accompany Durham as a private friend. Unfortunately the accord held the seeds of damaging disagreement. Durham considered he had specifically been authorized to offer Turton a post in the Canadian government if it seemed appropriate to do so after his arrival. That he sincerely believed this is beyond question. What Melbourne believed is more uncertain. Durham's leading biographer, Professor Chester New, is satisfied that he had indeed given Durham such an assurance. If so, his subsequent behaviour was dishonourable since he categorically stated in the House of Lords that no appointment for Turton, of any kind, had ever been envisaged. Such duplicity would be out of character, and is made still less likely by the fact that, in letters reporting his negotiations with Durham to Russell and the Queen, and in conversation with Duncannon, he stressed that Turton was going as a personal friend and gave not the slightest hint that he might be appointed to an official post once arrived in Canada. Given the mutual loathing between Durham and Melbourne and the latter's propensity to evade an issue if he possibly could it seems most likely that between them they left the matter vague: Durham convinced that he had *carte blanche*, Melbourne equally clear that, even if Durham had retained the possibility of appointing Turton, it was only to be after prior consultation with London.[29]

The damage, at all events, was done. Soon after Durham's departure the Tories began to rant about the perils of sending a sinner as notorious as Turton on such a mission. Melbourne made the statement referred to above and then hurriedly wrote to Durham, urging him on no account to put Turton forward – 'Beware of scamps and rogues . . . whatever their ability may be'. The fact that he thought such a letter necessary suggests that his instructions to Durham had been by no means so categoric as he now wished had been the case. Durham would probably have defied Melbourne with great relish; as it was he could truthfully reply that the appointment had already been made. '. . . it appears to me most wonderful', wrote Melbourne indignantly, 'that you should have done this so hastily, so precipitately and so entirely without consultation. If the public feeling here was such as to render it advisable that no appointment should be made here before you went, you could not suppose that it could either be satisfied or evaded by making the appointment on the other side of the water immediately upon your arrival.' When questioned about Turton's appointment in the House of Lords Melbourne entirely threw over his High Commissioner, said that he had learnt of it through the *Quebec Gazette* and stressed his surprise and regret at the news.[30]

No one can acquit Durham of arrogant indifference to the wishes of the government; equally, if Melbourne had been more decisive or perspicacious, the embarrassment could have been avoided. Now the stage was set for the next, still more mismanaged act of Durham's Canadian adventure. 'The colonies are saved to England as far as I am concerned', wrote Durham exultantly in mid-June, 'but you must be firm. Don't interfere with me whilst I am at work, after it is done impeach me if you will . . .' It seemed as if Melbourne might have to accept the invitation. As part of Canada's salvation and prior to declaring a general amnesty, Durham had issued an ordinance exiling eight of the former rebels to prison in Bermuda and sentencing them to death if they returned to Canada. Melbourne and Glenelg at once approved his action; Melbourne admittedly saying that 'some difficulties may be apprehended', but giving no indication that he foresaw real troubles. Next thing that Durham heard was a report in the American newspapers that the ordinance had been disallowed by the British government.[31]

In the meantime Brougham, realizing that Durham had acted unconstitutionally, had attacked his handling of affairs in the House of Lords. Melbourne was defenceless, particularly since Durham had omitted to provide more than a cursory sketch of his activities while Brougham had chapter and verse for every detail. 'We must stand by Durham stoutly in everything except Turton', Melbourne told Russell, but ministers still felt that there was no course open except to rescind the offending ordinance. Melbourne put up a defence of Durham's behaviour, but his dislike of the man and disapproval of his conduct was evident in all he said. 'What he did was often right', he told Lansdowne, 'but always so done as to be totally indefensible.' Grey called the government's attitude 'very shabby as regards [Durham], and very discreditable to themselves', while Howick thought 'anything so weak, so miserable and so wretched as the defence on our side there never was'. In Cabinet Howick was enraged to hear everyone agreeing that Durham was alone to blame when 'in my opinion much more than half of it is to be ascribed to the lamentable inefficiency of Glenelg . . . and to Melbourne's carelessness and indolence'.[32]

Melbourne had little doubt that Durham would now either resign in rage or rush through the rest of his legislative programme.[33] He was prepared to urge him to stay on but had no opportunity: as soon as Durham heard what had happened he fired off a proclamation defending his own conduct and took sail for London. He did not even wait to receive Melbourne's exposition of the difficulties that had arisen:

I have observed that those who are employed abroad almost in-
variably complain of the gross ignorance which prevails at home
respecting the countries in which they are serving, whilst ministers
at home accuse foreign governors and ambassadors of regarding only
the interests of that part of the world in which they are acting . . .
Both these complaints are very natural, probably well-grounded, and
arise from the respective positions of each party. The remedy of the
first evil is communication and explanation, upon all points and
particularly upon matters which appear upon the spot to be quite
obvious . . . I know that this is imposing a hard and tedious duty,
but it is very necessary and one which has hitherto been entirely
neglected in the Canadas.[34]

Melbourne and Brougham were burnt in effigy in British Canada and
public opinion at home seemed almost as exercised on Durham's behalf. Much alarm was shown at the prospect of the monster's return
but, when he arrived, he turned out to be sour and withdrawn but 'calm
and quiet enough'.[35] He dedicated himself to preparing the monumental
report on the future of Canada which, perhaps more than any other
single document, laid down the lines for the development of the
British Empire. If his report were to win acceptance, it could only be
thanks to the backing of Melbourne's ministry. The leadership of the
radicals was his for the asking, he could have destroyed the government
in a few weeks. That he declined the chance of revenge was a sign of
the greatness of the man, which transcended the vanity, the arrogance
and the pettiness that had marred his Canadian mission. He would have
been greater still if he could have brought himself to make some overture towards Melbourne but the two men disliked each other too much
for any reconciliation. Durham's rancour at what his wife described as
Melbourne's 'base and ungenerous' conduct remained with him all his
life.[36]

The Canadian rebellions left one embarrassing aftermath in the
swarm of exiles who remained poised as a constant threat along the
United States side of the frontier, making propaganda against the
British and the loyal colonials. Many hotheads urged violent action:
a punitive expedition across the border, perhaps even war with the
United States. Melbourne always spoke for prudence:

Would it not be right to try to arrange something upon these points
with the United States government? I am aware that it is a very
delicate matter, in as much as it touches their internal laws and constitution, and I am aware also that we do not abstain so far from the same

sort of conduct as to enable us to complain with a very good grace
. . . I think we should have great regard and make great allowance
for the situation of the American government and particularly that
we should if possible abstain from any violation of their territory.[37]

One must feel grateful that Palmerston heeded the advice.

While Canada absorbed so much of the government's time and
energies, ministers found themselves on yet another issue isolated from
a large body of their supporters. This time the issue was slavery. Negro
'apprentices' in British territories seemed to be receiving treatment
little if at all better than they had met with as slaves a few years before.
The status of apprenticeship was due to end in 1840 but the radicals
now pressed for its immediate abolition. It was embarrassing to appear
as champions of the slave-owners but equally ministers felt bound to
follow the programme laid down by the Grey administration when
slavery was abolished in 1833. They found themselves allied with the
Tories against the radicals and much of their own rank and file. Fowell
Buxton sent Melbourne a copy of his book *The Slave Trade and its
Remedy*, in which he advocated the establishment of posts throughout
Africa to check the continuing trade and civilize the continent. Glenelg
assured the proud author that Melbourne was most interested in the
book and had written to him about it in the strongest terms but the
Prime Minister's comment to Russell rings more true: 'Religion,
morality, law, eloquence, cruisers, will be all ineffectual when opposed
to a profit of cent per cent and more.' He maintained his belief that
slavery was undesirable but its formal abolition or subsequent pre-
vention never ranked high on his list of priorities. It came as no surprise to Hobhouse when, at a cabinet dinner, Melbourne defended Pitt
for abandoning the cause of abolition on the grounds that he had 'to
keep together a great party having a most important object in view'.[38]

Education promised to be a slightly less thorny topic, especially
since on this it could reasonably be hoped that Brougham would help
rather than obstruct. Russell was now the champion of a new and vastly
expanded scheme which was to place public education under the super-
vision of a committee of the Privy Council; to overhaul the grants
system and to make the size of the grant dependent only on population
figures; to allot grants equally to anglicans and dissenters and to set
up schools for teacher training. It was bold and imaginative, too bold
for the political realities of 1838 and 1839. Melbourne loathed it. At
cabinet he admitted that he was against the scheme. 'Thank God there

are some things even you cannot stop', blurted out Howick, 'and that is one of them.' Melbourne merely smiled.[39] He could afford to since he knew that only the most emasculated version of Russell's proud plan would eventually slip through the House of Lords.

He told Victoria that, though he would not dare say so elsewhere, he was against public education. It might do in Germany but 'the English would not submit to that thraldom'. The Queen asked whether Miss Murray's asylum for poor criminal children was not very good. 'I doubt it', answered Melbourne. Would the children not otherwise commit every sort of atrocity and wickedness? 'And so they will now, you'll see', was the reply. When he found Miss Murray herself with the Queen he grew still more outrageous. 'He doubts education will ever do any good, says all government has to do is to prevent and punish crime, and to preserve contracts. He is FOR labour and does not think the factory children are too much worked; and thinks it very wrong that parents should not be allowed to send their children who are under a certain age, to work.' He enjoyed quoting Walter Scott's dictum: 'Why do you bother the poor? Leave them alone'. 'Don't you think there's a great deal of truth in that?' he would ask. 'Nothing's learnt that way.'[40]

Howick was always dogmatic and truculent, early in 1839 his self-assertion reached the point almost of derangement. His relationship with the Chancellor of the Exchequer, Spring Rice, was particularly strained. The Treasury had granted special allowances to troops in North America without first consulting the Secretary of War. Howick insisted that they not only withdraw the allowances but grovel in abject apology into the bargain. '. . . you must not drive us to the wall', wrote Melbourne mildly. 'I dare say that what you ask for appears to you moderate and reasonable, and perhaps in fact is so, but recollect that it is asking the Treasury to say, "We have done wrong and we will never do so more", an avowal and promise sufficiently humiliating and never made, even by a child, except for urgent reasons and when placed in very unpleasant circumstances.' But Howick's wrath was not to be turned away by any soft answer. Within a few days Melbourne was telling the Queen that there had been another stormy cabinet, with Howick outrageous and 'very offensive to Rice. Upon the whole Lord Melbourne cannot but consider that affairs are in a most precarious state, and that whilst there is so much discontent fermenting within the cabinet itself, there must be great doubts of Lord Melbourne's being much longer able to hold the administration together.'[41]

Early in 1839 Melbourne was at last bullied into dismissing Glenelg from the Colonial Office. 'Many wonder that they ventured to make any change in such a rickety concern,' commented Greville. Mulgrave from Dublin, now the Marquis of Normanby, came back to fill the gap in the cabinet. Fred Lamb viewed such changes cynically. They were never carried through, he told his sister, 'without many disappointed pretensions, much heart-burning and vexation; these, I fear, will not have failed this time'. Certainly if Melbourne had supposed that tranquillity would fall over the cabinet as soon as this irritant had been expelled, he was swiftly disillusioned. At the cabinet on 9 February, only a week after Glenelg's dismissal, Howick's favourite topic of army reform was again raised. The meeting, wrote Lady Howick in her journal, was 'the most strong one they had ever had. The bitterness of dislike between Henry and Mr Thomson and Mr Rice has grown very great . . . I never saw Henry so warmed up and enraged as he is . . .'[42]

The reform of the Corn Laws now for the first time began seriously to be discussed and revealed another split in the cabinet, yet another case in which senior ministers found themselves isolated from their supporters and in alliance with the Tory opposition. The government's policy in Ireland was savagely criticized in the House of Lords and the radicals in the Commons went closer than they ever had before to defeating ministers when Russell appealed to them to vote confidence in the Irish administration. More than eighty of them voted for an amendment which linked their approval of the government's policy directly to the introduction of electoral reforms.

Morale within the cabinet had never been lower. Tavistock described it as being at its last gasp, 'disunited, dissatisfied and disgusted'. Their leader, wrote Greville, seemed to hold office 'for no other purpose but that of dining at Buckingham Palace'. Even the will to survive seemed to have flickered out: Fred Lamb, who now renewed life as Lord Beauvale, remarked that his brother had rushed through the grant of the peerage because he knew his ministry could not last more than another few weeks. The Queen had been alerted to the dangers ahead. On 9 April, when Melbourne was talking about the weaknesses of the government, Victoria said that it did not matter since the Tories could never stand alone. 'I don't know', replied the Prime Minister doubtfully. 'They are a very powerful party.' Victoria quoted Palmerston as saying they were divided. 'I know he thinks so, but I think they are less divided.' But surely the radicals would never turn out the government? pleaded Victoria. At least *they* could never stand alone. 'No', agreed Melbourne, 'they couldn't stand alone, but they like a general shuffle.' It seemed as if almost everyone in public life would like a general shuffle too.[43]

———◆◆◆———

CHAPTER 21

Bedchamber Treason
and Plot

WITH THE VOTE on Ireland behind them, the radicals congratulated
themselves that they had read the Whigs a sharp and salutary lesson.
The weakness of the government had been clearly demonstrated. On
22 March 1839 Victoria wistfully told her Prime Minister how helpless
she felt in the face of these dangers. 'We'll do everything we can to
avert it', he replied. 'I never thought we should have carried you on as
far as we have done.' Though she liked all the ministers, the Queen
confessed, *he* was the one she really cared for. 'But that can't be helped',
was Melbourne's not particularly consoling answer.[1]

The radicals took it for granted that they would now see some
movement in their direction by ministers: a promise of future action if
not the action itself. Their disappointment was rapid. On 3 May there
appeared Russell's letter to his electors at Stroud which restated with
undiminished fervour his opposition to any sort of constitutional
reform. It seems unlikely that Melbourne knew the letter was coming
– he would surely have suggested slightly less forthright phrasing if he
had – but to the radicals Russell spoke with the voice of the government. They did not need to look far to find an issue on which they
could be revenged. The government were determined to suspend the
corrupt and inefficient legislative assembly of Jamaica and to govern
the island by direct rule for five years. The Tories professed to find this
unwise and declared that they would vote against it. The radicals
threatened to vote with them, or at least abstain. Whether Peel wanted
to bring down the government on such an issue is doubtful but by the
time he saw what was happening the two parties were on collision
course. If the government were put in a minority, Melbourne warned
the Queen, 'it will be such a mark of want of confidence as it will be

impossible for your Majesty's government to submit to'.[2]

The critical vote came on 6 May. As an issue on which to assert their independence, the defence of a group of reactionary slave-owners can hardly have seemed ideal to the radicals, but their bitterness was now too great to permit of any restraint. Ten voted with Peel, more abstained. The government's majority fell to five. 'This decision seems to me decisive', wrote the Prime Minister to Russell. The news was brought to the Queen: 'This struck to my heart and I felt dreadfully anxious.' A crisis cabinet was called for the following morning. Melbourne stated bluntly that, in view of the radical revolt, there was nothing to be done but resign. Russell took the same line, and no minister spoke to the contrary.[3]

For Melbourne the decision was doubly painful: he was being driven from an office which he relished and he was to be the cause of great pain to the Queen. He called on her an hour before the cabinet met. 'It was some minutes before I could muster up courage to go in', wrote Victoria in her journal.[4] 'You will not forsake me! I held his hand for a little while, unable to leave go; and he gave me such a look of kindness, pity and affection and could hardly utter for tears, "Oh! no!" in such a touching voice.' After the cabinet he came again to explain what had been decided. He was going to announce the government's resignation that evening in the House of Lords. The Queen urged him to come back to the palace as soon as he had spoken. 'Yes, ma'am, I will', he replied, then thought for a moment and added, 'I don't think it would be right.' It would certainly be observed and commented on. Would he not dine? No, he was dining with Lady Holland. But you must come and see me, pleaded Victoria. 'Oh! yes, only not while these negotiations are going on.' In his farewell letter which he wrote as soon as he had got home, the retiring minister concluded:

> Lord Melbourne has felt his attendance upon your Majesty to be the greatest honour and pleasure of his life and your Majesty may believe that he will most severely and deeply feel the change. Nothing ever gave Lord Melbourne so much pain as to find himself obliged this morning to persuade your Majesty to excuse him from waiting on you this evening, but it is now necessary to act with the greatest prudence as the most vehement jealousy and suspicion will exist of Lord Melbourne's correspondence and communication with your Majesty.[5]

If this had been the end of it, then Melbourne's conduct would indeed have been impeccable, in political if not in human terms. When it came to the point, however, he could not bring himself thus to abandon her. Victoria was, in fact, soon to show that she was far from helpless, but to Melbourne it seemed at that moment that no man of chivalry could refuse her advice and succour. He prepared a short memorandum setting down the lines which he felt she should follow when she saw the Tory leaders. The paper ended: 'Your Majesty had better express your hope that none of your Majesty's household, except those who are engaged in politics, may be removed.'[6] Melbourne read the paper aloud, adding thoughtfully, 'I think you might ask him for that'. The note of doubt was to be amply justified.

Next morning Melbourne called again to brief her before the arrival of the Duke of Wellington. Victoria's approach, however, was very much her own. 'My Lord Duke', she began, 'I have sent for you with great reluctance. I am grieved to be obliged to part from my present ministers, and particularly Lord Melbourne, whom I look upon as a friend and almost a father, but I feel the necessity of doing so . . .' Wellington was unperturbed by this preamble, but even though he was at his most avuncular he could do no more than advise the Queen to send for Peel. This, Melbourne knew, would be the most dangerous moment. Peel was a man of awesome rectitude who had already proved himself a minister of vision and determination. The time was to come when the Queen would appreciate his qualities. In 1839, however, he seemed to her, 'a cold odd man', withdrawn and devious, austerely formal and ill at ease. Anyone would have had an unpleasant task as Melbourne's successor, Peel was almost uniquely ill-equipped to handle this moody, quick-tempered and deeply unhappy girl. Melbourne had made some effort to reconcile them. 'For God's sake, go and speak to the Queen!' he once whispered to Peel when the latter was standing awkwardly in a corner at a Buckingham Palace ball; and to the Queen he said: 'You must try and get over your dislike of Peel, he's a close, stiff man.' In both cases his advice was signally unsuccessful. Melbourne would have been less than human if he had not in part rejoiced at and even exacerbated this ill-feeling. When he spoke well of Peel and urged the Queen to note his good qualities one senses a faint flavour of patronage, even of malice in his words; the aging prima donna lauding the performance of the *jeune première* who has stolen her role.[7]

That first interview was a frosty affair. 'The Queen don't like his manner after – oh! how different, how dreadfully so, to that frank, open, natural, and most kind, warm manner of Lord Melbourne.' There was no direct clash, however; Peel contented himself with looking doubtful when Victoria followed the line suggested by Melbourne and said that she could not accept any changes in her household except in the case of gentlemen who were actively engaged in party politics. He may have imagined that this was no more than the opening gambit of an opponent who was ready to negotiate. Though Melbourne had once or twice made desultory efforts to introduce ladies of Tory complexion into the royal household, he had found it difficult to light upon satisfactory candidates. As a result its composition was starkly partisan; many of the more prominent ladies being wives, sisters or daughters of the former ministers. To Peel it seemed inconceivable that the Queen should remain secluded among this clique of his bitterest enemies. He withdrew, giving Victoria no indication of his feelings. Satisfied that she had deserved well of her mentor, Victoria wrote off to Melbourne, urging that they should meet 'accidentally' when riding in the park. 'Lord Melbourne may think this childish but the Queen really is so *anxious* it might be; and she would bear thro' all her trials so much better if she c'd just see a friendly face sometimes.' Melbourne's reply was a prudent compromise of the kind which would have been only too familiar to Lady Branden or Mrs Norton. He would ride in the park, he said, and would meet the Queen, 'but it will not do to show any emotion or to stop and speak. Such an occurrence would excite too much observation at this moment.'[8]

When Peel returned for his second interview he reverted to the question of the ladies. 'I said I could *not* give up any of my ladies', recorded Victoria, 'and never had imagined such a thing.' Peel asked if she meant to keep, literally, *all* her ladies, including the wives of prominent Whig politicians. 'All', she replied firmly. 'I never saw a man so frightened', wrote Victoria exultantly to Melbourne. Peel came back later with the Duke but the combined efforts of the two statesmen, in many ways the most formidable pair in Europe, could not shift by an inch the obstinate girl who confronted them. 'It is a high trial to our institutions', commented Greville, 'when the caprice of a girl of nineteen can overturn a great ministerial combination.'[9] She was left in little doubt that, if she would not yield on a single lady, she would have to look elsewhere for her ministers. The prospect, she made it equally clear, did not deter or even displease her.

Melbourne was dining with the Hollands that night and arrived late and much excited. Lady Holland at once accosted him, asking him to make Elphinstone an English peer before he finally quit office. 'Why are you in such a damned hurry?' asked Melbourne. 'How the devil do you know that I am out?' Then he embarked on the full story, 'related with great emotion and some humour and indicating the high

spirit and quick understanding of the Queen'. A cabinet was held at
ten the same night in Melbourne's house in South Street. Morpeth was
summoned from the opera, Normanby from the Olympic, Lansdowne
from dinner with the Archbishop. There are conflicting reports of
Melbourne's exact words, but in a letter which he wrote the same
evening to Palmerston he said that Peel had insisted he should have
'the power of removing the ladies of her bedchamber, not stating
distinctly or precisely the extent to which he intended to exercise this
power, but leaving upon Her Majesty's mind the impression that he
did intend to insist upon the present removal of the Mistress of the
Robes and the whole of the ladies of the bedchamber'.[10]

All the older members of the cabinet were hot in defence of the
Queen. John Russell in particular waxed eloquent: 'the Queen had
said to him "I have stood by you, do you stand by me", and would he
desert such a woman?' Hobhouse – drunk, said Howick – swore that
he would cut off his hand rather than advise the monarch to surrender
in such circumstances. Melbourne, though he made it plain that he
agreed, left the ranting to others and drily pointed out that, if the
Whigs were to stay in power, they would have to make concessions to
the radicals. It was left to Howick and Morpeth to argue that somebody
ought to find out Peel's real intentions. If only *some* of the ladies were
to be replaced then there would be no grounds on which they could
advise the Queen to refuse. Melbourne was prepared to support this
but he was overwhelmed in a wave of patriotic slogans from Russell,
Hobhouse and the Lord Chancellor. Howick's account of the meeting
is particularly interesting since it states explicitly what Holland and
Hobhouse only imply – that far from taking the lead in support of the
Queen, Melbourne was in fact one of the few doubters who would have
favoured an approach to Peel. When it came to the point, however,
he could not or would not maintain his view and only Howick eventually
stood out from the cabinet's advice to the Queen to stand her ground.[11]

Next day Melbourne's doubts were reinforced. He called on the
Palace and was given Peel's latest letter to read. 'He started at one part
where he says "*some* changes" ', noted the Queen, 'but some or all, I
said, was the same; and Lord Melbourne said "I must submit this to
the cabinet".' It seemed as if the basis on which the cabinet decision
rested might have been knocked away. Peel's letter, the Prime Minister
told Grey, showed that, 'there is either now a variation upon his part,
of what he said to the Queen, which I cannot believe, or there was a
great misapprehension'.[12] His doubts were further fostered by a letter
from Lady Egerton, who had spoken to the Duke and reported 'I can

positively affirm that the most complete and entire misapprehension does certainly prevail . . .' The Queen's wishes were to be consulted at every point – all that was proposed was that the political complexion of the household should be open to discussion. 'I understand from you that the Queen was considerably excited, my belief is that she [was] speaking in anger, did not convey the real state of the case.'[13]

Melbourne was now in great agitation. He realized that if the cabinet had known more of the facts the night before, their advice to the Queen would have been far more cautious. If Grey, who was much in evidence in the wings, had supported him, he might well have tried to reverse their decision. But Grey considered that Peel's letter, though 'artfully constructed to put himself in the right', did not alter the essential facts. The Queen, he was convinced, 'has the strongest claims upon you to support her . . . in the line which she has taken'. On such a point the views of the elder statesmen carried more weight than the appeal of Rice that all the ladies connected with the ministry should voluntarily withdraw. Yet Melbourne saw the force in Rice's argument that the reputation of the government would be destroyed if it appeared that they were clinging to power under the pretext of defending the Queen. 'You and John Russell have stated that you have not found your government to possess the confidence of the House of Commons,' observed Rice. 'How can we go on without it, and will this affair give it to us?'[14]

If ever there was a time for Melbourne to take a strong lead it was now. When it came to the point, however, he could not bring himself to throw his weight against the Queen and his loyalist colleagues. Hayward quotes him as admitting: 'I counted up more than two hundred of my intimate acquaintances, or their families, who would be half ruined and heart-broken by my going out'. '. . . I must think of the poor fellows who have to put down their broughams,' was another remark of similar portent. It would not do to make too much of such arguments, but in a finely balanced dispute it was inevitable that he would be swayed by self-interest. He did not want to give up his job, was prepared to fight for it, and therefore allowed his judgement to be clouded by a host of minor and essentially irrelevant criteria. Even though the cabinet on 11 May lasted for more than four hours no clear picture of what happened has ever emerged. It seems that Russell and Duncannon continued furious in defence of the Queen, that Howick alone felt that ministers should go back on their decision of two days before, and that Melbourne confined himself largely to discussing the finer points of drafting when the time came to draw up the formal

Cabinet Minute. In this document ministers stated that the ladies of the household should not be changed and that they were prepared to remain in office to ensure that the Queen's wishes in the matter were not overruled.[15]

They were sustained in this resolution by hints that the radicals were undergoing a change of heart. The day after the cabinet's decision to resign became generally known a group of the most extreme radicals – including eight of the ten who had voted against the government on the Jamaica Bill – met to discuss future policy. 'Twelve fools who dined at Sir W. Molesworth's last night and pretend to represent the Liberal party', as E. J. Stanley contemptuously described them[16] had thrashed out a programme of reform on the basis of which they were prepared to co-operate with the Whigs. Hume and Ward had been delegated to call on Melbourne and explain their terms though – 'Philip sober is different from Philip drunk' – Stanley doubted whether they would ever get as far as Downing Street. Melbourne had no idea what conditions the radicals would attach to their support and suspected they might be extravagant, but at least it was something that they were thinking in terms of a reconciliation. Yet even this consolation had its thorns. Lord Ashley, who had married Melbourne's favourite niece, found his new uncle 'evidently alarmed at the progress of radicalism and disgusted by the insolent and excessive demands of the Jacobinical hodge-podge in the House of Commons'. He was, thought Ashley, striving to save the Queen from the 'fangs of radicalism' by persuading her to give Peel the government. 'He must have it', he was supposed to have exclaimed, 'It is absolutely necessary, he must have it!'[17]

The following night Melbourne dined at the Palace. 'He was very much excited the whole evening', wrote the Queen, 'talking to himself and pulling his hair about, which always makes him look so much handsomer.' In spite of his suspicion that he had sown the seeds of eventual disaster, he could not curb his delight at what had happened. He must have felt apprehensive, however, when he heard that Brougham proposed to raise the ministerial crisis in the Lords and to demand an explanation. When the debate began, Melbourne's speech, outwardly a pattern of blunt sincerity, was in many ways equivocal.[18] He admitted that ministers had laid themselves open 'to the charge of intrigue, to the charge of personal considerations, to the insinuation of having beforehand settled this objection to render abortive any attempt to form another administration'. If people chose to believe this, he could do nothing about it. All he could do was to state categorically that, though he had advised the Queen to send for Wellington and ask the

Tories to form a government, 'as to the ladies of the household I gave her Majesty no advice whatever, for I fairly declare to you, my Lords, that I did not expect . . . I could not conceive that this proposition could be made'. Literally this form of words could perhaps be defended; but it would have been an embarrassment for the Prime Minister if anyone had been able to throw back at him his advice to the Queen that she should insist on retaining all her household except those directly engaged in politics.*

He concluded his speech with a noble peroration. He had given up the government, he said, because he did not think he had the parliamentary support which would enable him to carry on 'with honour to myself, or with advantage to the country'. He now resumed office 'solely because I will not abandon my sovereign in a situation of difficulty and distress'. The sentiment sounded worthy, but failed to meet the crucial point which Melbourne himself had made in cabinet: if a week before the government's support had eroded to a point at which it could no longer carry on, how had subsequent events strengthened their position? No hint was given in Melbourne's speech that any change of policy was intended – indeed it was stated clearly that no concessions to the left had been envisaged – yet how else could radical support be gained? Still less did he confront the basic absurdity of a Whig ministry with the Reform Bill to its credit, ignoring the fact that it could no longer command a workable majority in the House of Commons and holding on to office to defend the privileges of the monarch. Melbourne would undoubtedly have been more roughly handled in the Lords if Wellington, in what many of his followers considered an excess of gallantry, had not only acquitted his opponent of bad faith but even stated that he did not feel the vote on the Jamaica Bill had provided a good reason to resign in the first place.

Both Melbourne and Victoria realized that they had blundered. Hobhouse noticed Melbourne's gloom and irritation at a levée when addresses were being presented thanking the Queen for her action and Duncannon confirmed that the Prime Minister was 'greatly distressed' at developments. A few days later the Queen was asking Melbourne to look for 'some peeress who was a *moderate* Tory' who could be accommodated in the household without too much embarrassment. They were resolved that the problem should not recur. In May 1841, when the government was again about to collapse, Melbourne sent his former private secretary, Anson, to negotiate with Peel on his behalf. Anson said that three of the most prominent Whig ladies were ready to

* See p. 292 above.

resign, and indeed had been at the time of the earlier crisis. 'Had the Queen told me . . .' said Peel, 'that these three ladies immediately connected with the government had tendered their resignation, I should have been perfectly satisfied and should have consulted the Queen's feelings in replacing them.' So easily might the crisis been averted.[19]

Melbourne's enemies at the time delighted to portray him as a plotter who cynically manipulated the young Queen so as to serve his own political purposes. According to this thesis he foresaw Peel's determination that some at least of the ladies should be changed, instructed the Queen to provoke a clash on this issue and then struck Peel down before that guileless statesman had any chance to explain the innocence of his intentions. It is doubtful whether even the proponents of this theory took it very seriously. Certainly it is untenable today. Melbourne's confusion and uncertainty are patent in everything he said or did. If anyone was the victim it was he; if anyone did the manipulation it was the Queen.

More recently the established doctrine has been that Melbourne was a very perfect gentle knight, politically naive but splendid in his sentiments. He allowed his love for and loyalty towards the Queen to override his calmer judgement, and by his ardent oratory rallied his colleagues into a headlong charge against her enemies. This version is almost equally wide of the mark. The truth is that Melbourne at the time of the bedchamber controversy was as circumspect and as uncommitted as in any other great crisis of his life. He joined in the charge, certainly, but it was Russell who was in the van, Duncannon who bore the banner. If the decision had been left to him, he would probably have made a surreptitious approach to Peel or Wellington and worked out some compromise which he could have urged upon the Queen. Melbourne was neither Machiavelli nor Galahad and there would only be disillusionment for those who tried to force him into either mould. In this case at least his own preferred solution would have made better sense for the Whig party, for the Queen and for the nation.

CHAPTER 22

Playing Out Time

MINISTERS QUICKLY discovered that part of the price they must pay
for their return to office was the hostility of the London crowd. On 11
July they were heartily hissed and groaned at by a large body of people
who had assembled outside Buckingham Palace to see them arrive for
a council. 'Tories are capable of every villainy!' exclaimed the Queen in
indignation. Melbourne took the affair more lightly: 'A little hissing
and shouting does not matter much – almost as little as so much
applause.' But he found it hard to ride the storm with his usual nonchalance. He was eating and drinking too much, suffering from in-
digestion, sleeping badly, and being pumped full of worthless medicines
by the conscientious but limited Dr Holland. 'I think ministers should
be paid at an extra rate like any other unhealthy trade', remarked
Emily Cowper. 'Quicksilver mines and cotton mills are not so hurtful
as constant anxiety and work and worry.'[1]

The radicals soon reminded him that another part of the price now
fell due. Though Melbourne had managed to avoid making any precise
commitment he knew he would not be able to avoid concessions of
substance in the near future. The Tories believed, or professed to
believe, that he had sold the line on almost every front and that, in
particular, the Reform Act was about to be rewritten and vastly extended. Their concern was exaggerated. On 31 May in the House of
Lords he resoundingly declared that the principles of the government
remained unchanged. He was 'not prepared to adopt measures contrary
to my feelings, contrary to my opinions, contrary to my conscience,
for the sake of obtaining any support which they might obtain'. When
a motion about the suffrage was introduced into the Commons a few
days later, John Russell dismissed it in chilling terms – 'a good Tory

speech fit for the old times of Toryism', as one indignant radical described it.[2]

But such brave words did no more than cover the retreat on another, more exposed front. It would have been too much to expect the government actually to support the secret ballot – Russell could not possibly have swallowed such a rebuff – but the cabinet now concluded that it must be accepted as an open question. To abandon the official line on an issue which had tacitly been accepted as the litmus test of orthodox Whiggery seemed to some like weakness. Melbourne hopefully set out to Russell the precedents for similar free votes in the past which made their decision acceptable today: parliamentary reform in 1783; again in 1785; the slave trade. 'Facts like these', he urged, 'shiver all reasoning to pieces.' They notably failed to shiver the reasoning of his more conservative colleagues, who considered that a dangerous surrender had been made to the forces of the revolution. The radicals were equally exultant: 'Last night they sang hymns at the Reform Club', Ellice told Lady Holland.[3]

It is hard now to see any good grounds for their jubilation. Quite enough Whigs were still opposed to the ballot to make it almost certain that any motion would be defeated in the Commons; it stood no chance whatsoever in the Lords. Melbourne himself, while conceding that, in recent elections, 'intimidation and the power which station and wealth give one man over another has been exercised in a more reckless and unscrupulous manner than ever before', still made it plain that he would continue to oppose the introduction of this dangerous innovation. Worse still for the reformers, public attention was turning from issues of this kind to the critical economic problems of the day and even some of the parliamentary radicals were beginning to lose interest in what seemed an increasingly academic issue. 1840, the year after the Whigs' volte-face, was also the first year in which Grote did not bring forward his annual motion proposing a change in the law.

For the other great concession to the radicals Melbourne felt, if not enthusiasm, at least tolerant approval. The substitution of the penny post for the existing elaborate and expensive system had been the brainchild of Rowland Hill. It had not prospered, mainly because the Post-Master General, Lord Lichfield, considered it the most extraordinary of all 'the wild and visionary schemes' which had ever come his way. However, early in 1839, it was recommended by a Select Committee and eagerly espoused by the radicals. It seemed to Melbourne that here was a way of pleasing his allies without any sacrifice of principle. He agreed that Rice should include provision for it in his annual budget and himself undertook to make the main speech recommending it to the House of Lords. Hill called at South Street to brief him before the debate and, though it was one o'clock, found the Prime Minister still in his dressing gown:

> My reception was most kindly, and we presently went to work. In the course of the conversation I had occasion to speak of Mr Warbuton, when Lord Melbourne interrupted me with 'Warbuton! Warbuton! He's one of your moral-force men, isn't he?' I replied that I certainly believed Mr Warbuton's hopes of improvement did rest more on moral than on physical force. 'Well', he rejoined, 'I can understand your physical-force men, but as to your moral-force, I'll be damned if I know what they mean!' (Conversation then returned to the penny post) . . . until at length, seeming to have become possessed of his subject, he began to pace the room, as if arranging his speech; often moving his lips, though uttering no audible sound. [Then Lichfield arrived. Melbourne received him in the adjoining room.] A minute afterwards the hum of conversation sounded through the folding doors, and by-and-by, one of the voices gradually rose in distinctness and earnestness, taking at length an angry tone, in which I presently heard my own name pronounced. [Peace was restored, and Lichfield eventually left.] Lord Melbourne re-entering by the folding doors with the remark, '. . . I can't think why a man can't talk of penny postage without going into a passion!'[4]

The government swallowed Hill's assertion that the reduction in the cost of postage would lead to a vast increase in traffic and hence in revenue, but unfortunately assumed that this would happen over-night. In spite of pleas for caution from the opposition, and even from many liberals, the budget included what Gladstone described as 'the unexampled juggle of abandoning the Post Office revenue and recording by resolution a promise to find a substitute for it in the following year'.[5] The result was an overall deficit of £800,000 and the ministers, instead of winning deserved praise for their vision, were condemned for their ineptitude.

The last resort of a failing ministry is usually a reshuffle. Melbourne had resisted this as long as he could, arguing that 'the removal of one stone often disturbed the harmony or even shook the stability of the whole fabrick'. By the end of the 1839 session, however, he could no longer hold out. The most urgent need was to move Normanby, who had been almost as inefficient at the Colonial Office as his predecessor, Glenelg. Two months before Melbourne had told the Queen that

Normanby wanted to go to the Home Office but that he had handled
criminal affairs in Ireland with such incompetence that ministers 'would
put their finger upon that'. Now, in August, under pressure from John
Russell who wanted to exchange offices with Normanby, he proposed
this very appointment. Palmerston was dismayed because he believed
the double burden of the Colonial Office and Leadership of the
Commons would destroy the health of the notoriously frail Russell.
Others were still more concerned because they felt the switch would
be yet another concession to the radicals; Normanby, as Howick
angrily remarked to Melbourne, being 'identified in public opinion
with those who have a leaning toward further changes in our institutions'.[6]

For Howick this appointment was merely the last incident in a saga
of frustration. When the reshuffle became imminent he set out his views
in detail: Normanby should not go to the Home Office; the radical
Ward should not be offered a place; the cabinet should not be increased
in size; if anyone were promoted it should be his friend and kinsman,
Charles Wood.[7] At cabinet on 21 August it was decided that Normanby
should go to the Home Office; that Ward should be offered an under-
secretaryship; that the cabinet should be enlarged by two; and that
Labouchere should be promoted before Wood. After the meeting
Howick went over to Melbourne, who was talking in a corner to Rice,
and demanded angrily: 'Just let me ask you one question – is all I
objected to to be done?' 'Yes', replied the Prime Minister, with
honesty as admirable as it was unwelcome.[8]

After this Howick's resignation was inevitable. 'Nothing as it
appears to me can be more absurd than the grounds upon which he has
put it', Melbourne told Russell. 'I suppose the real reason is that he is
not Chancellor of the Exchequer', was the latter's comment. There was
some truth in this, but still more in Melbourne's belief that Howick
could no longer resist the pressure of his father. Grey, indeed, though
still restrained in public, was by now an inveterate enemy of government. For more than a year he had been pressing Howick to leave a
position in which he could not remain 'with honour to himself or with
advantage to the public'. Now at last he had prevailed.[9]

Melbourne so contrived things that the parting was amicable. He
spoke to Howick after the latter's resignation had been formally
accepted and the departing minister promised to support the government as much as he could. 'Oh, you have blown me up', said Melbourne
cheerfully. Howick said he would feel obliged to explain his retirement
in a statement to the House. It was quite a mistake to imagine that he

would be attacked for resigning office, retorted Melbourne, it was taking office that provoked attack. 'I wish it was possible', concluded Howick, 'to give the slightest idea of the frank, good-humoured manner, singularly joined with a shrewd and amused but cynical tone of observation, which makes it impossible to have a conversation even upon a disagreeable subject without coming away pleased with him.'[10]

In many ways it was a relief to be parted from the cantankerous and exigent Howick but it was also true that, however troublesome in cabinet, he was one of the most capable of the ministers. His withdrawal still further heightened what Howick himself described as 'the growing distrust and want of confidence' in the government felt by those moderates who, while liberal in principle, were averse to any striking new measures of reform. What was gained on the radical swings was lost with a vengeance on the right-wing roundabouts. The retreat of Poulett Thomson, now disgused as Lord Sydenham, to govern Canada, strengthened the same doubts. '... luxurious, affectedly indolent in manner ... and with a curious stamp of meanness', Harriet Martineau described him, but though one of the most disliked of ministers, he was also safe and sober, a competent debater and a man who knew his job. There were not so many such men in Melbourne's government that he could easily be spared. With Spring Rice, *bête noire* of the radicals, also retiring, the traditionalist wing of the ministry had been severely weakened.[11]

Their replacements, however, were hardly likely to arouse the fears of any except the most timorous. Morpeth, now promoted to the cabinet, certainly belonged to the more liberal fringe of the party but was also one of the most temperate of men. Clarendon, a diplomat by training, was not only no radical but was hailed by Greville as being likely to 'throw aside that wavering, truckling appearance', which gave such offence to those of conservative leanings. Macaulay was the most interesting recruit. When told the appointment was a possibility Brougham dismissed the report on the grounds that Melbourne would never consent to sit in cabinet with 'ten parrots, a chime of bells and Lady Westmoreland'. He underestimated the Prime Minister's capacity for tolerating oddities. When Macaulay was in spate, unleashing his eloquence and learning in great tirades which seemed sometimes to have little relevance to the subject under discussion, his other colleagues would fidget, but Melbourne would listen complacently, enjoying the entertainment and not in the least anxious to cut it short. Indeed, though so dissimilar in background and temperament, the two men had certain ways of thought in common. Macaulay, wrote Professor

Clive in his admirable biography, 'was not so much an Augustan as someone who . . . confronted the problem of finding himself in a transitional period between generations. Not so much, perhaps, an eighteenth century "survival" . . . as himself expressive of the dilemma faced by those in the early nineteenth century who could neither bring themselves to embrace the new nor to preserve the old without serious reservations.' Melbourne embraced the new with still less relish, clung to the old with greater fervour, but the dilemma was his also. He was never to resolve it.[12]

The reshuffle singularly failed to kindle public enthusiasm or to impress supporters of the government. 'A *rechauffée* of the old materials', Ellice called it contemptuously, while Holland in his diary denounced the new combination with measured gloom:[13]

> I own I perceive a want of energy, boldness and decision, and a sort of jealousy and fear of anything like ambition and intrepidity . . . That reflection makes me tremble for the fate of Lord Melbourne's government. I have stated to him my apprehension that in all branches, and especially in the Commons, it was fast assuming the fatal character of mediocrity and narrowness of views, and I was not a little startled to find that he thought a want of genius no great defect in the government of a great nation and quiet and ease more the aim of a wise statesman than popularity, authority or splendour.

In the autumn of 1839 it seemed as if the fate which Lord Holland predicted had almost overtaken the government. Two mismanaged by-elections cost them one safe seat and almost lost them a still safer. Ministers were hissed at the Guildhall dinner and the uproar was such that it was five minutes before Melbourne could make himself heard. 'It is certainly of no use to conceal the difficulties of the situation . . .' wrote Russell in sombre mood. '. . . I always thought the Whig party as a party would be destroyed by the Reform Bill.' And yet nothing happened. Infirm of purpose, the Tories still looked doubtfully upon their dagger and forbore to strike. 'A course of active hostility to the government has been announced', declared Aberdeen proudly, but when it came to the point the opposition seemed little more aggressive than in the past. Free trade, which would certainly have provided a battlefield, had lost its most active champions with the departure of Howick and Poulett Thomson. On the reform of the Irish corporations the Whigs had surrendered on so many of the points at issue that only the most fanatical members of the opposition were in favour of further resistance. On Canada a similar compromise was reached. It seemed almost as though Melbourne and Peel had entered into a compact to govern Britain between them in despite of their own more extreme supporters.[14]

Having no reforms which he wished to sponsor, Melbourne was well content with this supine policy. His main preoccupation was with the court, for the rest let the government jog along as best it might. The cabinet was a complete republic, said Greville, 'and Melbourne, their ostensible head, has no over-ruling authority, and is too indolent and too averse to energetic methods to think of having any, or to desire it. Any man of resolution and obstinacy does what he will with Melbourne.'[15] Greville over-simplified. Melbourne was still capable of intervening with authority and even energy if he thought it essential. But such occasions were increasingly rare and his efforts were exerted always for the maintenance of tranquillity, never in the interests of new activity. So far as that was concerned, he was satisfied, in the words of Mackworth Praed:

> To promise, pause, prepare, postpone
> And end by letting things alone:
> In short, to earn the people's pay
> By doing nothing every day.

The routine of a Prime Minister's life was now well known to him and on the whole he found it enjoyable. Patronage continued to occupy a disproportionately large amount of his time and he resented both the wasted hours and the pettiness of most of those who clamoured for favours. 'Nothing', he wrote in exasperation to Edward Pendarves, 'vexes a minister so much as jealousies, differences and conflicting claims amongst his friends and supporters . . .' When it came to giving away honours or other rewards, it somehow always seemed that the wrong person came to the fore – the wrong person, in Melbourne's mind, including the business-man, the attorney, the indigent, the radical, the nonconformist and the Jew. 'Holland wants to have I[saac] Lyon Goldsmid and other Jews made baronets . . .' he wrote in some dismay to Ellice. 'Jew commercial fortunes are less still than other commercial fortunes, which are not the finest things in the world.' Holland got his way in the end and Goldsmid became a baronet in 1841.[16]

Benevolence in the form of grants or pensions could be equally troublesome to administer. Mrs Fonblanque was widow of an eminent but, financially speaking, unsuccessful jurist; she was also mother of a distinguished journalist of radical ideas, Albany Fonblanque, editor of the *Examiner*. To award her a grant of £100 a year, it seemed to Melbourne, would both assist a needy old lady and propitiate a potentially dangerous enemy. Unfortunately he reckoned without the susceptibilities of Mr Fonblanque, who was alarmed at the damage that would be done to his status as an independent if the grant became known to the public and also indignant at the suggestion that his mother needed help which he was unable to provide her. Melbourne replied apologetically. He should have consulted the family first but he was sure that Fonblanque would agree 'that there was some difficulty in applying to a son in order to learn whether the representation of his mother was to be relied upon . . .'[17]

Like every prominent politician he received occasional threats from disaffected citizens. They caused him little alarm. Certainly he cannot have lost much sleep over the letter from Mr Hayward of Edinburgh which Thomas Attwood passed on to him.

I am and have been subject to the effect of *electricity* from my Lord Melbourne for more than one year past. As a stranger to the use of this power and feeling its effects in so dreadful an experience as that I have been subject to, I take the liberty of asking your advice. One of my children has already been killed by my Lord Melbourne through the use of electricity. I was persecuted in my mind by the same means . . . and was by electricity driven from my home and family . . . I have been informed through the medium of electricity that I am the son of George the Fourth . . . I cannot, will not bear the misery it produces in me. I am determined unless my Lord Melbourne desists from driving me about from town to town and his attempts to kill me that I will reach London by some means and kill him in the street if possible or anywhere where I can meet him.[18]

As his right hand in all such matters, and indeed more important matters too, Melbourne relied on George Anson, son of a former Dean of Chester and once a Whig candidate for parliament. Anson was close to being the ideal private secretary: sensible, discreet, industrious, above all, honest – 'a nature somewhat blunt and out-spoken, but utterly incapable of intrigue'.[19] He had no strong political views and fitted happily into a neutral role when transferred to Prince Albert after Queen Victoria's marriage. Melbourne then took as his new crutch his nephew, the young William Cowper, who had been working with Anson since 1837. Cowper lacked Anson's toughness and resilience, but he had a sensitivity which his predecessor lacked and which was of service to his master in negotiations with the Press. Press relations, indeed, were his speciality, but he found he was expected to be an authority on a wide range of subjects, usually connected with the court. Was a certain play suitable for the Queen? What was the length of private mourning for a first cousin? The depth? Should black gloves be worn? Were certain girls suitable to be maids of honour? – a delicate investigation which must have taxed Cowper's ingenuity to the full.

But for all their virtues neither Cowper nor Anson were remotely competent to advise the Prime Minister on the economic and social problems which underlay the difficulties of the government. Indeed there was nobody within the ministry or its immediate entourage who enjoyed even a hazy understanding of what was happening in the country. The explosive industrial growth of the last sixty years, though it had brought much misery and degradation to the working classes, had also created new opportunities. Of the vast prosperity generated by the new mines and factories, some small part at least had filtered down to those who did the menial work. On the whole living standards rose, even though fitfully and at a fearful price in human dignity. But the progress was by no means invariable, or spread equally around the country. In the last years of Melbourne's government there was a sharp recession. Wages remained static or fell back; export markets dwindled with consequential unemployment, particularly in the cotton mills; a sharp downturn in railway building gravely damaged the industries which had grown up largely to meet this demand. British agriculture was anyway unable to meet the needs of the rapidly swelling population, a series of bad harvests aggravated the problem, the Corn Laws impeded the obvious solution of importing cheap supplies from abroad. Add to this malign cocktail the workings of the new Poor Law, a system designed almost explicitly to ill-treat and degrade all those guilty of the crime of poverty, and a most explosive mixture was arrived at.

The remarkable thing is that the response of the working classes was so temperate and well ordered. The 'People's Charter' which was published in May 1838 contained certain precise political demands – all unacceptable to parliament though one, the secret ballot, was already the subject of much debate. Most of those who subscribed to it, however, were not so much concerned with political panaceas as with their immediate local problems. The Charter was a weapon with which to bring the ruling class to reason; Chartism, in Carlyle's phrase, 'A new name for a thing which has had many names'. Whipped up by the fiery demagoguery of Feargus O'Connor, the movement by the autumn of 1838 was presenting a serious threat to law and order.

Torchlight processions, drilling with pikes and pistols, even riots, became a feature of the season. Russell, preoccupied by the health of his wife and his difficult relationship with the party in the House of Commons, left the handling of affairs as far as possible to the Prime Minister.[20]

In this crisis Melbourne exhibited a total failure to understand the causes for the disturbances, mitigated by an admirable restraint in repressing them. His object always was to avoid extravagant gestures which might provoke fresh excesses from their victims. He delayed as long as possible before prosecuting the ring-leaders and, though he agreed with Russell that torchlight processions 'ought to be illegal', he only with reluctance and belatedly issued a royal proclamation to that effect. His view was always that there was no need for fresh legislation; if only the magistrates would act firmly but not provocatively, then the problems would melt away. But firmness and energy were necessary. In March 1839 he complained that the magistrates of Westmorland and Cumberland were supine. 'Without writing a public letter or a circular I think it would be well to stimulate them . . . I think some warning should also be sent to the mayors of towns where the arming is going on. I hope that our town councils will not be found deficient in energy or vigour.'[21]

In July 1839 the House of Commons refused even to consider the 'National Petition' which set out the Chartist demands. Uproar ensued and a mass demonstration in protest was fixed for 12 August. Two days before in cabinet someone raised the question of security. 'God bless us', said Melbourne, 'why, that is the day after tomorrow; 'tis time to be looking about us.' At dinner the same night Hobhouse noticed that the Prime Minister 'was silent and absent at first, and talked a good deal to himself' but cheered up later on. In the event precautions were taken in a low key and those few extra troops on duty were hidden from the public eye. Such restraint proved justified. The only crowd of any size assembled in Kensington Gardens and the alarm of the authorities was appeased when it was found that they merely wished to watch a Mr Hampton descend on them by parachute. The solitary victim was Mr Hampton himself who landed in a tree and was knocked unconscious.[22]

Further north things were busier. 'Alarms! Trumpets! Magistrates in a fuss. Troops! Troops! Troops! North, South, East, West, Lord how they make me swear', wrote the admirable General Napier, head of Northern Command and charged with the maintenance of law and order in his vast area of responsibility. Napier's common sense and goodwill, a lack of revolutionary zest on the part of the workers and the disappearance of the magistrates to shoot grouse as soon as the rules of the season permitted it: all helped to lower the temperature. Such rioting as there had been ceased and Campbell boasted that Chartism had been put down 'without one drop of blood being spilled'. The government rejoiced too soon. A few days later John Frost, a former mayor of Newport and an elder statesman of the Chartist movement, led a little army of colliers and ironworkers into a hopeless battle with the regular troops. Twenty-two Chartists were killed or later died of their wounds. In January 1840 Frost was condemned to death. The jury strongly recommended mercy.[23]

On 9 January the matter was discussed in cabinet. Melbourne said he saw no merit in the jury's recommendation: they were frightened and so was the judge. Hobhouse, with all the fervour of a reformed radical, remarked that, as the object of the Chartists was to knock them on the head and steal their property, they might as well go down fighting. 'Exactly so', said Melbourne, approvingly. It was a time for strong measures and he was ready to take them. Three weeks later he was still maintaining that Frost had been 'convicted of the highest crime known to British law . . .' and must be executed. With some doubts the cabinet deferred to his views, but the Lord Chief Justice himself now suggested that Frost's life should be spared. '. . . even Lord Melbourne admitted that it would be difficult to execute the man after such a hint.' Frost was transported for life and pardoned fifteen years later.[24]

By the middle of 1840 several hundred Chartists were in jail and the power of the movement was temporarily broken. An uneasy peace fell over the industrial areas. But Melbourne did not delude himself that this was more than a truce, nor that the root causes of the disorders had been eliminated. With the radicals complaining about the harshness of his repressive measures and the Tories professing a new aggressiveness, it seemed as if the balance of power in the House of Commons could not long be sustained. In April Melbourne told Hobhouse that the odds were ten to one against their being in office in another twelve months. He would not have found many takers at that price. As Lady Holland put it, the government now had nothing to rely on but the Queen and Paddy.[25]

The Queen stayed loyal. 1840 opened with her commitment to her Prime Minister and her government as total as ever. On 15 January, she rejoiced to hear that the ministry was doing well, 'for whom she *never* felt *more warmly* or more anxiously than she does now. Anything that *she* can do to uphold her government shall be done'. And yet what *she* could do, became increasingly uncertain. She could not manufacture a majority in the Commons, persuade the Lords into a less truculent frame of mind, cow the radicals, placate the ultras. At the most her influence extended to a score of waverers in either House who forbore to desert the government because of the displeasure they knew it would provoke. That she could have destroyed the government if she had wished to is, however, far more certain. Her failure to apply the *coup de grâce* to a government which had lost credibility and popular support seemed to the Tories a negation of the monarch's role as re-defined over the last fifty years. The Queen was 'blinded by her partialities', wrote Greville angrily. '. . . she does not perceive the magnitude of the evils which must flow from the mistrust, disunion and weakness which prevail in her government, and above all the deplorable but mischievous imbecility of her Prime Minister.'[26]

Yet already there had been developments at court which were in the end to undermine his position. As early as April of the previous year Victoria had raised with the Prime Minister the wish of her Uncle Leopold that she should marry her cousin, Albert of Saxe-Coburg. In her journal the Queen recorded that Melbourne pointed out the risk that there might be an alliance between Prince Albert and his aunt, the Duchess of Kent – '. . . if I was to make such a connection and then he was to go with Ma, that would be dreadful for me; I assured him he need have no fear *whatever* on that score'. Melbourne then cast around for other arguments against the match. The Coburgs were not popular abroad and were hated by the Russians; the Duchess of Kent, he commented sourly, was a good specimen of the family. Germans never washed their faces and, still worse, smoked – a particularly heinous crime; 'I always make a great row about it. If I smell tobacco I swear perhaps for half an hour'. Cousins, in general, were 'not very good things'. Any foreigner would be unpopular. Victoria pointed out that all the other European princes had arguments of equal force against them and that to marry a Briton would bring her into unwise equality with her subjects. Melbourne agreed that this was true. More and more it became clear that he was against any match: '. . . if one was to *make* a man for it, one would hardly know what to make'. Certainly he had genuine doubts as to whether Victoria was ready for marriage; equally he must have realized that a husband would threaten his own privileged position and have wished to postpone the evil moment for as long as possible. Whatever his motives, he had his way. The question of Victoria's marriage was quietly shelved.[27]

It did not remain on the shelf for long and Melbourne re-considered his attitude. By July he was coming round to Albert and saying that the fact that he was younger than the Queen was of no importance. But he still felt there was no hurry: 'better wait for a year or two, it's a very serious question'.

On October Albert arrived for what was to prove the crucial visit. It was quickly clear that Victoria was besotted with him. Nobody accepted the inevitable with better grace than Melbourne. He was 'certainly a very fine young man, very good looking', the Prime Minister agreed. His 'strong Protestant feeling' would also be a good thing provided it was not bigoted; which Victoria at once assured him it was not. He suggested she take a week to make up her mind but showed only pleasure when forty-eight hours proved enough. His report to Russell on the young Prince was more temperate than his remarks to the Queen but still friendly enough. Albert, he wrote, 'seems a very agreeable young man . . . and as to character, that we must always take our chance of'.[28]

Once the decision was made he was for carrying it out as rapidly as possible. There was no need for a long engagement nor would there be any popular objection, he assured the Queen with tears in his eyes. On the contrary: 'I hear there is an anxiety now that it should be; and I'm very glad of it. I think it is a very good thing, and you'll be much more comfortable; for a woman cannot stand alone for long, in whatever situation she is.' But in spite of these brave words, some part of him grieved at the changes which the marriage must inevitably bring. When the engagement was announced at Council, Croker, with characteristic relish, noted that the Prime Minister looked careworn and the meeting in general had a sombre air. He recorded too rumours that Melbourne and Lansdowne were to resign as soon as the marriage had taken place. Melbourne reassured the Queen that the story was absurd. 'I'm afraid that its our own people who spread these reports.' Ellice had come to him with the news. 'When people say a report prevails, it generally makes me suspect that they spread it.'[29]

At times over the next few weeks he must have wished that he had resigned already. The opposition delighted in the opportunities offered them to humiliate the government and get their own back on the Queen. On Melbourne's insistence and against Russell's advice the cabinet proposed that Albert should be given a lavish allowance of £50,000 a year.[30] The Tories announced their intention of reducing this by £20,000. One hundred and fifty liberals absented themselves when the time came to vote and the government were overwhelmingly defeated. On another point it was Russell who was at fault when he urged that no mention be made of Albert's religion in the formal declaration of the marriage. Wellington swooped on the omission and forced the government to insert the word 'Protestant' before 'Prince' in the first paragraph.

Albert's future precedence caused the Queen more pain and Melbourne more trouble than either of these issues. The Prime Minister was again misled by his desires into promising more than he could provide. It had been originally proposed that Albert should be given a British peerage but Melbourne had strongly opposed this on the grounds that it would involve him in national politics. The Queen insisted that, whatever else, her husband should have precedence over all other people in the realm. 'There'll be no difficulty about that', said Melbourne blithely. He confessed to doubts whether Albert could properly have precedence over a future Prince of Wales but did not feel the point sufficiently pressing to warrant a row. Then he wrote to the Dukes of Sussex and of Cambridge. It would, he pleaded, 'surely be inconvenient and in some degree unseemly that His Highness upon great occasions of state should be disjoined and placed at a distance from her Majesty'. Cambridge replied amiably, but Sussex was 'very petty and inclined to make great difficulties'. To his dismay Melbourne realized that he might have to disappoint the Queen.[31]

The attitude of Wellington was likely to be crucial. Clarendon was deputed to call on him and canvass his views. He found the Duke implacable. The precedence of the royal family, he said, was fixed by Act of Parliament, it would be an injustice to the royal dukes to change the law on this occasion. Clarendon pleaded the distress that the Duke's attitude would cause the Queen. He had had to deal with many sovereigns, replied Wellington loftily, and always found he could bring them to reason. But had he, asked Clarendon, ever had to deal with a young lady Queen in love? The Duke was unmoved. Glumly Clarendon went round to South Street to report the bad news. 'Lord Melbourne had gone to bed, but had left orders for George to be shown up to his bedroom when he came', recorded Lady Clarendon. 'George found him in bed, everything in the room in a great litter, the bed *dirty*, and books, pamphlets, papers, boots and shoes, all tumbling indiscriminately about.'[32]

Melbourne had no doubt that the point must be abandoned; if Wellington stuck to his guns the reward for persistence would inevitably be a humiliating defeat in the Lords. He could not find the courage to tell Victoria the news to her face but wrote apologetically to excuse his failure: 'In England new courses are always hazardous and precedent should be departed from as little as possible.'[33] He did not exaggerate her likely fury. 'Poor, dear Albert', she wrote in her journal, 'how cruelly are they ill-using that dearest angel! Monsters! you Tories shall be punished. Revenge, revenge!' On Wellington, at least, she saw a chance to carry out her threat immediately. He should not be invited to the wedding, she decreed. Melbourne argued that this would gravely offend both him and all his followers. 'This is what the Queen is *striving* to do!' she replied. 'What *does* she owe them? Nothing but hate.' In the end Melbourne got the Duke invited but he had to put up with some harsh treatment on the way. The Queen was 'teazed and worried and ill used', she complained. 'Lord Melbourne ought really to have thought of all this before, and not led the Queen to expect no difficulties . . .'[34]

Once or twice as the great day approached it seemed to the Queen that her Prime Minister was insufficiently serious about the married state. When Victoria said that she could never marry a man who had loved another woman, Melbourne cheerfully replied that one affair before marriage was nothing and should be permitted anyone. He got into still worse trouble when the Queen remarked that one of the things she liked most about Albert was the way he paid no attention to other women. Clarendon recorded the incident. 'Lord Melbourne *inadvertantly* (as he called it) answered, "No, that sort of thing is apt to come later", an odd remark to make to any woman on the eve of marriage – let alone *the Queen*. She said, "I shan't forgive you that". Lord Melbourne rubbed his hands when he told the anecdote and chuckled over it amazingly.' But she could never be seriously annoyed with him, even finding time to note in her journal the night before the wedding that he was boasting about the new full dress coat he had had made for the occasion. In point of work and trouble, he said, it was 'like building a 74 gun ship . . . I expect it to be thing most observed'.[35]

Lord Melbourne, wrote the Queen, 'was very much affected during the ceremony'. It would have been astonishing if he had not been. Though thoughts of his own position must have been in his mind, it would be unduly cynical to doubt that his first consideration was Victoria's happiness. He did not yet feel that he knew enough of Albert's character to be truly confident but he had already established that he was decent, honourable and conscientious. That there were squalls ahead was certain but it did not seem extravagant to hope that they might be successfully survived. 'It is impossible to predict the future', he had written to King Leopold some weeks before, 'it is impossible to conjecture what effect new situations, new interests and new passions may have upon young and plastic natures, but I feel much assured of a good and happy result.' He believed that the Queen 'will find the means of doing that, which is not altogether easy, namely of reconciling the authority of a sovereign with the duty of a wife'.[36]

The day after the ceremony Melbourne received a first, hurriedly scribbled message from the honeymooners at Windsor. She wrote of her 'most gratifying and bewildering' night and the splendid reception that had greeted them all along the route. 'The Queen cannot conclude without telling Ld Melbourne how *very, very* happy she feels. She never thought she could be so loved as she is by *dearest, dear* Albert . . . The kind and paternal interest Ld Melbourne has ever taken in the Queen makes her sure he will be happy to hear this. The Queen cannot finish without saying to Ld Melbourne most sincerely, God Bless You!'[37] Melbourne must have been deeply touched that the Queen should have thought of him when there was so much else to absorb her attention, but it would have been strange if he had not detected in her loving message some faint flavour of the valedictory.

It remained to come to terms with Albert. The relationship promised to be uneasy. To Melbourne, Albert must be to some extent a usurper; to Albert, Melbourne was the man whose privileged position threatened the influence he should properly exercise over his own wife. It says much for both of them that they not only respected but liked each other and that their differences of opinion were almost always regulated to the eventual satisfaction of both of them.

The two men had clashed six weeks before the wedding. Melbourne, at the suggestion of the Queen, wrote to Prince Albert setting out the principles which he thought should govern his life in England. The most important thing was that there should be no suspicion of dissension between the Queen and her husband. Albert should avoid involvement in party politics but 'it will be absolutely necessary that your Highness should be considered as sanctioning and countenancing the policy pursued by the actual government of the Queen, however that government may be constituted'. He should avoid appointing too many active parliamentarians to his household but should, nevertheless, select people generally favourable to the ministry of the day; otherwise, 'you will find yourself in spite of yourself taken up by the party in opposition and elevated to the post of the leader of the Tories'.[38]

Victoria thought this letter the most consummate wisdom: 'nothing could be better', she told her fiancé. Albert thought few things could be worse. No one could less relish the idea of dissension in the family, he told the Queen, but 'one's opinions are not to be dictated, for an opinion is the result of reflection and conviction, and you could not respect a husband who never formed an opinion till you had formed yours'. Melbourne was contradicting himself when he said that Albert should not take an active part in politics but should still countenance the policy of the government. To countenance a policy was to play an active part in politics. To the Prime Minister he complained that this proposal would mean his household changing with every government. He was resolved to have a permanent household composed both of Whigs and Tories yet as much outside politics as the Prince himself.[39]

Against the combination of Queen and Prime Minister poor Albert proved powerless. In spite of his protests his household was composed exclusively of Whigs, though certainly chosen from among the more moderate members of the party and not, as Graham had feared, from among 'their firmest and most crafty adherents'. His fiercest battle was against the appointment as his private secretary of George Anson, who had previously performed the same office for Melbourne. Here he won a minor victory since Anson did not, as was originally proposed, serve both masters at once, but resigned from Melbourne's employment on joining the court. In fact it took Albert only a little time to realize how wisely the Prime Minister had chosen. Anson served him with total loyalty, keeping open his lines of communication with Lord Melbourne but never using them with impropriety, and winning the confidence of the Tory leaders as completely as he retained that of the Whigs.[40]

Prince Albert was not a man whom Melbourne would have chosen as a friend: he found him too strait-laced, almost entirely humourless, narrow in outlook and heavy-handed in debate. Nevertheless he recognized that these characteristics, defects in a companion, might be no bad things in the husband of Victoria. He saw too, far more quickly than most, the qualities which won Albert the reluctant admiration of his adopted people. He told Greville that the Prince would 'acquire boundless influence', and he did his best to ensure that the process was rapid and painless. He urged that the Queen should show her husband all the state papers that he wished to see, made a point of discussing affairs with the Prince whenever occasion offered and encouraged him to express his views on all questions of public interest. Albert told his father that he often put his views on foreign affairs on paper to Lord Melbourne; 'He seldom answers me, but I have often had the satisfaction of seeing him act entirely in accordance with what I have said'. The remark betrays some naivety but it should not for that reason be assumed that Melbourne under-estimated the good sense of the young Prince. In almost his final letter to the Queen as Prime Minister he wrote:

> Lord Melbourne has formed the highest opinion of his Royal Highness's judgement, temper, and discretion, and he cannot but feel a great consolation and security in the reflection that he leaves your Majesty in a situation in which your Majesty has the inestimable advantage of such advice and assistance. Lord Melbourne feels certain that your Majesty cannot do better than have recourse to it, whenever it is needed, and rely upon it with confidence.[41]

But though he would have considered himself Albert's ally he was not prepared to engage in any serious confrontation with the Queen, or indeed to put himself out to further the Prince's interests. Baroness Lehzen, Victoria's former governess, had worked herself into a position of great influence at court and was reluctant to surrender it so as to make way for a mere husband. Melbourne had always had his doubts about Lehzen – 'She's a girl whom we don't quite understand', he told Howick – but had established a reasonable working relationship with her. 'The King [Leopold] says she dislikes me, but feels it necessary as well as safer for the Queen to confide entirely in me and submits accordingly.' The Queen was still devoted to her and ready to take offence at any attempt on the part of the Prince to interfere in affairs of state. When Stockmar, in mid-1840, asked Melbourne whether he would help Albert if it came to open conflict, the Prime Minister replied bluntly that he would not. On the contrary, if the rupture were over the Prince's desire to supplant Lehzen, 'I should support the Baroness. She has never stood in my way . . . She has always acted for instead of against us, we owe her much and ought to stand by her.'[42]

By February 1841 he had modified his views. The Prince's position had grown stronger, that of Lehzen correspondingly weaker. Melbourne was still reluctant to provoke an open row but was now ready to concede that the situation was becoming intolerable and that the only solution he could see was the eviction of the Baroness from the court. If he got an opportunity he would point out the dangers to the Queen; in the meantime Albert should act with 'great patience and great caution'. No one who knew Melbourne can have been surprised that a suitable opportunity never arose; it was a year after he left office before Lehzen was finally dispatched. But Anson and Stockmar had done their work well. 'The subject with its dangers and difficulties is weighing heavily upon Ld M's mind', recorded the former. Contrasting the Prime Minister's attitude in February with what it had been eight months before, Anson noted gratefully that 'there is sufficient variation of opinion in his mind to hope that he will be more alive to the danger'.[43]

On 22 January 1841 Melbourne wrote to the Queen at Windsor to say how pleased he was to hear that she was reluctant to come to London: '. . . there is no surer sign of complete happiness and contentment in the married life than a desire to remain quietly in the country'.[44] No one can doubt his sincerity but he must have realized that in this contentment lay the seeds of his own extinction. Victoria was still a devoted Whig, she was still convinced that Melbourne was and always would be her pattern of a perfect minister, yet he was no longer indispensable. Even though he fell, there would still be Albert. The reflection was in many ways a consoling one, but it was saddening too. It can never be pleasant to become expendable, to realize that those to whom your presence has been essential would now view your disappearance, if not with equanimity, at least with resignation. By early 1841 Melbourne had recognized that, if Whig support in the House of Commons once more collapsed, the Queen would accept the advent of the Tories; Albert, perhaps, even welcome them. The thought heightened his conviction that his government was almost over.

CHAPTER 23

Eastern Crisis

IN SPITE OF all the troubles at home it was a crisis in foreign affairs which came closest to destroying the Whig government in 1840. For Melbourne all questions of foreign policy were inextricably interwoven with his relationship with Lord Palmerston. Since the beginning of the year this relationship had become more than political. Palmerston had been Lady Cowper's lover for many years and had wanted to marry her since her husband's death. Now at last Emily Cowper decided that they would be good company for each other in their old age. 'I wrote to her she must do what she liked', Melbourne told the Queen. 'I couldn't advise her.' His sister said that all her children were delighted at the idea. Melbourne was sceptical, both about the reaction of the young Cowpers and the merits of Palmerston as a husband. 'You mustn't deceive yourself about it', he warned her, 'if you do this you must take the consequences.' In spite of such daunting advice, Emily Cowper stuck to her guns and was rewarded by many years of happiness. '. . . the union of the best-tempered persons in the world', Lady Holland called it. '*Never* did I see a man more in love . . .'[1]

The fact that Palmerston was now his brother-in-law did not make the Prime Minister any better disposed towards the more adventurous aspects of British foreign policy but it added an extra reason for avoiding a quarrel. Melbourne was even less inclined to concern himself with the intricacies of foreign affairs than the organization of the War Office or the duty on imported corn, and shrank from interference with a man as hot in defence of his own bailiwick as was the Foreign Secretary. To John Russell it seemed he shrank too visibly and too far. Palmerston, Russell conceded, was certainly the best man for his job, 'but anyone may be spoilt, and I think the entire want of control or contradiction has somewhat spoiled him. But for that you are more to blame than he is.'[2]

Melbourne could sometimes be firm. The Emperor of Russia made a speech in Warsaw which offended Palmerston's erratically liberal ideas. He wished to condemn the speech in forthright terms. 'Whatever may be your opinion of the prudence, feeling or propriety of the Emperor's reproaches for the past, and menaces for the future', wrote Melbourne, 'he has a right to employ them towards his subjects, if he pleases, and you have none to remark upon or remonstrate against his conduct in this respect.' When Palmerston complained of Russia's expansionist policies, Melbourne drily replied: 'I was pretty well aware of the acquisitions of Russia, of their extent, their direction and the time at which they had been made; a map of England with her acquisitions during the same period would make a very respectable figure and colour no inconsiderable portion of the globe.'[3] But such occasions were infrequent and grew more so as the years wore on. In general Melbourne preferred to let his Foreign Secretary go his own way.

Not everyone felt the same. Palmerston's policy was more assertive than certain senior ministers, notably Russell, thought proper. He also tended to run foul of the French in a way which seemed deplorable to the francophiles in the cabinet. When he wished to pursue a policy which was at once aggressive *and* ran counter to French interests, he therefore quickly assembled a formidable opposition in cabinet. Melbourne saw the force of everybody's arguments. Even within his family he was torn between his sister Emily who stood up for her husband and his brother, Fred Beauvale, now Ambassador in Vienna, who believed that Palmerston was an adventurer and his policy dangerous madness. His instinct was to lie low and let the main protagonists talk themselves out. But sometimes they would not do so. Palmerston was never a man to give in easily, yet neither was Russell. The government could not stand if either of them were to resign. If he had thrown his weight behind either of them Melbourne might have achieved the success of their policy, yet only at the price of disaffecting the other. His characteristic solution was to defer decisions and to blur the outlines of problems which to others appeared clear-cut. The longer a matter could be left open, the better the chance that it would solve itself, or that it would at least evolve in such a way as to make future debate less acrimonious. More sapient than Mr Micawber, Melbourne waited with equal optimism for something either to turn up or to go away. One or other thing usually happened. But the wait could be long and it was mainly thanks to Palmerston's tendency to go his own way without waiting for a cabinet ruling that no serious harm was done to British interests in the interval.

On no issue was the breach within the cabinet so wide or the stakes so high as on the Eastern Question. It is worth following the development of the crisis in some detail because of the vivid light it casts on Melbourne's somewhat individual practice of the art of leadership. He himself was always anxious not to become embroiled in the affairs of the area – 'The Black Sea and the Caucasus and these great Asiatic empires influence imaginations wonderfully' – but sometimes even he had to admit that activity was necessary. Mehemet Ali, the Turkish Sultan's Viceroy in Egypt, had assumed virtual independence and extended his power to cover Syria. By the summer of 1836 he was, in fact, mightier than his master. Some members of the cabinet believed that, provided his sovereignty over Egypt was formally secured, he would fall back from Syria and leave the rump of the Turkish empire to disintegrate in its own time. Melbourne was more sceptical. 'Mehemet Ali must be very different from the rest of mankind, and particularly from all other orientals, if having gained possession of such a country as Syria, at least equal in natural resources to Egypt, he is prepared to give it up at anyone's bidding. I know I never would, until I was forced out of it.'[4]

To Palmerston and his clamorous henchman, Ponsonby, Ambassador to the Porte and most ambitious of activists, the situation seemed intolerable. They wanted a strong Turkey able to resist Russia's expansionist ideas. To recognize the sovereignty of the man Palmerston once described as 'that aged afrancescado [francophile] freebooter' would be to seal the doom of the Turkish empire. From November 1835 the Foreign Secretary was arguing that Britain and France should together make a treaty with the Sultan aimed both against the rebellious Mehemet Ali and the Russians. Melbourne suggested bringing in Austria, which he once told Victoria was the only country sincerely friendly to Britain. Palmerston distrusted Metternich and was alarmed about the French, who seemed ready to go it alone. Melbourne was still doubtful whether we should involve ourselves so deeply. Backed by Grey from outside the cabinet he for once stood his ground. 'I have during the last six months', wrote Palmerston to Granville, 'used every endeavour in my power and employed every argument I could think of, but in vain. Melbourne remains immoveable and the natural consequence of that is, that, other members of the cabinet who originally agreed with me begin to partake of Melbourne's opinion.' A few months later the French government fell, the new incumbent, Thiers, preferred to fry his own fish in the Middle Eastern kitchen and the chance of a joint Anglo-French approach to the problem slipped away.[5]

Palmerston continued to call for intervention in favour of the Sultan but found little support among his colleagues. Then, in the summer of 1839, the Sultan precipitated matters by attacking Mehemet Ali in Syria. His forces were routed and Mehemet Ali proclaimed himself Viceroy of Syria. Melbourne was still against taking violent measures because, as he told the Austrian Ambassador, it would be 'a source of disunion among the great powers', but the Austrians and Russians were determined that the Sultan should be protected. Palmerston, of course, agreed, and felt still more strongly that the Russians could not be allowed to intervene without the British by their side. Only the French prevented the formation of a united front. They reckoned that they could do better out of Mehemet Ali than a patched-up Turkish empire and would have nothing to do with any of Palmerston's projects for forcing the rebellious dictator back to Egypt or, at least, to southern Syria. Palmerston had no doubt that, if such were their attitude, they should be left in the lurch while the other interested powers settled the matter as they thought best.[6]

The pro-French lobby within the cabinet began to stir uneasily. Holland was the most vociferous but Clarendon now lent him substantial aid. He told his wife that he considered the Eastern question to be in a disastrous state, and that, if his colleagues persisted in picking quarrels with France, he would resign. Lansdowne, though more reticent in the early stages, made it clear that he too had inherited the Foxite tradition while, from outside the cabinet, the arch-intriguer Ellice was called in to 'exert influence' on Melbourne and canvass for a pro-French line. 'Lord Melbourne', the Prime Minister wrote gloomily to the Queen, 'fears that he may have some difficulty in keeping the cabinet steady and united upon the oriental question.'[7]

He did not exaggerate the problems ahead. In May Palmerston discovered that no less than five senior ministers had let it be known to a private business-man that they were against his policy. In a rage he told the cabinet that he would resign if his strategy was disapproved. 'When Palmerston stopped speaking there was an ominous pause, Melbourne making no sign.'[8] Then minister after minister denied that they had been guilty of any disloyalty but attacked the Foreign Secretary's policy. Palmerston renewed his threat to resign and Melbourne at last intervened, urging that the matter be held over for a few weeks until the attitude of the French became more clear. To Palmerston's irritation but the general relief this compromise was accepted.

It could not last for long. By July Palmerston believed he had proof that the French were secretly trying to arrange their own settlement between the Turks and Mehemet Ali. Some decision had to be reached. First Melbourne tried to talk his brother-in-law into line. 'The more I think of the matter', he wrote, 'the more I am convinced that you will not be able to persuade a majority of the cabinet to concur in measures which may lead to long and difficult operations. Some are, as you know, entirely for Mehemet Ali; others will be apprehensive of the House of Commons and the country . . .' Palmerston was unimpressed; his resignation, he reminded the Prime Minister, could take effect as soon as was desired. This would, of course, lead to the immediate dissolution of the government, retorted Melbourne crossly; '. . . the consequences of which, both at home and abroad, . . . must be most grave'.[9]

Having failed with one side, Melbourne turned his attention to the other. Clarendon in his turn offered to resign. 'We must have no resignations', replied the Prime Minister. 'We cannot stand them, and what is more, the country cannot stand them . . .' He argued that either policy would do if it were quickly adopted and vigorously carried out, otherwise both of them would be disastrous.[10] Weighing up what he knew of his colleagues, Melbourne decided that Palmerston would certainly resign if frustrated; the others were less likely to. It followed that he must throw his weight behind the Foreign Secretary. He did so and was proved right. On 8 July the cabinet approved Palmerston's policy. Clarendon and Holland drew up a dissenting minute but did not resign.

Palmerston now quickly moved ahead. In the middle of the month the Treaty of London linked Britain, Austria, Prussia and Russia in a joint enterprise to force Mehemet Ali out of Syria. The French were left conspicuously to one side. Their resultant rage was fearsome and though Palmerston dismissed it as 'temporary swagger', to others it seemed more formidable. Guizot, the French Ambassador, made the flesh of the Foxites creep with stories of his government's indignation and their preparations for war, while Granville in Paris had his carriage stoned and the French fleet in the Mediterranean was reinforced. 'Affairs look awkward', Melbourne told Russell. Wellington had been with him and, while in general supporting the government line, urged that the French should be brought back into the alliance as soon as possible. 'All that is very well . . . but how the devil is that to be done?'[11]

By the end of August Melbourne was a deeply troubled man. More and more he became certain that the truculence of his brother-in-law was dragging Britain into a major war for which it had neither the weapons nor the will. British forces in the Mediterranean were inadequate for the scale of operations in which they might be involved. He pleaded with Palmerston to make some conciliatory move:

It is most highly desirable that something should be done to withdraw us from our present state of uncertainty. We are now dependent entirely upon accident for what may happen in the Levant, upon the caprice of Mehemet Ali, upon the irritation of the French people, of the tone of the French and of our own press. Depend upon it also you mistake Louis Philippe's character if you suppose that he will act solely according to his principles and not from passion.[12]

But he could not bring himself to summon the cabinet and reverse the policy which had been agreed a few weeks before. Instead he fretted impotently: 'I can neither eat nor sleep for anxiety', he told Russell.[13]

By early September it was clear that Melbourne was changing his tack. Emily Palmerston was so alarmed that she tried to get her brother Fred home from Vienna to stiffen his resolve. The most effective step she could have taken would have been to silence the pregnant Queen: '. . . for God's sake do not bring on a crisis', Victoria pleaded, 'the Queen really could not go through that *now*, and it might make her *seriously ill* . . .' A note of reproach began to creep into Melbourne's letters to Palmerston. 'You have forced the adoption of a line of policy . . . contrary to the opinion of two members of the cabinet, and but a very lukewarm consent and approbation upon the part of several others', he wrote. 'Never, I will answer for it, was a great measure undertaken upon a basis of support so slender and so uncertain.' Palmerston was not unreasonably put out by this attack. As he pointed out, whatever doubts there might have been, the cabinet had approved his policy and it was only fair that it should be given a proper trial. In riposte he complained bitterly about the activities of certain ministers, notably Holland, who not only publicly attacked the official line as vigorously as if he had been a member of the opposition, but thought nothing of passing on cabinet secrets to the French Ambassador over the port at Holland House.[14]

Now John Russell moved into action. He posted up from Scotland, complaining that nobody except Melbourne had any idea what the Foreign Secretary was doing. A cabinet must be called at once to thrash out the whole question. There must be some compromise. His appearance was enough to drive the Prime Minister back on to his trimming course: To Palmerston, Melbourne had revealed only his doubts about pursuing an active policy; to Russell, he emphasized the difficulties and dangers to be encountered in abandoning it. On 16 September he wrote:

> For heaven's sake do not be precipitate; consider this matter well.
>
> You have been a consenting party to the Convention; you cannot upon slight or subordinate grounds, withdraw yourself from the consequence of it.
>
> If the British government is broken up by the mere bluster and threats of the French, and by the sole apprehension of a difference with that country, what will be the impression, both upon Europe and upon France, of their strength and courage, of our weakness and humility?
>
> It will encourage France to such a degree that, even if it staves off war now, it will produce it very shortly.[15]

Palmerston himself could hardly have put the case more strongly.

To Greville it seemed that Melbourne had lost control over his cabinet and the situation. 'So melancholy a picture of indecision, weakness and pusillanimity as his conduct has exhibited, I never heard of.' He had been emasculated by living so much with the Queen, thought only about her health and how it might be affected by the present crisis, could not eat or sleep for worry and, in a few words, had been reduced to the level of 'a twaddling old woman . . . fitter to preside over the nursery than the Treasury'.[16] The other side of the coin, of course, shows him playing a cool and skilful game, little concerned about the principles at issue but determined to steer his cabinet out of a dangerous impasse without allowing it to break up. Viewed in this light his hesitation and inconsistency become mere tactical devices to avoid a fatal confrontation between the warring ministers. Which portrait is the true one Melbourne probably hardly knew himself but the events of the next few weeks were to show him far more in command of affairs than Greville imagined.

On 29 September the cabinet met to discuss the problem. It seemed that the fatal clash which Melbourne had tried so hard to avert was at last inevitable. Clarendon gave Greville an account of the meeting which the latter described as 'to the last degree amusing, but at the same time *pitoyable*'. Russell claimed that the country was on the brink of war and, turning on the Prime Minister, demanded his opinion on the subject. 'Nothing, however, could be got from Melbourne . . .' After an uncomfortable pause, Palmerston began to read lengthy extracts from the latest relevant despatches, 'in the middle of which operation someone happened to look up, and perceived Melbourne fast asleep in his armchair'. Russell and Palmerston then set out their different points of view at length and with some acrimony, various other ministers contributed their opinions and the meeting closed with an agreement that nothing could be decided until Lansdowne got back to London the following day. Melbourne had achieved his immediate purpose of postponing a split which could lead to resignations.[17]

Before the next meeting of the cabinet Melbourne worked busily to secure a compromise. Though retaining his posture on the fence he had decided that Palmerston must make some concession. To Russell he wrote in cautious terms, which must have left that statesman in doubt as to what was intended. Any overture to France would seem like surrender – 'But I should be inclined to submit to the imputation for the sake of preserving peace'; he doubted whether there was any real risk of war – 'but I should not like to act entirely upon that conviction'. To Palmerston, however, he was a great deal less ambiguous. Whatever happened in the Middle East, he argued, it must be a good idea to make some overture to France: 'If you fail, it is better to have taken this course before you learn of the failure. If you succeed, there will be no humiliation . . .' He reinforced his plea with letters from Victoria, Leopold and Albert, all urging the same course. Almost to Melbourne's surprise Palmerston fell in with the idea and at the cabinet on 1 October disarmed his opposition by his ready agreement to make some friendly approach to the French government. Melbourne presided over the resultant reconciliation with benign self-satisfaction: 'swaggering like any Bobadil', as Greville uncharitably put it, 'and talking about "fellows being frightened at their own shadows" and a deal of bravery when he began to breathe freely from the danger'.[18]

Unfortunately the new consensus proved illusory. Within a few days it became clear to Russell that Palmerston's idea of a conciliatory gesture was very different from his own. With the French still apparently bent on war, tension once again built up between the different groups of ministers. To add to Melbourne's other woes he was crippled by gout and suffering from a violently upset stomach, too sick even to pay his usual visit to Windsor. His illness left him still less inclined to take a decisive line. When Russell wrote to demand an immediate cabinet the Prime Minister replied wearily that it was too late to do anything. 'Lord John said that was always Lord Melbourne's way; that he always asked him to wait, wait, wait, and when he did wait, said it was then too late.'[19]

Once again disaster was averted, this time by a conciliatory note from the French. The lines of a possible compromise were thrashed out, by which Mehemet Ali would be left in peace in Egypt provided he would leave Syria to the Sultan. At the meeting where this was settled Melbourne once again was conspicuously loath to give a lead; he 'hardly said a word – lay sprawling on the sofa and took no part'. Palmerston undertook to see Guizot immediately and convey this offer to him; yet when Russell saw the Ambassador at Holland House two days later he discovered that no such overture had been made. Angrily he propelled Melbourne into battle with his brother-in-law: 'I hope you will see him tomorrow and urge him to instant action'. Melbourne did nothing of the sort. A combination of circumstances – the reluctance of the other European powers to agree to any fresh approach to the French; the news that the Turks, stiffened by Western support, had inflicted a sharp military set-back on Mehemet Ali; the serious illness of the arch-francophile, Lord Holland – had finally convinced him that the best chance for a successful settlement was to make Palmerston's policy work rather than to abandon or emasculate it. Abruptly he changed his tack.[20]

For the first time in the crisis he acted with energy. About 20 October he wrote a personal letter to King Leopold, intended for the eyes of Louis Philippe, in which he stated roundly that he could no longer tolerate French threats and that, if they continued, he would summon parliament and ask for the means to resist them. The text of the letter has not been found, yet enough references to it exist to give a clear picture of its uncharacteristic toughness, even truculence. According to Bülow he stated that he would 'lay before [parliament] the conduct of France, ask for supplies in order to increase our fleets. I will take care that they shall be placed upon the largest footing – this is, in a word, War, Sir. If I do take such a responsibility upon myself in the state in which is now her Majesty, I know that the interests and honour of my country require it and that I will be approved by the whole nation.'[21] The letter probably worked all the better for coming from a man so little bellicose as Melbourne. Its effects seemed almost magical. Though it would be a mistake to give the letter all the credit for a process which was under way already, Louis Philippe responded by dismissing the warlike Thiers and installing a government of which the anglophile and peace-loving Guizot was leader in all but name.

On 22 October Palmerston's position was further strengthened by the death of Holland. Holland had established himself as the most active enemy of Palmerston's policy – 'really quite foolish and super-annuated', Emily Palmerston described him, 'but with a name, and following, and dinners and activity of proselytism that was quite extraordinary'. Of recent months he had become more and more of a liability; his fanatical love of France driving him into behaviour that was indiscreet if not actually treasonable. Some weeks before, Melbourne had felt bound to write to him to urge slightly greater discretion. The warning had not been heeded. After his death the *Quarterly Review* attacked him for leaking secrets to the French government. Russell wanted an official denial to be issued. Melbourne flatly refused. 'Contradiction to be effective should be short, distinct and right in the teeth of the assertion contradicted.' Did Russell really feel certain that Holland had not passed information back to Thiers? 'I doubt whether he would have felt so much indignation at the mere proposal if he had thought that he could by it have assisted his own policy.' And yet in spite of it all Holland had been one of the most lovable of men: generous, affectionate, a loyal friend in trouble. He had been linked with Melbourne since childhood, had known as much as anyone of his tragic marriage, for more than forty years had offered a home in which Melbourne could feel at ease. His death, the Prime Minister told Ellice, 'was the heaviest blow, both personally and politically, which he had yet received'.[22]

The crisis had a twist or two to follow before it petered out. Though Mehemet Ali had been defeated he was still formidable and the great fortress of Acre remained firmly in his hands. Melbourne was a worried man, especially since his brother-in-law appeared to be suffering from a persecution complex, bombarding him with accusations against the treacherous machinations 'of some who ought to act differently'. Then, at the end of October, Beauvale wrote to suggest the setting up of a congress in which all outstanding differences could be settled peaceably. Palmerston rejected the proposal without even waiting to consult his colleagues. Russell took umbrage and once more tried to resign. 'It is much better', he told Melbourne, 'that Palmerston should lead in the House of Commons than that I should disgrace myself by pretending to an influence which I do not possess.'[23]

As he no doubt anticipated, the usual wails of protest arose from his colleagues. 'It must, of course, break up the government', wrote Melbourne resignedly. Even if it were possible to fill the gap and set up Palmerston as Leader in the House of Commons, 'I own I shall be unwilling [to continue] my present responsibility under the impression which would be created . . . by your retiring and Palmerston's remaining and acquiring additional weight and influence'. Palmerston for his part hastened to call on Russell and apologized handsomely for his misdemeanours. He found him at first 'very cross and somewhat sour', but he soon relaxed and ended up by discussing parliamentary business with all the interest of a man who expects to take part in it. '. . . so I think this little cloud has blown over', reported Palmerston to Melbourne with relief if not surprise. It only needed the sudden fall of Acre a few days later, followed by the collapse of Mehemet Ali's resistance, to cut what ground was left from under Russell's feet.[24]

The party had survived the crisis. Almost everyone was now in favour of the treaty, reported Emily Palmerston exultantly in mid-November. Only a 'little Cabal' within the cabinet and a 'few ignorant intriguers' outside it still denied that all had been managed with consummate skill. What was more, the government were backed by the Tories as well as 'the fanatical and religious elements, and you know what a following they have in this country. They are absolutely determined that Jerusalem and the whole of Palestine shall be reserved for the Jews to return to . . .' But it had been a close run thing and had done much damage to the party; indeed, concluded Lady Palmerston, if Holland had not died when he did, 'I really and truly think that our ministry would have fallen'.[25]

The victory was Palmerston's, yet Melbourne deserves credit for the fact that the cabinet had not disintegrated. Possibly he could have curbed Palmerston if he had intervened strongly before things had gone too far but, once positions had been taken up, he adopted the only tactics possible to achieve the end he desired. He conducted his campaign with skill, indifferent to the fact that whatever reputation he had for resolution or firm leadership would suffer by his behaviour. After all was over, Greville reported him as saying that, in his heart of hearts, he had been more opposed than anyone to Palmerston's policy. There is no evidence to support this in his letters, but it is still perfectly possible. At no point in the crisis was the justice or even the probable success of Palmerston's foreign policy a major consideration in Melbourne's mind. He had been concerned with the balance of power within the cabinet and the need to find some formula which would be tolerable to everyone. He had backed the right horse. The fact that British policy had been triumphantly successful was an agreeable bonus. It was small wonder that at Woburn in late December he was said to be 'like a boy escaped from school, in roaring spirits. They anticipate an easy session, and all Melbourne's alarm and despondency are quickly succeeded by joy at having got out of a scrape, and confidence that all difficulties are surmounted and all opposition will be silenced.'[26]

All opposition, of course, was far from being silenced. Even within the cabinet itself Melbourne a fortnight later was reporting that he feared bad feeling was 'still alive and lurking under the surface'. The radicals had been actively opposed to Palmerston's policy and were no more disposed to condone it now that it had turned out successful. The approval of the Tories was not likely to extend into any other field. The country was not particularly interested in or impressed by the government's handling of affairs in the Middle East; economic matters bulked larger in their minds. Aberdeen told Princess Lieven that, in spite of the Whigs' 'decisive and certainly brilliant success which has crowned their operations in the Levant, they have not in the slightest degree improved their position at home'. The facts were soon to prove him right.[27]

CHAPTER 24

Decline and Fall

FOR A FEW WEEKS it did indeed seem as if 1841 might provide the easy session that the Whigs had predicted. The power of the radicals had faded, the Irish were still generally loyal, there seemed no particular reason to fear that the Tories planned a switch to all-out assault. And yet Melbourne had no real confidence in the future. Clarendon told Greville of a conversation he had had with the Prime Minister at Windsor in which Melbourne, 'in his lounging way, as if thinking aloud', remarked that the government could not possibly carry on much longer. Palmerston, he casually threw in, was already in contact with the Tories. Startled, Clarendon enquired whether the Tories were making overtures to Palmerston or Palmerston to the Tories – 'To which Melbourne chuckled and grunted, laughed and rubbed his hands, and only said, "Oh, I don't know".' He would probably not have blamed Palmerston too harshly even if he had brought off this apostasy. The Whig cabinet, deeply divided, bereft of all policies, assailed from every side, was no place for an ambitious politician of conservative leanings. Melbourne was beginning to wonder whether it was the right place for him. He felt ill and tired. '. . . it's age and that constant care', he told Victoria. 'I'm nearly 61. Many men die at 63, and if they get over that, live till 70 . . . People like me grow old at once, who have been rather young for their age . . . I feel a great change since last year.'[1]

His mood of elegiac gloom was fostered by the disasters with which his party was meeting on the hustings. As early as December of the previous year the opposition had gained Carlow, a traditionally liberal seat in the south of Ireland. In February they won the county seat of Monmouthshire, the cathedral city of Canterbury and the industrial town of Walsall. It seemed as if the liberals were in retreat on every front. Still worse disaster struck in May when John Walter, proprietor of *The Times*, wrested Nottingham from the government with the help of a motley army of Tories, radicals and even Chartists. Melbourne continued to spend most of his time at Windsor, by no means detached from public affairs but seeming to view them as an irritating distraction from his primary function of safeguarding the well-being of the Queen. He usually attended cabinet meetings but his utterances there were often perfunctory and he made little secret of his wish to get them over as quickly as possible. '. . . a person might as well go to Brooks's to do business as to the cabinet', Clarendon told Howick in exasperation. The Prime Minister was 'utterly indifferent about public opinion which must lead the administration to a disgraceful end'.[2]

Things went no better in parliament. More to frustrate Stanley than from any real sense of urgency, the government put forward the reform of parliamentary registration in Ireland as their show piece for the session. To gratify their Irish supporters they proposed a considerably widened franchise: 'nothing short of a new reform bill for Ireland', Stanley described it. They scraped through with a tiny minority, but when Howick proposed his own, more moderate solution the opposition supported him and carried the day with some ease. To be thus defeated by one who had so recently been a member of the government made the blow doubly painful. Ministers agreed to water down their original ideas on the franchise and enraged the Irish and the radicals who in their turn voted against the government. Defeated once again, ministers stoutly denied any intention to resign, but privately admitted that their position was becoming intolerable: '. . . the Guelphs and Ghibellines of modern history are willing to destroy the country to further their own party interests', commented Emily Palmerston. Prince Albert sent Anson to ask his former master what was going to happen next. They would not go out on an issue like this, replied Melbourne, but if they were beaten on the budget, as seemed quite probable, then it would be another matter.[3]

It would indeed, for the budget was to be the last, desperate throw of a failing government. The defeat of the Whig candidate in the recent election at Walsall was largely attributed to the hostility of the Anti-Corn Law League.[4] It was in recognition of that fact that the government now decided to reverse existing policy and go to the country on a platform of, if not free, at least considerably freer trade. At the moment the agricultural interest was handsomely protected by a sliding scale of duties which were prohibitively heavy when corn at home was cheap

and only fell to a nominal level when the price at home was so high
that bread was already disastrously expensive. When harvests were
good, therefore, people tended to forget the issue; when they were bad,
the laws became a target for every malcontent. To the underpaid
industrial worker who had to refuse his child a second slice of bread
because the farmer's prosperity must be protected, the issue was clear
cut and violently emotive:

> Ye crop us up and tax our bread,
> And wonder why we pine.
> But ye are fat and round and red
> And filled with tax-bought wine.[5]

Melbourne cared little about the underpaid industrial worker.
Temperamentally he was unwilling, perhaps unable, to conceive what
it would be like not to have enough to eat. Arguments based on such
considerations were sentimental clap-trap advanced by people who did
not realize where the true interests of the country lay. Disraeli had
called on him about two years before as part of a deputation to urge
that there be no change to the laws. He found the experience amusing.
'Melbourne, frank and rollicking, evidently in his heart a thorough
Tory and agriculturist, rubbed his hands and laughed; when the evil
consequences insisted on, agreed to everything. "And my Lord", said
some Horwood from Ely, "will not the fund-holder be endangered?"
"Oh, of course", said the Prime Minister.'[6]
He had a range of more or less plausible justifications for his attitude.
Free importation of corn from abroad would reduce home production
and a dangerous dependence on foreign suppliers would follow. British
farmers who had poured money into the improvement of their land
would face ruin. A reduction in the price of bread would merely encourage employers to cut wages; indeed the Anti-Corn Law campaign
was largely stage-managed by malign master manufacturers with that
end in view. It was the wildest self-deception to suppose that concessions on corn would win comparable advantages for our industrial
products in foreign markets: 'If there were any chance you throw it all
away by carrying the measure here without negotiation.'[7] There was
something in all these arguments, and Melbourne found them conclusive. He was also sincerely convinced that, in defending the farmer
and landlord, he was preserving what was most valuable in British life.
But most of all he shrank from what he believed would be the *disruptive*
nature of a campaign against the Corn Laws. 'I own I dread it very
much', he told Russell, 'not so much from either the difficulty or

danger of the question itself . . . as from the conviction that it will not be settled either one way or the other without a very severe struggle . . . Nothing is so bad in my mind as abuse and condemnation of classes of society, and this naturally produces it.' Not only would it split the country, as the Reform Bill had done ten years before, but it would split the party. Years later Melbourne told Greville that he had resisted the clamour for reform for as long as he could and that, if he had given way before, 'his government would have fallen sooner'.[8]

Melbourne's strongest argument, therefore, was based on expediency rather than principle. Once he was satisfied that to retain the Corn Laws unchanged would be still more damaging to his government than to seek to amend them, he became a convert, albeit a reluctant and half-hearted one, to the cause of reform. Early in 1841 that point was reached. Without some such dramatic gesture as the abolition or the reduction of the duty on imported corn then the government was doomed; with it their position was still perilous but they might win back popular support. It was both a long shot and a distasteful expedient, but Melbourne had to admit that it was worth a try.

The background to the Chancellor's deliberations was sombre indeed. '. . . we have had the most unfortunate year in every way', Baring told Melbourne towards the end of 1840: a bad harvest; money in short supply; trade with America in the doldrums; the diplomatic row with France spilling over into the economic field; abnormally high prices for tea, copper and sugar. By February 1841 the picture had, if anything, darkened still further. The estimate of expenditure for the coming financial year was £50.9m. At least £1.5 more in revenue would be needed than in the previous year. 'Will you lay on a million and a half new taxes? My answer is Yes if necessary.' Melbourne's answer would no doubt have been the same but he was going to take a lot of convincing that measures so unpalatable to the country could not be avoided.[9]

Luckily another expedient was to hand. In 1840 a committee had been set up under Hume to consider the whole question of import duties. The committee reached the unexceptionable conclusion that, if the duty on certain raw materials was reduced, consumption would be greatly increased and the revenue would be a net beneficiary. Unfortunately it did not also point out that, as in the case of the penny post, the process could hardly be expected to work itself out at once and the immediate result would be a sharp fall in revenue. A more controversial element of the report was that British agriculture could in fact manage perfectly well without any or, at any rate, with much less protection. The doctrinaire radicalism of the findings would have inspired suspicion in ministers at any time but the present; as it was Baring saw that it provided a way out of his difficulties. To raise revenue without raising taxes was indeed a prospect to tempt an unpopular administration.

It was only after Baring had formally proposed the reduction of duties on imported sugar and timber that Russell raised the question of the Corn Laws. His original proposal was for a sharp reduction in the sliding scale of duties; by the end of April, after much hesitation, the cabinet came round to his point of view, though with the substitution of a fixed for the sliding scale of duty. They did so conscious that they could fairly be charged with inconsistency. 'Playing double or quits', Macaulay called it and there were those in the government who would have said that the odds were in fact heavily against success. Melbourne himself had the gravest doubts. 'You are bringing forward three great measures', he warned Baring, 'and raising all the great interests against you, without being sure of carrying either of them.'[10]

The 'great interests' of which Melbourne had written were quick to show themselves. The sugar and timber traders were indignant because the preference which their colonial products enjoyed over foreign rivals was to be whittled down or even eliminated. The farmers and landlords were appalled at the suggestion that they should be left unprotected in a hostile world. The proposal that sugar grown by slave labour should be more freely imported caused great offence to the emancipationists. Nor did the government's belated steps in the direction of free trade win them the support they might have hoped for. As Gladstone was to comment, it was too evident that their conversion was 'no more than a death-bed vow and gave them no more claim to credit than such bows commonly confer'. Melbourne, still down at Windsor where he was preparing the Queen for incipient disaster, received a particularly gloomy report from Ellice. A bizarre alliance of West India merchants and anti-slavers was forming to oppose the new sugar duties. Such Whig county members as remained were threatening to boycott the debate. 'It appears to me you will be beaten by a considerable majority.'[11]

The fatal debate began on 7 May. Two days earlier Melbourne had informed the Queen that defeat was almost certain and that resignation must follow. He told Anson that the Queen had been 'perfectly calm and reasonable'. She had wanted to send for Wellington but Melbourne had pressed the rights of Peel, at a pinch she might see them both at once. With Anson as intermediary and with the explicit blessing of the

Prime Minister, Prince Albert had already opened negotiations with Peel to ensure that the débâcle of the bedchamber ladies was not re-enacted in still more disastrous circumstances. Unobtrusively the scenery was being shifted in preparation for the next act. Melbourne surveyed the process with weary resignation. The Queen asked him outright whether he would mind going out of office. 'Why, nobody *likes* going out', he admitted, 'but I'm not well – I am a good deal tired, and it will be a great rest for me.'[12]

The curtain, however, had still to fall. The government were duly defeated on the sugar duties with eleven liberal defections to the opposition and still more abstentions. Resignation seemed the obvious if not the only course. Almost the only voice crying for another solution was that of the Queen. She had every confidence, she wrote to Melbourne, that he would do all that could be done 'to save the Queen from having to have recourse to those hated Tories. You will not desert me, that I know, from experience, and I will not ask for what cannot be; *all* I ask is, try if you *can* manage it either by a dissolution or any other way . . .'[13] Melbourne must have been deeply moved by this appeal but he was sure that the alternative that the Queen suggested, a general election, could only destroy his party yet more completely and leave Victoria helpless in the face of a triumphant Tory majority.

When the question was first discussed in cabinet, the Prime Minister took it for granted that resignation must follow. Only three ministers, though one of them the formidable Palmerston, were in favour of a dissolution. The cabinet considered the likely results of an election: their conclusions were not cheerful yet, as Melbourne gloomily told the Queen, 'more favourable than the reality would prove'.[14] But beneath the surface presented by the party potentates there was a strong ground-swell running in favour of battle. Some of the rank and file believed that the country was favourably impressed by the budget and would show its feelings at the polls. To the 'Whigs of Brooks's and the young and hot-headed', as Greville called them, it seemed intolerable that the government should give up without a fight. Clutching at every straw, they declared that the debate in the Commons had gone well for them, the anti-slavery cry of the opposition had failed, the Chartists were in disarray. What was quite certain, they claimed, was that if the government did not take their chance then Peel would surely dissolve as soon as he had a plausible excuse. With the weight of office behind him he would then win a crushing victory.

Melbourne was unconvinced. He spelt out his fears to John Russell.

From the manner in which the Tory party have gained upon us at the two last general elections; from the result of single elections, and the manner in which these events have been brought about . . . I feel persuaded that we shall be greatly beat at a general election, and that by giving the Tories that opportunity we shall give them a great advantage. We shall give them an appearance of strength greater than they really possess, and we shall ourselves show weaker than we really are.[15]

But it was the position of the Queen that worried him most. Indulging himself in one of those historical disquisitions which gave as much pleasure to him as to his hearer, he explained to Victoria that, ever since the time of Charles II, the crown had traditionally always had a majority returned in favour of its chosen party. William IV had provided something of an exception, but he at least had seen his candidates greatly strengthened. 'I am afraid that for the first time the crown would have an opposition returned smack against it; and that would be an affront to which I am very unwilling to expose the crown.' 'This is very true', commented the Queen dutifully, but she was only half won over.[16]

To his dismay his colleagues, one by one, began to show themselves as hesitant as the Queen. Palmerston, who had never had many doubts, battered his brother-in-law with arguments and confident assertions. All that was needed was some small modification to the poor law to give the party an irresistibly popular platform. The Tories, he declared hopefully, were filled with gloom. Lansdowne was soon convinced by his eloquence. Clarendon said that, if the Whigs shirked the challenge, he would not dare show his face in London for a month. Duncannon pleaded that the parliamentary rank and file should not be deserted; what was the point of adopting a bold financial policy if it was to be abandoned at the first challenge? Finally even Russell began to waver. Melbourne remained resolute. Emily Palmerston described him as 'always feeling as he does when two lines are open to him, rather desirous to take the one of least responsibility and the most inactive'. Her judgement of her brother was less perceptive than usual. To plunge the country into a general election in May 1841 would have been to Melbourne the easiest and most irresponsible course; to stand out against the pressure which was being brought upon him called for toughness and determination.[17]

The critical cabinet meeting came on 19 May. Melbourne called for a vote. Only Normanby, who had changed his mind in one direction while everybody else was moving in the other, unequivocally backed the Prime Minister. Minto was hesitant but acquiescent; everybody else, with varying degrees of enthusiasm, opted for an election. Melbourne spoke last. He reiterated his dislike of general elections, especially when public passions were aroused. Though the Corn Laws should no doubt be altered, this should be done 'deliberately and not under excitement'. He once again stressed his belief that the election would turn out badly for the liberals and for the Queen. But if that was what the party and his colleagues wanted, then he would not stand in the way. 'He said this with much, and serious, expression of feeling, and almost in tears.'[18]

Given the strength of Melbourne's convictions he should no doubt have told the other ministers that, if they wanted to fight an election, they would have to do so without him. Whether or not he had swung the day, he would still have played a better part in the eyes of posterity. Yet his behaviour is easily explicable. He knew that, if he once lost office, it was highly unlikely that he would ever return, at least to the post of Prime Minister. And yet he felt no more ready to retire now than he had done in 1839. In six months, a year perhaps, he would be ready to go; but not quite yet. Could it not be that Palmerston was right, that the country really was swinging behind the government? If there was even a slight chance of this it was surely wrong that he should let down his supporters, abandon the Queen. Pride, loyalty, self-interest, clamoured to be heard; and the voice of his better judgement was drowned amid the uproar. Hesitant, protesting, and yet in some part grateful to be coerced, Melbourne allowed himself to be impelled down the path that led to electoral defeat.

The euphoria of the liberal camp abated almost before it had arisen. By the time voting began, only the most hopeful still talked of victory, while the pessimists prophesied disaster. The liberals, indeed, fought a most dispirited campaign.[19] Less than half the 401 seats were contested and 27 liberal seats were lost without a candidate being put into the field. Incompetent organization certainly accounted for part of this but there was also a malaise among the party members. Melbourne himself played little or no part in the battle – such reticence was not unusual in a peer and a Prime Minister but his conspicuous distaste for the hustings can not have done much to stiffen the morale of his supporters. By 30 June his party had lost nine seats in the first forty or fifty results. 'Those who entertained more sanguine expectations will naturally feel disappointed and discouraged', he told the Queen, 'but Lord Melbourne expected this sort of result from the beginning . . .'[20]

In the event it proved a clear-cut defeat but not a rout. The opposition gained about fifty seats, enough to ensure that only they could form a future government. Ellice claimed that, but for the budget, things would have been even worse, yet there is little to show that budgetary issues really made much impression on the radicals and Chartists. They were concerned with the poor law, conditions in the factories and other such questions on which they thought there was a chance that Peel might satisfy them but had no hopes of Melbourne. Feargus O'Connor urged Chartists not to put up candidates of their own but to vote with the opposition, and though there can have been few constituencies in which this tipped the balance, it must have been dispiriting for the government candidate to find his enemy thus preferred by those who should rather have voted for anti-Christ than for a Tory.

The election caused Melbourne some personal as well as political embarrassment. With voters likely to sell their services to the highest bidder there was every reason for a candidate to keep his supporters under vigilant watch, or better still lock and key. The practice of 'cooping' voters, though officially deplored, was by no means uncommon. In June 1841 a score of voters whose greed was feared to be stronger than their principles were cooped at Melbourne Hall – driven to the gardens every morning, kept there all day behind locked gates and made drunk at night so as to eliminate any chance of their being suborned. When questioned about this the agent expressed injured surprise. So far as he knew these people had merely asked to walk in the gardens, the gates were locked so as to save them from being 'crowded by the people of the village'. There could be no possible connection with the election. More convincingly Cowper claimed that Melbourne rarely visited his Derbyshire home and that he had been in no way responsible for what had gone on there. Melbourne observed the efforts of his agent and his private secretary with benevolence but little hope. 'There was nothing wrong in what was done and it was very natural', he told Henry Fox. 'But I am afraid that we will not obtain much credit for the disclaimer of its having been done with my knowledge and by my authority.' Still, what was done was done and they must make the best of it. Probably it would matter little in the end.[21]

The Queen elected to demonstrate that her confidence in her ministers was undiminished by occupying part of the gap between the election and the meeting of the new parliament with a far-from-triumphal tour of various Whig stately homes. The first stop was Woburn, where an enormous house party had been assembled and many more of the local dignitaries came in by day. '. . . both their feeling and their behaviour was excellent', Melbourne noted approvingly. He told Russell that the Queen was calm and resigned. 'She was much agitated while the result could be considered in any degree uncertain, but now enjoys the tranquillity which always accompanies a decision.'[22]

From there they moved on to Panshanger where Emily and her son received them. The Queen found her visit still more enjoyable than at Woburn, the country beautiful, the house 'so pretty and *wohnlich*'.[23] But the chief delight of the tour was her stay at the humblest of the three houses, Lord Melbourne's home at Brocket. Lady Palmerston reappeared to act as hostess for a second time. Exultantly Emily described the visit to Mrs Huskisson.

> We had the most brilliant day at Brocket. I wish you could have seen Wm with his grey hair floating in the wind and the Queen on his arm as he walked her round the lawn to show her to the multitude assembled against the rails and all up the hill, so that it looked like an amphitheatre of heads. We all walked in procession behind, the Welwyn band playing and all Pen's old yeomanry flags brought out on the occasion. It really was a beautiful sight – and I had made poor dear old Brocket so smart with red cloth and carpets, and ornaments and flowers that you would hardly have known it again . . .
>
> The banquet was laid out for 36 in the ballroom, and very handsome; the centre of the table filled up by the three beautiful pieces of plate given to Melbourne by the Queen and Albert on their marriage. She then went over the house, admired everything with a curious eye, and then took the round of the lawn I before described and so on to the shrubbery, greenhouse, hot house, melon ground, to the shrubbery again and round by the water house. She had long wished to see Brocket, and it was evidently a very great pleasure and interest to her.[24]

Whether Albert enjoyed being dragged around this unsensational country house is open to question. The charm of Brocket lies in its setting; not its architecture, its great rooms or even its melon ground. To the Queen, however, who had heard so much about it from its owner and had pieced together still more by interrogating Melbourne's friends, it must indeed have been an experience to savour. 'Lord Melbourne', she told Lady Palmerston's daughter, Fanny Jocelyn, 'did the honours of his house exceeding well.' So too did Melbourne's sister, managing matters with just the right blend of stateliness and informality. The only fault, remarked Lady Lyttelton, 'is that they are immensely unpunctual, and make the poor Queen wait for dinner and drives till anybody but herself would be furious'.[25]

Towards the end of August the government faced parliament and was at once defeated decisively in both Houses. Though Melbourne was not formally to announce their resignation for another few days, the speech he delivered on this occasion was in all essentials his last as Prime Minister. It was, said Campbell, 'the most perfunctory, jejune and wretched performance I ever witnessed'. Other reports are little more flattering. Melbourne wholly misjudged the temper of the house; was flippant where he should have been earnest, arid where he should have been emotional and lacklustre on the one occasion when nobody would have begrudged him a modicum of hyperbole. He 'treated the change of government and the consequent crisis as matter for merriment', complained Hobhouse. When Wellington charged him with having changed his mind on the corn laws, he admitted that this was so and added for good measure: 'The fact is, we are always changing our opinions.' Members laughed loudly but were not impressed. It was a curious lapse from so experienced a speaker; one who, though never a great orator, rarely failed when it came to striking the note that would appeal to his audience.[26]

He had been bidding the Queen a long farewell since the fate of his ministry had been determined five months before, but the parting was still painful to both of them. To the Tories her visits to Woburn and Brocket had shown her at her worst – 'in the degrading character of the head of a beaten faction'. Melbourne had left her in no doubt how dangerous this could be and was anxious now to curb any excesses which could still further enrage the – for a few more days – opposition. When she had written to him a fortnight before to protest that her heart was breaking – 'She says little about it, but only because she *feels* it the more deeply' – his reply had been cool, even callous: 'events of this kind are necessary and incidental to your Majesty's high situation'. Yet now that the final crisis was upon them he could not disguise his sympathy for her suffering.[27]

On 28 August she wrote to him on the blackest of mourning paper (technically in honour of the Queen of Hanover). 'The sad, sad event has at length taken place . . .' she pointed out, somewhat superfluously.

'The reality is so *very, very* painful and dreadful to believe, and see!'
Melbourne replied with equal extravagance and equal sincerity. 'The
kindness of your Majesty's expressions emboldens Lord Melbourne to
say that he also feels deeply the pain of separation from a service which
has now for four years and more been no less his pleasure than his
pride.' But he could not merely join her in her mourning, he recognized
it as his duty to sustain her and make her path somewhat easier in the
dangerous stretches that lay ahead. '. . . If the first gloom is brushed
away', he told her, 'confidence and hope and spirits return, and things
begin to appear more cheerful.' He himself, he added with a slight
relapse into pessimism, had slept well but woken early, 'which he
always does now, and which is a sure sign of anxiety of mind'.[28]

He was, indeed, deeply disturbed, 'very much vexed' as his sister put
it, but he presented his usual equable appearance to the outside world
and only those who knew him best even guessed at his distress.[29]
This distress was not primarily for himself. He *did* regret losing office
but there were compensations in increased ease and relaxed tension.
What he felt most acutely were the pain and the alarm of the young
Queen who once again found herself abandoned among her enemies.
One part of him knew well that she was more than capable of looking
after herself and that, even if his hand were not there to guide her,
Peel and Prince Albert could do the job as well. But such voices provided little consolation. The fear that without him the Queen was lost
was a spectre to haunt his nights and ensure his early waking; yet the
suspicion that without him she would manage very well was almost
equally unwelcome.

At least he would go out with clean hands. When Anson went to his
room at Windsor early in August the Prime Minister told him that
Albert had urged him to accept the Garter before resigning. He was
determined not to do so. '. . . it may be a foolish weakness on my part,
but I wish to quit office without having any honour conferred upon me;
the Queen's confidence towards me is sufficiently known without any
public mark of this nature. I have always disregarded these honours, and
there would be an inconsistency in my accepting this.' It was not a
matter of pride; if he had been a poor man he would have been happy
to receive a place or a pension: 'only I *don't wish* for a place, because I
do not *want* it'.[30]

Later in the same conversation Melbourne told Anson that he
doubted whether he would ever again form part of any administration.
It was a reasonable supposition. He was only sixty-three but his health
was not good, he felt himself to be an old man and Peel might well

remain in office for a decade or more. Yet such avowals did not mean that he planned to withdraw from public life. When, in September, he replied to the addresses presented to him by the citizens of Derby and of Melbourne he emphasized his 'impaired strength, less buoyant spirits, and diminished powers of exertion', but claimed too that he would never withdraw from the public service while he could be of use. Though defeated, his hat, he declared with some pride, was still most definitely in the ring.[31]

CHAPTER 25

The Race of Glory Run

TO LOSE GRACEFULLY is relatively easy; to remain graceful in a state of permanent inferiority is more testing to the patience. Melbourne found opposition hard to take. He did not begrudge Peel the appurtenances of Downing Street, the trappings of power, but he did miss bitterly the privileged position at court on which so much of his influence and indeed happiness had depended. 'I never heard of anybody, who had once got fairly within the atmosphere of the court, being able to live out of it', observed Grey wisely in 1828. 'It becomes as necessary to the life of a courtier as water to that of a fish.' For Melbourne, to mix the metaphor, the water had been champagne; the court had occupied his life to an extent unique among nineteenth-century statesmen. '... he will feel it more than any of us', wrote Campbell. 'He not only loses the occupation and excitement of office, but his whole existence is changed. With him it is as if a man were to have his wife and children, with whom he had lived affectionately and happily, torn from him when he falls from power.'[1]

Melbourne's response was to pretend that it had never happened. He started, indeed, with behaviour of the greatest propriety. While Peel's government was still forming, Prince Albert sent Anson to see Melbourne. His task was to persuade the outgoing Prime Minister to advise the Queen that, since he himself was no longer available, she should in future turn to the Prince when she wanted guidance on political questions. Melbourne agreed, and furthermore passed on some excellent advice to Peel on the need to write to the Queen 'fully ... and *elementarily*', since she hated to be kept in the dark about anything that was going on. But in his heart he must have known that the Queen was not yet ready to accept Albert or Peel as her mentor, nobody could usurp his own position. When he wrote to tell her how highly he esteemed her husband's 'judgment, temper and discretion', he was not being insincere, yet he can hardly have avoided the comforting reflection that the Queen was not likely to be over-impressed. In speaking so kindly of the Prince he was doing no more than repay the latter's courtesy. Only the day before Albert had sent a message to say that Melbourne's advice had always been 'peculiarly sound', particularly on 'private concerns and family concerns' and that he hoped it would continue to be made available in the future. Melbourne accepted the compliment and kept his own counsel about the qualification that it was only on personal matters that his advice would be welcome.[2]

He was well aware what protocol and propriety demanded. Several months before, when the fall of the government seemed imminent, he had told Anson that the Queen should never ask his advice direct once the change-over had occurred – 'if she required his opinion there would be no objection to her obtaining it through the Prince'. The intervening period had in no way changed his views. He realized that all those Tories who had most resented his privileged status would now be on the watch for any sign that it had not ended with his term in office. Their mood was not merely anti-Melbourne, it was anti-royalist. 'He would be looked upon as Lord Bute had been in his relation to George III – always suspected of secret intercourse and intrigue.' The dangers for the crown were obviously considerable.[3]

The attitude of Peel himself was certainly reassuring. The new Prime Minister was highly pleased by the steps his predecessor had taken to avoid any recurrence of the bedchamber affair and was disposed to be chivalrous. Melbourne was equally ready to smooth Peel's path so far as was in his power. 'Have you any means of speaking to these chaps', he asked Greville when he met him at dinner, and when Greville assured him that he did, passed on some excellent advice on how best to handle the Queen. Greville for his part assured Melbourne that Peel would not feel in the least upset if Victoria continued to see him; 'so far from taking umbrage at such continuance of the social intercourse between him and the Queen, he was perfectly content it should continue.'[4] But neither Peel nor Prince Albert envisaged that such conversations should go beyond 'personal matters' or 'social intercourse'; Melbourne's role, in fact, was to keep the young Queen more or less contented while she got used to life under the new regime.

Neither Melbourne nor the Queen saw things in that light. From the moment the Whig government fell Victoria bombarded her old friend with letters, commenting on everything Peel did and asking

Melbourne's advice. On the whole Melbourne's replies were responsible. When the Queen complained about the appearance of her new ministers, he remarked that he did not think they could have really looked cross; 'most probably they did look shy and embarrassed. Strange faces are apt to give the idea of ill-humour.' It could just be argued that Melbourne's position made it proper for him to comment on appointments to the royal household. Jermyn was 'foolish, pompous and ridiculous'; the Queen should think twice before she accepted Lord Galloway who was 'prim, precise, pragmatical; sour and conceited, religious in the extreme'. But Melbourne did not confine himself to such relatively trivial appointments. He expressed his views forcibly on the principal diplomatic appointments. Stratford Canning was 'a strong, quarrelsome, conceited, punctilious man. Lord Melbourne does not see that he can give much trouble, but if he can, he will.' Sir Charles Bagot would be a disastrous selection for Canada – 'inadequate and inefficient' – and she should certainly stop it if she could. In general, he suggested, Peel should be left a pretty free hand with his choice of Ambassadors, though the Queen should not accept somebody like Londonderry. He did not even draw the line at criticizing Peel's cabinet appointments. To put Lord Haddington at the Admiralty seemed to him unwise. It was 'better than the Duke of Buckingham but that is all that can be said of it. Lord Melbourne wishes we could have had an Englishman at the head of the Admiralty. A Scotchman is almost always much given to jobbery.'[5]

In defence of Melbourne it can be said that the Queen took the initiative in these exchanges and protested vigorously if his replies were not prompt, long and frank enough to satisfy her demands. It would not have been easy for him to rebuff her overtures. Nevertheless, he should have done it and knew he should. To Victoria he constantly emphasized that the existence of their letters must be a secret between them; he failed to pass on a message to the Duchess of Bedford on the grounds that 'though he considers her by no means indiscreet, he did not like to furnish anybody with such . . . evidence of communication'. Anson begged Melbourne not to pass on any titbits of news given him by the Queen to his sister Emily, who would undoubtedly trumpet them all over the town. Melbourne 'seemed much struck . . . and promised to be careful in future'.[6]

It seems to have been Baron Stockmar – upright, rigid and doctrinaire – who first took alarm at what he rightly felt to be an indiscreet, if not actually unconstitutional proceeding. He saw the damage it would do to the Queen if it were discovered that she was seeking the advice of her former instead of her present ministers. According to Greville, Stockmar saw a letter which Melbourne had written to Victoria telling her that the time had come to dispose of Sir Robert Peel and giving her advice as to how best to do the deed. If such a letter were ever written – which sounds almost impossible – it certainly does not survive in the archives at Windsor: nevertheless, any one of a dozen of Melbourne's letters would have been enough to stir the susceptible Stockmar into a frenzy of dismay. He at once cornered Anson and said that the correspondence must be stopped. Anson was inclined to pooh-pooh the Baron's fears, claiming that Peel would not object if he knew about it. He might consent out of chivalry, Stockmar darkly observed, 'but look to the result. Distrust being implanted from the first, whenever the first misunderstanding arose, or things took a wrong turn, all would, in Peel's mind, be immediately attributed to this cause.'[7]

The force of the argument was too obvious to be ignored. Reluctantly Anson agreed to beard his former master and point out the peril to which he was exposing the Queen. An opportunity arose almost immediately. Melbourne, half-jokingly, described his alarm when he had thought one of Victoria's letters had gone astray. At once Anson passed on Stockmar's opinion, which gave Melbourne 'a *grave fit*'. His immediate reaction was to scoff. He had been quite certain, he said, that William IV kept up some sort of correspondence with the opposition, and indeed had hoped this was the case. He made his views still more clear by writing to the Queen the following day, once more complaining about Haddington's appointment to the Admiralty and adding for good measure some criticism of Wharncliffe's 'dictatorial and overbearing' character.[8]

Stockmar bided his time. Early in October the Queen invited Melbourne to Windsor. With unusual prudence Melbourne wrote to ask Albert his opinion and Albert in his turn referred the question to Stockmar and Anson. As luck would have it, only the day before Melbourne had delivered one of his rare partisan speeches in the House of Lords, attacking Lord Ripon with particular vigour. The three men concluded not only that Melbourne should stay away from Windsor but that his correspondence with the Queen must end. With relish Stockmar drew up a memorandum. The 'secret interchange' he said, was unjust to Sir Robert Peel and dangerous to the country. It was unreasonable to ask Prince Albert for his opinion about this or about possible visits to Windsor. 'In this particular matter nobody has paramount power to do right or wrong but the Queen, and more especially Lord Melbourne himself. To any danger which may come out of this to Her Majesty's character, the caution and objection must come from him, and from him alone.'⁹

Once more the unfortunate Anson was charged with talking Melbourne into reason. He handed over the memorandum, which Melbourne read carefully twice; and added that the previous day's speech in the Lords had made things still worse. 'Melbourne, who was then sitting on the sofa, rushed up upon this, and went up and down the room in a violent frenzy, exclaiming – "God eternally damn it!" etc. etc. "Flesh and blood cannot stand that. I only spoke up on the *defensive* . . . I cannot be expected to give up my position in the country, neither do I think that it is to the Queen's interest that I should." ' Anson pressed on, and asked Melbourne if *he* did not see dangers in the correspondence. After a long pause Melbourne said, or is reported as having said, 'I certainly cannot think it right'; though he immediately qualified this admission by arguing that he never gave any opinion in opposition to Peel's and that he would always advise the Queen to stick by her government 'unless he saw the time had arrived at which it might be resisted'. Stockmar was far from satisfied with this response. He would have been unhappier still if he had known that Melbourne, apparently forgetful of his resolution not to oppose Peel's opinion, was dismissing Stuart de Rothesay, one of the Tory government's new ambassadorial appointments, as 'a low gossiping, intriguing character' and Bulwer, another choice, as good and clever but 'more ridiculous than ever. He is perched upon heels ½ a foot high, which pitch him upon the foremost extremities of his feet so as continually to endanger his tumbling over upon his nose.'¹⁰

Another three weeks went by and Stockmar returned to the charge, this time taking upon himself the task of setting Melbourne straight. It is impossible not to respect the worthy, upright, unimaginative German; impossible not to see that he was essentially right; impossible not to feel sympathy for Lord Melbourne in his rearguard action. What Stockmar saw as a relationship which Melbourne was reluctant to give up because of the importance it gave him in the eyes of the party was to the other man something far more significant, half a sacred charge, half a social delight. Stockmar said bluntly that Melbourne, through his own weakness and against his own better convictions, had given the Queen 'a most pernicious bias' which was likely to undermine her relationship with all her future Prime Ministers. It was hardly surprising that Melbourne became 'visibly nervous, perplexed and distressed'. Indeed, he behaved with remarkable restraint: he listened to the Baron with courtesy, took note of the view that the correspondence should cease as soon as the Queen had had the baby with which she was now pregnant, and left Stockmar with the comforting conviction that his words had sunk in. Perhaps they had, but when Melbourne saw the Queen again the following day it so delighted him that he even wrote to apologize: 'he hopes that his high spirits did not betray him into talking too much or too heedlessly, which he is conscious that they sometimes do'. Any good intentions were forgotten and a stream of letters, on matters political and personal, followed the meeting.[11]

The warnings had some effect, however. His appearances at the palace were now few and far between; not, as he told the Queen, because he feared what Peel and the other Tory ministers might think of his visits, but because of the danger of public notice. 'A public cry, however unfounded and absurd, has more force in this country than objections which have in them more of truth and reality.' Stockmar was unimpressed by this belated discretion. His conviction that the correspondence must end was hardened by a conversation he had with Peel in which the Prime Minister had said he would never concern himself with the private life of the Queen but that, if he discovered she was taking advice from anybody but him on public affairs, he would at once resign. Yet this was exactly what she was doing, with the enthusiastic co-operation of Lord Melbourne. Stockmar determined to tackle Melbourne once more, if that failed to approach the Queen and, as a last resort, to leave the country. He had a useful tool in the indiscretion of Mrs Norton, who had been dining out on the contents of letters from Victoria which she claimed Melbourne had showed her. 'This latter argument', as Stockmar pointed out with some relish, 'would be a strong weapon to use with the Queen whose pride would be offended by feeling that her confidence was so betrayed.'[12]

Melbourne's response to this barely veiled blackmail was a brisk acknowledgement and a promise to write further on the matter in the next few days. Hopefully the Baron waited, while Queen Victoria continued to receive her letter two or three times a week. Anson wrote cheerfully that the correspondence seemed no longer to be in its 'pristine vigour' but there was still more than enough political content to make Stockmar's hair stand on end. Nor would Peel have been gratified if he had known that his predecessor was telling the Queen in February 1842 that the government's corn plan was not 'as good as ours and the Corn Law repealers will of course condemn it more loudly . . .' Nevertheless the flow of letters did diminish and the proportion of chat to politics steadily increased. He continued to offer advice but it was now usually on such innocuous matters as whether to continue the pension paid to Lord Munster – William IV's eldest bastard – after the former's suicide; or what should be bought at the sale of Horace Walpole's effects from Strawberry Hill – 'Lord Melbourne would not give much money for a mere curiosity, unless there were also some intrinsic merits or beauty. What is the value of Cardinal Wolsey's cap, for instance? It was not different from that of any other Cardinal, and a Cardinal's cap is no great wonder.' He offered sage counsel on the choice of a lady to look after the elder children: at all costs let her be an aristocrat, '. . . women of the middle rank have frequently little education and less sense, they are possessed by strong prejudices, they have low and interested connections, and they are more liable to have their heads turned by their elevation'. When the Queen went on a visit to the north he was amiably cynical about the Scots. The scenery was indeed beautiful: 'There is nothing to detract from it, except the very high opinion that the Scotch themselves entertain of it'. The clans were indeed picturesque and romantic: 'It is quite as well, however, particularly for the monarchy, that they are but remains, and that no more of them have been left.'[13]

Stockmar was still uneasy but he neither found it necessary to approach the Queen nor to leave the country. Even before Melbourne's stroke in the autumn of 1842 violently interrupted the correspondence it had dwindled both in scale and import. Stockmar could legitimately congratulate himself on this happy outcome but he did no more than speed a process which was anyhow inevitable. Absence usually makes the heart grow harder, particularly when one of the hearts belongs to somebody as active, as occupied and as egocentric as the Queen. Letters were no substitute for conversation, and with Albert ever in attendance, it was inevitable that Melbourne should be replaced at court as well as in office. His special chair vanished and now everyone settled down to whist as soon as dinner was over. Re-reading her diary of two years before the Queen noted a reference to Melbourne's transcendent virtues. 'I cannot forbear remarking what an artificial sort of happiness *mine* was *then*', she noted, 'and what a blessing it is I have now in my beloved husband *real* and solid happiness . . . it could not have lasted long as it was then, for after all, kind and excellent as Lord Melbourne is, and kind as he was to me, it was but in society that I had amusement.'[14]

That this caused Melbourne regret, even chagrin, can hardly be doubted but it would be wrong to paint too vividly the portrait of a forlorn old man pining over the ashes of his former life. In a letter to the Queen he wrote touchingly of driving past Buckingham Palace in his carriage and looking in at the lighted windows of the royal sitting-room. No doubt the sight did inspire some nostalgia, a wistful regret at his exclusion from Elysium, but the fact remains that he was on his way to dine with the Palmerstons and later the same night would call on Mrs Norton. Paradise might be lost, but at least a measure of independence had been regained.

He was also quite as busy as he felt inclined to be. The concept of 'Leader of the Opposition' was, of course, unknown and few people anyway believed that Melbourne could return in his former role. 'He never can be minister again', said his nephew by marriage, the future Lord Shaftesbury. '10 men would not follow a future government of his and Lord John will be looked up to by the movement party . . .'[15] But even though this were generally accepted – and there were few who would have stated it with such confidence – Melbourne was still one of the leaders of the party, the most important Whig in the House of Lords. No major decision could be taken without his approval, no strategy evolved without his co-operation. Until long after the stroke which effectively removed him from the parliamentary scene, Monteagle, Normanby, even Russell regularly reported to him on developments in their particular fields, with Palmerston he would deplore the vagaries of Tory foreign policy and decide the lines on which it should be attacked.

Nor were the Whigs supine after their defeat. Even while they were still digesting their electoral setback Melbourne assured Russell that there was no risk of the party breaking up. On the contrary its morale was strikingly high; 'in the best possible spirits and confident of ultimate success', wrote Lady Palmerston. By October Buller was prophesying that the Tory government was so badly split that it could not hold together for another six weeks. 'This I hold to be extravagant', Russell told Melbourne. 'But next session must either destroy the Tory ministry, or give a heavy blow to Tory principles.' Melbourne therefore lived in the constant expectation that he would shortly find himself back, if not in supreme power, at least in a position of dignity and authority. He found that the irresponsibility of opposition when coupled with a serious hope of returning soon to power suited him well. In almost every report of him at this period there is a note of relieved yet slightly irritated surprise, the cry of a Cassandra when doom obstinately refuses to strike. 'I know not what is to become of him', wrote Campbell sorrowfully in early September. 'The shade of the trees at Brocket will be very funereal.' And yet there he was at Lady Holland's a week later, '. . . very gay, and I begin to think he will carry it off the best of us all'; and six weeks later, 'I see Lord Melbourne almost daily at Brooks's . . . He sets an excellent example to all ex-officials. Instead of languishing, as I expected he would, he is as merry as a grig. Without affectation, he really seems cheerful and happy.' 'I have seldom seen Lord Melbourne in such good spirits', commented Thomas Moore; while the young Lady Cowper, staying at Broadlands, found Palmerston bitter and resentful at being out of office, 'whereas Lord Melbourne shines beside him by his candour. Thinking everybody means well and will do well'.[16]

There were many compensations for the loss of office. He told the Queen that he intended 'to see a little of the bloom of spring and summer, which he has missed for so many years'. He got one or two horses and began to ride again; Haydon saw him hacking up South Audley Street with a white hat on, 'I never saw him look so well, brown, sunny and good-humoured'. In May 1842 he went to see a magnificent show of rhododendrons, azaleas and kalmias in the King's Road a hundred yards beyond Chelsea Hospital. The plants had come from Mr Waterer's nursery garden near Bagshot; well worth the trouble of driving down to see them, thought Melbourne. He felt relaxed and fitter than he had been for a decade at least. 'Whatever other disagreeable circumstances may belong to it', he told the Queen, 'there can be no doubt that being out of office is much healthier than being in.' He moved from country house to country house, indulging that propensity to slothfulness which to some extent he had had to curb in recent years. 'Country houses', he wrote with satisfaction, 'are the most dawdling work in the world, so much time is lost in lounging and in gossiping after breakfast.'[17]

In politics that innate conservatism which he had tried to disguise when Prime Minister now rose unchecked to the surface. He attended the House of Lords with fair regularity but treated it more as an annexe to his club than a forum for legislative labours. 'He would have made little objection to a general resolution that all bills proposed during the session should pass . . .' wrote Campbell. Indeed he some-times seemed disposed actively to aid their passage. When a bill for abolishing the Assembly of Newfoundland came before the House he upset the more doctrinaire liberals by announcing that he approved strongly of it. Indeed, all colonial legislatures ought to be abolished. The worst thing that the Tories had ever done was defeating the Whigs when they tried to abolish the Assembly in Jamaica. To Victoria, early in 1842, he said that he was anxious to avoid commitments; '. . . his strong opinion at present is not to encumber himself for the future by opposition to measures, which he thinks to be very expedient, if not absolutely necessary, and than which he does not perceive any other, which is equally efficient and less objectionable'.[18]

His increasing alienation from his party at times caused him concern. In March 1842 the details of Peel's new budget were discussed at a party meeting in Melbourne's house in South Street. Melbourne and Russell were both in favour of accepting its main provisions but Baring argued that income tax at seven pence in the pound could never be tolerable to the British people. This point of view was finally accepted but Melbourne, though by no means sure that the 'spirit and patriotism' of the country was great enough to endure so fearsome a burden, still felt that it was right to impose the tax. By May he was in increasing doubt. His problem, he told the Queen, was 'to try to discover some means of satisfying his friends and at the same time his own conscience and consistency'. The Queen had no doubt as to what was proper; if Melbourne would listen chiefly to his own conscience he could not go wrong. Melbourne was not so sure. In the event he adopted a shifty compromise; voting for Lord Lansdowne's amendment but 'arguing as strongly as he could in favour of the tax'.[19]

The Corn Laws revealed an even sharper divergence from his party. After the events of 1841 Russell felt that the party was committed to a radical change of the existing system; Melbourne, on the other hand, swung back into the resistance to reform which had been his posture for so many years. 'My esoteric doctrine', he told Russell blandly, 'is that, if you entertain any doubt, it is safest to take the unpopular side in the first instance. The transition from the unpopular is easy and prosperous travelling. But from the popular to the unpopular the ascent is so steep and rugged that it is impossible to master it.' He had certainly picked the unpopular side over the Corn Laws, but unfortunately, when it came to beginning the easy transition to the popular, he seemed to have become obstinately stuck. Lady Clanricarde, one of the very few women who consistently spoke ill of him, denounced his conduct, accused him of insincerity and claimed that he was ready to break up his party so as to curry favour with the Queen. Her accusation is hard to understand; Melbourne's insincerity had come a year before when he had supported a change in the laws.

The danger to the party, however, was real. If he stuck to his guns, unity would be shattered on what should have been a cardinal point of policy and one of their few potential election winners. He obstinately refused to budge, maintaining that all the reports of hardship among the poor were grossly exaggerated and that the lot of the farmer and landlord was quite as hard. Russell pleaded with him to open his mind: 'I do not see why the exaggeration of the distress should prevent you taking into view the actual suffering . . . Your extreme doctrine has the effect of hurting yourself, for though you may find it very easy to change your course, it is not done without a diminution of your character for foresight and practical wisdom.' Melbourne was unmoved, and equally reluctant to believe that Peel was more likely to change his course than he was himself. 'Peel would be an imbecile if he were to break up his party . . .' he told Russell. 'He will remain quietly in his present position.' And beside him, it was clear, would remain Lord Melbourne.[20]

Russell was not the only person to notice a new rigidity in Melbourne. He seemed to be losing the sensitivity which had enabled him in the past to be outrageous without ever becoming offensive. Sydney Smith had been a friend for many years. He was one of the few people to have stopped Lord Melbourne from swearing, for an evening at least, by suggesting with some irritation that they should agree everything and everyone was damned and come to the point. Then in May 1842, when Smith was holding forth at a large party, Melbourne interrupted rudely with a loud: 'Sydney, you always talk damned nonsense, and when you write you are worse.' Smith said nothing at the time but brooded over the insult and next day wrote to protest. The reply which he got was apologetic but flippant, Melbourne promising to abstain in future 'from anything that can be construed into unseemly irreverence or discourtesy'. Perhaps Smith deserved no better but there was dignity and truth in his final rejoinder: 'I have never accused you of an *intention* to give pain – but you exercise the privilege of thinking aloud, of saying what comes uppermost, and are totally indifferent whether you give pain or not, considering yourself as superior to all ordinances.' Even a year before such a reproach would hardly have been merited.[21]

On 23 October 1842 Melbourne was staying at Brocket when he suffered a severe stroke. For two days his life was thought to be in danger, for several weeks the left side of his body was paralysed. Six months later he could still only use his left arm and leg with difficulty. The muscles of his face, however, were scarcely affected and, intellectually, he suffered no direct damage. Though Greville referred to it as an 'attack of palsy' and said that Melbourne thought so little of the disease as to suppose it was lumbago, it is clear that the victim had no doubts about the severity of his illness. 'Lord Melbourne has had a very

awkward and severe illness', he told the Queen, in the first letter he
wrote her a month after the stroke, 'and he cannot deny that he is much
annoyed and disheartened by this attack coming upon him as it did,
at a moment when he thought his health better . . . than it had been for
some time past. Lord Melbourne however is much better and hopes
that he is now really getting well and strong.'[22]

His brother Fred Beauvale was with him at the time. In the past Fred
had never been as close to Melbourne as George or Emily, but they
were remarkably similar in their conservatism, their ability, their idleness and their robust good humour. At the age of sixty he had married
a twenty-year-old Austrian, Countess Alexandrina Maltzahn, Adine as
she was always called, who cared for him devotedly for the rest of her
life. Melbourne took to her immediately: 'the delight and comfort of
our lives' he called her, and she brought light and youth into what
would otherwise have been a sombre household. The couple were
looking for a house in London at the time of Melbourne's stroke, now
the idea was tacitly shelved and the Beauvales settled down to make a
home for Melbourne at Brocket. When Beauvale was offered the
Embassy at Paris in 1846 he turned it down, partly because of his own
health but mainly since he knew that his brother was now wholly
dependent on him. 'My brothers are still at Brocket', wrote Lady
Palmerston about the same date, 'living in retirement like two phil-
osophers, and very happy – they take great interest in the events of
the outside world, but refuse to work.' Nor was Emily herself less
attentive. 4 November found Lord and Lady Palmerston hastening to
Brocket after only a few days at Broadlands because Melbourne was
too ill for general company but it cheered him to have his family around
him.[23]

By the early summer of 1843 Melbourne was on a fair way to recovery. Though he had aged ten years in six months and his movements were clumsy and ponderous, he was capable of travel. Anson,
who was sent down by the Queen in early May, reported that he was not
much improved and that he ate and drank far too much for prudence.[24]
Melbourne would have replied that he ate and drank no more than
before and that lolling around in boredom at Brocket was certain to
drive him to greater excesses. He was beginning to grow restless and to
say that he was needed in the House of Lords. His colleagues urged
prudence. There was no question of his returning as Prime Minister;
Russell had assumed the mantle by default. Emily Palmerston, deeply
concerned for her brother's happiness, was torn between encouraging
Melbourne to play an active role and urging caution:

The considerations it involves are too serious, and a failure or an exhibition on the part of Wm would render it much more difficult for him to resume his place there hereafter when his cure shall be as complete as we are now authorized to hope it will be. I suspect that some of his ladies have been pressing him to come up, and I know him to have confided in them that he finds his life here very dull. If he is ordered to give up the House of Lords, he may not improbably give up London along with it, and in that case what can be done to amuse him? He will not move, here I believe him to be unamusable, and I take a state of apathy and ennui to be a great drawback to his perfect recovery . . .[25]

He did not long delay in returning to London and taking his seat in the House. Superficially the other members found him largely unchanged but underneath he had become an old man, with all the weaknesses which are traditionally, though often unjustly, ascribed to those in that condition: forgetfulness, slowness of thought, rigidity of mind, failure of concentration. '. . . there was no speculation in his eye', wrote Campbell, 'sometimes when he spoke his voice was broken as if he had been going to burst into tears.'[26] He would sit for hours slumped in silence; his friends in two minds whether to pass him by and risk the accusation that they were neglecting him, or approach him and put him to the strain of a conversation. Though the party leaders might formally consult him they did so out of courtesy, not with the expectation of enlightenment.

The Queen had dutifully enquired after his health from time to time and had been saddened by his illness, but with Albert, her children and affairs of state, she had little time for musing over the past. Melbourne was like an old album of photographs; to be cherished, flicked through occasionally on a wintry evening with sentimental sighs, but resident permanently in some remote cupboard. She was slow to answer his letters, urged him to take his time before coming back to London, invited him to dinner or to Windsor when he did return but did not treat him with any special attention. Melbourne was hurt by her neglect but seems to have resigned himself to it with the same apathetic indifference as to all the other symptoms of senescence. Indeed he seems sometimes to have contributed as much to the dwindling of their relationship as the Queen herself; failing to answer her letters for two or three weeks, not making the effort to go to receptions at which he knew she would be present. 'Lord Melbourne is glad that your Majesty thought him in good health and spirits when he had the honour of dining at the palace but he has neither health nor spirits in any degree comparable to those, which he enjoyed, when he first had the honour and pleasure of becoming acquainted with your Majesty. He tries not to repine, because he thinks it wrong, but finds it difficult.'[27]

He still offered her advice on matters in which he should not have interfered – a passage in the Queen's speech which betrayed too great an anxiety to avoid war with the United States, the folly of the government in allowing 'lawless riotings in South Wales to go on with success and impunity . . .' – but it seems unlikely that Victoria did more than glance at his quavering missives. Not even the suspicious Stockmar can now have felt that his influence at court was improperly great. By 1845 months would slip by without them meeting or even corresponding. Occasionally, pricked by conscience, the Queen would make an overture towards her former Prime Minister but it was usually perfunctory and not followed up with zeal. At the end of July she found herself having to write: 'The Queen is extremely sorry to leave England without seeing Lord Melbourne, and without having seen him all the season; but something or other always prevented us from seeing Lord Melbourne each time we hoped to do so.' 'Something or other' would not have been allowed to play so obstructive a role a few years before.[28]

It is easy to over-paint the picture of a sad, old hulk, without wife or child, rejected by the Queen, ignored by his party, brooding disconsolate in the empty halls of Brocket. Such a portrait would not be wholly untrue. He did have bouts of depression, periods of ill-health, moments of loneliness and disappointment. Yet on the whole he was contented. At Brocket the Beauvales were in almost constant attendance and the rest of the family were loyal and affectionate. 'Who have you got there?' asked Mrs Norton. 'Does Emily hang her long gowns up, like banners of victory in the cupboard? Does Lady Holland cut herself in four to help and serve you?' In London he would always find friends at Brooks's and there were as many hostesses anxious to receive him as any semi-invalid in his mid-sixties could require. Hobhouse met him frequently at Holland House, almost always apparently in high spirits. He recounted with relish how he had dined a day or two before at the palace and shocked a maid of honour by exclaiming: 'This dish is damned bad. On ordinary occasions I should try to leave out the adjective, but on this it is not worth while, it is so damned bad.' He went with Mrs Norton to the theatre to see Ben Jonson's *Every Man in His Humour* and bellowed across the pit, 'I knew this play would be dull, but that it would be so damnably dull as this I did not suppose'.

Even though life had lost some of its savour it was still enjoyable to behave outrageously.[29]

His political aspirations, though dimmed, were still alive. Lord William Russell met him at the Palmerstons' in February 1844 and found him talking hopefully of a return to power, and speculating about the advice he should give the Queen if the Commons defeated the government. Greville, who was also there, was saddened by the spectacle: 'Whilst all indicates the decay of his powers, and his own consciousness of it, he assumes an air and language as if he was the same man, and ready to act his old part on the stage . . .' Indeed, in his more lucid moments, Melbourne knew he could undertake no position of real responsibility. Only a fortnight before the Palmerstons' dinner he had gone down to the House primed with a list of important points he was anxious to make. Then, when it came to the point, he found that he did not feel equal to the exertion and held his peace. '. . . the evidence of decadence is a very hard and disagreeable trial', he wrote sadly a few weeks later. In April 1845 he lost his balance when getting out of his carriage, fell heavily and sprained his shoulder. At first it was thought that he had had another stroke and, even though this fear was soon dispelled, he was in considerable pain and confined to his room for almost two months. Bored by his isolation, fretful at the slow mending of his failing body, he grew depressed. By that autumn, though substantially recovered, he could still only walk with difficulty and was dismayed to find that he could no longer concentrate while reading. His pleasure in life, as he forlornly told the Queen, seemed fast to be fading.[30]

Political crisis came to rescue him from his apathy. In 1845 bad harvests all over Britain and the failure of the potato crop in Ireland lent sharp spurs to the crusade for free trade and, above all, for a lower duty on imported corn. Melbourne could not conceive any measure, he had told the Queen in 1842, 'which it is in the power of the government to take for the relief of suffering'. The fact that hunger had now given way to famine in no way altered the realities of the situation. Indeed he refused to contemplate that famine could exist. Fears for the Irish were 'much exaggerated and the apprehensions of a dearth of corn still more so'. A few propagandists were trying to stir up trouble by inflating minor and local difficulties into a national disaster. Luckily the Tories showed no signs of yielding to the pressure of revolutionaries, 'and he hopes that they will persevere in it'.[31]

John Russell, however, better informed and less rigid than his former leader, was convinced that matters had already been allowed to go too far. Early in December he wrote an open letter to his constituents which stated more or less explicitly that he supported the entire and immediate repeal of the Corn Laws. Melbourne was appalled. 'I certainly do not approve nor concur in John Russell's letter . . .' he told Palmerston. 'Not only is it hasty and reckless and unfair towards those with whom he expresses himself [?] to be acting, but it is in my opinion erroneous and mischievous in itself.' He was hardly less outspoken to Russell himself. The only concession he would make to the latter was to promise that he would not actually vote *against* his proposal in the House of Lords but would confine himself to 'stating the reasons why I think the measure doubtful'.[32]

Till the last minute he pinned his hopes on the Tories but Peel now believed the repeal of the Corn Laws to be of such critical importance that, if necessary, he was prepared to destroy his party to achieve it. On 7 December the Queen wrote to Melbourne to give him the news that Peel had resigned. She had sent for John Russell, she told him, because the state of health of her former Prime Minister did not make it reasonable that he should be asked to take up the burden of office again. Her hope was that 'Lord Melbourne will not withhold from her new government his advice which would be so valuable to her'. It was a letter intended to soothe an old man's susceptibilities and it did its task; 'in the highest degree kind, considerate and amiable', he described it to Brougham.[33]

He took it for granted that he would be offered some place of dignity though without departmental duties. He may well have been correct; a sketch of a future Whig government jotted down by Palmerston eight months before showed Russell as Prime Minister and Melbourne as President of the Council. He hesitated for two days over what he should do. If Russell became Prime Minister his first measure must be the repeal of the Corn Laws. Melbourne could not bring himself to support such a position; but equally, he told Anson, he did not want to come out against his former colleagues. In the end he told the Queen that, while he would support Russell's government, he would not join it. His soul-searching proved unnecessary. Russell failed to cobble together a ministry and, in Disraeli's elegant phrase, 'handed back with courtesy the poisoned chalice to Sir Robert'.[34]

Melbourne was convinced that Peel had betrayed both his party and his country. There was an unpleasant scene at Windsor in early January when he insisted on discussing the Corn Laws in the middle of dinner, booming out in a voice which he no longer found it easy to control that Peel's was a 'damned dishonest act'. The Queen laughed and tried to change the subject, but after dinner Melbourne continued his tirade to Albert and Lord Aberdeen, saying that the policy was 'the greatest piece of villainy he had ever heard of'. Aberdeen wisely did not reply and the old man subsided into grumbling silence. It was a sad display of fading judgement and self-control but, as he told the Queen more temperately a few weeks later, 'it a little annoys him to reflect that if the Tory Party had given him . . . a little support in 1841, and only a little support was necessary, he would have been able easily to prevent all this evil and danger'.[35]

On 23 May 1846, the Whig peers met at Lansdowne House to discuss their attitude towards Peel's legislation for the repeal of the Corn Laws. In the Commons, of course, the support of Russell guaranteed the Prime Minister a safe majority but the landed interest was far stronger in the Lords. Indignation against the measure ran high and Melbourne's was as high as anyone's. Peel had disgraced himself to all eternity, he declared, and he hoped the House of Lords would not do the same. If he had stuck to his guns he might have rallied a majority of the peers behind him and defeated the government. But he was still the old Melbourne at heart: he had promised the Queen two months before that he would not oppose the measures; he did not wish to offend Russell and his other friends; after all, it would make no difference in the end, what was the point of causing trouble? Since everyone was resolved on taking a mischievous course, he finally announced, he would assist in doing the mischief. 'All unanimous against the bill, and all unanimous not to oppose it', was Palmerston's terse summary of these deliberations.[36]

In June Peel, having supped of the poisoned chalice, duly perished. It fell to John Russell to compose his new government. Melbourne still expected to be offered some honorific post. He wrote to Anson complaining that nothing had been proposed to him and that, even though he would not necessarily have taken it up, he would have liked the offer of a seat in the cabinet. Word got back to Russell of his old leader's discontent and he at once wrote off to excuse himself. He had only not offered any post, he said, 'because I do not think your health is equal to the fatigues which any office must entail'. Even a Lord Privy Seal, in these hard days, had to take charge of committees and help the Leader of the House. Melbourne accepted the olive branch with good grace. Russell had judged 'very rightly and kindly', he told him. 'I am subject to such frequent accesses of illness as render me incapable of any exertion.' He wrote valiantly to the Queen to assure her that he would not have accepted any post even if it had been pressed upon him, and that he had told Ellice this several weeks before.[37]

His public life was over. He was still to hobble occasionally into the House of Lords. His last vote – pleasantly enough, in view of his traditional anti-semitism, in favour of removing legal disabilities on the Jews – was not cast until 25 May 1848. Russell would still write to him occasionally to ask his views. But these were the last stirrings of a dormant volcano. Greville found him muttering sadly to himself the lines from *Samson Agonistes*:

> So much I feel my genial spirits droop,
> My hopes all flat, Nature within me seems
> In all her functions weary of herself.
> My race of glory run, *not* race of shame,
> And I shall shortly be with those that rest.[38]

The last eighteen months of Melbourne's life were passed almost entirely at Brocket; uneventful months in which the quiet tranquillity of day-to-day existence was varied only by increasingly frequent on-slaughts of ill-health. He was not unhappy, yet life had little to offer him. Ironically, for a man who believed poverty to be an offence against society, he was haunted by the conviction that he himself was in serious financial difficulties. At the end of 1847 he told the Queen that he was 'low and depressed in spirits for a cause which has long pressed upon his mind'. His debts were now so large, his commitments so pressing, that he feared he was on the point of bankruptcy. The real reason that he had refused the Garter a few years before had been that he could not find the £1000 or so which had to be laid out in expenses.[39]

There was some basis for his worry. He had run his houses in London and in Hertfordshire extravagantly, or to be more precise had not run them at all but had permitted his servants to do as they pleased. There was said to be much drunkenness among the staff, but as he never saw it himself he did not feel he could complain. People told him Brocket was run on absurdly lavish lines – 'he does *not* think the expense very great, in fact he says it *cannot* be, as he is so little at home'. Fred, on his return to England was dismayed to find the house and stables in South Street costing £1300 a year and tried, without success, to persuade him to find a smaller home. Women, too, were an expensive luxury. He was still paying Lady Branden £800 to £1000 a year and made frequent presents to Mrs Norton. 'I dare say we shall find more debts than we reckon upon', wrote Brougham after Melbourne's death to his coexecutor, Edward Ellice. 'What a sad pillage! *Women of course.*'[40]

And yet his troubles largely existed in his imagination. The estate accounts for 1847, still at Melbourne Hall, show that though he sold the Over Haddon estate for some £35,000, he invested almost as much in other land and in railway shares. His income from land, including £1800 from the Derbyshire collieries, amounted to £19,162. Though this property was mainly entailed on his brother and sister, quite enough remained free of any charge to provide security for a loan if such was needed. Anson, who was sent down to Brocket on a fact-finding mission by the Queen, reported that Beauvale had told him his brother 'was quite unfit to attend to his own affairs' but would not allow any of his family to interfere in them and passed his days brooding over his largely mythical difficulties. 'I think Lord Melbourne altered for the worse a good deal since I saw him', wrote Anson, 'and no wonder, for nothing can exceed his imprudence in living, and after an unwholesome dinner and much more wine than he ought to drink, he generally goes to bed *before* 9 oc. His doctor and head nurse are not the least check upon him.'[41]

In the event Queen Victoria lent him £10,000 at 3% interest to enable him to repay the same amount to his broker. 'This is a great, substantial and timely benefit', wrote Melbourne gratefully, 'and quite enables me to go on which otherwise I should not be able to do.' Yet his solicitor told Anson that he could easily have raised the loan on the open market. Not content with this, he now asked the Queen to arrange for him to receive a pension, 'considering the offices which he has filled and the time during which he has filled them . . . If Lord Melbourne could obtain an annual payment of £2000 it would probably improve his circumstances, but £3000 will render him affluent.' Beauvale was horrified at the proposal, which he rightly felt would mar his brother's reputation, and Russell, when the Queen somewhat gingerly approached him, replied that, to merit such a pension, Melbourne would have to show that he did not enjoy 'a private fortune adequate to his station in life'. Since he was obviously a rich man by any standard, he was ineligible. Regretfully Melbourne agreed with the Queen that, in view of Russell's letter, the matter could be pursued no further.[42]

Nothing could show more clearly than this degrading episode how far Melbourne had deteriorated. The good judgement and moderation which had marked his life seemed suddenly to have worn thin. On 21 June 1848, he wrote to Anson for the last time on affairs of public interest. It was a curious letter for a former Whig Prime Minister to write about the ministers with whom he had been so long associated.

The government he said, apparently with relish, was 'sinking much in the public estimation and becoming very unpopular'. When it fell, as seemed likely to happen soon, he would advise the Queen to send for Peel. This was not because Melbourne thought well of the Tory leader, on the contrary he had committed 'great and national errors' and was likely to repeat them, but the opinion of the 'important classes' in his favour was so prevalent that it could not be ignored. As a compound of disloyalty and defeatism the letter could hardly have been improved. To all who valued his good name it could only be a relief that the end was near.[43]

It would indeed be wholly unfair to judge him by his performance during his last few months of life. In April 1848 a further stroke had finally crippled him and still further befuddled his tired mind. During the summer a silly scandal started by his former secretary Young preyed on his mind, so that he feared he might be accused of complicity in a half-baked plot to set up a military revolt at the time of the Reform Bill. By August he was visibly sinking, frequently fainting and the victim of increasingly painful bilious attacks. Jaundice followed and in the second week of November he suffered two apoplectic seizures. He was conscious and able to recognize those around him, but dozed almost all the time and seemed unaware of his condition. In the last few days of his life a series of epileptic fits racked his body, then he mercifully drifted into unconsciousness. The end came on 24 November. 'He died and gave no sign', wrote Shaftesbury, 'all *without* was coldness and indifference; God only can discern what was within . . . It was not the death of a heathen; he would have had an image or a ceremony. It was the death of an animal.' This savage judgement showed Shaftesbury in his most atrabilious vein but it was certainly a godless end. Not even the pious Lady Beauvale, who would have manufactured a religious brick if offered even a wisp of straw, could pretend that his relationship with the Almighty greatly preoccupied him during his final weeks. He died pragmatic and uncommitted as he had lived, reserving his judgement on the nature or existence of an after life and ready, as always, to adapt himself to whatever obligations the future might impose upon him.[44]

'Our poor old friend Melbourne died on the 24th', wrote Victoria to King Leopold. 'I sincerely regret him for he was truly attached to me, and tho' not a good or firm minister he was a noble, kind-hearted generous being.'[45] It is curious to reflect how far more radiant a panegyric she would have written only a few years before. Certainly the cool verdict of 1848 was nearer the truth than her earlier ecstasies. Yet was it wholly fair? Was Melbourne indeed 'not a good . . . minister'? It depends, of course, on what a minister must do to be esteemed 'good'. If he must be an autocrat, a Chatham or a Churchill imposing his views on colleagues and country by the force of his personality, then indeed Melbourne would fail the test. If he must be an innovator, challenging accepted doctrine, actively promoting departures from accepted policies, then the accolade would be still less appropriate. Yet Melbourne could reasonably have argued that such had never been his intention, nor did he feel it should have been. He took over in 1834 a great reforming ministry which was running out of steam. Important things were still to be done, but all of them had been initiated before he came to power. In such circumstances a Prime Minister can either stoke up the boilers with a new load of reform or preside gracefully over the slowing-down of the party engine. Melbourne would have maintained that by 1834 the British people had had as much reform as they could stomach, by 1836 they were sated. What was needed was a period for digestion. On this hypothesis, all that he could legitimately be blamed for was seeking to prolong the period of inertia beyond the point at which any objective observer could believe that it served the interests of the country. In so doing he debilitated his own party and allowed the country to drift rudderless towards disaster.

From the accession of Victoria he could claim a new responsibility and a new title to the gratitude of the country. His primary task was now to guide the inexperienced Queen, to give her the knowledge, the judgement and the self-confidence which would be essential if she were to reign successfully after his going. From 1837 he sought by every device to keep his government in power, not just for the sake of the party or because that was the way the game was played, but so as to preserve his place at court. This place, he believed, he was uniquely qualified to fill. If he had been required to name one achievement by which posterity should judge him it would have been his tutelage of the young monarch. He had good reason for his pride. His handling of her education is indeed open to criticism but on the whole it is hard to believe that anyone else would have done it as well, let alone better. There are many ways in which Peel was better qualified than Melbourne to preside over the youth of a Queen destined to rule until the twentieth century. He would have taught her, or tried to teach her, many useful lessons which to Melbourne would have seemed mischievous, irrelevant or dull. But he could never have so wholly occupied her attention. He had neither the tact nor the charm to exercise the authority which Melbourne could wield over the impressionable but headstrong girl. Inevitably the two would have clashed. Victoria had to have some man of preponderant influence in her life and if she had felt antipathy towards the minister who ought to have filled that role then she would have looked elsewhere. In such circumstances there would have been a real danger that she might have taken some favourite who would have usurped the proper position of the Prime Minister and headed a court faction in opposition to the legal government. There was no room for such a man in the London of the 1830s. If such a threat had developed, its consequences for the country could have been grave and for the monarchy catastrophic.

Though Victoria therefore was probably right in dismissing Melbourne as 'not a good or firm minister' she should still have acknowledged the debt which she and the monarchy owed to his endeavours. Through a trick of circumstances his value was greater than his merits. When it came to her praise for his generosity and kind-heartedness, there need be no such qualification. 'Of all the public men I have ever known', wrote Campbell, 'Lord Melbourne was approached with the greatest pleasure and satisfaction . . . From the first instant of meeting, all who came into his presence felt themselves on a footing of perfect equality with him. He seemed to have no reserves and to make everyone his confidant.' Almost everyone who knew him testified that he was the most delightful of companions: a man of warmth and humour, self-deprecating without being falsely humble, self-assured without being arrogant. He was every man's ideal brother-in-law: a figure on whose interested benevolence one could depend, yet who would never make unreasonable demands or insist upon an oppressive intimacy.

Yet that was the end of it. Perhaps it is unreasonable to expect more, but when all his glowing qualities have been counted and assessed there still lingers about Melbourne a sense of deficiency, an incompleteness. His closest associations were all to some degree impaired by his inability to commit himself. Always something was held back; some still, objective voice reminded him that displays of strong emotion were unseemly, that it was weakness to expose oneself too far, that the game was not really worth the candle. Melbourne was not a cold man – he was too vital, too sentimental – yet he was cool. His shrinking from the ultimate involvement was shown most vividly in his relationships with women: his wife, Mrs Norton, Lady Branden. They made demands on him to which he was emotionally unable to respond, which he could not even understand. He offered them affection, tolerance and mutual freedom and was genuinely perplexed when they showed themselves abandoned and distraught. The eighteenth century could not communicate with the nineteenth; classical could not speak to romantic; Wilcox to Schlegel. None of these glib formulae explains Lord Melbourne, yet all do something to illuminate him. It is not necessary to experience a grand passion to prove oneself a man, but he to whom the term is meaningless still leads a life to some extent impoverished. In public or in private, a thin streak of indifference ran pallid through Melbourne's life.

'I know thy works', runs the *Revelation of St John the Divine*:

'I know thy works, that thou are neither cold nor hot: I would thou wert cold or hot. So because thou art lukewarm, and neither hot nor cold, I will spew thee out of my mouth.'

It is a fearful doctrine and it would be harsh to apply it to Melbourne. No one who was loved by so many people, who gave so much pleasure by the delights of his society, who sounded so eloquent a call for tolerance, moderation, decency, could deserve so brutal a verdict. Yet its application is too evident to be ignored. All his sins can be forgiven him but perhaps because to be lukewarm is not a sin it is less easy to forgive. A good man, a generous man, a decent man, but something less than a full man. That must be the last word on Viscount Melbourne.

APPENDIX I:
MELBOURNE'S FIRST CABINET

(formed July 1834)

Prime Minister and First Lord of the Treasury:	Viscount Melbourne
Lord Chancellor:	Lord Brougham
Lord President of the Council:	Marquess of Lansdowne
Lord Privy Seal:	Earl of Mulgrave
Chancellor of the Exchequer:	Viscount Althorp
Home Secretary:	Viscount Duncannon
Foreign Secretary:	Viscount Palmerston
Secretary for War and Colonies:	T. Spring Rice
First Lord of the Admiralty:	Lord Auckland
President of the Board of Trade:	C. E. Poulett Thomson
President of the Board of Control:	C. Grant
Master of the Mint:	J. Abercromby
Chancellor of the Duchy of Lancaster:	Lord Holland
Secretary at War:	Viscount Howick
First Commissioner of Woods and Forests:	Sir J. C. Hobhouse
Paymaster General:	Lord J. Russell

APPENDIX II:
MELBOURNE'S SECOND CABINET

———◆◆◆———

(formed April 1835)

Prime Minister and First Lord of the Treasury:	Viscount Melbourne
Lord Chancellor:	
April 1835 to Jan. 1836:	In Commission
Jan. 1836:	Lord Cottenham
Lord President of the Council:	Marquess of Lansdowne
Lord Privy Seal:	
April 1835 to Jan. 1841:	Lord Duncannon
Jan 1841:	Earl of Clarendon
First Commissioner of Woods and Forests:	Lord Duncannon
Chancellor of the Exchequer:	
April 1835 to Aug. 1839:	T. Spring Rice
Aug. 1839:	Sir F. T. Baring
Home Secretary:	
April 1835 to Sept. 1839:	Lord J. Russell
Sept. 1839:	Marquess of Normanby
Foreign Secretary:	Viscount Palmerston
Secretary for War and Colonies:	
April 1835 to Feb. 1839:	C. Grant (created Lord Glenelg, May 1835)
Feb. 1839 to Sept. 1839:	Marquess of Normanby
Sept. 1839:	Lord J. Russell
First Lord of the Admiralty:	
April 1835 to Sept. 1835:	Lord Auckland
Sept. 1835:	Earl of Minto
President of the Board of Trade:	
April 1835 to Aug. 1839:	C. E. Poulett Thomson
Aug. 1839:	H. Labouchere
President of the Board of Control:	Sir J. C. Hobhouse
Chancellor of the Duchy of Lancaster:	
April 1835 to Oct. 1840:	Lord Holland
Oct. 1840 to Jan. 1841:	Earl of Clarendon
Jan. 1841:	Sir G. Grey
Secretary of War:	
April 1835 to Sept. 1839:	Viscount Howick
Sept. 1839:	T. B. Macaulay

NOTE ON MANUSCRIPT SOURCES

The bulk of Lord Melbourne's official papers (referred to in the notes as 'RA MP') have been deposited in the archives at Windsor Castle. These were in the process of being catalogued when I worked on them. My style of reference is therefore sometimes inconsistent but should always suffice for the tracing of any individual paper. The treasure-house at Windsor, containing as it of course also does Queen Victoria's papers (RA and Vic.Add. MSS.) and her diary (Victoria's Journal), is by far the most important source for a biography of Melbourne. Many of his personal papers (Panshanger MSS.) are to be found in the County Record Office at Hertford. These include some 25,000 words of Melbourne's own autobiography and large parts of his correspondence with Mrs Norton and Lady Branden. Some papers are also in the British Museum (Add. MSS.) and eight boxes of Lamb family papers have been placed under embargo till 1980. Frustrating though this is, I am assured by those fortunate enough to see the papers at an earlier stage that almost all those relevant to Lord Melbourne were published by Lady Airlie in her two books *In Whig Society* and *Lady Palmerston and her Times*. The most interesting of those unpublished are said to relate primarily to the affairs of the Duchess of Devonshire. The Public Record Office contains papers relating to Melbourne's period as Home Secretary (P.R.O.). Finally the estate papers and a handful of personal papers remain in the muniment room at Melbourne Hall in Derbyshire (Melbourne Hall MSS.).

The most important body of papers outside the various family collections are those from Broadlands, currently in the possession of the Historical Manuscripts Commission (Broadlands MSS.). This contains not only Palmerston's correspondence with Melbourne and other contemporaries but also many letters exchanged between Melbourne and Anson, Lord Cowper and, much the most important, Lord John Russell.

The correspondence of the 2nd and 3rd Earls Grey, now in the possession of Durham University (Grey MSS.) contains a great deal of importance and the University also holds the invaluable diary kept by the 3rd Earl and his wife (Howick Diary). This is currently being edited for publication by Dr A. M. Burton. The papers of Edward Littleton, Lord Hatherton, now in the County Record Office at Stafford (Hatherton MSS.) are also of great value, in particular his diary (Littleton Diary). A third diary of the greatest importance is that of Lord Holland (Holland Diary Add. MSS.) now in the British Museum. The Holland House MSS., including the correspondence of Lord and Lady Holland and Lady Holland's Dinner Book (Add. MSS.), as well as this diary, are essential for a biography of Melbourne.

Other collections of importance are those of the Duke of Devonshire at Chatsworth (Cavendish MSS.), of Lord Lansdowne at Bowood (Bowood MSS.), of Edward Ellice and Lord Minto in the National Library of Scotland (Ellice and Minto MSS.), of Lord Brougham in the Library of University College, London (Brougham MSS.) and of Lord Fitzwilliam in the Sheffield City Library (Fitzwilliam MSS.). I have been fortunate enough to see transcripts of relevant papers from three other most important collections, those of the Duke of Wellington (Wellington MSS.), Lord Althorp (Spencer MSS.) and Lord Durham (Durham MSS.). Other collections in the British Museum (Add. MSS.) which contain relevant material are those of the Duke of Leeds, Bishop Butler, Mr C. Babbage, Lord Wellesley, Mr Huskisson and Sir Robert Peel.

I have been allowed to consult the unpublished theses of Dr D. M. Close on the General Elections of 1835 and 1837 (Oxford, 1966); of Dr I. D. Newbould on the Politics of the Cabinets of Grey and Melbourne (Manchester, 1971); and – of particular value – of Dr Donald Cameron on Lord Melbourne's Second Administration (London, 1970).

NOTES

———— ••• ————

CHAPTER 1 (pp. 13–20)

1. *The Passing of the Whigs. 1832–86*. Donald Southgate. London, 1962. p. 76.
2. Panshanger MSS. Box 17.
3. *In Whig Society*. Lady Airlie. London, 1921. p. 2.
4. *The Girlhood of Queen Victoria*. ed. Viscount Esher. London, 1912. Vol. 2, p. 69.
5. *Sketches of Eminent Statesmen and Writers*. Abraham Hayward. London, 1880. Vol. 1, p. 332.
6. *Girlhood of Victoria*. Vol. 1, p. 250.
7. *The Journal of Elizabeth, Lady Holland*. ed. Lord Ilchester. London, 1908. Vol. 1, p. 98.
8. *Byron's Letters and Journals*. ed. Leslie Marchand. London, 1974. Vol. 3, p. 93.
9. *The Memoirs of Mrs Sophia Baddeley*. Mrs Elizabeth Steele. London, 1787. Vol. 2, p. 199.
10. Transcript by Lord Rosebery of Spencer Cowper's manuscript notes in the margin of an essay by Abraham Hayward. In the author's possession.
11. P.R.O. 6838. No. 18.
12. *Recollections of a Long Life*. Lord Broughton. London, 1911. Vol. 5, p. 180.
13. Hayward. Vol. 1, p. 336.
14. Panshanger MSS. Box 18. 22 May 1845. Panshanger MSS. Box 58.
15. *Girlhood of Victoria*. Vol. 1, p. 280. *In Whig Society*. p. 63.
16. ibid. Vol. 2, p. 305.
17. ibid. Vol. 1, p. 246.

CHAPTER 2 (pp. 21–32)

1. *Girlhood of Victoria*. Vol. 2, p. 30.
2. ibid. Vol. 1, p. 348.
3. ibid. Vol. 2, p. 56.
4. Panshanger MSS. Box 9.
5. *Eton College Lists*, 1678–1790. ed. R. Austen Leigh. Eton, 1907, and *Eton College Register*, 1753–1790. ed. R. Austen Leigh. Eton, 1921.
6. *Girlhood of Victoria*. Vol. 1, p. 312.
7. 16 Oct, 1835. Add. MSS. 51558. f. 88.
8. *Trinity College. An Historical Sketch*. G. M. Trevelyan. Cambridge, 1943. p. 75.
9. *The Prelude*. Book 3, Lines 545–9. 1850 version.

10. *Girlhood of Victoria.* Vol. 2, p. 133.
11. *Trinity College.* Trevelyan, p. 85.
12. *A History of the University of Glasgow.* James Coutts. Glasgow, 1909. p. 310.
13. ibid. p. 305.
14. *The University of Glasgow, 1451–1951.* J. D. Mackie. Glasgow, 1954. pp. 211–35.
15. 14 Jan. 1800. Panshanger MSS. Box 17.
16. *Lady Bessborough and her Family Circle.* ed. Lord Bessborough and A. Aspinall. London, 1940. p. 143.
17. Undated. Panshanger MSS. Box 17.
18. 8 Jan. 1800. ibid.
19. 27 March 1800. ibid.

CHAPTER 3 (pp. 33–41)

1. See, e.g. *Crossroads of Power.* L. B. Namier. London, 1962. p. 231.
2. to Holland. 17 Jan. 1817. Grey MSS. See also *The Whigs in Opposition.* Austin Mitchell. Oxford, 1967.
3. *Passing of the Whigs.* p. 21.
4. *Journal of Lady Holland.* Vol. 1, p. 225.
5. *Lady Bessborough and her Family Circle.* p. 116. *The Sovereign Lady, A Life of Elizabeth Vassall, third Lady Holland.* Sonia Keppel. London, 1974. p. 101.
6. *Hary-O. Letters of Lady Harriet Cavendish.* ed. Sir G. Leveson-Gower and Iris Palmer. London, 1940. p. 44. *Girlhood of Victoria.* Vol. 2, p. 123.
7. *Memoirs of Viscount Melbourne.* W. M. Torrens. London, 1878. Vol. 1, p. 41.
8. 17 Jan. 1798.
9. Torrens. *Melbourne.* Vol. 1, p. 48.
10. *Life of Lord Campbell.* ed. Mrs Hardcastle. London, 1881. Vol. 1, p. 63.
11. *Girlhood of Victoria.* Vol. 2, p. 291. *In Whig Society.* p. 182. *Private Correspondence of Lord Granville Leveson-Gower.* ed. Countess Granville. London, 1916. Vol. 2, p. 229.
12. *The Diary of Benjamin Robert Haydon.* ed. W. B. Hope. Harvard, 1963. Vol. 4, p. 203.
13. *Private Correspondence of Lord Granville.* Vol. 2, p. 9.

CHAPTER 4 (pp. 42–57)

1. to J. Wedderburn Webster. 18 Sept. 1815. Copy in Panshanger MSS. Box 17.
2. The best portrait of Caroline Lamb is that by David Cecil in *The Young Melbourne* (London, 1939). The most recent study is that of Mr Henry Blyth, *Caro, The Fatal Passion,* (London, 1973).
3. *Byron's Letters and Journals.* Vol. 2, p. 170.

4. *Byron's Letters and Journals.* Vol. 2, p. 170. *Girlhood of Victoria.* Vol. 2, p. 64.
5. *Hary-O.* p. 23.
6. *Private Correspondence of Lord Granville.* Vol. 2, p. 67. Duchess of Devonshire to Lady Spencer. 4 May 1805. Cavendish MSS. 1804.
7. *Lady Bessborough and her Family Circle.* p. 130.
8. *Private Correspondence of Lord Granville.* Vol. 2, p. 68. *Lady Bessborough and her Family Circle.* p. 130.
9. *Private Correspondence of Lord Granville.* Vol. 2, p. 67. Duchess of Devonshire to Lady Spencer. 4 June 1805. Cavendish MSS. 1812.
10. Lady Spencer to Duchess of Devonshire. 9 June 1805. Cavendish MSS. 1813.
11. *Girlhood of Victoria.* Vol. 2, p. 225 and Vol. 1, p. 257.
12. ibid. Vol. 2, p. 158.
13. London, 1816. p. 152.
14. *Memoirs, Journal and Correspondence of Thomas Moore.* ed. Lord John Russell. London, 1853–6. Vol. 7, p. 4. *Hary-O.* p. 145.
15. *Georgiana. Extracts from the Correspondence of Georgiana, Duchess of Devonshire.* ed. Lord Bessborough. London, 1955. p. 275. *Private Correspondence of Lord Granville.* Vol. 2, pp. 126–51. *Lady Bessborough and her Family Circle.* p. 140. *Hary-O.* pp. 41; 124–36. *The Diary of a Lady in Waiting.* Lady Charlotte Bury. London, 1908. p. 282.
16. *Correspondence of Sarah Spencer, Lady Lyttelton.* ed. Mrs Hugh Wyndham. London, 1912. p. 79. *The Life of Viscount Palmerston.* Henry Lytton Bulwer. London, 1871. Vol. 1, p. 119. *Hary-O.* p. 124. *The Memoirs of Harriette Wilson.* London, 1909. Vol. 2, p. 612. Melbourne to Cowper. Broadlands MSS. MEL/CO/49.
17. *Girlhood of Victoria.* Vol. 2, p. 283.
18. *Hary-O.* p. 242. Caroline Lamb's Commonplace Book (formerly in the possession of Lady Salmond). *Lady Bessborough and her Family Circle.* p. 182.
19. Add. MSS. 51558. f. 125.
20. *In Whig Society.* p. 119.
21. 27 May 1809. Panshanger MSS. Box 17.
22. *In Whig Society.* p. 117. Add. MSS. 51558. f. 1. *The Sovereign Lady.* p. 180.
23. *Letters to 'Ivy' from the First Earl of Dudley.* ed. S. H. Romilly. London, 1905. p. 162. Byron to Lady Melbourne. 30 Sept. 1812. *Byron's Letters and Journals.* Vol. 2, p. 222.
24. *In Whig Society.* p. 129. *Private Correspondence of Lord Granville.* Vol. 2, p. 447.
25. Melbourne to Grey. 25 Jan. 1831. Grey MSS. *Girlhood of Victoria.* Vol. 1, p. 303.
26. *Letters to 'Ivy'.* p. 162.
27. *In Whig Society.* p. 131.
28. ibid. p. 154.

29. Byron to Lady Melbourne. 12 Jan., 26 June and 5 Oct. 1814. *Byron's Letters and Journals.* Vol. 4, pp. 27, 132 and 195.
30. *Letters of Harriet, Countess Granville,* ed. F. Leveson-Gower. London, 1894. Vol. 1, pp. 40–1.
31. 25 Oct. 1814. *Miss Eden's Letters.* ed. Violet Dickinson. London, 1919. p. 3. Byron to Lady Melbourne. 5 Feb. 1815. *Byron's Letters and Journals.* Vol. 4, p. 266.
32. Byron to Annabella Milbanke. 9 Oct. 1814. *Byron's Letters and Journals.* Vol. 4, p. 203.
33. Byron to J. Wedderburn Webster. 18 Sept. 1815. Panshanger MSS. Box 17.
34. 18 July 1815. *Letters of Harriet Granville.* Vol. 1, p. 57. *In Whig Society.* p. 171.
35. *Letters of Harriet Granville.* Vol. 1, p. 74.
36. *Girlhood of Victoria.* Vol. 2, p. 86.

CHAPTER 5 (pp. 58–83)

1. 3 Aug. 1827. Bowood MSS.
2. *In Whig Society.* p. 86. *The Later Correspondence of George III.* ed. A. Aspinall. Cambridge, 1968. Vol. 4, p. 499.
3. *His Majesty's Opposition.* 1714–1830. A. S. Foord. Oxford, 1964.
4. *The Creevey Papers.* ed. Sir H. Maxwell. London, 1904. Vol. 1, p. 144. *An Embassy to the Court of St James.* F. Guizot. London, 1862. p. 133.
5. In fact Mr Grey till his father became an earl in April 1806; then Lord Howick till November 1807 when his father died.
6. *Letters and Journals.* ed. R. E. Prothero. London, 1898–1900. Vol. 5, p. 176.
7. *Lord Brougham and the Whig Party.* A. Aspinall. Manchester, 1927. p. 21.
8. Macaulay to Hannah Macaulay. 10 June 1833. cit. John Clive. *Macaulay. The Making of a Historian.* London, 1973. p. 212.
9. *Private Correspondence of Lord Granville.* Vol. 2, pp. 162–4.
10. to Lady Melbourne. Undated but about end 1806. Panshanger MSS. Box 17.
11. *The Letters of Richard Brinsley Sheridan.* ed. Cecil Price. Oxford, 1966. Vol. 2, p. 307.
12. *Lady Bessborough and her Family Circle.* p. 163.
13. 28 April 1810. RA MP 1/71.
14. *Girlhood of Victoria.* Vol. 2, p. 210.
15. 25 May 1810. Hansard 17. 203.
16. *Lord Melbourne's Papers.* ed. Lloyd Sanders. London, 1889. p.19. Lord Howick's Diary (Grey MSS.). Feb. 1841. *The Letters of Lady Palmerston.* ed. Tresham Lever. London, 1957. p. 173. *Private Correspondence of Lord Granville.* Vol. 2, p. 342.
17. *The Greville Journal.* ed. Strachey and Fulford. London, 1938. Vol. 2, p. 46.

18. 18 Feb. 1812. *Hansard* 21. 848. 10 July 1812. *Hansard* 23. 984.
19. 26 Feb. 1812. RA Add. 19316. *Private Correspondence of Lord Granville.* Vol. 2, p. 465.
20. *In Whig Society.* p. 108.
21. *In Whig Society.* p. 109. *Private Correspondence of Lord Granville.* Vol. 2, p. 461. Brougham to Grey. 24 Oct. 1812. *The Life and Times of Henry Lord Brougham.* Written by Himself. London, 1871. Vol. 2, p. 70.
22. *In Whig Society.* pp. 109 and 111.
23. 3 Nov. 1812. Grey MSS.
24. 12 Nov. and 29 Nov. 1812. Grey MSS. *Whig Principles and Party Politics. Earl Fitzwilliam and the Whig Party.* Antony Smith. Manchester, 1975. p. 528.
25. *Brougham's Life and Times.* Vol. 2, p. 24. *Private Correspondence of Lord Granville.* Vol. 2, p. 466.
26. 10 Dec. 1815. Add. MSS. 51558. f. 37.
27. 30 June 1815. Fitzwilliam MSS. 26 and 28 March 1816. Add. MSS. 51558. ff. 39 and 41.
28. *Notes.* Sir Robert Heron. Grantham, 1851. p. 225.
29. 28 Jan. 1817. *Hansard* 35. 26.
30. *The Whigs in Opposition.* p. 103. 28 Feb. 1817. *Hansard* 35. 799–801.
31. *Letters of Lady Palmerston.* p. 21. Brougham. *Life and Times.* Vol. 2, p. 350. 8 Oct. 1819. Fitzwilliam MSS. 11 March 1818. *Hansard* 37. 999–1009.
32. Lambton to Grey. 12 Feb. 1819. Grey MSS.
33. 11 March 1820. *The Private Letters of Princess Lieven to Prince Metternich.* ed. Peter Quennell. London, 1937. p. 13. *The Life of Francis Place.* Graham Wallas. London, 1925. p. 136.
34. Melbourne to Hardwicke. 12 Oct. 1819. Add. MSS. 35652. f. 274. *Letters of Lady Palmerston.* p. 20.
35. 31 Jan. 1821. *Hansard.* NS 4. 261. *Letters of Lady Palmerston.* p. 70. *Lady Palmerston and her Times.* Mabel, Countess of Airlie. London, 1922. Vol. 1, p. 91.
36. *In Whig Society.* p. 185. *The Creevey Papers.* ed. Sir H. Maxwell. London, 1904. Vol. 1, p. 204.
37. 27 May 1816. Add. MSS. 51558. f. 35.
38. *Letters of Lady Palmerston.* p. 15. *Huskisson and His Age.* C. R. Fay. London, 1951. p. 191.
39. *Letters of Lady Palmerston.* pp. 15 and 96. *Lieven–Metternich Letters.* p. 204. *Elizabeth Lady Holland to her Son.* ed. Lord Ilchester. London, 1946. p. 28.
40. 26 Oct. 1822. Cavendish MSS. *Lady Palmerston and her Times.* Vol. 1, pp. 61 and 44.
41. *The Diary of Frances Lady Shelley.* ed. R. Edgcumbe. London, 1913. Vol. 2, p. 6. Lady Cowper to Fred Lamb. 9 March 1818. Panshanger MSS. Box 17.

42. *Extracts from the Diary of the Late Dr Robert Lee.* London, 1897. p. 106. 21 Oct. 1825. Panshanger MSS. Box 17.
43. *Letters of Lady Palmerston.* pp. 62 and 71. *Elizabeth Lady Holland to her Son.* p. 69.
44. *Memoirs of Thomas Moore.* Vol. 2, p. 306.
45. *Life of John, Lord Campbell.* Mrs Hardcastle. London, 1881. p. 409.
46. 7 Oct. 1822. *Letters of Lady Palmerston.* p. 111.
47. *The Life of Edward Bulwer, 1st Lord Lytton.* The Earl of Lytton. London, 1913. pp. 119–22. *Memoirs of Harriette Wilson.* Vol. 1, p. 323.
48. 19 May 1824 and April 1825. Cavendish MSS. 996 and 1128.
49. 10 April 1825. Cavendish MSS. 1129. 16 May 1825. Panshanger MSS. Box 9.
50. to Fred Lamb. Panshanger MSS. Box 17.
51. *Girlhood of Victoria.* Vol. 2, p. 141. Lamb to Fitzwilliam. 22 June 1825. Fitzwilliam MSS. Althorp to Devonshire. 7 June 1825. Cavendish MSS. 1153.
52. *Letters of Lady Palmerston.* pp. 136 and 137. *Lady Palmerston and her Times.* Vol. 1, p. 119.
53. *Lady Palmerston and her Times.* Vol. 1, p. 119. *Letters of Lady Palmerston.* p. 139. *Three Howard Sisters.* ed. Lady Leconfield and John Gore. London, 1955. p. 49. Sir George Tuthill's Report. 19 Oct. 1825. Panshanger MSS. Box 17. *Lady Bessborough and her Family Circle.* p. 286.

CHAPTER 6 (pp. 84–99)

1. Lamb to Ward. 29 Sept. 1822. RA MP 27/96.
2. 30 Sept. 1820. *Lady Palmerston and her Times.* p. 68. Lamb to Mrs George Lamb. 24 Dec. 1838. Brougham MSS.
3. 3 Dec. 1827. Panshanger MSS. Box 9.
4. 16 April 1823. *Hansard.* NS 8. 1028.
5. 22 April 1823. *Letters of Lady Palmerston.* p. 123. *Miss Eden's Letters.* p. 107.
6. 27 April 1826. *Hansard.* NS 15. 712. *Letters of Lady Palmerston.* p.149.
7. *Letters of Lady Palmerston.* p. 146. W. Lamb to Fred Lamb. 13 April 1826. Panshanger MSS. Box 9.
8. Torrens. *Melbourne.* Vol. 1, p. 213. *Letters of Lady Palmerston.* p. 148.
9. *Lady Palmerston and her Times.* Vol. 1, p. 126.
10. Londonderry to Wellington. 12 April 1827. Wellington MSS.
11. Of particular value for the study of the subsequent negotiations are A. Aspinall's *Lord Brougham and the Whig Party* (op. cit.) and *The Formation of Canning's Ministry.* Camden Third Series. Vol. LIX. London, 1937.
12. 18 April 1827. Broadlands MSS. GC/ME/507.
13. 21 April 1827. Harewood MSS. cit. *The Formation of Canning's Ministry.* p. 142.

14. Torrens. *Melbourne*. Vol. 1, p. 223. *Memoirs of Thomas Moore*. Vol. 5, pp. 164 and 198.
15. 27 April 1827. *Letters of Lady Palmerston*. p. 165. John Allen's Memorandum of 26 April 1827. Holland House MSS. Canning to Portland. 27 April 1827. cit. *Formation of Canning's Ministry*. p. 190.
16. 24 April 1827. *The Letters of George IV*. ed. Aspinall. London, 1938. Vol. 3, p. 223.
17. Howick Diary. August 1839.
18. Lady Cowper to F. Lamb. 1 and 8 May 1827. Panshanger MSS. Box 17.
19. 11 May 1827. *Creevey Papers*. Vol. 2, p. 117. 29 April 1827. Bowood MSS.
20. to Rev. W. Leigh. 19 May 1827. Hatherton MSS. 10 July 1827. *The Early Correspondence of Lord John Russell*. London, 1913. Vol. 1, p. 249.
21. cit. *One Leg. The Life and Letters of Henry William Paget, First Marquess of Anglesey*. The Marquess of Anglesey. London, 1961. p. 260.
22. 15 Feb. 1825. *Hansard*. NS 12. 444.
23. *Lord Melbourne's Papers*. p. 210. Lamb to Brougham. 14 Oct. 1827. Brougham MSS.
24. *Lord Melbourne's Papers*. p. 103.
25. Anglesey to Lamb. 17 Sept. 1827. Paget MSS.
26. 9 June 1827. *The Correspondence of Daniel O'Connell*. ed. M. O'Connell. Dublin, 1974. p. 321. ibid. pp. 325 and 369.
27. Lamb to Lansdowne. 3 Aug. 1827. Bowood MSS. Colonel Meyrick Shawe to Knighton. 15 Aug. 1827. *Letters of George IV*. Vol. 3, p. 287.
28. Lamb to Brougham. 28 Sept. 1827. Brougham MSS. to Lansdowne. 19 Sept. 1827. Bowood MSS.
29. *Girlhood of Victoria*. Vol. 2, p. 5. Torrens. *Melbourne*. Vol. 1, p. 229.
30. to Caroline Lamb. 9 Oct. 1827. Panshanger MSS. Box 9.
31. 11 Nov. 1827. Bowood MSS. 28 Aug. 1827. *Letters of Lady Palmerston*. p. 174. *Greville Journal*. Vol. 1, p. 144.
32. RA MP 8/63. W. Lamb to F. Lamb. 3 Dec. 1827. Panshanger MSS. Box 9. Lamb to Brougham. 4 Sept. 1827. Brougham MSS.
33. Cavendish MSS. 1553 and 1554. W. Lamb to F. Lamb. 3 Dec. 1827. Panshanger MSS. Box 9. Auckland to Minto. 12 Jan. 1828. Minto MSS. 2E f. 416.
34. Lamb to Wellington. RA MP 17/57 and 58. W. Lamb to Fred Lamb. 12 Jan. 1828. Panshanger MSS. Box 9.
35. Broadlands MSS. 13 Jan. 1828. GMC 18; 18 Jan. 1828. GMC 25; 21 Jan. 1828. GMC 32.
36. 20 Jan. 1828. *Three Howard Sisters*. p. 101. 28 Jan. 1828. Panshanger MSS. Box 9. See also *The Last of the Canningites*. A. Aspinall. E.H.R. Vol. 50, p. 639.
37. Lansdowne to Minto. 18 Jan. 1828. Minto MSS. 2E f. 416. Devonshire to Lady Granville. 24 Jan. 1828. Cavendish MSS. 1655. *Chronicles of Holland House*. Lord Ilchester. London, 1946. Vol. 2, p. 94.

38. Durham to Ellice. 23 Jan. 1828. Ellice MSS. E.29 f. 19.
39. *Letters to Ivy.* p. 337.
40. 26 May 1828. Add. MSS. 40397. f. 14.
41. Bulwer. *Palmerston.* pp. 273–5.
42. to F. Lamb. 28 May 1828. Panshanger MSS. Box 17.

CHAPTER 7 (p. 100–110)

1. to Caroline Lamb. 21 Aug. 1827. *Lady Bessborough and her Family Circle.* p. 289.
2. 28 Jan. 1828. Panshanger MSS. Box 18.
3. 19 June 1928. ibid. Box 18.
4. Lady Branden to Melbourne. Undated. Panshanger MSS. Box 18.
5. Melbourne to F. Lamb. 12 June 1828. ibid. Box 17.
6. *The Life of Mrs Norton.* Jane Perkins. London, 1910. p. 85.
7. 6 Jan. 1828. *Lady Bessborough and her Family Circle,* p. 290.
8. 18 Jan. 1828. Panshanger MSS. Box 18. Caroline to Lady Duncannon. *Lady Bessborough and her Family Circle.* p. 290.
9. 23 Jan. 1828. Panshanger MSS. Box 18. Emily Cowper to F. Lamb. *Lady Palmerston and her Times.* Vol. 1, p. 129. *In Whig Society.* p. 186.
10. *Three Howard Sisters.* p. 107. *Lady Palmerston and her Times.* Vol. 1, p. 129. Lamb to Lady Branden. 18 Feb. 1828. Panshanger MSS. Box 18.
11. 23 July 1828. Panshanger MSS. Box 18.
12. 1 March 1828; 14 May 1830; 9 Aug. 1828. Panshanger MSS. Box 18.
13. Mrs Susan Cuessod to Melbourne. 5 April 1842. Panshanger MSS. Box 17. I am indebted to Miss Margot Strickland for drawing my attention to this letter.
14. 19 Dec. 1839. Panshanger MSS. Box 37.
15. *Greville Journal.* Vol. 4, p. 152. 3 March 1828. Panshanger MSS. Box 18.
16. *Creevey Papers.* Vol. 2, p. 160. cf. Emily Cowper to F. Lamb. 11 June 1828. Panshanger MSS. Box 17.
17. 27 and 29 May 1828. Panshanger MSS. Box 18.
18. *Life of Lord Campbell.* Vol. 2, p. 83.
19. 12 Nov. 1829. RA MP. Personal Box.
20. 11 Dec. 1831. ibid.
21. Emily Cowper to F. Lamb. 12 June 1828. Panshanger MSS. Box 17. Melbourne to Lady Branden. 24 June 1828. Panshanger MSS. Box 18.
22. 23 July and 9 August 1828. Panshanger MSS. Box 18.
23. 7 Nov. 1829. ibid.
24. 26 Dec. 1844. RA MP. Personal Box.

CHAPTER 8 (pp. 111–126)

1. 23 June 1828. *The Journal of Mrs Arbuthnot.* ed. F. Bamford, London, 1950. Vol. 2, p. 195.

2. *Journal of Mrs Arbuthnot.* Vol. 2, p. 235. cf. *Correspondence of Princess Lieven and Lord Grey.* ed. G. le Strange. London, 1890. Vol. 1, p. 218.
3. *Journal of Mrs Arbuthnot.* Vol. 2, p. 159.
4. See, in particular, *The Last of the Canningites,* p. 667.
5. *The Whigs in Opposition,* p. 217.
6. 24 Aug., 3 Sept., 28 Sept. 1828. *Lieven–Grey Correspondence.* Vol. 1, pp. 135–43.
7. 24 Oct. 1829. *Journal of Mrs Arbuthnot.* Vol. 2, p. 311.
8. 29 Jan. 1830. Cavendish MSS. 1909. Grey to Howick. 8 Jan. 1830. Grey MSS. Howick Diary. 2 Dec. 1829. *Lieven–Grey Correspondence.* Vol. 1, p. 421.
9. Howick Diary. 5 May 1830. Grey to Howick. 9 March 1830. Grey MSS.
10. to Lady Branden. 20 Sept. 1830. Panshanger MSS. Box 18.
11. *Miss Eden's Letters.* p. 167.
12. For these negotiations see Palmerston's undated memorandum, Broadlands MSS. GMC/33.
13. 13 Sept. 1830. RA MP 28/55.
14. Torrens. *Melbourne.* Vol. 1, p. 336. Palmerston to Littleton. 25 Sept. 1830. Hatherton MSS. Howick Diary. 27 Sept. 1830.
15. 18 Sept. 1830. Cavendish MSS. Palmerston to Littleton. 25 Sept. 1830. Hatherton MSS. Palmerston to Grant. 25 Sept. 1830. Broadlands MSS. GMC/35. 21 and 30 Sept. 1830. Cavendish MSS. 1909 and 2012.
16. *Letters of Dorothea, Princess Lieven, during her Residence in London.* ed. L. G. Robinson. London, 1902. p. 254. *Journal of Mrs Arbuthnot.* Vol. 2, p. 395. Melbourne to Palmerston. 13 Oct. 1830. Broadlands MSS. GMC/40.
17. Wellington to Lady Salisbury, cit. M. Brock. *The Great Reform Act.* London, 1973. p. 118.
18. Howick Diary. 7 Nov. 1830.
19. See N. Gash. *Essays Presented to Sir Lewis Namier.* London, 1956. p. 287.
20. to Duke of Devonshire. 17 Nov. 1830. Cavendish MSS. 2092.
21. *Blackwood's Magazine.* Vol. 87. Edinburgh 1860.
22. *Correspondence of Lady Lyttelton.* p. 328.
23. 12 Feb. 1833. Ellice MSS. E 28 f. 2.
24. *Lord Melbourne's Papers.* p. 307. *Girlhood of Victoria.* Vol. 2, p. 149.
25. RA MP 14/27. *Girlhood of Victoria.* Vol. 2, p. 277.
26. *Life of Richard Whately.* E. Jane Whately. London, 1866. Vol. 2, p. 452.
27. *An Embassy to the Court of St James.* F. Guizot. London, 1862. p. 9.
28. *Lord Melbourne's Papers.* p. 505.
29. *Girlhood of Victoria.* Vol. 2, p. 156.
30. *Greville Journal.* Vol. 4, p. 365. 15 May 1842. RA A4/67.
31. Howick Diary. 1 May 1835. *The Diary of Benjamin Robert Haydon.* Vol. 4, p. 139.
32. *Second Letter to Archdeacon Singleton. Collected Works.* Vol. 2, p. 278.
33. Broughton. *Recollections.* Vol. 5, p. 25.

34. ibid. Vol. 5, p. 169.
35. Lytton. *Edward Bulwer, 1st Lord Lytton.* p. 483.
36. 25 Sept. 1840. RA MP 23/82.
37. 12 Feb. 1835. *Early Correspondence of Lord John Russell.* Vol. 2, p. 91.

CHAPTER 9 (pp. 127–140)

1. *Letters during Residence in London.* p. 274.
2. ibid. p. 286.
3. Undated. RA MP 1/87. Brock. *Great Reform Act.* p. 132.
4. *Greville Journal.* Vol. 2, p. 114. *Memoir of Viscount Althorp.* Denis le Marchant. London, 1876. p. 400.
5. *Greville Journal.* Vol. 2, p. 322.
6. *Creevey Papers.* Vol. 2, p. 296. *The Letters of Runnymede.* 30 Jan. 1836.
7. to Palmerston. 28 Aug. 1834. Broadlands MSS. GC/ME/18.
8. 7 Sept. 1837. Broadlands MSS. MEL/RU/396.
9. *Life of Lord Sidmouth.* G. Pellew. London, 1847. Vol. 3, p. 395.
10. The classic study of this period lies in J. L. and B. Hammond's *The Village Labourer* (London, 1911). I have found of particular value E. J. Hobsbawm and George Rudé's *Captain Swing* (London, 1969) and, for a narrower canvas, J. P. Dunbabin's *Rural Discontent in 19th Century Britain* (London, 1974).
11. 1 July 1812.
12. 20 Nov. 1830. Cavendish MSS. 2098.
13. Undated Memorandum. RA MP Gen.
14. to Lt.-Col. J. Wodehouse. 6 Dec. 1830. RA MP R4
15. H.O. 52/8.
16. *Captain Swing.* pp. 303–58.
17. 1 Feb. 1831 and 26 Nov. 1830. RA MP.
18. 27 Nov. 1830 and 13 Nov. 1831. RA MP 17/59 and RA R1.
19. 19 Dec. 1830 and 14 Jan. 1831. RA MP 35/37 and /38.
20. Circular of 8 Dec. 1830. RA MP R3.
21. 16 Sept. 1831. *Hansard.* 3rd Series. 7.86. *Lord Grey of the Reform Bill.* London, 1920, p. 251.
22. *Captain Swing.* p. 29. *Lord Melbourne.* Bertram Newman. London, 1930. p. 97.
23. 21, 25 and 26 Jan. 1831. RA MP R1.
24. *Life of Francis Place.* p. 253.
25. *Three Early Nineteenth Century Diaries.* ed. Aspinall. London, 1952. p. 118. *Life of Francis Place.* p. 303.
26. e.g. Melbourne to Grey. 24 April 1832 and 20 March 1834. Grey MSS.
27. Torrens. *Melbourne.* Vol. 1, p. 368.
28. *Girlhood of Victoria.* Vol. 2, p. 305.
29. 7 June 1831. Paget MSS. Melbourne to William. 30 June 1831. RA MP.
30. 26 and 27 Nov. 1830. Hatherton MSS.

31. *Greville Journal*. Vol. 2, p. 87. Brougham to Devonshire. 5 Dec. 1830. Cavendish MSS. 2111. Brougham. *Life and Times*. Vol. 3, p. 380.
32. 5 Sept. 1831. Add. MSS. 51867.

CHAPTER 10 (pp. 141–149)

1. 11 June 1831. Grey MSS.
2. 16 Jan. 1831. *Journal of Mrs Arbuthnot*. Vol. 2, p. 411. *Three Nineteenth Century Diaries*. pp. 39 and 205. Le Marchant. *Althorp*. p. 294.
3. *Politics in the Age of Peel*. Norman Gash. London, 1953. p. 11. 4 Oct. 1831. *Hansard*. 3rd Series. 7.1176.
4. J. A. Roebuck. *History of the Whig Ministry of 1830*. London, 1852. Vol. 2, p. 87.
5. Melbourne to John Key. 29 April and 2 May 1831; William IV to Melbourne. 2 and 3 May; Melbourne to William IV. 3 May; RA MP. 21 June 1831. *Hansard*. 3rd Series. 4.138.
6. Brock. *Reform Bill*. p. 275. Holland Diary. 5 Sept. 1831. Add. MSS. 51867. f. 126.
7. For what follows, as for so much connected with the period of the Reform Bill, I am particularly grateful to Dr Michael Brock for his invaluable work on the subject (op. cit.).
8. H.O. 48.28 f. 135.
9. H.O. 40.28 f. 26.
10. to Brougham. 31 Oct. 1831. Brougham MSS.
11. Nov. 1831. Draft in RA MP.
12. RA MP 1/83 and 84. Melbourne to Grey. 30 Oct. 1831. Grey MSS.
13. H.O. 64.11. Lawless to Melbourne. 22 Oct. 1831. RA MP R2. Holland Diary. Add. MSS. 51868. f. 210.
14. Melbourne to Grey. 18 Nov. 1831. Grey MSS. H.O. 41.10.
15. Add. MSS. 51568. f. 217. cf. Palmerston to Melbourne. 20 Nov. 1831. RA MP 11/3.
16. *Greville Journal*. Vol. 2, p. 226.
17. *Greville Journal*. Vol. 2, p. 244. Brougham. *Life and Times*. Vol. 3, p. 165. Holland Diary. 2 Jan. 1832. Add. MSS. 51868. *Life and Letters of Sir James Graham*. Charles Parker. London, 1907. Vol. 1, p. 135.
18. 10 Oct. 1831. Broadlands MSS. GC/ME/12.
19. *Greville Journal*. Vol. 2, p. 277. Cecil. *Lord M*. p. 185.
20. Broughton. *Recollections*. Vol. 4, p. 214.
21. *Lady Holland to her Son*. p. 137.

CHAPTER 11 (p. 150–166)

1. Torrens. *Melbourne*. Vol. 1, p. 364. June 1832. *Lord Melbourne's Papers*. p. 186.
2. 21 Jan. 1833 and 14 July 1832. Paget MSS.

3. cit. R. B. McDowell. *Public Opinion and Government Policy in Ireland, 1801–46*. London, 1952. p. 154. This book provides an excellent introduction to Irish politics of the period.

4. 31 Dec. 1830. Paget MSS.

5. 28 and 29 Dec. 1830. Paget MSS. *Lord Melbourne's Papers*. p. 174. 26 Feb. 1831. Paget MSS.

6. Melbourne to Stanley. 7 Jan. 1831. *Lord Melbourne's Papers*. p. 171. Melbourne to Anglesey. 30 July 1832. Paget MSS.

7. *Lord Melbourne's Papers*. p. 175.

8. Melbourne to Anglesey. 26 Feb. 1831. Paget MSS.

9. 28 Sept. 1832. RA MP 8/77. *The Passing of the Whigs*. p. 43. Grey to Lansdowne. 2 Jan. 1833. Bowood MSS. Brougham. *Life and Times*. Vol. 3, p. 247. Melbourne to Grey. 11 Jan. 1833. Grey MSS.

10. *One Leg*. p. 265. Melbourne to Grey. 11 Oct. 1833. Grey MSS.

11. 13 May 1833. Paget MSS. *Girlhood of Victoria*. Vol. 2, p. 181. *The Later Correspondence of Lord John Russell*, ed. G. P. Gooch. London, 1925. Vol. 1, p. 69.

12. *Lord Melbourne's Papers*. p. 122. Brougham. *Life and Times*. Vol. 3, p. 323.

13. *Chartist Studies*. London, 1959. p. 6 (though see also E. J. Hobsbawm. *Labouring Men*. London, 1964. Chapter 8).

14. cit. Asa Briggs. *The Age of Improvement*. London, 1959. p. 247. This book provides admirable background to Melbourne's problems with the unions (and the unions' problems with Melbourne!)

15. 26 Dec. 1830. Grey MSS. Copy of Nassau Report in Panshanger MSS. Box 16.

16. Sir H. Taylor to Melbourne. 23 Sept. 1831; Melbourne to Taylor. 24 Sept. 1831. RA MP.

17. Littleton Diary. 28 Oct. 1831.

18. Melbourne to Lawley. 10 and 16 Nov. 1831; Lawley to Melbourne. 14 Nov. RA MP. Melbourne to William IV. 24 Nov. 1831. RA MP.

19. H.O. 41.10.

20. 26 Sept. 1831. *Lord Melbourne's Papers*. p. 133.

21. 15 June 1833. Melbourne MSS. RA MP R4. Howick Diary. 13 Jan. 1834. Melbourne to E. B. Portman. 10 Feb. 1834. RA MP R3.

22. 28 March 1834. RA MP R2.

23. Joyce Marlow's *The Tolpuddle Martyrs*. (London, 1971), provides an excellent account of this episode. Walter Citrine's *The Martyrs of Tolpuddle* (London, 1934) contains more extensive documentation.

24. e.g. Melbourne to Frampton. Add. MSS. 41567. f. 125.

25. *Life of Francis Place*. p. 357.

26. Broughton. *Recollections*. Vol. 4, p. 334.

27. 25 April 1834. *Letters during Residence in London*. p. 372. Melbourne to William. 2 April 1834. RA MP. 21 April 1834. Add. MSS. 35154.

28. *Haydon Diary*. Vol. 4, p. 186.
29. 8 Aug. 1833. *Memoirs of Thomas Moore*. Vol. 6, p. 332. Broughton. *Recollections*. Vol. 4, p. 277. *Memoirs of Thomas Moore*. Vol. 7, p. 4.
30. Oct. 1831. RA MP 32/9–11. Melbourne to Howick. 27 Feb. 1834. Grey MSS. Broughton. *Recollections*. Vol. 6, p. 106. *Greville Journal*. Vol. 2, p. 229.
31. 8 Sept. 1832. RA MP.
32. to T. Sanctuary. 6 Jan. 1831. *Lord Melbourne's Papers*. p. 127.
33. 20 Jan. 1834. *Hansard*. 3rd Series. 24.612.
34. 1 Aug. 1833. *Hansard*. 3rd Series. 20.247. Melbourne to Grey. 18 June 1832. Grey MSS.
35. *The Life and Letters of George, 4th Earl of Clarendon*. Herbert Maxwell. London, 1913. p. 82. Melbourne to Grey. 5 Jan. 1834. Grey MSS.
36. Howick Diary. 3 and 7 Jan. 1834. Grey to Melbourne. 6 Jan. 1834. RA MP 5/118.
37. Howick Diary. 13 Jan.–31 March *passim*.
38. *Girlhood of Victoria*. Vol. 2, p. 148.

CHAPTER 12 (pp. 167–180)

1. 24 Jan. 1834. *Letters During Residence in London*. p. 364. Howick Diary. 13 Jan. 1834.
2. Howick Diary. 29 Jan. and 25 April 1834. *Creevey Papers*. Vol. 2, p. 274. *Greville Journal*. Vol. 3, p. 88. *The Political and Occasional Poems of Winthrop Mackworth Praed*. London, 1888. p. 276.
3. *Lives of the Lord Chancellors*. Vol. 8, p. 93.
4. *Memoir and Correspondence relating to Political Occurrences in June and July, 1834*. E. J. Littleton. ed. Henry Reeve. London, 1872. cf. *Lord Brougham and the Whig Party*. A. Aspinall. pp. 195–8.
5. 8 July 1834. Broadlands MSS. GC/ME.
6. 8 July 1834. Bowood MSS. Duchess of Dino. *Memoirs*. Vol. 1, p. 118.
7. Lytton. *Life of Palmerston*. Vol. 2, p. 203n.
8. Holland Diary. Add. MSS. 51870. ff. 736 and 37.
9. Melbourne MSS. RA MP 1/112.
10. *Greville Journal*. Vol. 3, p. 76.
11. 10 July 1834. Add. MSS. 40303. f. 198. Wellington to William. 12 July 1834. RA Add. 15/8020. Peel to William. 13 July 1834. Add. MSS. 40302. f. 1.
12. Grey to Melbourne. 10 July 1834. RA MP 5/124. *The Correspondence of Charles Arbuthnot*. ed. A. Aspinall. Camden 3rd Series. London, 1941. Vol. LXV, p. 187. *Hansard*. 3rd Series. 25.22.
13. e.g. Lord Essex. Le Marchant. *Althorp*. p. 517.
14. Howick Diary. 17 July 1834.
15. Melbourne to Holland. 10 July 1834. Add. MSS. 51558. f. 62. *Hansard*. 3rd Series. 25.47. Brougham to Wellesley. 19 July 1834. Add. MSS.

37311. f. 201. 29 July 1834. Grey MSS.

16. Broughton. *Recollections*. Vol. 4, p. 356. Howick Diary. 15 July 1834.
17. Melbourne to Brougham. 16 July 1834. Brougham MSS. William to Melbourne. 13 July 1834. RA MP. *Lord Melbourne's Papers*. p. 204.
18. *Letters During Residence in London*. p. 378. Broughton. *Recollections*. Vol. 4, p. 356. Palmerston to Melbourne. 12 July 1834. RA MP 11/6. *The Times*. 12 July 1834.
19. *Life and Times*. p. 408.
20. *Creevey Papers*. p. 286. Broughton. *Recollections*. Vol. 4, p. 356. *Hansard*. 3rd Series. 25.466.
21. *Correspondence of Daniel O'Connell*. ed. W. J. Fitzpatrick. London, 1888. Vol. 1, p. 451. Althorp to Spencer. 13 July 1834. Spencer MSS.
22. *Joseph Parkes of Birmingham*. Jessie Buckley. London, 1926. p. 159. *Life of Bulwer*. p. 488.
23. Parker. *Graham*. Vol. 1, p. 208.
24. *Life of Lord Campbell*. Vol. 2, p. 145. *The First Lady Wharncliffe and her Family*. ed. C. Grosvenor. London, 1927. Vol. 2, p. 200. Haydon. *Diary*. Vol. 4, p. 234. Howick Diary. 18 July and 6 Oct. 1834.
25. Brougham to Melbourne. Sept. 1834. RA MP 1/118.
26. Melbourne to Palmerston. 28 Aug. 1834. Broadlands MSS. GC/ME/18. *Lieven–Grey Correspondence*. Vol. 3, p. 18. *The Correspondence of Lord Aberdeen and Princess Lieven*. ed. E. J. Parry. Camden 3rd Series. London, 1938. Vol. LX(I), p. 19. Grey to Russell. 15 Nov. 1834. *Early Correspondence*. Vol. 2, p. 57.
27. *Lord William Russell and his Wife*. Georgina Blakiston. London, 1972. p. 337.
28. to Lord John Russell. 16 Aug. 1834. *Lord Melbourne's Papers*. p. 208.
29. Palmerston to Melbourne. 30 Aug. 1834. Broadlands MSS. GC/ME/509. Melbourne to Brougham. 16 Aug. 1834. Brougham MSS.
30. Haydon. *Diary*. Vol. 4, pp. 222–312 *passim*.
31. Moore. *Memoirs*. Vol. 7, p. 47. *Miss Eden's Letters*. p. 245.
32. 24 Oct. 1834. Grey MSS. 17 Oct. 1834. Brougham MSS.
33. Broughton. *Recollections*. Vol. 5, p. 23. William to Melbourne. 31 Oct. 1834 and Melbourne to William. 1 Nov. 1834. RA MP.
34. 1 Aug. 1834. Broadlands MSS. GC/TE/227. *Girlhood of Victoria*. Vol. 2, p. 181. *Lord Beaconsfield's Correspondence with his Sister*. London, 1886. p. 42.

CHAPTER 13 (pp. 181–192)

1. *Memoirs*. Baron Stockmar. ed. Muller. London, 1872. Vol. 1, p. 332. *Lord Melbourne's Papers*. p. 220.
2. 10 Nov. 1834. Holland Diary. Add. MSS. 51870. *The Lieven–Palmerston Correspondence*. ed. Lord Sudley. London, 1943. p. 60.
3. *Girlhood of Victoria*. Vol. 2, p. 149.

4. *The Croker Papers*. ed. Louis Jennings. London, 1804. Vol. 2, p. 243. *The Letter Bag of Lady Elizabeth Stanhope*. London, 1913. Vol. 2, p. 154.
5. *The Eve of Victorianism*. Lady Brownlow. London, 1940. p. 190.
6. Add. MSS. 40303. f. 227.
7. 24 Feb. 1835. *Hansard*. 3rd Series. 26.88. *Chronicles of Holland House*. Vol. 2, p. 188.
8. 20 Nov. 1834. Brougham MSS. Campbell. *Brougham*. p. 460.
9. *Lady Holland to her Son*. p. 155. *Lieven–Palmerston Correspondence*. p. 61. *Miss Eden's Letters*. p. 246.
10. Grey to Holland. 16 Nov. 1834. Add. MSS. 51557. f. 37. Grey to Melbourne. 16 Nov. 1834. RA MP 5/126. *Miss Eden's Letters*. p. 248.
11. 14 Nov. 1834. *Lord Melbourne's Papers*. p. 224.
12. *Croker Papers*. Vol. 2, p. 246. *Greville Journal*. Vol. 3, p. 147. Melbourne to Holland. Add. MSS. 51558. f. 74.
13. Undated. RA MP 2/15.
14. RA MP.
15. 23 Jan. 1835. *Lord Melbourne's Papers*. p. 235.
16. *Greville Journal*. Vol. 3, p. 111.
17. Broughton. *Recollections*. Vol. 5, p. 27. Holland to Melbourne. 8 Dec. 1834. RA MP 7/8.
18. Brougham to Melbourne. 4 Dec. 1834. RA MP 2/18. Melbourne to Lansdowne. 7 Dec. 1834. Bowood MSS.
19. 24 Jan. 1835. RA MP 7/11.
20. cit. *The Politics of the Whigs in Opposition*. A. D. Kriegel. Journal of British Studies. Vol. 7, No. 2, p. 65.
21. 24 Feb. 1835. *Hansard*. 3rd Series. 26.75. 13 Dec. 1834. Lambton MSS. Grey to Melbourne. 18 Nov. 1834. RA MP 5/127. Duncannon to Grey. 14 Jan. 1835. Grey MSS.
22. The best estimate is probably that of Ellice – 281 Tories, 239 Whigs, 112 Radicals, 34 O'Connellites. 18 Feb. 1835. Lambton MSS.
23. 21 Jan. 1835. Add. MSS. 51558. f. 68. *Lord Melbourne's Papers*. p. 235.
24. *Greville Journal*. Vol. 3, p. 144. Littleton Diary. 5 March 1835.
25. Melbourne to Lansdowne. 29 Dec. 1834. Bowood MSS. Melbourne to Holland. 10 Feb. 1835. Add. MSS. 51558. f. 61. Palmerston to Melbourne. 2 Dec. 1834. RA MP 11/12.
26. Broadlands MSS. MEL/RU/143.
27. 13 Feb. 1835. *Early Correspondence*. Vol. 2, p. 92.
28. 1 Feb. 1835. ibid. p. 85.
29. See Kitson Clark. *Peel and the Conservative Party*. 2nd Ed. London, 1964. p. 246.
30. 12 Feb. 1835. Broadlands MSS. MEL/RU/143.
31. Grey to Melbourne. 1 Feb. 1835. PRO 30/22/1E. f. 21. Howick to Grey. 1 March 1835. Grey MSS. Ellice to Durham. 24 May 1835. Durham MSS. Howick Diary. 22 March 1835.

32. Durham to Ellice. 3 Feb. 1835. Ellice MSS. E 29 f. 178. Grey to Melbourne. 3 Feb. 1835. RA MP 5/129. Melbourne to Russell. 29 Dec. 1834. Broadlands MSS. MEL/RU/133. Melbourne to Grey. 6 Feb. 1835. *Lord Melbourne's Papers.* p. 244.
33. Melbourne to Russell. 16 Jan. 1835. Broadlands MSS. MEL/RU/138. Melbourne to Rice and vice versa. 13–31 Jan. 1835. RA MP 9/69–74.
34. Moore. *Memoirs.* Vol. 7, p. 68. *Croker Papers.* Vol. 2, p. 262. *Greville Journal.* Vol. 3, p. 216. *The First Lady Wharncliffe.* Vol. 2, p. 236.
35. to Russell. 5 Feb. 1835. Broadlands MSS. MEL/RU/141.
36. Howick Diary. 1 March 1835.
37. RA Add. 15/8042. Broadlands MSS. MEL/RU/147. Grey to Taylor. 12 April 1835. RA Add. 15/8044.

CHAPTER 14 (pp. 193–207)

1. Melbourne to William. 13, 14, 15 April 1835. RA 50522–25; William to Melbourne. 15, 16, 17 April. RA Add. 15/8040 and RA MP.
2. Grey to Melbourne. 1 Feb. 1835. *Early Correspondence of John Russell.* Vol. 2, p. 86. Russell to Melbourne. 9 Feb. 1835. RA MP 13/40.
3. Littleton Diary. 9 and 18 April 1835.
4. Melbourne to Wellesley. 19 April 1835. Add. MSS. 37311. f. 254; Add. MSS. 37316. f. 52. Brougham to Wellesley. Undated. Add. MSS. 37311. f. 258.
5. *The Eldest Brother.* Iris Butler. London, 1973. p. 551.
6. 7 Feb. 1835. Broadlands MSS. MEL/RU/142.
7. 14, 17 and 20 Feb. *Lord Melbourne's Papers.* pp. 257–65.
8. 18 Feb. 1835. Spencer MSS. Littleton Diary. 15 April 1835. Grey to Lansdowne. 9 April 1835. Bowood MSS. *Greville Journal.* Vol. 4, p. 114.
9. April 1835. RA MP 2/33. 24 April 1835. Brougham MSS.
10. Campbell. *Brougham.* p. 468. *Hansard.* 3rd Series. 27.974.
11. Howick Diary. 11 April 1835. Palmerston to Melbourne. 12 April 1835. RA MP 11/13. Melbourne to Ellice. 11 April 1835. Ellice MSS. E28 f. 6.
12. Howick Diary. 16 April 1835.
13. Ellice to Durham. 11 April 1835. Lambton MSS.
14. Undated memo by Colonel Grey. RA A80/101. Grey to Melbourne. 14 April 1835; Melbourne to Palmerston. 14 April; Palmerston to Melbourne. 15 April; Broadlands MSS. GC/ME 26/2, 4 and 5.
15. *The Foreign Policy of Palmerston.* Charles Webster. London, 1951. Vol. 1, p. 418. *Lord Palmerston.* Jasper Ridley. London, 1970. p. 161.
16. Le Marchant. *Althorp.* p. 538. Althorp to Melbourne. 13 April 1835. RA MP 15/113.
17. e.g. Littleton Diary. 10 April 1835.
18. *Greville Journal.* Vol. 3, p. 197. O'Connell. *Correspondence.* Vol. 2, p. 4. PRO 30/12/28/5 f. 274. 18 April 1835. *Hansard.* 3rd Series. 27.974.

19. *Greville Journal*. Vol. 3, p. 194. Broughton. *Recollections*. Vol. 5, p. 34.
20. *Autobiography*. London, 1873. p. 195.
21. *Lord Melbourne's Papers*. p. 58.
22. Littleton Diary. 10 Aug. 1835. Howick Diary. 20 April and 10 June 1835. *Lord Melbourne's Papers*. p. 479.
23. Howick Diary. 5 March 1836. Webster. *Foreign Policy of Palmerston*. Vol. 1, p. 36n.
24. Howick Diary. 20 April 1835. Melbourne to Ellice. 14 Sept. 1837. Ellice MSS. 28E f. 48.
25. Holland Diary. 27 May 1835. Add. MSS. 51871.
26. 19 Dec. 1840. RA MP 17/32.
27. to Ellice. 19 Sept. 1834. Ellice MSS. 28E f. 6.
28. Russell. *Early Correspondence*. October 1835. pp. 132–46.
29. Melbourne to Russell. 19 July 1841. *Lord Melbourne's Papers*. p. 511. Torrens. *Melbourne*. Vol. 2, p. 211.
30. 18 Jan. 1836. *The Letters of Runnymede*. p. 79. *The Private Letters of Sir Robert Peel*. ed. G. Peel. London, 1920. p. 156. Howick Diary. 30 Jan. 1836. Melbourne to Holland. 25 March 1837. Add. MSS. 51558. f. 145. *Creevey Papers*. Vol. 2, p. 308.

CHAPTER 15 (pp. 208–225)

1. Melbourne to William IV. 16 June 1835. *Lord Melbourne's Papers*. p. 285. Melbourne to Lansdowne. 29 Oct. 1835. Bowood MSS.
2. 20 Aug. 1835. *Hansard*. 3rd Series. 30.715.
3. RA MP 32/40. Disraeli. *Whigs and Whiggism*. London, 1913. p. 58. *Greville Journal*. Vol. 3, p. 243.
4. 26 Sept. 1835. Broadlands MSS. MEL/RU/174. Howick Diary. 28 Nov. 1835.
5. *Lord Melbourne's Papers*. p. 278. 22 Oct. 1835. *Early Correspondence*. Vol. 2, p. 148. 9 Dec. 1835. Melbourne to Palmerston. Broadlands MSS. GC/ME/59.
6. 18 and 19 Oct. 1835. RA MP.
7. Buckingham. *Memoirs*. Vol. 2, p. 186. Melbourne to Lansdowne. 30 June 1835. Bowood MSS. 28 and 29 June 1835. RA MP 4/2, /3, /4 and /7.
8. Broughton. *Recollections*. Vol. 5, p. 47.
9. Melbourne to Russell. 5 July 1835. Broadlands MSS. MEL/RU/163. Draft in RA MP. 7 June (July?) 1835. Broadlands MSS. MEL/RU/158. Holland Diary. 15 July 1835. Add. MSS. 51871. Melbourne to Russell. 26 Aug. 1836. Broadlands MSS. MEL/RU/259.
10. *Girlhood of Victoria*. Vol. 2, p. 405. Broughton. *Recollections*. Vol. 5, p. 42.
11. Littleton Diary. 28 Aug. 1835. *Letters of Sir Walter Scott*. ed. H. J. Grierson. London, 1932. Vol. 2, p. 268. Holland Diary. 22 April 1835.

Add. MSS. 51870. Melbourne to Brougham. 13 Oct. 1835. Brougham MSS.

12. *The Municipal Corporation Commission and Report.* G. B. Finlayson. BIHR XXXVI. p. 93. (May 1963).

13. Parkes to Durham. 1 June 1835. Lambton MSS. Melbourne to Rice. 2 June 1835. *Lord Melbourne's Papers.* p. 282.

14. Howick Diary. 4 Aug. 1835.

15. *Hansard.* 3rd Series. 30.330.

16. Parkes to Durham. 14 Aug. 1835. Lambton MSS. *Greville Journal.* Vol. 3, p. 235. *Aberdeen–Lieven Correspondence.* Vol. 1, p. 29.

17. *Joseph Parkes of Birmingham.* p. 125. *Creevey Papers.* Vol. 2, p. 308. Torrens. *Melbourne.* Vol. 2, p. 156.

18. Howick Diary. 23 May 1835. *Girlhood of Victoria.* Vol. 1, p. 386. Melbourne to Cowper. 21 July 1840. Broadlands MSS. MEL/CO/40. *Girlhood of Victoria.* Vol. 2, p. 250. Melbourne to Dunfermline. 20 April 1841. *Lord Melbourne's Papers.* p. 416.

19. *Reaction and Reconstruction in English Politics.* Oxford 1965. p. 61.

20. *The Victorian Church.* Owen Chadwick. London, 1966. Vol. 1, p. 129.

21. 9 Nov. 1840. Broadlands MSS. MEL/CO/43.

22. *Hansard.* 3rd Series. 35.33. Melbourne to Lansdowne. 2 March 1837. Bowood MSS. [The Bishop of Salisbury]. *Lord Melbourne's Papers.* p. 467.

23. *The Victorian Church.* op. cit. Vol. 1, pp. 113–25.

24. 15 Feb. 1836. *Lord Melbourne's Papers.* p. 408. Queen Victoria's Journal.

25. *Greville Journal.* Vol. 3, p. 267.

26. Add. MSS. 37311. ff. 260 and 264. Add. MSS. 37297. ff. 433 and 434. *The First Lady Wharncliffe.* Vol. 2, p. 258. Wellesley to Holland. 13 Nov. 1839. Add. MSS. 37312. f. 181. Wellesley to Melbourne. 3 March 1839. RA MP 39/80.

27. Parkes to Durham. 14 Aug. 1835. Lambton MSS.

28. *Greville Journal.* Vol. 3, p. 225. Campbell. *Brougham.* p. 474. Melbourne to Russell. 2 Dec. 1835. Broadlands MSS. MEL/RU/196.

29. Howick Diary. 16 Dec. 1835. Torrens. *Melbourne.* Vol. 2, p. 174. Melbourne to Brougham. 25 Dec. 1835. Brougham MSS.

30. Jan. 1836. RA MP 2/38. June 1836. RA MP 2/45.

31. Brougham to Melbourne. June 1836. RA MP 2/45. e.g. Howick Diary. 7 May, 18 May, 14 Nov. 1835. Littleton Diary. 3 July 1835. Melbourne to Russell. 28 Oct. 1835. Broadlands MSS. MEL/RU/191. O'Connell. *Correspondence.* Vol. 2, p. 45.

32. 29 Jan. 1836. Copy in Grey MSS.

33. *Letters of Thomas Carlyle.* ed. C. E. Norton. London, 1888. Vol. 2, p. 322. *Reaction and Reconstruction in English Politics.* p. 166. *Life of Sir William Molesworth.* Mrs Fawcett. London, 1901. p. 70. Maxwell. *Clarendon.* p.107.

34. *Girlhood of Victoria.* Vol. 2, p. 204. Melbourne to Ellice. 17 Nov. 1836. Ellice MSS. E.28 f. 42. Melbourne to Thomson. 1 June 1835. *Lord Melbourne's Papers.* p. 288.

35. Howick Diary. 20 May and 28 June 1836. Russell to Holland. 26 May 1836. Add. MSS. 51677. f. 162. Howick Diary. 10 July 1836. Parkes to Durham. 27 July 1836. Durham MSS.

CHAPTER 16 (pp. 226–243)

1. Littleton Diary. 7 July 1832.
2. *The Life of Mrs Norton.* Jane Perkins. London, 1910. p. 2. This sensible and well-written biography is the source of much that follows, though Mrs Perkins did not see any of Mrs Norton's letters to Melbourne now in the County Record Office at Hertford.
3. *Lord Beaconsfield's Letters.* London, 1887. p. 80.
4. *Record of a Girlhood.* Frances Kemble. London, 1878. Vol. 3, p. 194. Haydon. *Diary.* Vol. 4, pp. 47 and 180.
5. Maxwell. *Clarendon.* p. 82. *Three Howard Sisters.* p. 192. Haydon. *Diary.* Vol. 4, p. 287. *The Letters of Queen Victoria.* ed. Benson and Esher. London, 1908. Vol. 1, p. 362.
6. *Record of a Girlhood.* Vol. 3, p. 194.
7. 1 Aug. 1831. Panshanger MSS. Box 37. The bulk of these letters have recently been published in *The Letters of Caroline Norton to Lord Melbourne.* ed. J. Hoge and C. Olney. Ohio, 1974.
8. 12 Aug., 22 Aug., 25 Aug., 6 Dec. 1831. Panshanger MSS. Box 37.
9. Haydon. *Diary.* Vol. 4, pp. 224 and 271.
10. *Memoirs of an Ex-Minister.* Earl of Malmesbury. London, 1884. Vol. 1, p. 66. Littleton Diary. 31 July 1835. *The First Lady Wharncliffe.* Vol. 2, p. 271. Howick Diary. 11 Dec. 1835.
11. Melbourne to Holland. 6 April 1836. Add. MSS. 51558. f. 101. Melbourne to Mrs Norton. 6, 8, 10 and 19 April 1836. *Mrs Norton.* pp. 83–6.
12. Cavendish MSS. 3519.4. 23 April 1836. *Mrs Norton.* p. 92.
13. Mrs Norton to R. B. Sheridan. 22 April 1836. Add. MSS. 42767. f. 5. Melbourne to Mrs Norton. 9 June 1836. *Mrs Norton.* p. 93.
14. Howick Diary. 5 June 1836. *Correspondence of Charles Arbuthnot.* p. 192. *Creevey Papers.* Vol. 2, p. 311.
15. *Correspondence of Charles Arbuthnot.* p. 194.
16. Howick Diary. 22 June 1836. *Extraordinary Trial. Norton V. Viscount Melbourne.* London 1836. *Chronicles of Holland House.* Vol. 2, p. 219. *Creevey Papers.* Vol. 2, p. 311.
17. *Mrs Norton.* p. 93. Fred Lamb to Emily Cowper. 28 June 1836. *Lady Palmerston and her Times.* Vol. 1, p. 190. Granville to Holland. 27 July 1836. Duke University Library.

18. *Greville Journal.* Vol. 3, p. 350. *Correspondence with Lord Grey.* Vol. 3, p. 200. Broughton. *Recollections.* Vol. 5, p. 54. *Chronicles of Holland House.* Vol. 2, p. 219. Malmesbury. *Memoirs.* Vol. 1, p. 71. Haydon. *Diary.* Vol. 4, p. 482.
19. Broughton. *Recollections.* Vol. 5, p. 54. *Life of Campbell.* Vol. 2, p. 83.
20. Referred to, *inter alia*, in *Mrs Norton.* p. 213.
21. Devonshire to Lady Granville. 24 June 1836. Cavendish MSS. 3519. f. 5.
22. *Elizabeth Lady Holland to her Son.* p. 32.
23. Howick Diary. 25 July 1838.
24. Lady Granville to Devonshire. 11 Nov 1830. Cavendish MSS. 2082. *Miss Eden's Letters.* p. 215.
25. Panshanger MSS. Box 16. *Miss Eden's Letters.* p. 258.
26. *Girlhood of Victoria.* Vol. 1, p. 302. *Lord Melbourne's Papers.* p. 93. Littleton Diary. 18 April 1835.
27. 26 and 28 Sept. 1835. Broadlands MSS. MEL/RU/174 and 5/1. Lady Lyttelton. *Correspondence.* p. 285.
28. Torrens. *Melbourne.* Vol. 2, p. 333. Broughton. *Recollections.* Vol. 5, p. 136. *Life of Clarendon.* p. 207.
29. Melbourne to Russell. Broadlands MSS. MEL/RU/276. Torrens. *Melbourne.* Vol. 2, p. 212. Post Mortem of 28 Nov. 1836. Panshanger MSS. Box 13.
30. Broughton. *Recollections.* Vol. 5, p. 64.

CHAPTER 17 (pp. 244–255)

1. *The Times.* 19 Aug. 1836. *Hansard.* 3rd Series. 35.1303. Campbell. *Lyndhurst.* p. 116.
2. 3 Sept. 1836. Broadlands MSS. MEL/RU/263. Broughton. *Recollections.* Vol. 5, p. 59. Torrens. *Melbourne.* Vol. 2, p. 201. *Greville Journal.* Vol. 3, p. 360.
3. Undated and 28 Oct. 1836. cit. Torrens. *Melbourne.* Vol. 2, p. 209.
4. Add. MSS. 51871.
5. Howick Diary. 25 Oct. 1836.
6. 10 Oct. 1836. Lambton MSS. *Joseph Parkes of Birmingham.* p. 161.
7. 11 June 1836. Brougham MSS.
8. cit. Gash. *Reaction and Reconstruction.* p. 37.
9. Broughton. *Recollections.* Vol. 5, p. 57. 13 Oct. 1835. Brougham MSS.
10. 13 Oct. 1835. Brougham MSS. Melbourne to Russell. 5 June 1836. *Early Correspondence.* pp. 185–7. Melbourne to Lansdowne. 29 Dec. 1836. Bowood MSS.
11. *The Passing of the Whigs.* p. 65.
12. 21 Jan. 1837. Grey MSS. Melbourne to Russell. 9 Feb. 1837. Broadlands MSS. MEL/RU/306.
13. 21 Jan. 1837. Grey MSS.

14. 1 April 1837. Broadlands MSS. MEL/RU/320. *Croker Papers.* Vol. 2, p. 306.
15. Wharncliffe to Peel. 13 May 1837. Add. MSS. 40423. f. 227.
16. Melbourne to Hummelauer. 29 May 1836. *Lord Melbourne's Papers.* p. 340. *Greville Journal.* Vol. 4, p. 357.
17. July 1836. RA MP. Personal Box. Webster. *Foreign Policy of Palmerston.* Vol. 2, p. 786.
18. 9 Jan. 1836. Grey MSS. Roger Bullen. *Palmerston, Guizot and the Collapse of the Entente Cordiale.* London, 1974. p. 3. Melbourne to Granville. 21 July 1834. RA MP 22/76. Melbourne to Palmerston. 12 Sept. 1836. Broadlands MSS. GC/ME/123.
19. Melbourne to Russell. 31 May and 12 June 1835. Broadlands MSS. MEL/RU/155 and /160. Melbourne to Palmerston. 11 June 1835. Broadlands MSS. GC/ME/31.
20. 4 March 1836. Broadlands MSS. GC/ME/77. Broughton. *Recollections.* Vol. 5, p. 51.
21. William IV to Melbourne. 18 Aug. 1836. RA MP.
22. 26 Nov. 1836. Walpole. *Russell.* Vol. 1, p. 269.
23. 27 April 1836. Broadlands MSS. GC/ME/97.
24. Melbourne to Taylor. 17 and 22 May 1837. RA A and C M7/2 and /30.
25. Duchess of Kent to Melbourne. 21 May 1837. RA A and C M 7/24. Melbourne to William IV. 22 May 1837. RA A and C M 7/30. Queen Victoria's Journal. 5 Sept. 1838.
26. June 1837. Add. MSS. 51871.

CHAPTER 18 (pp. 256–265)

1. Holland Diary. 22 July 1837. Add. MSS. 51871.
2. For everything connected with Queen Victoria I am particularly indebted to Lady Longford's *Victoria R.I.* (London, 1964); by far the best of the innumerable biographies.
3. *Girlhood of Victoria.* Vol. 1, p. 197. Melbourne to Lansdowne. 20 June 1837. Bowood MSS. Broughton. *Recollections.* Vol. 5, p. 77.
4. These quotations, and others similar, come from the Journal of Queen Victoria in the Royal Archives.
5. An analogy for which I am indebted to Mr Richard Olland.
6. Broughton. *Recollections.* Vol. 5, p. 97.
7. *Greville Journal.* Vol. 4, p. 169. *Aberdeen–Lieven Correspondence.* Vol. 1, p. 72. *Creevey Papers.* Vol. 2, p. 327. *Greville Journal.* Vol. 4, p. 93.
8. Holland Diary. August 1837. Add. MSS. 51871.
9. Holland Diary. Christmas 1837. Add. MSS. 51872. 24 Aug. 1841. *Hansard.* 3rd Series. 59.77.
10. *Greville Journal.* Vol. 4, p. 230.
11. 9 March 1839. RA C 1/20. *Creevey Papers.* Vol. 2, p. 332. Arbuthnot. *Correspondence.* p. 197.

12. *Victoria R.I.* p. 68. *Girlhood of Victoria.* Vol. 2, p. 312.
13. *Political and Occasional Poems.* p. 323.
14. 16 Sept. 1838. *Aberdeen–Lieven Correspondence.* Vol. 1, p. 113.
15. *Croker Papers.* Vol. 2, p. 320.
16. 28 June 1837. RA Add. A 11/32. Broughton. *Recollections.* Vol. 5, p. 122.
17. 6 July 1838. *Aberdeen–Lieven Correspondence.* Vol. 1, p. 110. 5 July 1837. Vic. Add. MSS. A 11/32. *Greville Journal.* Vol. 4, p. 198.

CHAPTER 19 (pp. 266–273)

1. Memorandum by Stockmar. 28 Oct. 1837. RA M 7/68.
2. 14 April 1812. *Hansard.* 3rd Series. 22.352. Melbourne to Russell. 17 Dec. 1837. Broadlands MSS. MEL/RU/426.
3. Holland Diary. 3 July 1837. Add. MSS. 51871. June 1837. RA M 7/68.
4. Holland Diary. Christmas 1837. Add. MSS. 51872.
5. 16 Feb. 1838. Ellice MSS. E 28 f. 60. Melbourne to Victoria. 28 Feb. 1835. RA A 1/107.
6. July 1840. RA MP.
7. Holland Diary. Jan. 1838. Add. MSS. 51872.
8. Broughton. *Recollections.* Vol. 5, p. 130. Greville to Melbourne. 7 April 1838. RA MP 26/104. Melbourne to Palmerston. 23 Jan. 1838. Broadlands MSS. GC/ME/187.
9. *Aberdeen–Lieven Correspondence.* Vol. 1, p. 109.
10. *Lord Beaconsfield's Letters.* edited by his brother. London, 1887. p. 140. Howick Diary. 29 June 1838.
11. Anson's Memorandum of 13 Dec. 1841. RA Y 54/99. *Sir Robert Peel.* Charles Parker. London, 1899. Vol. 2, p. 404. *Greville Journal.* Vol. 6, p. 441.
12. 13 July and 17 Dec. 1839. RA MP 32/10 and 19/11.
13. 15 April 1839. *Lord William Russell and his Wife.* p. 419.
14 20 Feb. 1839. RA Z/486/4.
15. 17 March 1839. RA Z/486/24.
16. 19 and 20 June 1839. RA Z/486/29, /30 and /31. Victoria's Journal. 9 Oct. 1839.
17. *Statement of the Case of the Late Lady Flora Hastings.* The Marquess of Hastings. London, 1839. Fred Lamb to Lady Cowper. 12 May 1839. *Lady Palmerston and her Times.* Vol. 2, p. 16.
18. *Greville Journal.* Vol. 4, p. 133.
19. Holland Diary. 1839. Add. MSS. 51872.

CHAPTER 20 (pp. 274–289)

1. *Letters of Lady Granville.* p. 239. Melbourne to Howick. 8 Aug. 1837. Grey MSS.
2. Melbourne to Russell. 2 Aug. 1837. Broadlands MSS. MEL/RU/382. Melbourne to Lady Holland. 10 Aug. 1837. Add. MSS. 51560.

3. D. M. Close. *The General Elections of 1835 and 1837 in England and Wales.* Unpublished Thesis. Oxford D.Phil., 1966.
4. Newman. *Melbourne.* p. 240. *Aberdeen–Lieven Correspondence.* Vol. 1, p. 85.
5. Melbourne to Russell. 13 Aug. and 7 Sept. 1837. Broadlands MSS. MEL/RU/387 and /396.
6. 7 Sept. 1837. Broadlands MSS. MEL/RU/396.
7. 20 Nov. 1837. *Hansard.* 3rd Series. 39.65. *Girlhood of Victoria.* Vol. 2, p. 20.
8. 14 Feb. 1839. Grey MSS.
9. 27 Dec. 1837. *Lord Melbourne's Papers.* p. 370.
10. Melbourne to Russell. 8 Aug. 1837. Broadlands MSS. MEL/RU/383.
11. *Nobody in London, 1838.* 17 Dec. 1837. Broadlands MSS. MEL/RU/426.
12. *Girlhood of Victoria.* Vol. 1, p. 244. *Aberdeen–Lieven Correspondence.* Vol. 1, p. 96.
13. 7 Sept. 1837 and 11 May 1838. MEL/RU/396 and /485.
14. *Letters of Lady Granville.* Vol. 2, p. 243.
15. 11 March 1838. Broadlands MSS. MEL/RU/465.
16. 10 May 1838. RA MP 32/73.
17. Howick Diary. 11 June 1838.
18. *Girlhood of Victoria.* Vol. 2, p. 240. Howick Diary. 13 July 1838.
19. e.g. Duncannon to Melbourne. 20 Oct. 1838. RA MP 3/53. Russell to Melbourne. 14 and 18 Oct. 1838. Broadlands MSS. MEL/RU/61 and /62.
20. Melbourne to Russell. 26 Oct. 1838. *Lord Melbourne's Papers.* p. 383.
21. 25 Oct. 1838. RA A 1/198. Ellice to Melbourne. Undated. RA MP 5/21.
22. Monteagle MSS. cit. R. H. Cameron. *Lord Melbourne's Second Administration and the Opposition.* Unpublished Thesis. Oxford D.Phil., 1970.
23. A useful analysis of the situation is provided by *Crisis in the Canadas: 1838–39. The Grey Journals and Letters.* W. Ormsby. London, 1965.
24. Melbourne to Howick. 2 Jan. 1839. Grey MSS.
25. Melbourne to Fitzwilliam. 15 Jan. 1838. RA MP 25/63. Melbourne to Victoria. 27 Dec. 1837. RA A 1/73(E). Howick to Melbourne. 29 Dec. 1837. RA MP 7/77.
26. Melbourne to Howick. 21 Jan. 1838. Grey MSS. *The First Lady Wharncliffe.* Vol. 2, p. 287.
27. Melbourne to Russell. 7 July 1837. Broadlands MSS. MEL/RU/367. Durham to Ellice. 27 Aug. 1837. Ellice MSS. E 30 f. 37. Broughton. *Recollections.* Vol. 5, pp. 105 and 118. Durham to Grey. 15 Jan. 1838. Grey MSS. *Lord Durham.* Chester New. Oxford, 1929. p. 351.
28. Melbourne to Russell. 9 April 1838. Broadlands MSS. MEL/RU/475. Durham to Melbourne. 12 April 1838. RA MP 4/129. Melbourne to Russell. 18 April 1838. Broadlands MSS. MEL/RU/476.
29. New. *Durham.* pp. 370–85. 30 April 1838. *Hansard.* 3rd Series. 42.673. Melbourne to Russell. 11 April 1838. Broadlands MSS. MEL/RU/477.
30. Melbourne to Durham. 1 May 1838. Lambton MSS. and 2 July 1838. RA MP 4/36. 2 July 1838. *Hansard.* 3rd Series. 43.1167.

31. Durham to Melbourne. 16 June 1838. RA MP 4/33. Melbourne to Durham. 28 July 1838. Lambton MSS.
32. Melbourne to Russell. 4 July 1838. Broadlands MSS. MEL/RU/514. Melbourne to Lansdowne. 14 Dec. 1838. Bowood MSS. *Grey–Lieven Correspondence*. Vol. 3, p. 278. Howick Diary. 10 Aug. 1838.
33. Melbourne to Russell. 25 Aug. 1838. *Lord Melbourne's Papers*. p. 432.
34. Melbourne to Durham. 22 Aug. 1838. RA MP 4/46.
35. Melbourne to Russell. 8 Dec. 1838. *Lord Melbourne's Papers*. p. 440.
36. Lady Durham to Lady Grey. 10–18 Jan. 1839. cit. New. p. 484.
37. to Palmerston. 15 Dec. 1838. Broadlands MSS. GC/ME/260.
38. *Memoirs of Sir Thomas Fowell Buxton*. ed. C. Buxton. London, 1848. p. 434. *Lord Melbourne's Papers*. p. 376. Broughton. *Recollections*. Vol. 6, p. 12.
39. Broughton. *Recollections*. Vol. 5, p. 168.
40. *Girlhood of Victoria*. Vol. 2, pp. 117, 122 and 148.
41. Melbourne to Howick. 28 Jan. 1839. Grey MSS. Melbourne to Victoria. RA A2/16.
42. *Greville Journal*. Vol. 4, p. 123. *Lady Palmerston and her Times*. Vol. 2, p. 7. Howick Diary. 9 Feb. 1839.
43. *Greville Journal*. Vol. 4, pp. 123 and 138. *Diary of Philip Von Neumann*. ed. E. Chancellor. London, 1928. p. 116. *Girlhood of Victoria*. Vol. 2, p. 149.

CHAPTER 21 (pp. 290–298)

1. *Girlhood of Victoria*. Vol. 2, p. 137.
2. 26 April 1839. RA C 43/5.
3. Melbourne to Russell. 7 May 1839. RA MP 14/26. *Girlhood of Victoria*. Vol. 2, p. 159. Broughton. *Recollections*. Vol. 5, p. 188.
4. Queen Victoria's Journal, in the Royal Archives, is the source of this and other unattributed quotations in this chapter.
5. 7 May 1839. RA C 43/13.
6. RA C 43/1.
7. *Lady Palmerston and her Times*. Vol. 2, p. 12. *Greville Journal*. Vol. 4, p. 237. *Girlhood of Victoria*. Vol. 2, p. 168.
8. Parker. *Peel*. Vol. 2, p. 403. *Croker Papers*. Vol. 2, p. 315. Melbourne to Victoria. 9 May 1839. RA C 43/18.
9. *Greville Journal*. Vol. 4, p. 167.
10. Holland Diary. Add. MSS. 51872. Broadlands MSS. GC/ME/334.
11. Broughton. *Recollections*. Vol. 5, pp. 190 and 195. Holland Diary. Add. MSS. 51872. Howick Diary.
12. Melbourne to Grey. 10 and 11 May 1839. Grey MSS.
13. contained in letter to Palmerston. Broadlands MSS. GC/ME/328.
14. Grey to Melbourne. 10 and 11 May 1839. *Lord Melbourne's Papers*. pp. 397–8. Rice to Melbourne. 9 May 1839. RA MP 10/22.

15. *Sketches of Eminent Statesmen.* p. 384. *Lord Melbourne's Papers.* p. 390.
16. Stanley to Melbourne. 13 May 1839. RA MP 36/124. O'Connell in his letter to P. V. Fitzpatrick (*Correspondence.* Vol. 2, p. 183) said there were sixteen at dinner.
17. Ashley to Peel. 21 May 1839. Parker. *Peel.* Vol. 2, p. 404.
18. 14 May 1839. *Hansard.* 3rd Series. 47.1008.
19. Broughton. *Recollections.* Vol. 5, p. 199. 29 June 1837. RA C 1/7. Anson to Melbourne. 9 and 10 May 1841. Broadlands MSS. MEL/AN/1.

CHAPTER 22 (pp. 299–317)

1. *The First Lady Wharncliffe.* Vol. 2, p. 297. RA C 1/49 and A 2/69. *Lady Palmerston and her Times.* Vol. 2, p. 18.
2. *Correspondence of Charles Arbuthnot.* p. 201. *Hansard.* 3rd Series. 47.1161 and 1366.
3. *Lord Melbourne's Papers.* p. 399.
4. *Life of Sir Rowland Hill.* By his nephew. London, 1881. Vol. 1, p. 358.
5. Southgate. *The Passing of the Whigs.* p. 118.
6. Holland Diary. Add. MSS. 51872. *Girlhood of Victoria.* Vol. 2, p. 217. Palmerston to Melbourne. 25 Aug. 1839. RA MP 12/7. Howick to Melbourne. 25 Aug. 1839. RA MP 8/46.
7. Howick to Melbourne. 10 Aug. 1839. RA MP 8/41 and 21 Aug. 1839. RA 8/42. cf. Melbourne to Macaulay. 17 Sept. 1839. RA MP 30/5.
8. Howick Diary. 24 Aug. 1839.
9. *Early Correspondence.* Vol. 2, pp. 258 and 260. RA MP 8/44. *Lieven–Grey Correspondence.* p. 310.
10. Howick Diary. 29 Aug. 1839.
11. Howick to Grey. 26 Aug. 1839. Grey MSS. Martineau. *Autobiography.* London, 1877. Vol. 2, p. 131.
12. Clarendon. *Life and Letters.* p. 174. *Greville Journal.* Vol. 4, p. 211. Broughton. *Recollections.* Vol. 5, p. 219. *Queen Victoria's Girlhood.* Vol. 2, p. 259. Clive. *Macaulay. The Shaping of the Historian.* p. 80.
13. Ellice to Durham. 29 Aug. 1839. Lambton MSS. Holland Diary. Add. MSS. 51872.
14. Russell to Melbourne. 9 Sept. 1839. *Early Correspondence.* Vol. 2, p. 264. *Aberdeen–Lieven Correspondence.* Vol. 1, p. 132.
15. *Greville Journal.* Vol. 4, p. 276.
16. Melbourne to Pendarves. 7 Dec. 1839. RA MP 33/62. Melbourne to Ellice. 28 May 1838. Ellice MSS. E 28 f. 70.
17. RA MP 25/98, /99 and /100.
18. RA MP 18/93.
19. *The Early Years of the Prince Consort.* Lt.-Gen. Grey. London, 1867. p. 323.

20. *The Age of Improvement.* Asa Briggs. London 1959 and *Chartist Studies.* ed. Asa Briggs. London, 1962. I have also found of much use F. C. Mather's *Public Order in the Age of the Chartists.* Manchester, 1959.

21. Melbourne to Russell. 19 March 1838. RA MP 14/4. Melbourne to Palmerston. 9 Dec. 1838. Broadlands MSS. GC/ME/259.

22. Broughton. *Recollections.* Vol. 5, p. 222.

23. *Revolution and the Napier Brothers.* Priscilla Napier. London, 1973. p. 270. *John Frost. A Study in Chartism.* Cardiff, 1939.

24. Broughton. *Recollections.* Vol. 5, pp. 240–4.

25. ibid. Vol. 5, p. 259.

26. RA C 2/5. *Greville Journal.* Vol. 4, p. 322.

27. Victoria's Journal – *passim.* In particular entries for 18 April, 12 July and 6 Aug. 1839.

28. Victoria's Journal. 13 Oct. 1839. Melbourne to Russell. 13 Oct. 1839. RA MP 14/70.

29. Victoria's Journal. 14 Oct. 1839 and 14 Jan. 1840. *Croker Papers.* Vol. 2, p. 360.

30. Broughton. *Recollections.* Vol. 5, p. 233.

31. Victoria's Journal. 16 Oct. and 11 Dec. 1839. Melbourne to Sussex. 17 Dec. 1839. RA Z 270/21. Melbourne to Russell. 23 Dec. 1839. RA MP 14/85 and to Holland. 22 Dec. 1839. Add. MSS. 51559.

32. Clarendon to Melbourne. 1 Feb. 1840. RA MP 3/10. Clarendon. *Life and Letters.* p. 179.

33. Melbourne to Russell. 2 Feb. 1840. RA MP 14/97. Melbourne to Victoria. 2 Feb. 1840. RA Z 270/56.

34. Melbourne to Victoria. 1 Feb. 1840. RA Z 270/53. Victoria to Melbourne. 1 and 2 Feb. 1840. RA C 2/21 and /23.

35. Victoria's Journal. 6 Nov. 1839. Clarendon. *Life and Letters.* p. 181.

36. 8 Dec. 1839. RA Z 270/15.

37. 11 Feb. 1840. RA C 2/40.

38. 29 Dec. 1839. RA Z 270/22.

39. Albert to Victoria. 13 Jan. 1840. *Letters of the Prince Consort.* ed. Jagens. London, 1938. p. 51. Albert to Melbourne. 13 Jan. 1840. RA Z 270/29.

40. Graham to Peel. 18 Dec. 1839. Add. MSS. 40318. f. 163. Gash. *Reaction and Reconstruction.* p. 23n.

41. *Greville Journal.* Vol. 5, p. 39. *Early Years of the Prince Consort.* p. 321. Melbourne to Victoria. 30 Aug. 1841. RA C 21/83.

42. Howick Diary. 1 Nov. 1837. Anson Memorandum. 17 Feb. 1841. RA Y 54/17.

43. Anson Memorandum. 19 Feb. 1841. RA Y 54/17.

44. RA A 3/125.

CHAPTER 23 (pp. 318–329)

1. *Girlhood of Victoria.* Vol. 2, p. 260. *Lady Holland to her Son.* p. 181.
2. 29 Sept. 1840. Broadlands MSS. MEL/RU/124.
3. 14 Dec. 1835 and 17 Feb. 1836. Broadlands MSS. GC/ME/57 and /72.
4. Melbourne to Palmerston. 23 Jan. and 16 June 1836. Broadlands MSS. GC/ME/67 and /104.
5. Clarendon. *Life and Letters.* p. 185. Victoria's Journal. 1 Jan. 1840. Palmerston to Granville. 9 Feb. 1836. Broadlands MSS. GC/GR/1595.
6. Webster. *Foreign Policy of Palmerston.* Vol. 2, p. 653.
7. Clarendon. *Life and Letters.* p. 184. Clarendon to Ellice. 5 March 1840. Ellice MSS. E 56 f. 65. Melbourne to Victoria. 5 Jan. 1840. RA A 3/2.
8. Clarendon. *Life and Letters.* p. 193.
9. Melbourne to Palmerston. 4 and 6 July 1840; Palmerston to Melbourne. 5 July 1840. Broadlands MSS. GC/ME/393, /394 and /535.
10. 7 July 1840. Clarendon. *Life and Letters.* p. 195.
11. Palmerston to Melbourne. 28 July 1840. RA MP 12/46. Melbourne to Russell. 19 Aug. 1840. *Lord Melbourne's Papers.* p. 460.
12. 25 Aug. 1840. Broadlands MSS. GC/ME/412.
13. 26 Aug. 1840. RA MP 14/449.
14. Victoria to Melbourne. 26 Sept. 1840. RA C 3/67A. Melbourne to Palmerston. 14 Sept. 1840. Broadlands MSS. GC/ME/418. Palmerston to Melbourne. 16 Sept. 1840. RA MP 12/53.
15. RA MP 15/1.
16. *Greville Journal.* Vol. 4, p. 291.
17. ibid. pp. 300–1.
18. Melbourne to Russell. 30 Sept. 1840. RA MP 15/7. to Palmerston. 29 Sept. 1840. Broadlands MSS. GC/ME/429. *Greville Journal.* Vol. 4, p. 305.
19. Clarendon. *Life and Letters.* p. 212.
20. *Greville Journal.* Vol. 4, p. 314. Russell to Melbourne. 11 Oct. 1840. RA MP 10/125.
21. Webster. *Foreign Policy of Palmerston.* Vol. 2, p. 723. Leopold to Melbourne. 23 Oct. 1840. Broadlands MSS. GC/ME/542/5. Beauvale to Palmerston. 14 Nov. 1840. Broadlands MSS. GC/BE/352.
22. *Letters of Lady Palmerston.* p. 234. *Chronicles o, Holland House.* p. 282. Melbourne to Russell. 28 Dec. 1840. RA MP 15/22. *Chronicles of Holland House.* p. 284.
23. Palmerston to Melbourne. 25 Oct. 1840. RA MP 13/5. Russell to Melbourne. 31 Oct. 1840. Broadlands MSS. MEL/RU/127.
24. Melbourne to Russell. 1 Nov. 1840. *Lord Melbourne's Papers.* p. 491. Palmerston to Melbourne. 31 Oct. 1840. RA MP 13/9.
25. 13 Nov. 1840. *Lieven–Palmerston Correspondence.* p. 196.
26. *Greville Journal.* Vol. 4, p. 338.
27. Melbourne to Victoria. 17 Jan. 1841. RA G 1/55. *Aberdeen–Lieven Correspondence.* Vol. 1, p. 163.

CHAPTER 24 (pp. 330–342)

1. *Greville Journal*. Vol. 4, p. 344. Victoria's Journal. 20 Jan. 1841.
2. Howick Diary. 27 Feb. 1841.
3. 4 Feb. 1841. *Hansard*. 3rd Series 56.274. *Lieven–Palmerston Correspondence*. p. 209. Melbourne to Anson. 29 April 1841. RA C 21/4.
4. *Morning Chronicle*. 12 Jan. 1841.
5. Ebenezer Elliot. *Corn Law Rhymes*. cit. Briggs. *The Age of Improvement*. p. 313.
6. *Lord Beaconsfield's Letters*. p. 147.
7. Melbourne to Russell. 29 Dec. 1838 and 20 Jan. 1839; to Mark Philips. 25 Dec. 1839; RA MP 13/12, 13/127 and 33/89.
8. Melbourne to Russell. 29 Dec. 1838. RA MP 13/117. *Greville Journal*. Vol. 5, p. 151.
9. Baring to Melbourne. 1 Sept. 1840 and 8 Feb. 1841. RA MP 1/52 and 1/64.
10. Trevelyan. *Macaulay*. Vol. 2, p. 87. Broughton. *Recollections*. Vol. 6, p. 20. *Lord Melbourne's Papers*. p. 416.
11. Add. MSS. 44745. Ellice to Melbourne. 5 May 1841. RA MP 5/32.
12. Victoria's Journal. 9 May 1841.
13. 6 May 1841. RA C 4/11.
14. 8 May 1841. RA C 21/12.
15. 14 May 1841. *Lord Melbourne's Papers*. p. 417.
16. Victoria's Journal. 15 May 1841.
17. Palmerston to Melbourne. 14 May 1841. RA MP 13/24. Duncannon to Melbourne. 16 May 1841. RA MP 3/103. *Letters of Lady Palmerston*. p. 251.
18. Broughton. *Recollections*. Vol. 6, p. 27.
19. See Betty Kemp's *The General Election of 1841*. *History*. Vol. 27, p. 146.
20. RA A 3/179.
21. The details of this episode and Melbourne's letter to Fox of 20 May 1842 are to be found among the MSS. at Melbourne Hall.
22. 31 July 1841. RA MP 15/47.
23. to Leopold. 3 Aug. 1841. *Letters of Queen Victoria*. Vol. 1, p. 296.
24. *Lady Palmerston's Letters*. p. 253.
25. *Lady Palmerston's Letters*. p. 255. Lyttelton. *Correspondence*. p. 316.
26. Campbell. *Brougham*. p. 518. Broughton. *Recollections*. Vol. 6, p. 41.
27. James Graham to Arbuthnot. *Arbuthnot Correspondence*. p. 229. 15 Aug. 1841. RA C 5/6 and C 21/69.
28. 28 and 29 Aug. 1841. RA C 5/19, C 21/82 and A 3/203.
29. 28 Aug. 1841. *Lady Palmerston's Letters*. p. 256.
30. 7 Aug. 1841. RA Y 54/61.
31. Torrens. *Melbourne*. Vol. 2, p. 370.

CHAPTER 25 (pp. 343–365)

1. Brougham. *Life and Times.* Vol. 3, p. 14. *Life of Lord Campbell.* Vol. 2, p. 159.
2. Melbourne to Victoria. 30 Aug. 1841. RA C 21/83. Albert to Melbourne. 29 and 30 Aug. 1841. RA Y 54/66 and /67.
3. Melbourne to Anson. 4 May 1841. RA C 21/8. Melbourne to Victoria. 30 Aug. 1841. RA Y 54/67.
4. *Greville Journal.* Vol. 4, pp. 409–10.
5. 4 Sept. 1841. RA A 4/2; 2 Sept. RA C 22/11; 8 Sept. RA A 4/5 and 12 Sept. RA A 4/8.
6. 14 Sept. 1841. RA A 4/9 and RA Y 54/72.
7. *Greville Journal.* Vol. 7, p. 68. 21 Sept. 1841. RA Y 54/78.
8. 22 Sept. 1841. RA A 4/13.
9. *The Letters of Queen Victoria.* Vol. 2, p. 339.
10. RA Y 54/83 and /85. Melbourne to Victoria. 10 and 14 Oct. RA A 4/22 and /25.
11. *Letters of Queen Victoria.* Vol. 1, p. 352. Melbourne to Victoria. 26 Oct. 1841. RA A 4/29.
12. 7 and 19 Nov. 1841. RA A 4/37 and RA Y 54/9. *Letters of Queen Victoria.* Vol. 1, p. 360.
13. 26 Dec. 1841; 10 Feb., 31 March, 25 March and 29 Sept. 1842. RA Y 54/99, A 4/53, A 4/60, M 12/17 and A 4/82.
14. Victoria's Journal. 1 Oct. 1842.
15. RA Y 54/59.
16. *Lord Melbourne's Papers.* p. 510. *Lieven–Palmerston Correspondence.* p. 217. Russell to Melbourne. 16 Oct. 1841. RA MP 15/57. *Life of Lord Campbell.* Vol. 2, pp. 159–61. Moore. *Memoirs.* Vol. 7, p. 313. Ridley. *Palmerston.* p. 184.
17. RA A 4/60. Haydon. *Diary.* Vol. 5, p. 169. Melbourne to Victoria. RA A 4/68, A 4/73. Melbourne to Cowper. 20 Nov. 1841. Broadlands MSS. MEL/CO/44.
18. *Life of Lord Campbell.* Vol. 2, p. 164. Melbourne to Victoria. 30 May 1842. RA A 4/68.
19. Broughton. *Recollections.* Vol. 6, p. 58. RA A 4/68, C 6/33 and A 4/71.
20. *Lord Melbourne's Papers.* p. 514. Broughton. *Recollections.* Vol. 6, p. 72. Russell to Melbourne. 9 Aug. 1842. Broadlands MSS. MEL/RU/131. Melbourne to Russell. 5 Jan. 1843. RA MP 15/64.
21. *Emma Darwin, a Century of Family Letters.* ed. H. Litchfield. London, 1915. p. 142. RA MP 33/55, /57 and /58.
22. *Greville Journal.* Vol. 5, p. 45. Melbourne to Victoria. 30 Nov. 1842. RA A 4/85.
23. Melbourne to Victoria. 9 April 1843. RA A 4/100. *Lieven–Palmerston Correspondence.* p. 295. Palmerston to Lansdowne. 4 Nov. 1842. Bowood MSS.

24. 7 May 1843. RA Y 55/11.
25. *Lady Palmerston and her Times*. Vol. 2, p. 90.
26. *Life of Lord Campbell*. Vol. 2, p. 173.
27. 8 July 1844. RA A 4/126.
28. Melbourne to Victoria. 3 Feb. and 22 June 1843. RA A 4/91 and /105. Victoria to Melbourne. 31 July 1845. RA C 6/43.
29. Mrs Norton to Melbourne. *Lord Melbourne's Papers*. p. 523. Broughton. *Recollections*. Vol. 6, p. 105. Perkins. *Mrs Norton*. p. 196.
30. *Lord William Russell and his Wife*. p. 488. *Greville Journal*. Vol. 5, p. 166. Melbourne to Victoria. 9 Feb. and 3 April 1844. RA A 4/119 and /121. Victoria to Leopold. 29 April and 6 May 1845. RA 99/21 and /22. Melbourne to Victoria. 2 Dec. 1845. RA A 4/140.
31. Melbourne to Victoria. 19 July 1842 and 2 Dec. 1845. RA A 4/74 and /141.
32. Melbourne to Palmerston. 7 Dec. 1845. Broadlands MSS. GC/ME/496. *The Later Correspondence of Lord John Russell*. Vol. 1, p. 88.
33. Victoria to Melbourne. 7 Dec. 1845. *Lord Melbourne's Papers*. p. 51. Melbourne to Brougham. 24 Dec. 1845. Brougham MSS.
34. 8 April 1845. Broadlands MSS. GMC. Melbourne to Victoria. 9 Dec. 1845. RA C 44/29 and /30. Disraeli. *Lord George Bentinck*. p. 21.
35. *Greville Journal*. Vol. 5, p. 283. *Letters of Lady Palmerston*. p. 271. *Lady Palmerston and her Times*. Vol. 2, p. 107. Melbourne to Victoria. 8 Feb. 1846. RA C 23/49.
36. *Greville Journal*. Vol. 5, p. 323. Broughton. *Recollections*. Vol. 6, p. 173. Melbourne to Victoria. 8 Feb. 1846. RA C 23/49.
37. *Greville Journal*. Vol. 5, p. 405. Russell to Melbourne. 3 July 1846. RA MP 15/84. Melbourne to Russell. 3 July 1846. RA MP 15/85. Melbourne to Victoria. 21 July 1846. RA A 4/145.
38. *Greville Journal*. Vol. 6, p. 136.
39. 30 Dec. 1847. RA A 4/153.
40. *Girlhood of Victoria*. Vol. 1, p. 342. *Lady Palmerston and her Times*. Vol. 2, p. 84. Brougham to Ellice. Ellice MSS. E 28 f. 131.
41. 8 Feb. 1848. RA A 4/174.
42. 27 Jan. to 16 Feb. 1848. RA A 4/172 to /178.
43. 21 June 1848. RA C 57/3.
44. Battiscombe. *Shaftesbury*. p. 207. Lady Beauvale to Lady Douro. 19 Nov. 1848. RA A 4/157. Lady Palmerston to Mrs Huskisson. Add. MSS. 39949. f. 250.
45. 27 Nov. 1848. RA Y 94/5.

INDEX

Se Dio ti lasci,
lettor, prender frutto
di tua lezione

The Agnes Irwin School